Leavin' a Testimony

Focus on American History Series
Center for American History
University of Texas at Austin
Don Carleton, Editor

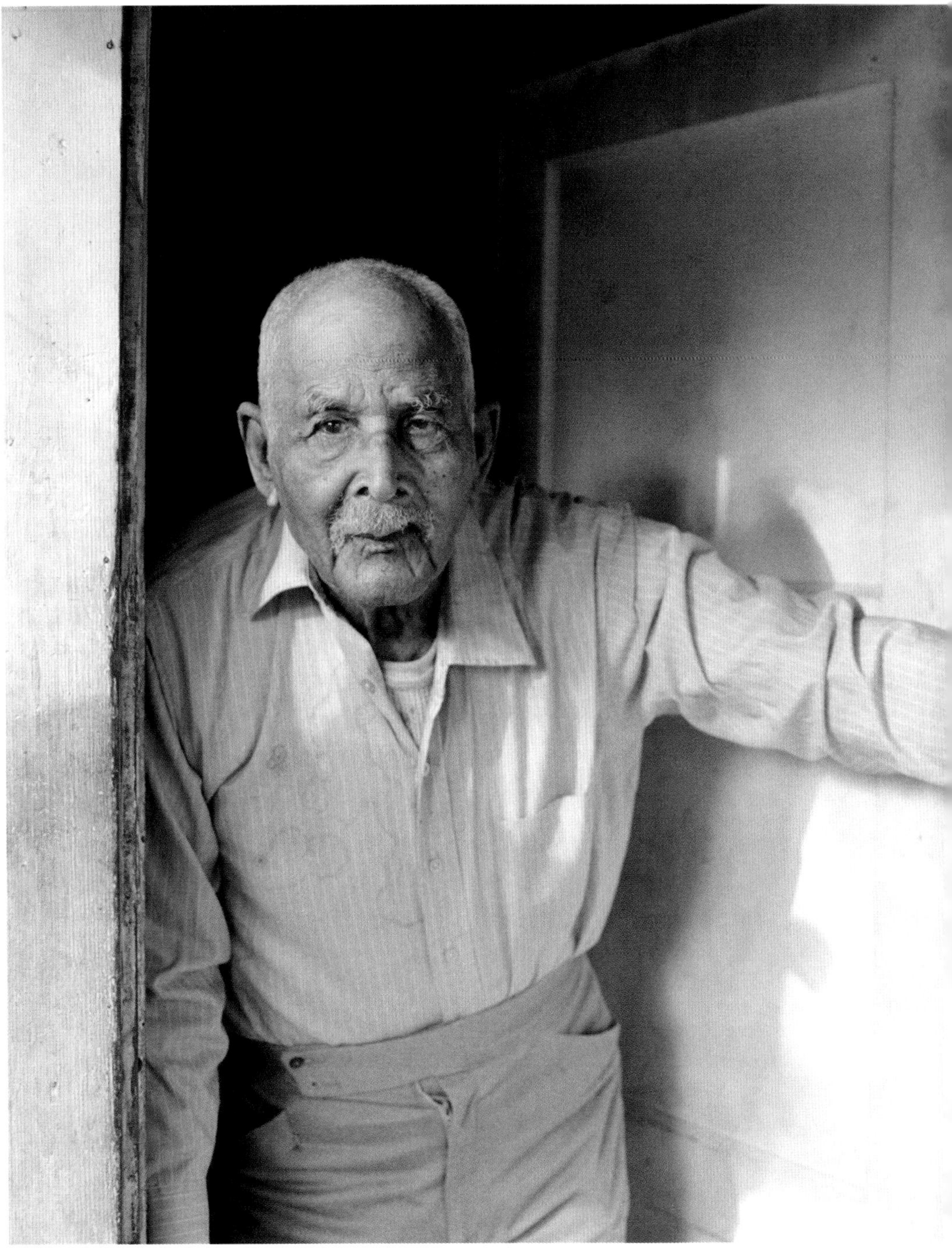

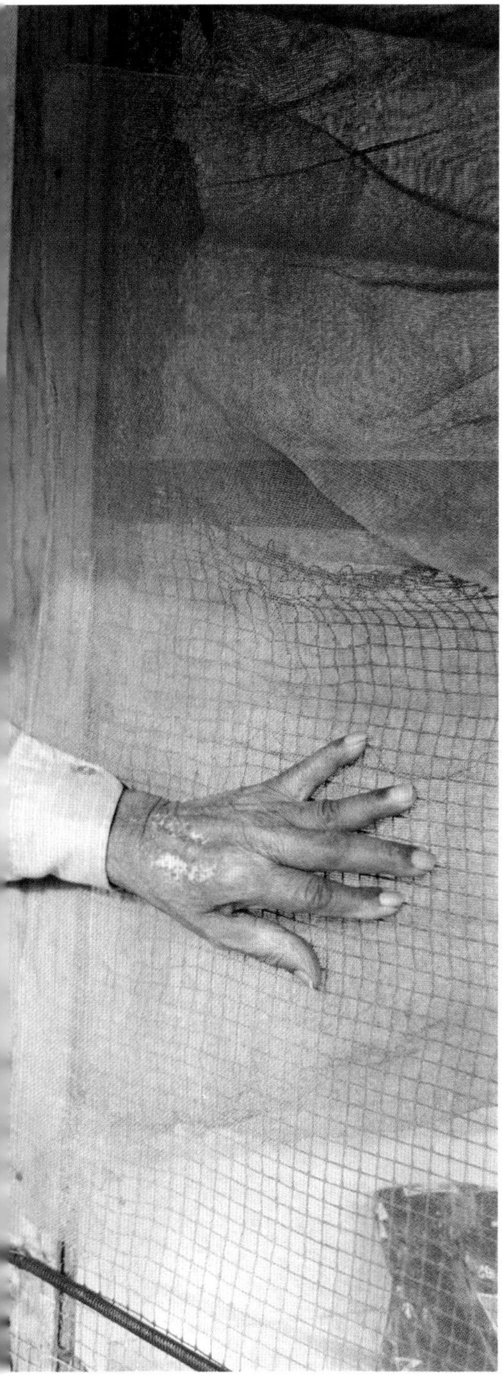

Leavin' a Testimony

Portraits from Rural Texas

by Patsy Cravens

Foreword by John B. Boles

Afterword by Bob Patten

University of Texas Press, Austin

Publication of this book was aided
by the generous support of the
University of Texas Advisory Council.

Printed in China
First edition, 2006

♾ The paper used in this book meets
the minimum requirements of
ANSI/NISO Z39.48-1992 (R1997)
(Permanence of Paper).

Library of Congress Cataloging-in-Publication Data

Cravens, Patsy
Leavin' a testimony : portraits from rural Texas /
by Patsy Cravens ; foreword by John B. Boles ;
afterword by Bob Patten.— 1st ed.
p. cm. — (Focus on American history series)
ISBN-13: 978-0-292-71305-5 (cl. : alk. paper)
ISBN-10: 0-292-71305-3 (cl. : alk. paper)
1. Colorado County (Tex.)—History. 2. Colorado County (Tex.)—
History—Pictorial works. 3. Colorado County (Tex.)—Social conditions.
4. Colorado County (Tex.)—Social conditions—Pictorial works.
5. Oral history—Texas—Colorado County. 6. Colorado County (Tex.)—
Biography. I. Title: Leavin' a testimony. II. Title. III. Series.
F392.C58.C73 2006
976.4'253—dc22

2005037094

I want to dedicate this work with great love and affection to my first grandchild, Johnny Arcidiacono, who was with us from 1985 till '98, a boy with a big heart, loved by all who knew him. His generous spirit was evident when he said pensively of his great-grandmother after she died, "Meme's so lucky—she's gonna get to heaven and meet Martin Luther King before I do." None of us knew then how quickly Johnny would follow her. He was a child with a rare sense of love, wisdom, and gentleness, like an old soul. We miss him.

And I'm preparin' every day for a better home. . . . And I'm proud to tell what I know because one of these days I will go to a new home. And when I go, I want to leave a testimony, and that is that I've done my best.

Rosezena Woodson

Contents

Foreword

John B. Boles

Colorado County, Texas, lies about one hour due west of Houston, but it can seem a thousand miles away. One heads out on Interstate 10, all twelve lanes swarming with cars and trucks just past the beltway around the city, and for endless miles the urban sprawl, with its frenetic pace, sweeps westward almost until one reaches the Brazos River. Finally housing developments give way to prairie, and an observant driver eventually notices that the land becomes slightly more rolling and life less hectic. One has reached Colorado County. Its county seat, Columbus, is bisected by the Colorado River, which, beginning far away in the southern section of the Panhandle, runs southeastwardly across the state, through Austin, and on through Columbus before emptying into the Gulf of Mexico at Matagorda. Colorado County is about a thousand square miles in size, with a growing season of 280 days and an annual rainfall of 41 inches—a perfect climate, it turns out, for cotton.

Several American Indian groups first inhabited the region at least twelve thousand years ago, and in the late seventeenth and early eighteenth centuries explorers from both France and Spain traversed what became the county. But the first permanent Anglo settlers began arriving in 1821 as part of the original colonists brought to Texas by Stephen F. Austin. Colorado County was organized in 1837, a year after the Texas Revolution, and its population began to grow rapidly as settlers migrated from the Old South, often bringing their slaves, intending to grow cotton on the virgin soil of the new county. By 1860, Colorado County produced the fifth-largest cotton crop of any Texas county, and 45 percent of its population were African American slaves.

There was also from the 1830s and 1840s a smattering of settlers from Germany, and later in the nineteenth century other immigrants came from Czechoslovakia and Austria. It would not be until the last few decades of the twentieth century that significant Hispanic immigration further diversified the population. In the census of 2000, Hispanics made up 20 percent of the county's population and the blacks only 15 percent, but that shift in ethnicity was a development of the last twenty-five years or so. Before 1960, Colorado County's population remained quite similar to the way it had been in the nineteenth century, largely Anglo and black with some families of German and Czech ancestry.

So this old Texas county, with its antebellum heritage of cotton and slavery, seasoned with a sprinkling of mostly non-slaveholding European settlers, entered the twentieth century with a history not unlike that of many other counties in East and Central Texas (except that those to the east had largely been settled only by whites and blacks from the Old South). Colorado County's agriculture, its folkways and culture, its religious traditions, and its pattern of race relations closely resembled those of much of the state. Because it escaped the rapid urbanizing experience of Harris County and Houston, Colorado County retained significant portions of its early character and traditions almost until the end of the twentieth century. Not that modernity had not intruded along with new people and new ideas—one saw TV antennas and fast-food restaurants—but much of the county remained culturally in touch with its past to an extent seldom seen in modern urban Texas.

Patsy Cravens realized almost two decades ago that the past really did extend into the present in Colorado County and was there to be captured by her camera and tape recorder. With consummate skill and patience, a sympathetic ear, and a winning smile, she set forth to discover, to excavate, to recover, and to record what she saw and heard. But she was not looking for the Colorado County of today as much as that of yesterday, which was slowly fading away. She had come to realize that as the older population died—those whose lives were grounded in the rural and small-town past—a veritable time capsule would be lost. (Many of her interviewees represented here have in fact died since she recorded their stories.) Patsy therefore set forth on an incredible journey to learn and preserve the memory of lived experience, to prepare a folk history of this county whose heritage resembles so many others in the state and yet is subtly different.

And the authors of this folk history would be those very senior citizens who, because they are "just ordinary people," are so often omitted from the accounts of the past. Not a modern sociological cross section of the citizens of present-day Colorado County but rather an unscientific, intuitive representation of those people who had dominated the county a half century or more ago, the result turned out to be this remarkable portrait of Colorado Countians of yesteryear. The ethnic mix of her characters is that of about 1950, not 2000. To a stunning degree, Patsy Cravens has revealed more about the tone and texture of life in one Texas county than most would have thought possible. Here one finds storytellers of consummate skill and others almost too shy to talk, town folk and ranchers, storekeepers and farmers, husbands and wives, mothers and grown children, musicians and artists, the mainstays of the church and reprobates, gardeners plain and fancy, paeans to spouses and good-riddances to sorry partners, characters so colorful and lively and varied they seem to have been produced by a kaleidoscope. This book is a triumph of the human spirit, both Patsy Cravens's and that of her subjects.

The photographs and the words of Patsy's subjects speak to us with power, with insight, and with courage. Occasionally they are funny, always they are honest, sometimes they are bitter, usually they are more generous than we might have expected, always they come across as so emphatically human that we feel we have actually met them ourselves. The stories they tell often shock the modern ear, and they reveal a past that was often hard, brutal, unforgiving. Here is grinding poverty, racial prejudice, violence—even a shocking lynching (one of several, in fact) that was mostly covered up for more than a half century before Patsy teased out its history. Here too one hears over and over again of the abiding strength, the healing balm, provided by heartfelt religion. I think many urban readers today will especially be surprised by the poverty so many of these people, black and white, suffered—those were hard times back in the thirties, mean things happened to people, and yet most of those who lived through that era somehow found a resiliency, a capacity to endure, that can only evoke admiration.

These stories reveal personal tragedies, lives at first battered and warped but eventually straightened out, a simply amazing ability to keep on struggling in the face of adversity and hatefulness and ignorance. Despite the hardship and disappointment described decades ago, nearly every person interviewed evinced a sense of humor, compassion, forgiveness, and a positive orientation toward life in the present. One cannot help being struck by the strength of character these interviewees reveal despite, or perhaps because of, what they have come through. Not everyone experienced the same degree of hardship, and of course only the African Americans (and the few Mexican Americans) suffered the double blow of bone-breaking poverty and soul-wounding racism. Yet one comes away from the experience of encountering all the people who populate the pages of this remarkable book feeling more confident of the ability of the human spirit to prevail in the midst of the travails of life. This is a shocking, powerful, moving, disturbing, ultimately hopeful book. We all stand in debt to Patsy Cravens for having the imagination, the determination, the skill, and the heart to capture this almost-forgotten portion of the past and to preserve those fragile memories that could so easily have been lost. They are now, thanks to her, a permanent part of our state's history.

Acknowledgments

Many thanks and much love to my four sons, Pepe (James), Johnny, Joe Henry, and Peter Arcidiacono, wonderful men and great friends to me.

Love to their wives, four incredible women, and thanks for my eight grandchildren—each special and beautiful in his or her own way.

Thanks to Theresa May, my editor at the University of Texas Press, for her belief in me, her patience, her understanding, her sensitivity to my work, and her ability to teach and make new concepts clear without being "preachy." Theresa, you are a wonder. I remember gratefully the day she pointed out how the voices of the people in these stories are musical, while our voices, my voice, is interruptive of their flow. In other words, speak lightly, let the force of their words have sway, without interference. Thanks to Don Carlton and Linda Peterson, from the Center for American History at the University of Texas, and to Bill Bishel of UT Press, for your support.

Special thanks Robert Al Walee, my "Black Guardian Angel" as he calls himself, who has taught, helped, and encouraged me in many ways, for many years. Thanks to Bob Patten, a dear friend, and Bill Camfield, both from Rice University, and to Mimi Crossley and Mary Margaret Hanson who have believed in my "eye" and my abilities as a photographer. They all have been supportive of my work for years and have pushed and prodded me to keep on when I was in doubt and hesitation.

Thanks to Jessica and Louisa, friends I could count on from early childhood. Thanks to my friends and teachers of social justice, Jackalyn Rainosek and Liz Cloud especially, who taught me so much about racism and the other "isms," those vicious and insidious dividers of people. They helped me examine my previously unrecognized white privilege and its accompanying arrogance, guiding me in how to learn and change my thinking, actions, and attitudes, plus many other challenging and invaluable lessons.

Introduction

These are stories of hard times. They could be set in many different parts of the country, but they actually took place in South Central Texas, in Colorado County.

I have been coming to this area since my parents bought a farm here, over fifty years ago. I am a photographer and a lover of the Texas landscape. I spent many hours walking through the fields and woods, exploring and taking pictures, but I never really knew the people, and that felt sad to me.

So I decided to pay a visit to an elderly neighbor, Ivory Steward, to take his picture and hear his story. Somehow I knew I had a lot to learn from him. Ivory was a church deacon, a farmer, and a "water witch." We sat at his kitchen table, and I listened while Ivory reminisced, cried, and told funny stories. I was amazed by his openness, wisdom, and generosity.

Ivory died soon after that, but with that gentle man, and in that quiet way, I began a project that was to last many years and change my life enormously: the gathering of people's stories. It became a journey of great learning for me.

So I bring you some of these special friends with their stories of hard times and survival, faith and forgiveness, friendship and celebration, for your enjoyment and learning.

These are the words that opened the oral history video I wrote and produced in 1995, *Coming through Hard Times.* It featured many of the same individuals you will meet in this book, and the words that introduced the video now welcome you to this book as well.

How did the project begin? Innocently, through that first visit to Ivory Steward, camera and tape recorder in hand. I had only one idea in mind: to spend time with Ivory and get to know him better before he died. But Ivory had a lot to teach—and I had a lot to learn. It never entered my mind that this one visit would lead to twenty years of work: browsing the area, seeking and meeting interesting people, building lifelong friendships, creating a traveling photography show called "Colorado County Memories: Everybody Has a Story to Tell" (which I carried by rent truck from place to place), the award-winning video *Coming Through Hard Times,* and now this book.

I never meant to be a documentary photographer. A professional photographer and friend once told me, "You're not a photographer. You're an artist with a camera."

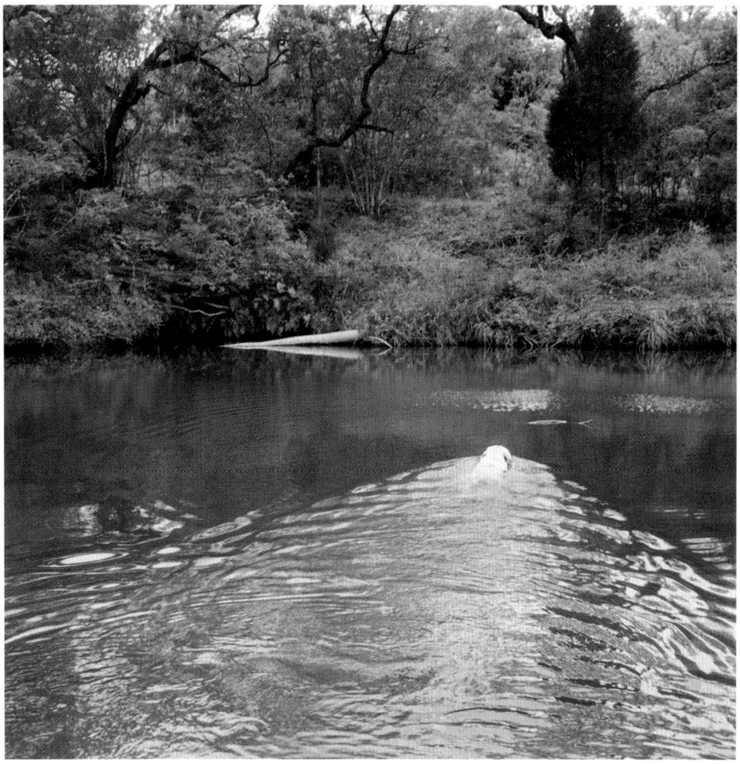

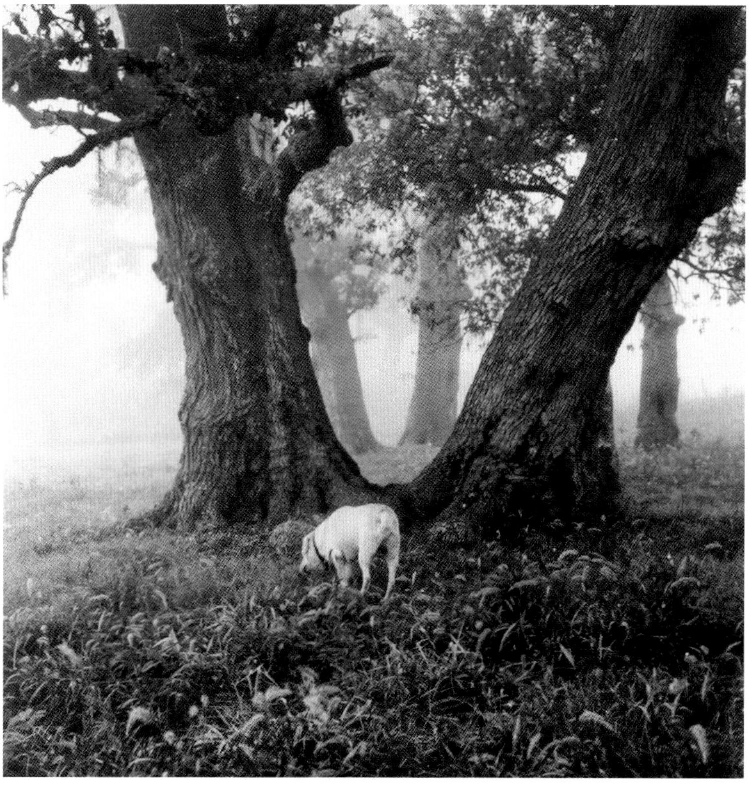

And that was fine. Yet here I am, documenting people. A friend once called this process of working without a fixed goal "going ass-backwards into things." It works fine for me.

Ivory provided my first taste of the kind of wisdom I was to discover later in many other individuals in his rural community. I found these folks, often with minimal education, to have extraordinary skills for self-expression. They seemed to have an image of their life in its entirety, seeing patterns and relationships in a way very unlike the people I'd been familiar with, people who tended to see their lives in terms of achievements, education, and job titles. My rural friends see more patterns in life; they seem to possess a broader, more circular, holistic view of life that has been inspiring.

Their goodwill, the abiding humor and joy, the courage, resiliency, and faith they possess in the face of poverty and hard times, racism and bigotry, are amazing. That they emerged with spirits intact seems incredible. I took an audiotape of one conversation to a transcription service, and when I went to retrieve the document, the woman who had done the work came out from her desk to say "thank you." She said that it was the most enjoyable work she had ever done in that business. And she explained that she had no one among her older relatives and friends with the high spirits, positive attitude, and sense of fun that she found in the woman whose interview she had transcribed. She was feeling more hopeful for her own later years.

I wish you could actually hear their voices, so you could better appreciate the thoughts of my editor, Theresa May, on the poetry and melody to be found there. A high school English teacher once told me he was using *Coming Through Hard Times* in teaching a poetry class. Notice the deeply romantic way Lonzo Dorn and John Webb describe falling in love with their wives-to-be from the first glimpse, when they were youngsters—it's very open, loving, and heartfelt. Hear Mamie Johnson when she describes losing her baby girl at "one year, four months, and sixteen days"; the pain is palpable still, after more than seventy years. Enjoy the naughtiness in Eva Mae Glover and Lillie Williams as they tell stories of "dancin' bad," doing the "Maw Grind" and the "Sassy Wiggle." Eva Mae was a "bad wo-*man*," as she said. What fun they were having even in their last years—and what role models for the rest of us!

I found these to be people of great goodwill. As they welcomed this stranger into their houses, they also opened their hearts and were gracious in a way that was new to me. This generosity came even though the purpose of my work was vague at best. I never envisioned it as anything like a book or a film. Only once do I remember being turned down when asking for a picture. Folks were much more apt to say, as one woman did, "Sure, come on in the house. I'll show you the family album." No questions asked. No fear—only the willingness to share.

In the midst of this goodwill, there were times when I felt disturbed. One was an instance of meanness and racism when a white man mocked a mentally handicapped black man and called him "Creepin' Jesus." Another was when an elderly white man used the "N word," that cruel, demeaning term. Yes, he was from an era when the word was commonly used, and he was getting senile. Yet my discomfort was deep, because it is painful to hear, ever. Otherwise, most individuals were like Lillie Freis, who spoke with love and caring of her black neighbors, describing how they helped each other and shared food and vegetables out of their gardens. The Kasper family at the meat market helped care for the jobless Jack Fields by giving him food. Everybody seemed to be treated equally at Kasper's.

Each photograph is set in the subjects' personal environment, wherever they were comfortable—living room, front yard, porch, or working environment. I loved the way Eva Mae Glover jammed her hat onto her head, pulling it down with both hands, getting ready for her picture. That was Eva Mae—cocky and confident as always.

It is important to remember that these stories are people's memories—they are not "the Truth," but are simply individuals' recollections. I remember a man who wrote the PBS station in Houston when it first aired *Coming Through Hard Times,* in which several of these same individuals spoke. In the video, Eva Mae Glover talked about the lynching that had happened sixty years earlier, in the hometown she shared with the angry author of the letter. He was furious and canceling his membership in the station because of what Eva Mae had said. He thought she had dishonored his friend, the dead girl's brother, and was "apt to cause major damage" in the community. Since lynching is about instilling fear and maintaining power and control, one can be sure that parts of the white community were worried when the story was finally spoken aloud after sixty years of fearful silence. Eva Mae was a courageous woman indeed, a fighter. The director of programming for the station wrote back to the angry man and pointed out that the stories had not been presented as factual. I feel honored to have been entrusted with these precious memories and want to do them honor. Thank you, Eva Mae.

There is one point I want to make regarding the lynching and the other acts of bigotry, racial meanness, cruelty, and discrimination as related in these stories. In no way do I intend to imply that these horrific attitudes and incidents were particular to Colorado County or that they define the people of Colorado County. Rather, racism, bigotry, discrimination, and acts of terrorism were (and still are to a degree) commonplace from California (where the targets were usually Asian or Hispanic) to the East Coast, across most parts of the United States. Both Columbus and Weimar are towns with charm, warmth, and a sense of welcome. These racist attitudes and behaviors were widely accepted across America without question—South Central Texas was not immune.

Gresham Marmion, a retired Episcopal bishop who tried to stop the lynching, also appeared in the video. I want to thank him in memoriam. He too had great courage. When we talked, he admitted, humbly, that he could easily have been one of the lynch mob if he had not had some fortunate life opportunities that changed him: a chance to travel and to attend divinity school. And he was so frightened on the night of the killing that he remembered almost nothing about it. He simply knew he had tried to stop the murder, standing alone on the hood of a car, the only dissenter, before a large crowd of angry and determined citizens. Someone said there was a rope for him too, if he kept on—he didn't remember this part clearly. And he knew he had no choice—he left. He could remember no faces afterwards, yet he knew some of them were his parishioners, few of whom ever mentioned the awful deed. Gresham came to realize that his entire life had been altered by this one event, that he had ever since taken an active part in the civil rights movement—a good man.

And where did this interest in the lives of others, especially the black community, come from? It's hard to say, yet I do believe that always, even as a small child, there was in me a deep curiosity about other people, and a puzzlement and confusion around many of our society's secrets. I remember asking questions of my mother about the people who worked in our house, a cook and a nurse: If we loved and cared for them, how come we never went to their house, or had them over for dinner, or shared Christmas? It was clear they loved us and we them—so what did it all mean? I remember being disturbed by some racist and demeaning cartoons we sometimes saw at the movies; even then, they were troubling to me and not funny, although some people laughed. The African American man who walked to our house with his mower and tools to do yard work—where did he go when he disappeared so suddenly and mysteriously? (The answer was that he went to prison and to his execution, facts I did not know for years. All the whispering and mystery around him was troubling, and this is a story in itself.) My questions were met with the equivalent of "Don't ask, don't worry, everything is fine," and then silence.

To me, my life growing up seemed small and limited in some ways. I wanted to get out and explore, wander and learn more, go into people's homes and lives, share with them. So it seems natural to end up doing this type of work, the work of exploration with camera and recorder. And it's interesting to recognize that although I always disliked history class and found it dry and boring, I was later called a historian. That felt strange initially. Yet, learning directly from individuals' words about their lives, that is history that has life and meaning for me.

I was asked by an African American woman, how could I *not* have known the extent of racism and racial violence all around as I grew up? In truth, the system of silence, secrecy, and white privilege works so effectively that the truth is well hidden from us, the privileged white folks. I was shushed so often that after a while my questions stopped, and the discomfort got tamped down. I knew no one who talked about or questioned the system. As a grown woman, I believe this is shameful, and I feel sad, angry, and embarrassed about it. Without the friends whose beautiful images appear here, I would never have had the wider understanding they gave me.

I appreciate the words I read recently on "whiteness" in an exhibition at the International Center of Photography in New York. I admire the clarity with which the author, Maurice Berger, expresses himself:

> To be white in American culture today means occupying a social norm so powerful and pervasive that it is rarely even acknowledged. As a marker of identity, whiteness remains an ever-present, and largely unexplored, state of mind and body. This exhibition offers a critical examination of how white skin and white privilege inexorably shape images of the world—and suggests ways we might be able to change them.
>
> Until recently, discussions about race and representation have focused almost exclusively on the experience and struggles of people of color. Such investigations were—and continue to be—essential to peeling back the complex layers of the very idea of race. But they most often left aside the category of "whiteness," which has remained largely invisible, unconscious, presumed. Yet failing to mark whiteness—to probe it and assign it meaning—means failing to take a hard look at a vital component of the social construction of race. In the end, to overlook representations of whiteness is not only to encourage their predominance but also to neglect their potential frailties and weaknesses. No full discussion of race can be complete without addressing these often elusive images.
>
> . . . the works in "White" strive to challenge traditional notions of race, urging us to look beyond entrenched stereotypes, surprising blind spots, and the received ideas that help keep the race debate restricted to comfortable, familiar modes of discussion.*

I believe that even today, we white folks have little recognition of our privilege, the privilege we enjoy without earning it, simply by benefit of our skin color. Black friends have told me stories of things I never experienced—for example, being taught as a child that it was not safe to cross Main Street, the primary city artery. My friend who told me this was finally driven across that dreaded barrier as an adult, by his friend Mickey Leland, against my friend's better judgment. Another black friend still recalls being teased and intimidated as a child by the white policemen in his neighborhood, men who were supposed to be there to protect him, not torment him. There was the man who had the letters "KKK" cut into his chest, in Hermann Park in central Houston in the 1960s. Chilling, isn't it?

We whites do not experience people watching us furtively over their shoulders when we are walking behind them. We have been expecting and receiving acceptance and privilege in the workplace, in school and hospital admissions, in lines at

*Maurice Berger, from the introduction to "White: Whiteness and Race in Contemporary Art," an exhibit at the International Center for Photography, New York, 2005.

To learn more about "whiteness," see the chapter entitled "Representations of Whiteness in the Black Imagination," in *Killing Rage: Ending Racism,* by bell hooks; *To Be One: A Battle against Racism,* by Nathan Rutstein; *Killers of the Dream,* by Lillian Smith; and *A Lynching in the Heartland: Race and Memory in America,* by James H. Madison.

the movies, virtually everywhere. A younger black friend told me how glad she and her friends and family were when finally, one day a week, they were allowed to visit the Museum of Fine Arts in Houston. Many an African American was refused hospital care in the past, so I am proud that my maternal grandfather gave funds for the first Houston hospital where black doctors could practice and black patients be admitted. We have a lot to learn still about all of this.

My hope is that you, the reader, will experience some of the wisdom, joy, and proud spirit I have enjoyed from these extraordinary folks as they speak to us from their hearts. I have learned so much and have enjoyed doing this work profoundly. I feel fortunate and richly rewarded. May you be also.

The Stories

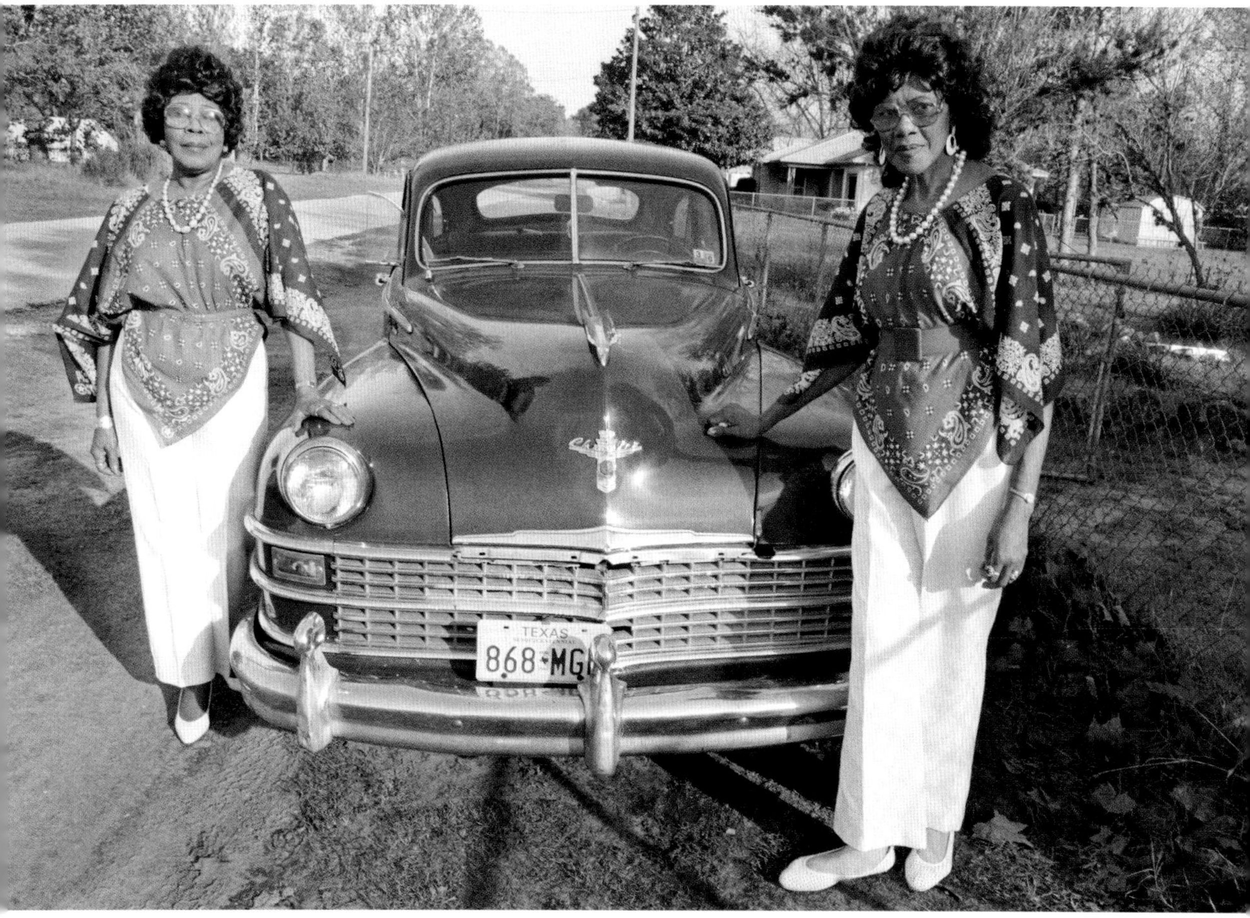

Ethel and Hattie Lee Wilson with their '49 Chrysler

Ethel & Hattie Lee Wilson

I first noticed the dashing Wilson sisters at the Colorado County Fair, dressed in matching red, white, and blue bandanna outfits that Ethel had sewn. It was clear right off that they would be great women and we needed to meet.

It turned out they had spotted me too, staked me out as a photographer. "We knowed as soon as we seen you, you'd wanta take our picture," they said, with winning smiles. Then Ethel described her 1949 Chrysler, the two-owner car with the long, shiny body, and we were in business. By good fortune, we became friends through this chance meeting at the fairgrounds.

"We always lived in Colorado County," said Hattie, with a sense of pride in her cultured voice. "We were born on the Tait Ranch. It's a plantation," she explained grandly. The Wilson family had lived there on the ranch, a few miles out from Columbus, and worked for the Taits for many years. "Colonel Tait brought our family from Georgia and placed them out there. Dr. William Tait brought my great-grandmother here as a slave.

"Our great-grandmother's name was Jenny, Jenny Blake—and she had only one child, a son she named Plez," Hattie continued. "Plez was my mother's daddy. They all lived out on the plantation until they passed. Just as the kids was married, they would move away. Mother married and left. Then our daddy died when I was a little girl, and Mother moved back with the Taits. And so we been with them ever since." The charming Wilson sisters were never far from Columbus.

"We was happy as larks," Ethel said of their childhood. "We could get up and play. We raised chickens. We raised our own turkeys, hogs, cows, made our own milk, and butter. We raised our own vegetables. We were raised right up in the Tait house—we slept in the home with the kids. We slept with those kids. And they were gonna go anywhere, they'd just gather up and go on and leave us with the kids."

They worked in the fields until Ethel figured a way to get out of that chore: "I didn't like field work! I stopped workin' in the fields, and I went and stayed at the house and just done housework, 'cause I didn't *like* field work. It's *very* hard work, and I didn't like it. I *still* don't! Be cryin'! I was afraid of worms—you know how worms gets on the cotton leaves and things—and I be standin' up in the fields *fightin'* the worms and *cryin',* and Mama say, *'Goooo* to the house before I kill you.' And that's the way I got out of fields, and I never *did* go back! You can take me and run me all over town with one worm—I still don't like 'em!

"Our mother was Sophile Wilson and our daddy was Náthaniel, and we also had a brother, Leamon, but he got hurt workin' in a gravel pit, and he died. So that was the end of our family. So after Brother died, Sister and I, we just decided to dedicate our lives to takin' care of Mother. And we taken care of her till she passed [at ninety-seven]." She, Leamon, and Leamon's son were all buried in the Willing Workers Cemetery in Columbus.

Ethel worked for the Taits for forty-eighty years and raised the Taits' daughter, Millie, "like my own daughter," she said fondly. "I was like a mother to her. And boy, I had a room upstairs where I'd just go up there and sleep, just Millie and me. And I keep the baby near me."

After Sophile's death, Hattie and Ethel moved into town, Hattie into a house belonging to the Taits, which she embellished with wind chimes in the trees, wine bottle–lined walkways, painted stones, upended bricks in patterns, and a front porch heavy with mobiles, couches, chairs, and mirrors framed in seashells. She thus created an inviting presence. Ethel moved into a rent house a few streets away, with her dog and The Car, which the ladies still drove, slowly, around town.

The Wilsons' lives were anything but empty after their move in from the ranch. Hattie "did a little bit of everything." She decorated the church, helped out at funerals, "made welcome," sang in three choirs, and worked in the community at the Red Cross, the March of Dimes, Magnolia Homes Tour, and the senior citizens program. She sang once on the radio and did interior and wedding decorations. Ethel also worked in the Magnolia Home Tours and at St. Paul's United Methodist Church, where she sang in the women's choir and played piano for the men's. She had taught herself to cook and sew by watching her mother and later learned to play the piano by ear. She raised one daughter, Joyce, who moved to San Antonio and became a nurse.

When asked what was important to her late in life, Ethel responded, "A lot of things are important to me. I just want to have a good, healthy life and love people, do for people, whatever I can for 'em. Be able to help wherever I can for whoever I can. That's my theory, to do the best I can in life, live to the best of my abilities and serve the Lord—because I'm almost too old to do anything else!" And she laughed cheerily.

The two ladies were almost always in each other's company, visiting at one of their houses or driving slowly in their elegant Chrysler, laughing and talking, the best of friends. The Wilson sisters were not quite like anyone else. They stood alone and special, with a sense of openness to life that was a pleasure to share.

Hattie died unexpectedly in 1992, leaving Ethel devastated. Seven pastors from around the area spoke at Hattie's funeral. Ethel lived until 1998, leaving behind her daughter, Joyce, her car, and her beloved fox terrier, Peewee.

Ivory "Pie" Steward

"We've gotta help somebody, we gotta give a portion of what you know, of what you have, to the other fellow. This world is fixed so your brother is tied to you—can't go to heaven without him, got to carry him along with you. You can't love God until you love your fellow man. I don't see no color, I love *everybody*. If I got an enemy, I don't know it." These are Pie Steward's loving words.

Ivory Steward, called Pie by his family and friends, lived his entire life in Colorado County, and on the same plot of land for eighty-five years, from 1903 until he died in 1988. His parents were Riss Jackson Steward, from the Borden community near Weimar, and Will Steward, from nearby Osage. Will ran a small grocery store there on their farm. "A country store," recalled one of Pie's friends. "We'd go over there and get coal oil for 'bout a nickel." Friends say Ivory's nickname came from childhood, when his older brother was called Sweetie, and Ivory, who followed, naturally became Pie.

When we first talked in 1985, Pie was already eighty-seven years old. He was having some problems with his legs, but clearly none with his mental faculties. He was alert, eloquent, and brimming with wise thoughts and funny stories. He was living with his second wife, Katherine, whom he called Katerina, in the house where his parents had once lived and run their tiny rural store.

It was a small white frame house set in a yard full of chickens on a farm-to-market road. Pie had a fine collection of gaudily feathered roosters to tend to the many hens, all scratching around the large pile of firewood he cut for his stove. Pie said he enjoyed living near the road because he loved to watch people drive by on their way to town. He also liked to keep an eye on the neighborhood activities.

He talked a lot about his church, Pleasant Hill Missionary Baptist, and he served his church loyally. He was a clerk there and often spoke during the services. It was a source of great pride for him to have been honored for his forty-five years of service on the board of the La Grange Missionary Baptist Association. It was clear that people respected Ivory.

He had been a farmer, a digger of water wells, and a "water witch" all his life. He explained that he used both peach and willow branches equally well as divining rods, or "wands," in his search for water. He said he had learned his skills from other local water diviners. He was known to miss the mark only rarely. I was with him in the woods as he searched for water one day, and I experienced the wand turning in my hands, pointing down to the ground against my will. Pie was a gentle and patient teacher.

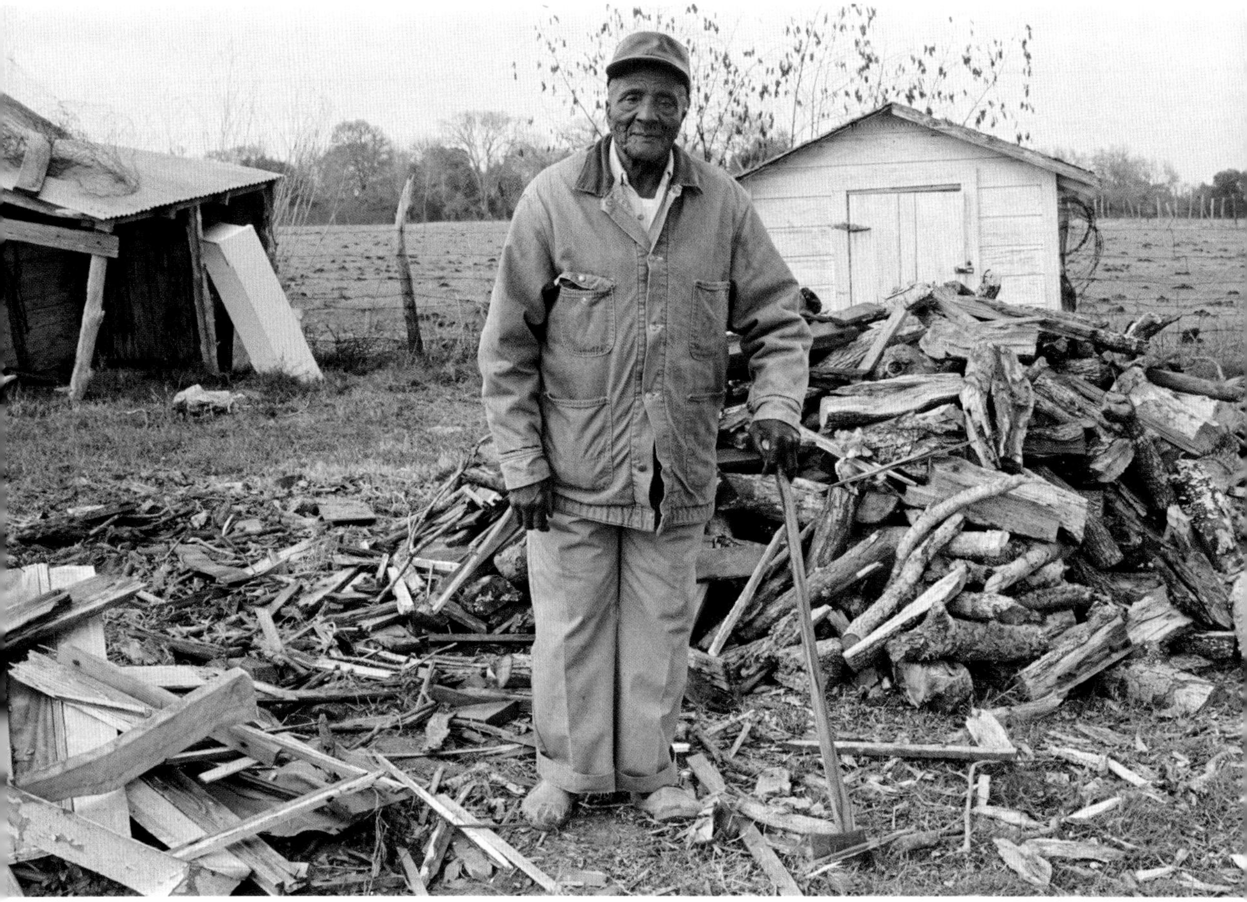

Ivory "Pie" Steward at the woodpile

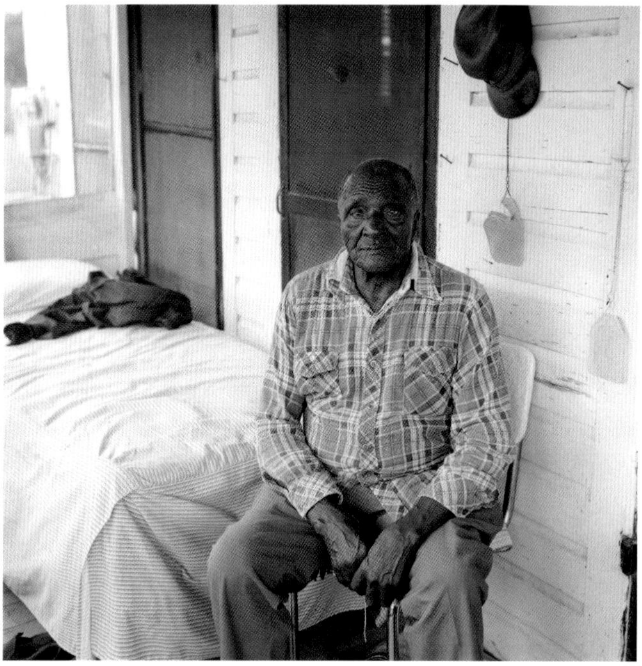

Ivory "Pie" Steward

When we sat together that day in his kitchen, Pie spoke with dignity and clarity, telling stories about his life and the life around him in Colorado County. "I'm glad to tell you things that I passed," he said sincerely and pointed out that he was the only "colored" left living in the country—but he added that his white neighbors looked out for him. "I enjoy what you're doing now. I'm glad to tell you things I've passed over, because you can't go back over this life. You live it only one time."

He described the risks of being a young man coming home in an open-sided wagon after a night on the town. He explained that the trick was to sit in the very center of the wagon so that if you fell over you wouldn't fall off the wagon and get left behind. He said it also helped to have a horse or mule that could find its own way home if you were so incapacitated you were unable to direct it. Pie assured me he did not drink or ride a wagon anymore.

"Well, a young man is foolish to a whole extent," he said, "but he doesn't see that until he get old. But when you get old, where you can't do what you used to, can't think like you used to, and all like that, you can learn to take things as you find it, and thank Jesus for your friend—that's if you want to do the right thing."

Here is some more of Ivory's wisdom as it was recorded that day: "That's my determination, to be friendly. Because, you know, you can't go back over this life. You live it one time. And same way about having so much here—you can't carry it with you, and you can't come back after it, no, no.

"It's a blessing to be poor to me. What I mean, a 'poor man' is one who don't have no health—that's what you call 'poor.' If he got health and strength, a good sane mind, if he has a good will, he can please hisself, he can please God, he can please

Jack Fields

Jack Fields was known to one and all in Weimar, where he spent his days sitting on a bench on the sidewalk outside of Kasper's Meat Market, on the main street of town, a store where everyone shopped and where he is seen standing in this photograph. Jack sat there daily, watching the street life and greeting people as they passed.

Born Fields Thomas in Weimar in 1910, he was called Jack by all. No one could tell where he got his nickname, but Jack Fields was his only name as far as most people knew. Jack did not drive a car. He never married. He had not held a steady job for long. He lived in a small house in the backyard of a local family and walked wherever he needed to go. Folks looked out for him, as far as one could see. Kasper's market gave him meat and snacks. People sometimes drove him places. He had once worked as a dock loader at M-G Feeds but was without a job all the time we were acquainted.

Jack had an intense stammer that made him quite hard to understand, and he had a habit of saying "Ooooo, ooooo, ooooo" over and over when he got excited. He attended Greater Macedonia Baptist Church, where he was treated with great respect by the other parishioners. He was asked to say some words each Sunday ("Can we hear from you, Brother Jack?" the preacher would say). And he was listened to gravely and respectfully as he stammered his few words. It was hard to know if anyone understood him, and yet he had everyone's full attention. He always had a few coins to put in the collection plate.

Jack was an ideal subject for photography since he was so calm and still in front of the camera. When I gave him a copy of his photograph, he looked utterly amazed and delighted, tapping himself gently on the chest, saying over and over, "Oooo, oooo, oooo, that's good! That's me. That's Jack! Oooo, oooo." And he carried the photograph into Kasper's to show around. Folks said that for weeks afterward Jack was still showing the picture proudly, to whoever would look. Once, when this photograph was part of an exhibit at the Weimar Heritage Society Museum, Jack wanted to take the framed picture to show around. He was genuinely surprised that he couldn't remove it from the museum. It was a treat to see him have so much pleasure in something that most people take for granted, a photograph of himself.

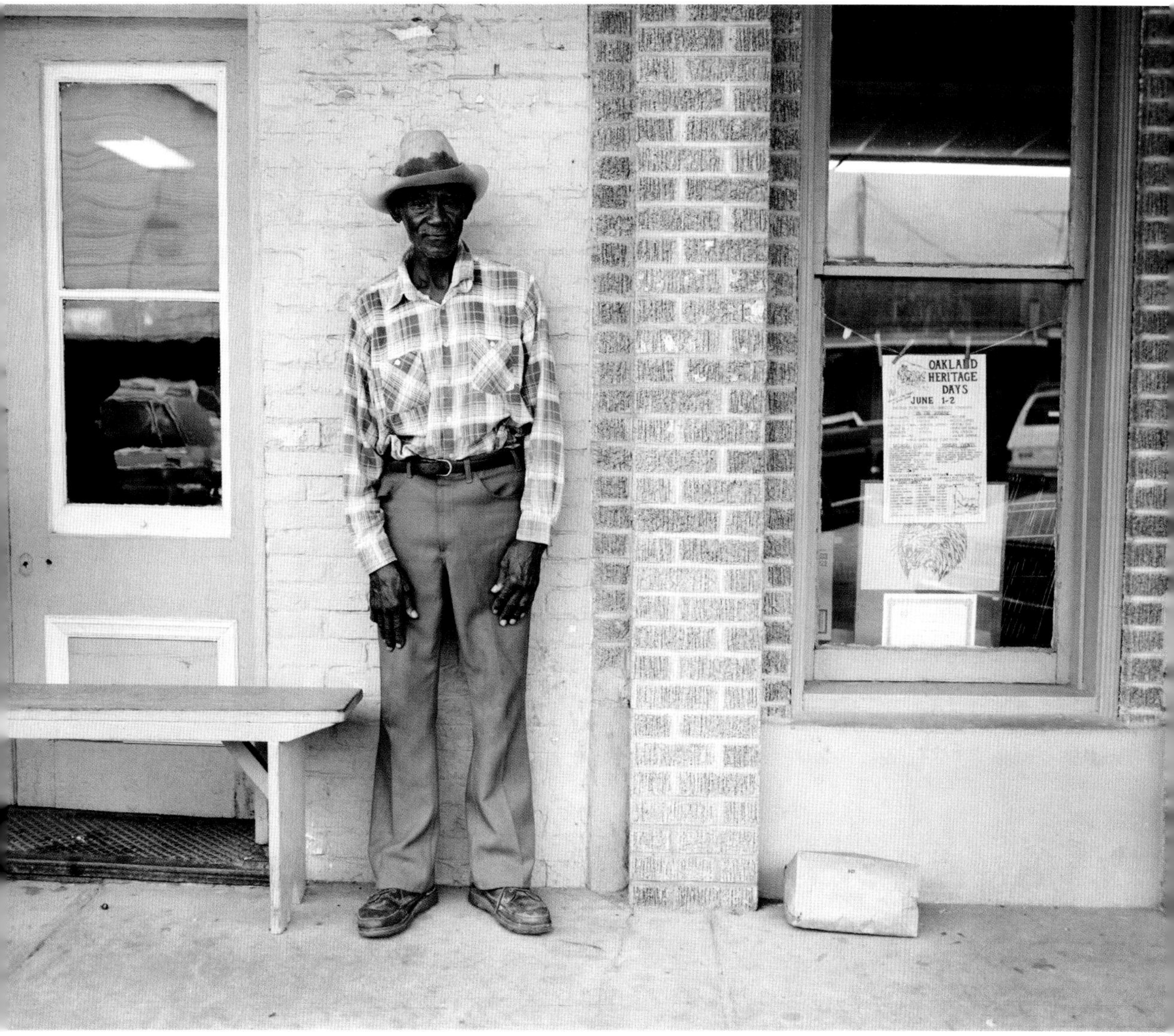

Jack Fields

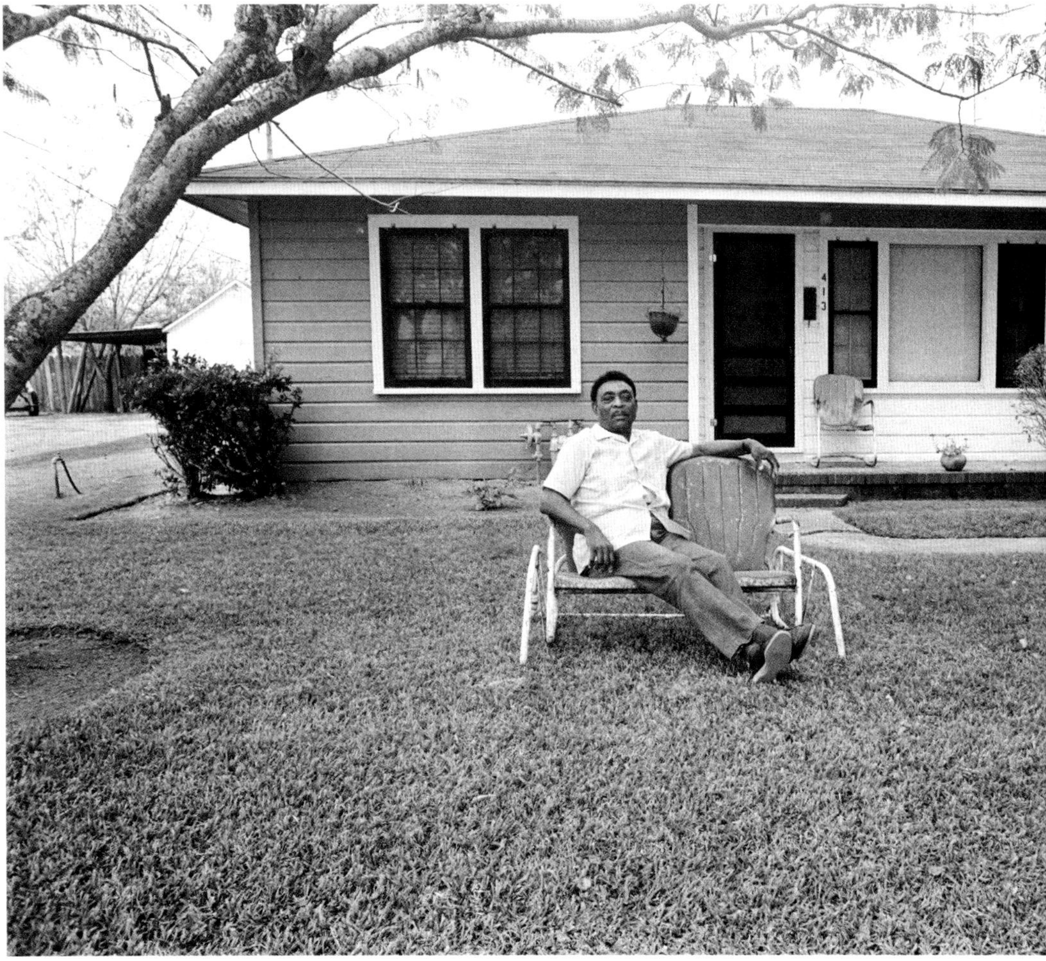

George Braziel

George Braziel

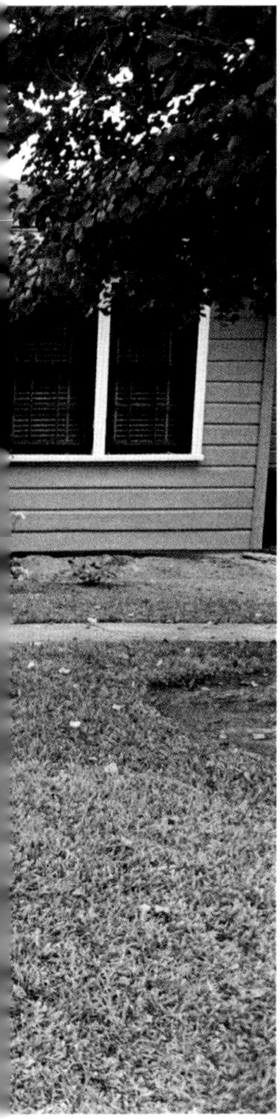

"I'm George Braziel Junior, and my granddaddy told my daddy that he was a slave on the Adkins Plantation, that he was a slave man, the yardman at Old Man Adkins' at that time. He was enslaved." These were George Braziel's first words as he began to tell his story. "He died in the same year I was born, 1910. But he told my daddy a whole lot of what he went through."

George was born the son of a tenant farmer on the Herder Plantation, outside of Columbus: "I was raised in the country, born out there and raised. I come up a young man in Columbus."

His parents were Pinkey and George Braziel; his siblings were his three sisters, Selesa, Gertrude, and Annie Mae, and one brother, Nathan. All were born on the Herder place and worked there at their parents' sides from their earliest years until adulthood, as the Braziel family tried without success to get ahead, leave their servitude, and acquire a farm of their own.

"The Herders had a big farm back there down on the river, had a bunch down there workin' for 'em, like the ole slaves was when my daddy's daddy was comin' up. But we was inched up a little bit from what they were—we wasn't slaves, but just like slaves, you could say—had seven or eight families stayin' in one place.

"We had it hard all the way, *cold,* no food—*all* the way. Papa could hardly make it. We toughed it out. Some years he'd make ten or fifteen bales of cotton, and you never *could* sell it. Mr. Herder and them sold it and give my daddy some seed money. You had to do what he said—you couldn't get nothin' to eat if you didn't do that.

"Whatever Herder said you owed, that's what you had to pay. And then he'd tell them, 'Well, you *just* about got squeezed out.' You didn't get no money—*they* got the money. Herder and them got the money. You worked on it all year, and they said if you got out of debt, then they would give you some. But he fixed it so you never *did* get out of debt. You always a little bit, just *a little bit* from gettin' out of debt. We had a *hard* way to go. We still was naked and didn't have no clothes hardly to wear.

"You know the sacks what they put cotton in? I wore that many a day. They taken old sacks, sacks what they put cotton in. Mama cut out the hole and slide it on over us. Just cut the corners out and make a hole in it, slip it over, and cut it on off. I wore that many a day. Slip it over your head, and you go on and play, just like you had good clothes on. Did that many a day. Wore that. Felt just like a old rough shirt. Who cares, long as it hid your nakedness?

"I asked Daddy many times why he had to stay there. He said, 'Well, there's nothin' else you could do. *What I gonna do?* I don't know *nothin' else to do*.' See, that's why a lot of people got rich like that. They got rich on people workin' out there and takin' everything from 'em and sellin' it and givin' 'em whatever they wanted to give 'em. That's why I say we had such a hard way to go."

What did the tenants get to eat? "What they sent back from the commissary," George said. "Old rank lard, and yellowed. And old half-rotten potatoes. Fed 'em like you do cattle. They brought truckloads of food what Herder's brother had there in Weimar. He had a store. Things they were gonna throw away, they brought it to the farm. People grabbed a gallon bucket and go to the commissary to get what the man brought 'em. And he brought it down there and throwed it to my Daddy and them, when I was comin' up.

"That's why I didn't get no further in school. I didn't get a chance to go to school. Only when it rained we got a chance to go to school.

"Them little books and things there, Papa wadn't able to buy none hardly. 'Cause he had to buy you books. The state didn't furnish no books—*you* had to buy 'em. I had to quit. Just learned how to write my name and read a little bit, that's what I did. And when we was big enough to work, Papa kept us busy workin'—you didn't have no days to go to school. Did learn to read and write just a little." George sometimes said he quit after the first grade, sometimes that he made it to third. No matter, it was too little to benefit him much either way. "That's why I could have been further than I am now, if I could've had any kind of education," he added.

"So we stayed till I got grown. Then I said, 'Well, when I get grown, I don't believe I'm gonna live this way. I'm gonna get me a job where I can work and earn my money, and get it where I get paid every weekend.'

"See, my daddy, his daddy was enslaved. And the generation comin' on up was just a little bit better. He was the same as enslaved 'cause he had to do what they said to do. If they tell you to do somethin', well, we had to do it. If he didn't do it, Herder and them would 'cut his mouth off,' meanin' he would give him nothin' to eat.

"Well, see, like I got 'low IQ.' When I went in the army, I got 'low I.Q.' and they put all us of 'low IQ'—well, we were given common labor to do, drain oil, stuff like that." So George did "common labor" until he was chosen to become the company barber and help run the PX.

"I been barberin' ever since I was about fifteen years old. I learned to barber from a boy out there in the sticks—wasn't no barber shop, least at that time. I started cuttin' hair on the stump, for nothin'. We cut each other's hair. Then I growed up to be a man and I picked it up, and I can cut any kind of hair. Just kept the trade a-goin'.

"Army life was all right with me. It was nice. Saved a little money there—made enough to build a house."

The land where George's grandfather was held in bondage was in Osage, near Weimar, on land now belonging to the Trefny family. George remembered many stories from his grandfather, Wash, told to him as a boy by his father. One favorite was how Wash helped build a log barn for his owner, Mr. Adkins. The story went that when he was getting old, Mr. Adkins began to think about protecting his money. According to George, the old man "went to town in his jig and he bought some large brass pots" and buried his money in the pots underneath the barn floor. Legend had it that the money sat undisturbed for years. George laughs about the time he and some friends went to the farm to look for the buried treasure. It was about 1929, and the old barn had fallen in. The young men dragged away the floorboards with a tractor and dug for the gold pots. "I just knowed we was rich then!" he said with a chuckle. "I thought we were poor goin' up there, be rich comin' back! Got up there and dug all over that barn, couldn't find nothin'. I sure was disappointed," and he laughed again.

Charles Trefny, too, remembered stories of buried treasure: "During the Civil War, supposedly they buried their gold that they had. They didn't have banks in those days or any other place to put their valuables. So they either had a strongbox in the house, or a lot of people just hid things. They hid 'em out in the woods or in the creeks, under the rocks, under the corners of the house, or under the corners of the barns and all. There are all kinds of tales about where the money is buried and what's been dug up. And lots of folks have dug around looking for treasure and found nothin'."

The only evidence remaining of the Adkins house was the front steps, which sat in the Trefnys' backyard. Charles walked me around the hillside where the slave graves were supposed to have been. We searched and found only a few low humps of dirt, no evidence of gravesites. He said there used to be lots of superstition around the spot and lots of talk of ghosts and spirits.

After the army, George ended up in Weimar. There he remained, and that was where he proudly moved his elderly parents, providing them with a small house and their first time ever of rest and comfort. "Mr. Holt sold us a little ground for a hundred and some dollars, and we built a little box house there. My father died in that same house. It was back in '41 or '42. Papa and them on relief then, so they could get food."

George worked for years in Weimar, driving trucks for Walter Beken, Brasher Motors, and Carl Saunders. "When I was growed up and got a man, after I came to Weimar and growed up and be gone, I taken care of all my children," George said. "They went to school. All of 'em finished high school. Got two graduates out of college. I got here and started workin', and things got better. My kids didn't come up like I did. This is my home now. This is the house where all my children were raised up grown, and after, they left, moved some in San Antonio, some in Houston. And I own the home—this is my home," he repeated with pride in his voice.

George had six children—four in San Antonio, two in Houston—all doing well in their professions. His son, Melvin, was named president and CEO of the San Antonio Housing Authority in 1998 and was described in the local newspaper, the *Weimar Mercury,* as "well-known and well respected" in the public housing industry. One granddaughter graduated from law school.

George said, "Young people these days, they got a *good* way to go. In them days when I come along, wasn't no cars. Wasn't nothin' but mules, horses and buggies. Wasn't no way for you to get to town 'less'n you walk. Wasn't no airplanes—*just* beginnin' to come in. I remember the first airplane to come along—everybody runnin' along, just like the world comin' to an end. Didn't know *what that was* in the sky.

"Was hard times when I was comin' up. Things done got better now than what they used to be. We livin' a whole lot better now. I own my own home and everythin'. Now retired, getting' to old age. So I'm doin' pretty good now. It was rough back then, when we come along—it was rough! But the Lord brought us on, brought us on through it all. It's all over now. We don't have to live that way no more. It's all over—we live better than we did then. He taken care of us some kind of way until he seen fit for things to change. The Lord fixed it so it wouldn't last."

When George died in 2003, the local paper wrote that he had been known as "Mr. Sugar" because he would keep the American Legion hall open "for the children to buy candy and have a place to play pool."

Eva Mae Glover

"My name is Eva Mae Glover," she began, "but they call me Geneva for a nickname.

"My grandchil'ren call me Big Mama. I'm Big Mama to everybody what come here. Well, see, that don't make me no nevermind—I *like* it, 'cause some come along since I come along, has gone in. But the Lord, he left me here for a good reason. He must have.

"Well, there's been so much done happened to me, I don't want to tell it. It's so *much* done happened to me, I just don't want to tell it, 'cause I have been through some *bad stuff in my time*," Eva Mae said, with serious emphasis.

When I first went to Eva Mae's house, she slammed the door on me. I had taken a photograph of her son, B.C., at a Weimar parade and wanted to leave a copy at his mom's home. Finding the Glovers' house, I knocked, the door opened, and there was Eva Mae—towering in the doorway, frowning, and looking formidable—as if anyone would be foolish enough to challenge a woman with that posture and that look on her face.

Standing on the lower step, I asked her carefully if she would ever let me take her picture. "Not for a million dollars!" she snapped, and pushed the door shut.

How we became friends is hard to say, but somehow, over time, we did. And we spent some fun and happy hours together. She became a "star" in my documentary, *Coming through Hard Times*, flirting with the male crew members and comfortably telling her stories—sometimes naughty, sometimes funny, sometimes tragic—for the camera.

I found Eva Mae to be direct, gutsy, spirited, fun-loving, intelligent, and courageous. She was wary of the law and the establishment, slow to trust, loyal to her family and friends, and totally faithful to her god. Who else in all of Colorado County was willing to talk about the 1935 lynching of two young teenage cousins? No one but Eva Mae. She had experienced more hard times and tough challenges than most of us can even imagine. She had survived hard work, terrible economic hardship, and a rough relationship with her husband; had intervened when a sheriff tried to shoot her father; had given birth to thirteen children at home, lost three of her adult children, one newborn baby, and three grandchildren, including two grandsons who died violently—not to ignore the harsh reality of being black in a white-dominant world, with all that that implies.

Eva Mae grew up on a farm in the country near Columbus. "I was the boy and the girl both at home. I could cook, I could plow, would go to the fields and I would plow. My

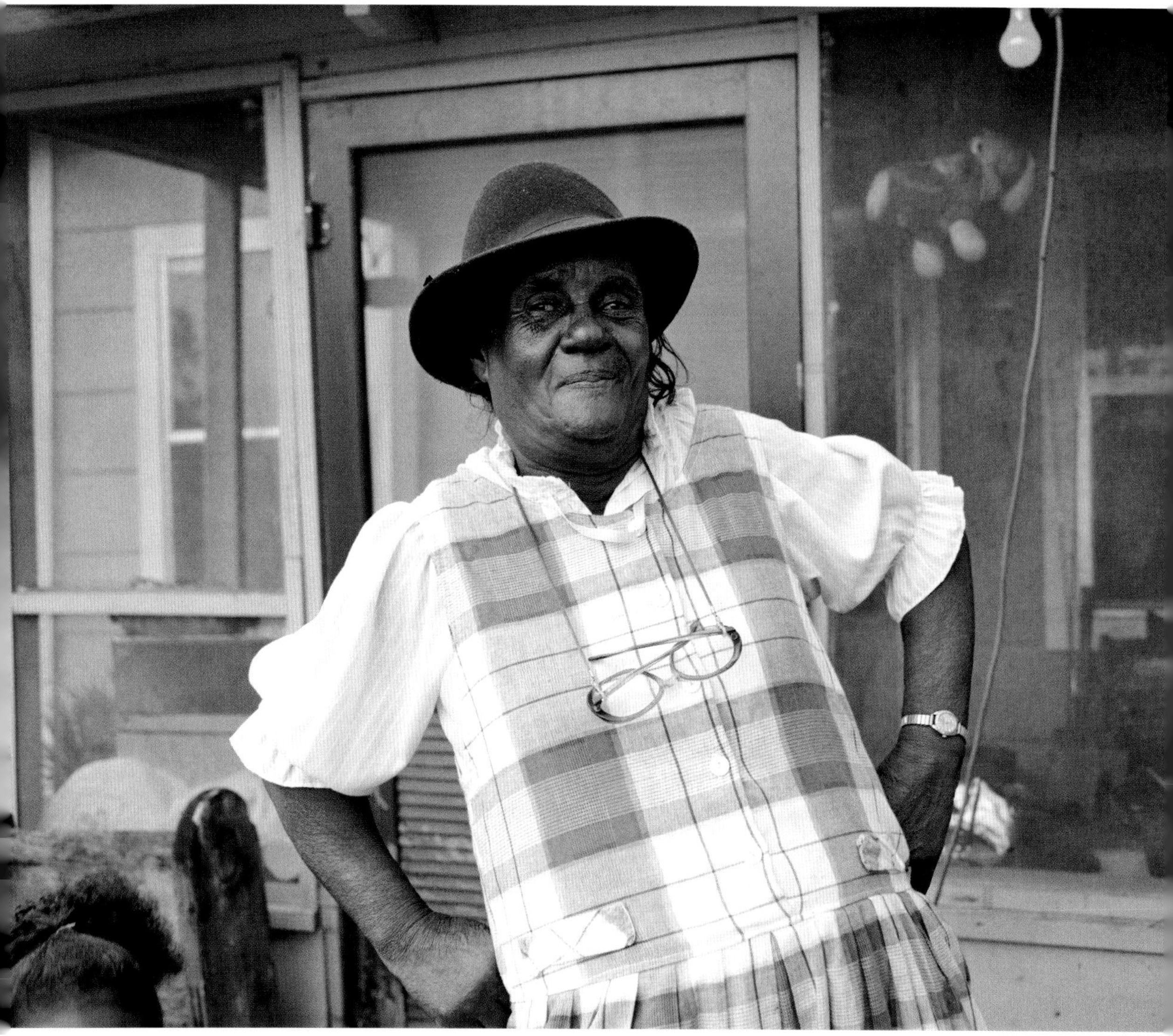

Eva Mae Glover

daddy—we had these old plows—and sometimes he would, we called it 'bustin' middles' [breaking the soil so the seed could be planted]. And sometime I busted middles, and he would do the plantin'. Sometime I do the plantin', and he busted middles.

"I'm tellin' you, I've come a long ways, and I thank the Lord for it, 'cause it could have been worse, but it wasn't—it was good. And he brought me a long, long ways, and I thank him for that.

"We would have so much fun when I was a girl. It was a bottom—there was a bottom where we was stayin', and we would roll that bottom down! And there were some trees out there they call huckleberry trees. We would eat them huckleberries. And there were some trees out there you call 'rat tail,' had little black things on 'em. We would get them rat tail, and we would eat them rat tail. And take like these prickly pears, we would get those prickly pears and rub the stickers offa there. We would eat that, and we never did get sick. But now, you try that now, and see what happen! You have to go to the doctor or either die. We used to have nice times roamin' them pastures and things, eatin' some of them wild lemons. We would get anythin' wild out of the bottom—it wouldn't make us sick. And I enjoyed it myself. I wouldn't care if we could bring them days back, but them days done passed. You can't bring them days back 'cause they're gone.

"I told my daddy he cheated me out of most of my learnin' 'cause when I should've been goin' to school, I was home, plowin'. And I could hear the other chil'ren on the road goin' to school, and they was laughin' and hollerin' and goin' on, and I would just *grieve* to myself about it. And I told him, I said—I called my daddy 'Ed'—'Ed, you cheated me out of much of my learnin'.' But I *learned*—it was by the help of the good Lord. I didn't go to no high school or nothin'. I just had a good 'mother wit.' that's what took me on—nobody didn't learn me nothin'. What I learned, I learned on my own. *Good mother wit*, and I thank the Lord for it.

"I can't talk plain 'cause I got Mex'can in me, I got Indian in me, and I got colored in me. Now, my grandma, her daddy was Spanish. My grandfather's daddy was an Indian. And my daddy is a colored man," she said with a laugh. "And now, see, I got all of that mixed up in me." She was clearly delighted with this.

Eva Mae married at seventeen, to an older man. "And I had babies, and he be in the street," she said. "I went along with that. Married at seventeen. And when I was purgnant, carryin' babies, shoot, it wasn't nothin' too good for my husband to 'get up in my stomach.' It's lucky any of my chil'ren livin', 'cause he would get up in my stomach with his knees. But the Lord makin' sure I overcome all of that. I said, 'Well, I gonna see who gonna be the longest-liver. You go on doin' what you're doin', and see what's gonna happen to you. You tryin' to get me down, man,' I say. 'But I be here when you be gone.' And that's the way the Lord fixed it!"

What about her children? "I tried to bring 'em up the right way," she said, "and the good Lord wanted me to. While they were home, I done my part. They *love* me, I'm Mama.

"I come up the hard way, the hard way, but I thanks the Lord for it. He brought me this far, to seventy-six years old, and I liable to get to one hun'red. I don't know. It gonna depend on how you treat your life. If you treat your life rugged, it gonna come up to you rugged. But if you treat your life nice, everythin' will fall in line and will be all right like that. You'll see. And I come up the hard way. But I ain't got no cause to grumble 'cause God, he ain't gonna put more on you than he want you to bear. And that's what we got to learn. I'm able enough to bear whatever he brings to me.

"If you carry yourself in Christ's way, well, you'll come out more better. If you try hangin' onto things and tryin' to work things your way, things ain't never gonna fall in line. They'll always be out of line. And I try to keep myself in line. And that the way I'm tryin' to bring my gran'chil'ren up—not to lie, not to steal. Whatever you want, ask for it. If it's too good for him to give to you, leave it alone!

"I likes to treat everybody nice. And I want folk to treat me like I treat them. That the way I am. And ain't nothin' too good I wouldn't give to you if I had it. I believe whatever the Good Book says. I got that much faith to believe in him, 'cause I know too much about it. Nobody can tell me that he ain't real, 'cause I know he is. He have done so *much* for me! He has brought me a whole lot."

Eva Mae recalled the lynching in 1935: "There's a tree right 'cross the river over there, they call it the hangin' tree, where they hung them two colored boys. I'm gonna tell you 'bout those boys, when they got those boys over there and hung 'em. I'm gonna tell you the truth now, the way it were. See, it was a white girl raped, and they said that the boys raped the girl. There was a colored boy, and this white girl, she was out in the pasture, and she play like the boys've raped her. *But they did not!* She done fooled with her own brother, and then it was too late.

"After then, the brother took sick and told it on his deathbed, 'cause he messed with his own sister. And they laid it on them colored boys.

"They drug them chil'ren up and down the road, put a rope on 'em. Then they *hung* them chil'ren—they *hung* 'em, killed both of 'em together. They were *young chil'ren*! They was two first cousins. They drug them boys all down this road out here, blowin' horns and things, drug them poor little boys and took 'em over yonder there to that tree, and they hung 'em to that tree. And the doctor what examined the girl, see, she had this skin up under her fingernails, and it was white skin, wasn't no black skin. They couldn't prove that those kids done that. And the doctor what told the truth, they hated him—they didn't want him in Columbus. He finally moved somewhere else. And so, when her brother got ready to die, he told them that he was the one what raped his sister. But they laid it on them colored boys.

"And the colored undertaker, they made him bury them in the *same grave*. And you know that was *turr'ble*! That was somethin' to see. They were racin' their motors and goin' on and everythin' when they was takin' them chil'ren out there. It was turr'ble! I would hate *mighty* bad for that had been my chil'ren. It was *sad*. They wouldn't want nobody to do their chil'ren like that. Oh, yes, everybody was scared after that, hmmm, hmmm."

I asked Eva Mae if she believed that her God forgives for such brutal acts. She pondered a moment, then said, "No, uh-uh, he don't forgive things like that—but I don't know, you know." She hesitated. "They say you forgiven for everythin' but self-murder. I don't believe that. He don't forgive for things you do to other people.

"I always said, I don't want nobody's bloodstain on my hand, nobody's. Uh-uh, 'cause that's a hard thing to go with. 'cause my uncle killed a man, and that worried him. That *worried* him—he told me that. He would *see* this man. This man was tormentin' him—he was mean, wouldn't let 'im rest. Uhh-uhhhh, no, Lord, I don't want nothin' like that, 'cause that's hard, hard, hard."

Regarding the trustworthiness of white people, Eva Mae said, "All of 'em were the same. They pulled together. All of 'em were the same. What against them is one colored? You ain't got no more say than the man in the moon. Uh-uh, Lord, no, I don't trust 'em. 'Cause I just get out and tell 'em just what I think. And I know what right, and I know what wrong, 'cause God didn't make me no fool. And I like to treat everybody right. I ain't got no kick against you 'cause you white. I treat you like I treat one of my colored. That the way I am. I won't treat the white no badder than I would one of my colored. That the way I am. Just 'cause they got white skin, that don't mean nothin'.

"All the law was mean," she said, a statement corroborated even by some members of the white community. "My sister had a run-in with 'em. Take Harvey Lee [a law officer]—he wanted to whip my sister, but she didn't go for it. She wasn't gonna let no white man whip her! They did fight. They sure didn't whip her. She was tough! One law went and got a ax handle, and she went and got her a ax handle, and I betcha he didn't bother her 'cause she gonna rassle right down with him." After a pause, she remarked, "It's a little better today."

Eva Mae continued: "I'm the mother of thirteen chil'ren, nine boys and four girls. And I didn't have no doctor. All of my chil'ren was born at home but one—that's the baby. My chil'ren's names is Myrtle, Roy, Eddie, Johnny, Bobby Joe, Bennie Charles, Leroy, Billy Jean, Luevayda, Minnie, Shirley, and Terry. And the baby what died, he name Reggie."

She recalled Reggie's birth and death, showing great sadness: "The little baby lived a day and a half, and then he took real sick. The doctor said it was a good thing it was the baby in place of me, but I didn't want it to be neither one of us. That was the *saddest thing* done happened to me—*sad*. But look like I killed 'im, caused 'im to have heart trouble—that was the way it was with me." When she was nine months pregnant and awaiting the baby, there was an altercation between her cousin and his wife, and the police were called in. "The law shot the old man [Eva's uncle], and he turned around to my daddy. They thought they were gonna shoot him too. Me, I

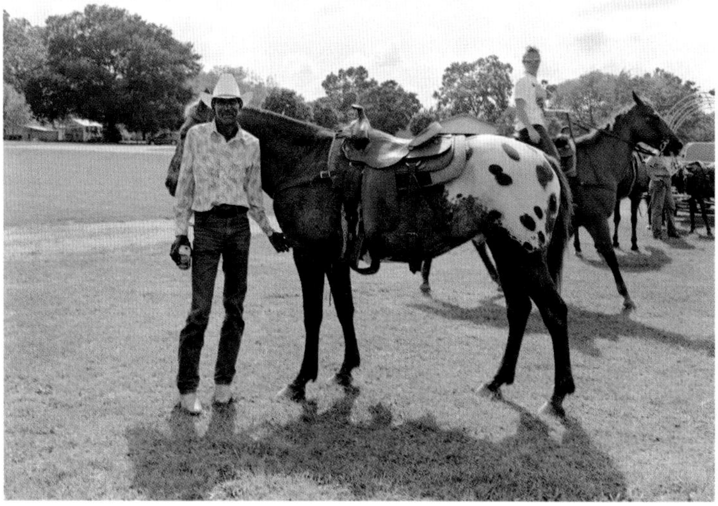

B.C. at the "Gedenke!" Parade in Weimar

B.C. added proudly, "I got a little boy, Li'l B.C.—he's seven—and a stepdaughter, and my wife, Betty Jean Glover."

After his mother's death in 1996, B.C. seemed to age very quickly. His hair began turning gray, and his body became bent and stooped. Before long, he developed cancer, against which he made a successful struggle for a while. Then the disease returned, weakening him and forcing him to quit his job on the ranch, the work he enjoyed so much. He worried about Li'l B.C., by then a teenager and not so little, who had been involved in a serious automobile accident on a foggy morning and was in some trouble. Further news of the boy and his father was hard to come by. B.C. was a dear friend, but a man who often let phone calls and cards go unanswered. Contact with him was a chance meeting at his mother's old house or news from his older sister, Myrtle.

So this is the story of handsome B.C. Glover. In December 2001, two of B.C.'s sisters, Myrtle and Minnie, called to say that he had died from the cancer. His wife, Betty, invited me to the funeral. The way people spoke of B.C. at his funeral was impressive, showing their tears and their tenderness. Person after person, preachers and friends alike, stood and told about their personal experiences with his warmth, kindness, and generosity of heart. The most touching tribute was from a man who told, with great feeling, how B.C. had welcomed him into his life and helped him get back on his feet at a time of great personal difficulty, when he was trying to recover and reestablish a normal life. This was a side of B.C. I'd not known before—how many loving friends he had and how many lives he had affected. It was a beautiful tribute to his life.

Myrtle Glover Toliver

Myrtle Glover Toliver was Eva Mae Glover's daughter and next-door neighbor. Because of Eva Mae's powerful presence, Myrtle and I did not become friends until after her mother's death, but then we became close.

It turned out that Myrtle was the mother of Marshall "Ricky" Toliver, Eva Mae's thirty-year-old grandson who had died in police custody in 1992. I knew of him through his grandmother, who had shared first her fear and, later, her grief at his death, a grief compounded by the knowledge that Ricky had been embalmed and put into a coffin by the police before his family even knew he was gone. Eva Mae had frantically told the story over the phone, piece by piece and day by day, as it unfolded. "My baby grandson is dead" were her final words as she rang off for the last time, adding, "I'm tired, I'm ready to hurt, and I don't want to do that." She sounded heartsick and exhausted.

It took time to learn more of Myrtle's story. She told it gradually. It turned out her older son, Thomas, had also died violently, by gunfire—killed over a girl he was dating. And it became clear that Myrtle possessed a singular capacity for restorative prayer and gratitude.

Wanting to write about Ricky's story, I was uneasy about doing it without his family's permission, and it was too painful to bring up with Myrtle. While I was sitting at my desk and thinking about Ricky soon after Eva Mae had died, Myrtle made a surprise call. She wanted to talk about her son and gave her permission for me to write about him.

"Couple Sues County Cops in Son's Death; Claim Brutality, Negligence," read the headline in the *Weimar Mercury* on October 8, 1992.

Eva Mae had called weeks before to say that Ricky had been arrested, adding that he had been arrested before, earlier that year. During the previous arrest, he had been kicked and physically abused by the Columbus police, according to Eva Mae. Because of this alleged mistreatment, Ricky suffered abdominal pain, blood in his urine, despondency, and a great fear of the police. So when he called his family to say he'd been arrested again (on charges of drunkenness and disorderly conduct), they became deeply worried. Eva Mae described Ricky as anxious and fearful over the phone, protesting that the charges were false. Eva sounded frightened. A few short days later, Ricky was dead. The police said he had hung himself, and they claimed they had forgotten to remove his belt when he was admitted to the jail.

In time, the police chief and one of his officers were named as codefendants in a damage suit filed by Myrtle and her husband, Edward Lee Toliver, who alleged "un-

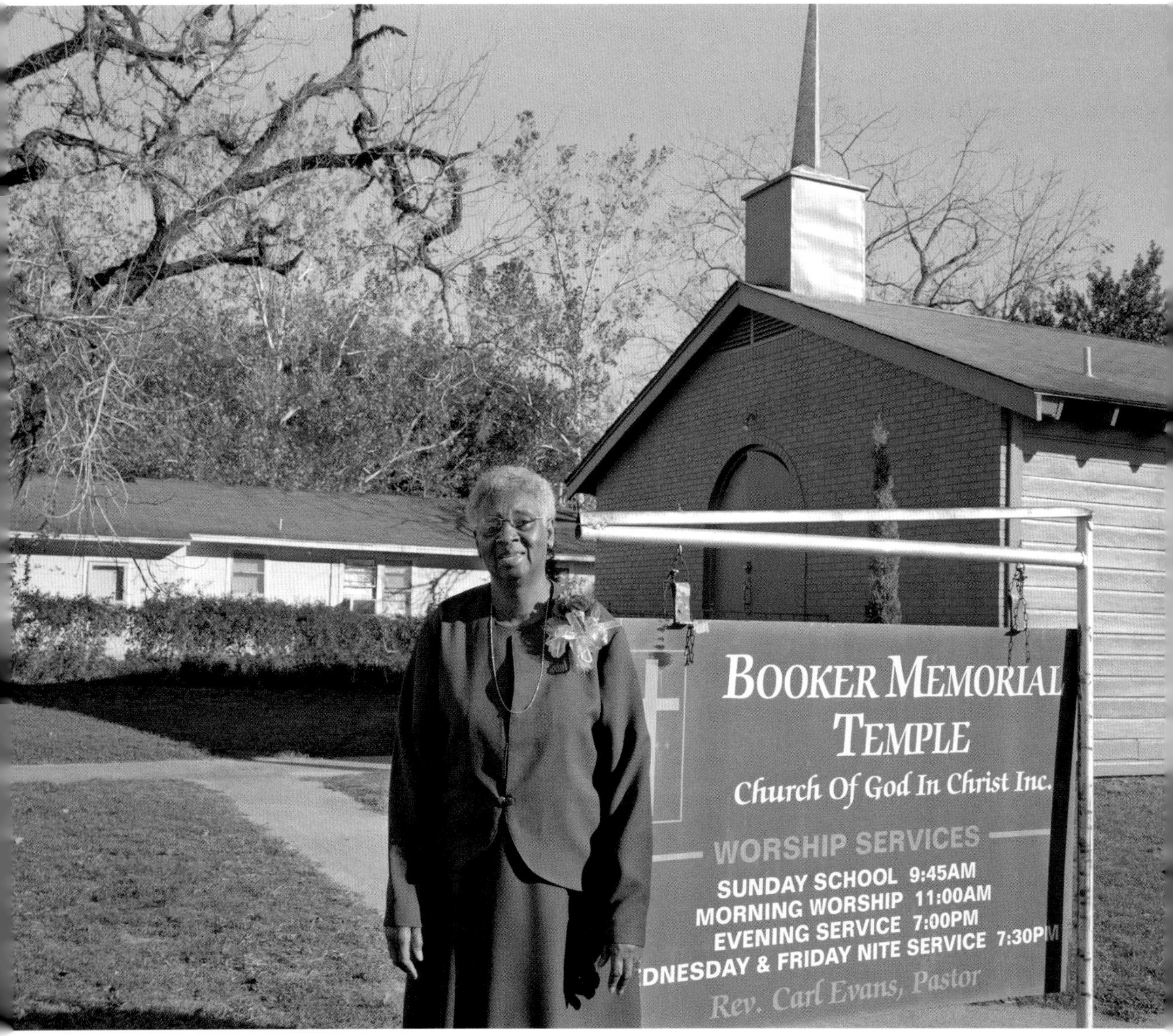

Myrtle Glover Toliver

reasonable and excessive force" in the earlier incident and negligence in this last case. The young man's death was finally ruled a suicide, but numerous questions were never resolved. Why was he left with his belt? Why was there a delay in informing his family? Why was he put into a coffin so quickly? The justice of the peace found no wrongdoing by the police. Yet Myrtle said that the family saw marks on his neck that indicated strangulation. And still the police insisted Ricky had hung himself.

Myrtle was working six days a week as a cook in a Columbus restaurant, from early morning to day's end. But she got a break every afternoon for an hour to go home, rest, and restore herself. She said she followed the same routine every day—she spent the first fifteen minutes praying, thanking God for all her blessings, then took a short nap, able to return to work refreshed again.

How could anyone be grateful after losing her two sons so sadly? "Well," she answered, "I'm grateful to God for all I *do* have and for all I *have* had. My mother taught me to pray like that, so I do it every day. I thank God for all he's given me, and I name all my blessings." Then, she said, she could rest quietly and feel at peace.

Myrtle stalled and stalled about having her picture taken. When at last she relented, she said that she did not like the picture much. But here she is, in front of the church she so faithfully served, Booker Temple. It is the cleanest and best tended church one could find, outstanding with red carpets, red seat cushions, and large, color photographs of church ministers and dignitaries lining the walls. Booker Memorial Temple was Myrtle's spiritual home and her place of service. She worked hard there and attended services faithfully.

Myrtle had been married two times and had given birth to seven children. Ricky and Thomas were her last two. Ricky was her "baby boy"—as she always said lovingly, "my baby boy."

So Ricky Toliver was gone, and the Glover family was deep in grief once more and powerless to do much besides pray. Eva and Myrtle were devastated and, at the same time, familiar with hateful and violent acts toward their family and friends. Ricky's father, Edward Lee Toliver, wrote to me in 2004: "You may not know you are just like a sister into this family & God & Jesus Christ. For us to make it into heaven we must all become like brothers and sisters in Jesus Christ. For all that was done to my 2 sons, I hold no hate on no Race of people's. Because if I did I would be in the same shape they are in and hell bound. Oh yes." And so their life went on.

Leroy Glover

Leroy Glover was born in 1954 to Eva Mae, one of her fourteen children. He was usually found somewhere around his mom's house and was easy to visit with, affable and friendly, wearing his signature black cowboy hat, always with the brim turned up. As friendly as Leroy was, he was pretty short on words, and it wasn't until the funeral of his brother B.C. that he told something of his life's details. He seemed like such a loner that it was a surprise to hear he had six children. As we stood outside the church, waiting for the procession to the cemetery, he remarked quietly that he was "goin' back in the church at last, 'cause my time is comin' and you never know when."

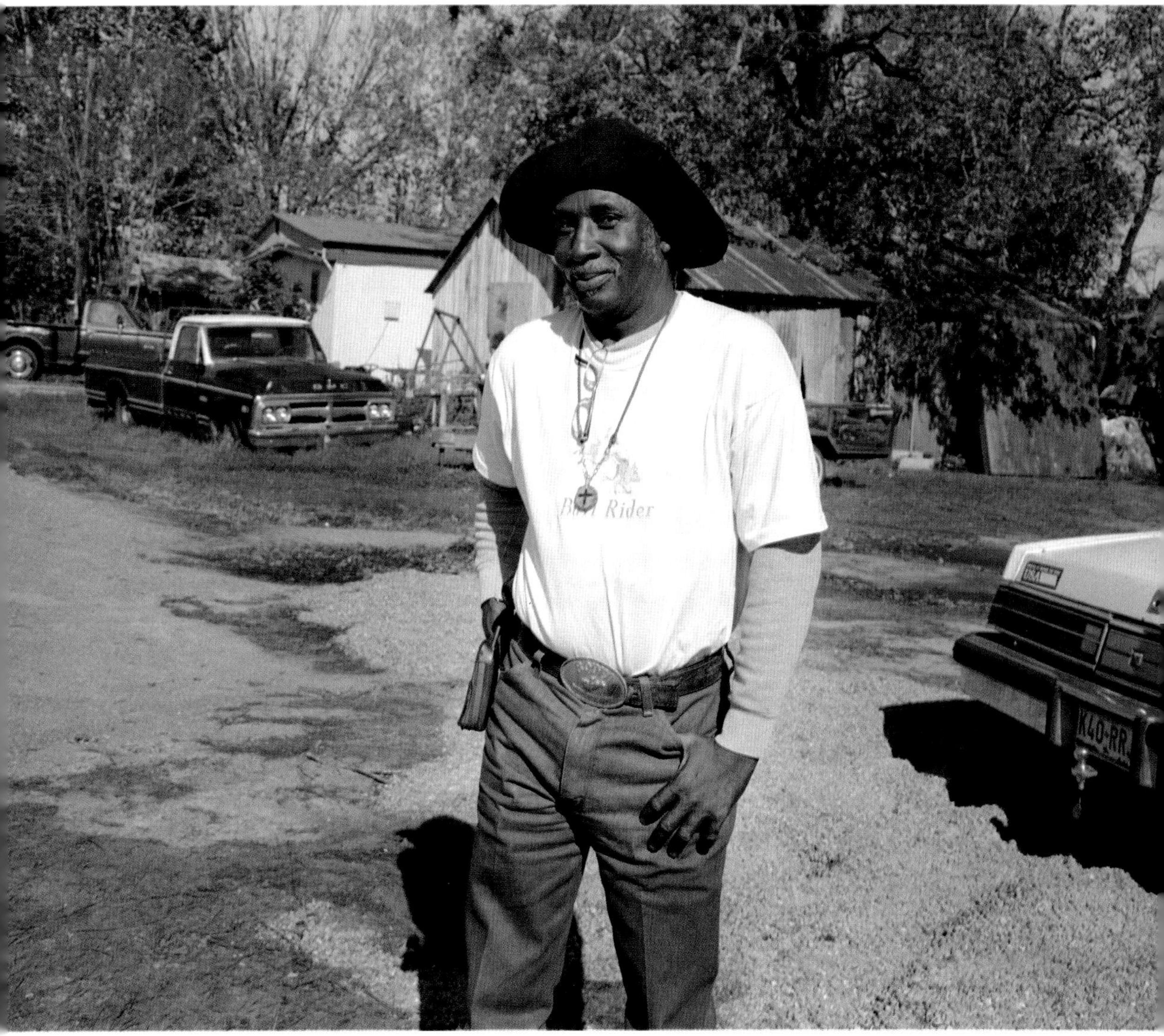

Leroy Glover

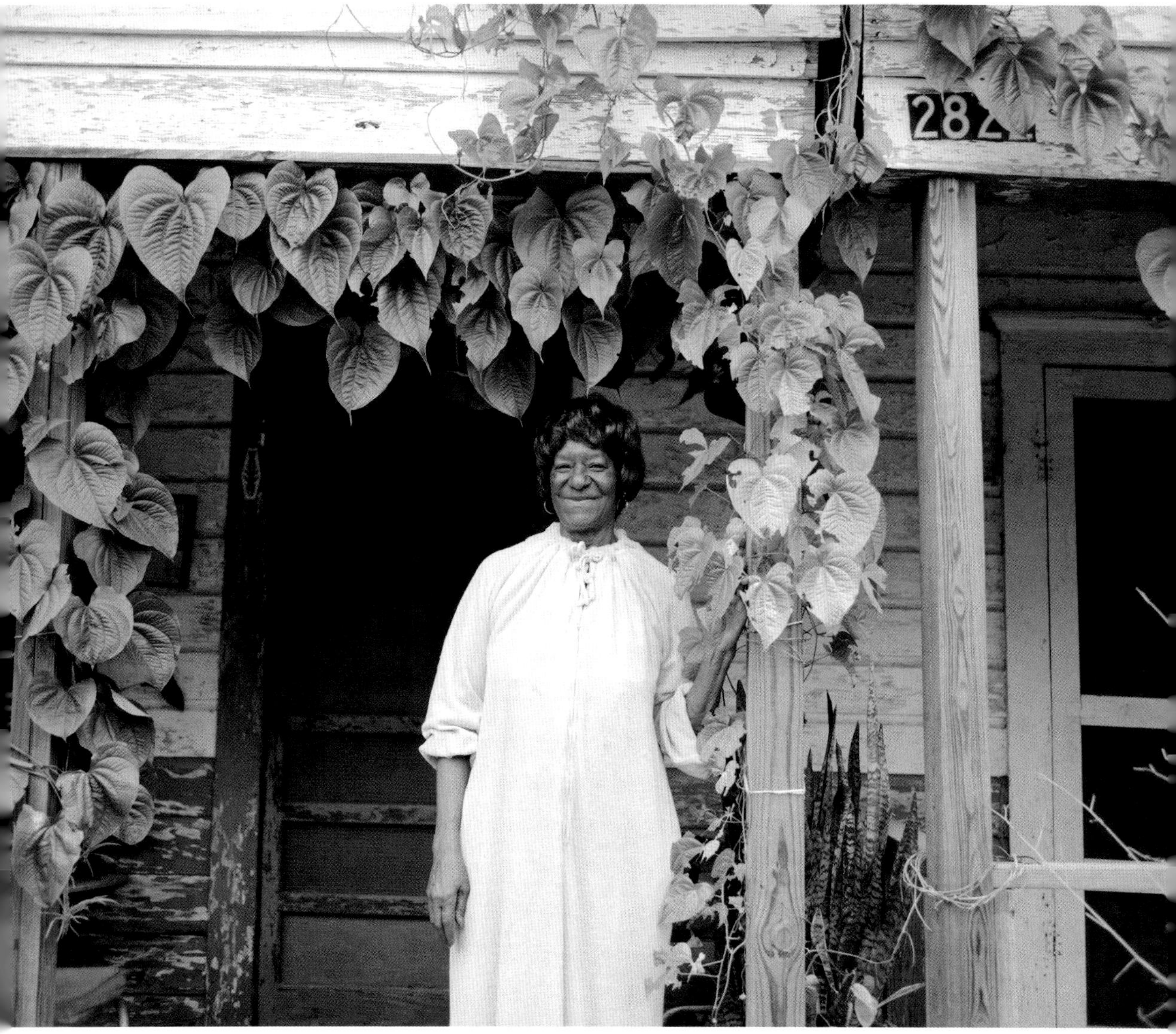

Ida Mae Mitchell

Ida Mae Mitchell

Ida Mae Mitchell was born in 1924, "the twenty-sixth day of the fourth month in the twenty-fourth year," she said, smiling, forcing me to think hard. She was one of fourteen children born to Laura Collins and Bennie Mitchell, of Columbus. Laura died young, in her mid-thirties—from having so many kids, suggested Ida Mae. One can see her reasoning—childbirth was hard and perilous. But that is surely only a small part of Laura Mitchell's story. I think of the pain she must have experienced when her fourteen-year-old son, Bennie, was lynched by a mob of local white citizens, along with his fifteen-year-old cousin—hung from a tree in a double murder by a crowd of white men and women.

I heard this story from Eva Mae Glover, who had been a youngster at the time of the lynching but remembered it clearly. Eva Mae was the only person willing to talk about this ugly event. She recalled with chilling clarity the honking of the mob's cars and seeing their license plates covered with burlap. And she was one of many who believed that the sheriff was in cahoots with the lynch mob and had let them know which road he would be taking when he brought the boys back from the Houston jail, so they could be easily seized by the crowd. Eva told stories she had heard of a black man who had climbed a tree near the crime, armed with a shotgun, determined to stop them. His friends pulled him down from the tree, hid him in a wagon, and hurried him out of town.

It's hard to believe that women and children were in the watching crowd. (An aunt told me that when she was in grammar school in Corsicana, Texas, the children were dismissed early one day to attend a lynching. My grandfather came to the school and took all his children and some of their friends to his house, refusing to let them watch.)

One can imagine the cold terror of the two young boys when they realized what was happening. Two members of the white community in Columbus who were alive in 1935 said that they knew many white residents who *never* believed the boys were guilty. Yet only one person tried to stop the lynching, a young Houston-born, Episcopalian minister, Gresham Marmion, who later became the bishop of Kentucky. He stood on the hood of a car alone, before this large group of his peers, and begged for them to stop. Someone told him there was one more rope for him, if he persisted—"I saw there was nothing I could do, and I left," he said softly sixty years later. He was so frightened that he could never afterwards remember the face of even one member of the mob—even though he was sure some were members of his congregation. Only a couple of white acquaintances ever even mentioned it to him, both women who spoke with warmth and gratitude for his actions. He received many cards, news clippings, and telegrams with accolades from all across the United States.

Ida Mae was the next child to be born after her brother Bennie and felt very close to him. She spoke about Bennie only once or twice—saying how much she loved him—and this she said with a sense of being still in deep pain, sixty years after he had died. Ida Mae left her hometown immediately after Bennie's murder, before she turned fifteen, and she never lived there again.

She went to Houston to stay for a while with her aunt, then moved to New York, and eventually returned to Houston. We met because a neighbor-friend, Jill, introduced us. During the years I knew her, Ida Mae was living happily in one-half of one of the tiniest of houses in Houston's Fifth Ward, on a street that dead-ended near her house at several fenced-off industrial buildings. It was just Ida Mae, her several much-loved white cats, and a front yard with a junk-filled ditch, a porch full of potted plants, and a small bed of beautiful, carefully tended roses.

When Ida May watched the video *Coming Through Hard Times,* which includes the story of her brother's killing, she said she skipped the entire part on his death. She added that the hanging was first planned to take place on the tree in her family's backyard. It's hard to comprehend the viciousness of this. Some believe that lynchings are about justice. Others believe they are about control of others through fear, terror, and intimidation.

When I think of Ida Mae, I remember her dangling earrings, her devotion to her cats, her loyalty to her deteriorating neighborhood, her tenderness toward my friend Jill, and the spunk, spirit, and good humor she showed in spite of all she had endured.

Charles Trefny Jr.

"My name is Charles Trefny, and I was born and raised on this old plantation out here, which was called the Adkins Plantation originally, because that was the landowner that settled this plantation out here. I was born and raised here, spent all of my life here, besides the two years I spent in military service from 1954 to 1956. I've seen a lot of changes come about. Being born in 1933, it was sort of the middle of the Depression days, and I can vaguely remember the last of the real hard times before things got better during World War II and thereafter. I can remember the last of the big floods that came down the river and flooded the whole bottomland, the whole floodplain where the pecan trees and everything are. I was about four years old when the last one did that."

The Trefnys are a family of farmers. For several generations they have lived and worked on the same land near Osage, several miles out of Weimar. Charles Senior died in 1989; his wife, Emma, in 1996. Charles Junior and his wife, Donna, reside on the family farm with their oldest son, Russell, and his wife, Michaelanne, who have their own house a short way down the lane from his parents'. Their second son, Mike, lives in Houston with his wife, Katherine, and their three kids. The Trefnys' daughter, Kimberly, teaches school in Klein, near Houston.

Charles knows more family history than most people, and he clearly recalls his grandfather, Ignas Trefny. "Grandpa Trefny came over from Czechoslovakia about 1870 or something. Supposedly he came from Praha, Czechoslovakia, which is pronounced "Prague." He just would not say anything about his past history in Czechoslovakia. He seemed like he just wanted to forget that.

"When he landed in New York, Ignas could not find a single person to speak Czech to. Somehow or another, he must have found out that there was more Czech-origin people in Chicago, and this is where he went. And he stayed in Chicago for a year, and then he heard about Ammansville, Texas, as being a place where a lot of Czech people were moving to that wanted to farm and live out in the country. So as we know it, he came to Ammansville then, and he married a second time down here, and this is when he raised his family, which was my dad and his two other brothers and four sisters.

"Osage, that's where my father grew up. And after the boys got big enough, they did the farmwork out on the farm. And I think Grandpa Trefny had been a shoemaker, or he was taught the trade of making shoes in the old country, so he naturally moved to Weimar after he retired from farming, and he had a shoe shop there where he re-

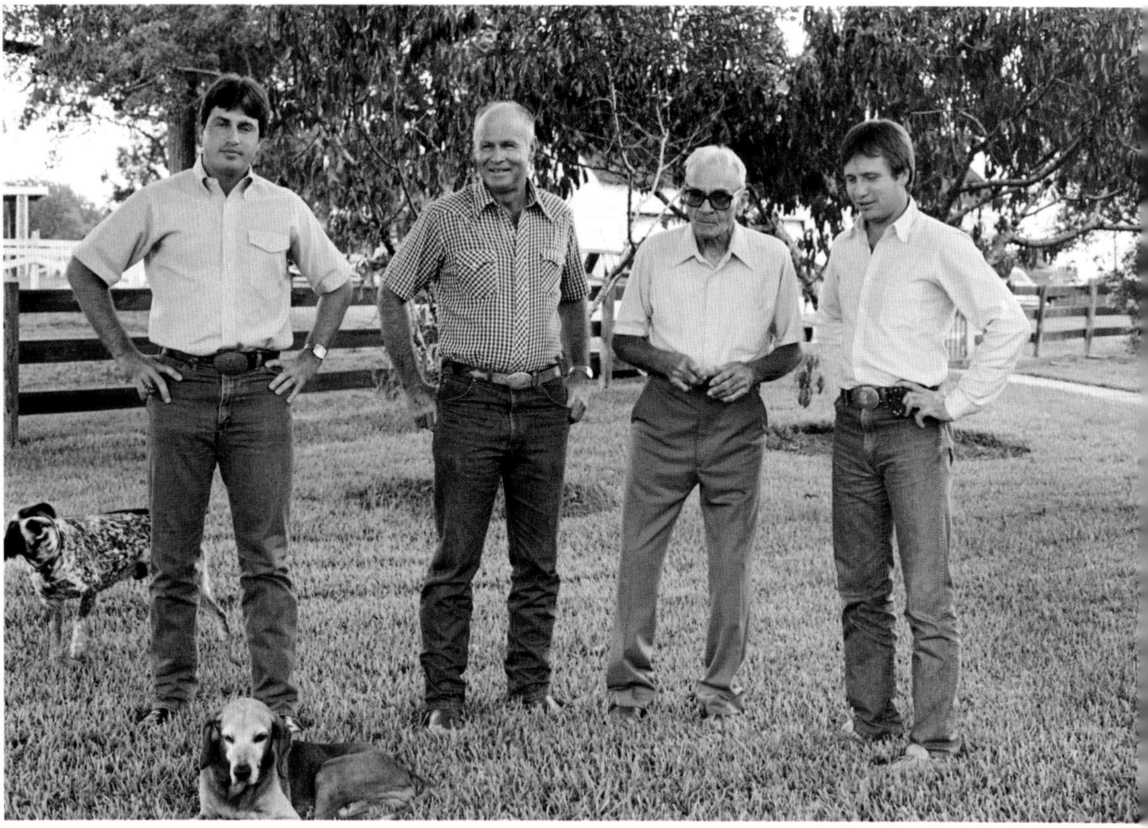

The Trefny men: Mike, Charles Junior, Charles Senior, and Russell

paired shoes, and even made shoes, and did everything that needed to be done with leather and harnesses and everything else there. I can remember playing in his shoe shop as a young boy—really it was kind of a babysitting service. I would go spend my Saturday afternoon with Grandpa Trefny in the shoe shop, while Mama and Daddy did their trading and doing the things they need to do in town."

Emma Brandt Trefny's family came over from Germany in the late nineteenth century. Said Charles, "My grandparents, Eilert Brandt and his wife, Wilamina, came over here in about 1888, I think it was. They landed first in New York, and then they took another ship down to Galveston, and then from Galveston to Weimar on the railroad—completed here in 1875 to Weimar. And they went from Weimar due north out to the community called Holman. They were almost a year looking for a place to settle the family. And they found another 1,500 acres here, in a community that was called Osage, which is where I was born and raised, here on this place. They bought it for thirty dollars an acre, if I recall right.

"Well, they had had a fairly good-sized farm in the northern part of Germany along the Baltic Sea, north of Hamburg upon the North Sea coast, the lowlands. Most of the people there were farmers or stock people. They raised livestock and did agricultural work, row crops, wheat.

"And they left there primarily because Germany was goin' through a series of small wars at the time, and they didn't want to get their sons killed off. You know, times were hard in Germany, and all the young men had to go and serve—you had military terms. And my grandparents, having five living sons, they weren't too interested in seeing them going off and fighting in the wars of Europe. So they had heard stories about immigration to the United States, and particularly to Texas, and the good lands that was available to 'em, so they sent two of their oldest boys over here that were nineteen and twenty years old. The two boys looked for land, and then when they found it, they sent back for the parents to come on over. And the story was that Grandma didn't wanna come, that she didn't want to leave the place. But that was part of the plan—to send the two oldest sons over here—and the dad knew that, with the oldest boys over here, that would help pull Mama over.

"From the tales that I hear that it was a whole community that moved from Germany. There was the Onckens, the Brandts, the Poppes, the Menises, Herbrichs, Schwegmanns, just a whole multitude of people that came over on this boat and settled in and around the Weimar area.

"There was fourteen of them born in that family, and I know there was only five of them that grew to adults. That's why Grandpa Brandt always said, 'It's just the tough ones that survive.'

"An interesting thing is that my mother's family was the Brandts, and between the Brandts and Trefnys there was three of these sisters and brothers that married, and there was one cousin, a Brandt, which was my mother, that married a Trefny. And they were all small-time farmers.

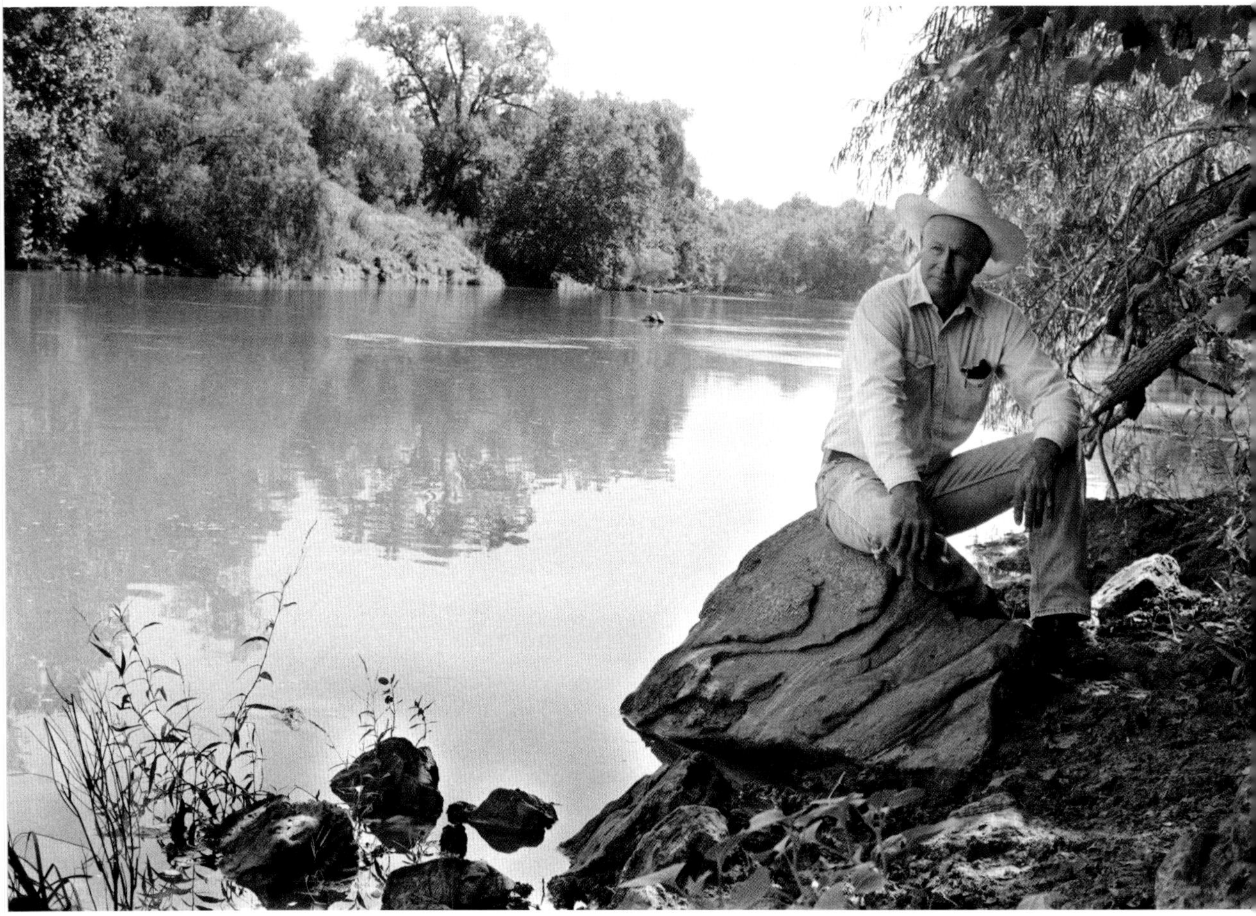

Charles Trefny Jr. at the river

Charles Trefny Talks about the River

It was a rare treat to float the Colorado River with Charles Trefny. Charles grew up around the river, and he knows it well. He talked about the river as we traveled downstream, slowly, slowly turning in our inner tubes, taking it all in. He knows each marker along the way—each creek and sandbank, each piece of property, each sunken tree that you or I would not even know existed were it not for the slight eddies above them. He said that some of these submerged trees have been in the river since his grandfather was a boy, preserved under the water. He talks about how the river has changed since the dams were built upstream, and he sounds saddened and frustrated by the changes and problems threatening his beloved waterway.

Every farmer I have talked to around here has told stories of fierce floods during the 1930s. And they remember clearly still the number of animals and crops lost to the floodwaters before the dams were built in Austin and, even afterwards, when water would sometimes be released from the dams without fair warning for the farmers downstream.

Charles said, "I can remember my parents, one time from the years about '35 to '38, there was four losses out of five years here, to floods, meanin' they didn't harvest any cash crop of cotton." And Richard Freis, another farmer neighbor, recalled with frustration in his voice, "Man, I tell you! We lost three crops on the river—washed away! Three years, 1935, '36, and '38, river floods took our crops, and one time, we had a *big* crop. The corn was gettin' mighty ripe—it was just time to pick cotton, and then them suckers turned that water loose on us. They had a big boat race. They wanta have a boat race; then it rained so much, they had to open the gate and *they flood us!*"

Several times in recent years there have been moves to build a large dam at Columbus and to flood the river bottoms along here, where people float, fish, and swim—to submerge the river as it exists, along with the rich, fertile land that borders it, along with the orderly, manicured pecan groves, cattle herds, and cultivated fields. And for what? No one seemed to me to have a clear and reasonable answer to that question. A number of years ago, a group of us went on a fact-gathering tour with local farmers and the board and staff of the LCRA (Lower Colorado River Authority). There was talk of taking land from the farmers and ranchers here to give water to the rice farmers downstream. The LCRA people admitted that much of the land would be under very shallow water, which would quickly evaporate. One farmer walked us through his pecan grove, talking about his love of the trees and remembering when the different trees were planted by his parents—one at this sister's birth, another at his arrival sixty or more years earlier, and so on. It was sad to think of these beauties submerged and dead just so that someone downstream could plant rice.

In time, it seemed the dam threat had diminished, and Charles was more concerned over the quality of the water in the river. They say it is sometimes too polluted for swimming or rafting but safe, at times, still for fishing. Yet, even the fish population seems to be dwindling. At any rate, the river is not in good shape. Charles said this is because of the enormous increase in population, increased sedimentation, a lack of adequate sewage treatment, chemical runoff from farms, and industrial runoff.

In 2001 the talk was about supplying water to the city of San Antonio and buying water from rice farmers to sell to the city. What's next, no one knows.

Rosie Lee Hasty

When Rosie Lee and I talked in August 2000, it was after she, a virtual stranger, had written me an inviting note, in which she wrote that her family story was "very depressin'." The letter continued: "I have a lots of talk for you about my brother and my hold [*sic*] family. Its very depressin' but I keep my head up, an' go on. Yes it was ten of us, but all gone 'cept three of us. I'm 'bout the last chicken in the yard—I had to bury just 'bout all of 'em."

So we got together, and Rosie calmly began, "I was born on Hatterman Lane, back down on Hatterman Lane down there—they call it Skull Creek. Mama was stayin' down there at Mr. Gus Williams' home, stayin' down there washin' for them, for rent—'cause we kind of had a sorry dad. Our daddy was *sorry!* Mama would always go to places and get a house, you know, to rent. I was the seventh child.

"After we moved away from there, we moved back over to my grandpa's house, over 'cross the river, called it the Ellinger area. We stayed over there 'til Mama fucked up Papa. My papa and his daddy got into it, because Daddy wanted to fight the biggest sister. My dad wanted to fight his daughter. Knocked her teeth out! Ain't that awful? He was just *mean*.

"We moved on, moved to Tucker's, a place down there at Glidden—the name is Tucker's place. We had another child named Hosey, Hosey Junior. So we stayed down there. Mama was a-washin' for those people, you know, for rent.

"And Papa didn't do nothin' but cut cordwood and hunt. He cut cordwood and hunt—didn't work for nobody much. So we stayed down there; then we moved up there to Borden, in my grandma and them's house, Grandma and Grandpa's. And it was so raggedy—whenever it would rain, it rained *in the house*. We had to pull in the beds at night, you know, try to find a dry spot. We stayed there for the longest. And then, my stepbrother, my papa's son from an outside lady, he come there and saw what kind of condition we was livin' in. His name was Birdie, my father's son by another lady—stepbrother. And he went to the army and made a check out for us to eat and buy clothes. He said he couldn't stand for his little sisters and brothers to live that way, so he helped us. Then my older brother, Sherman, he was in Houston all the time stayin' with my great auntie. He had run off from Mama, run off from home to stay with my great auntie, Delphie Woolridge. And she got him and sent him to school. And then, when he got big enough, he come back and was workin', tryin' to feed us."

"Was your daddy still there?" I asked.

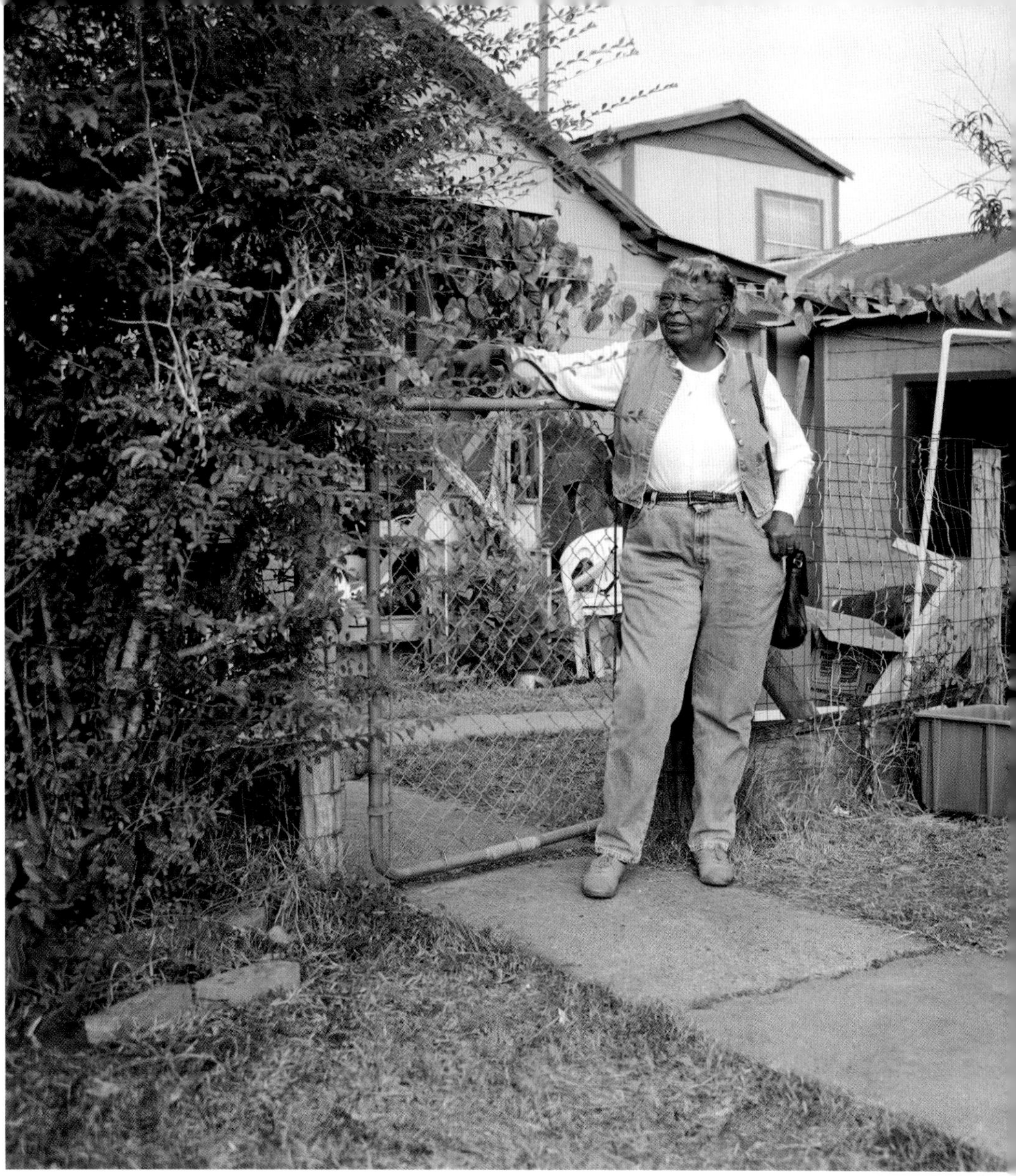

Rosie Lee Hasty

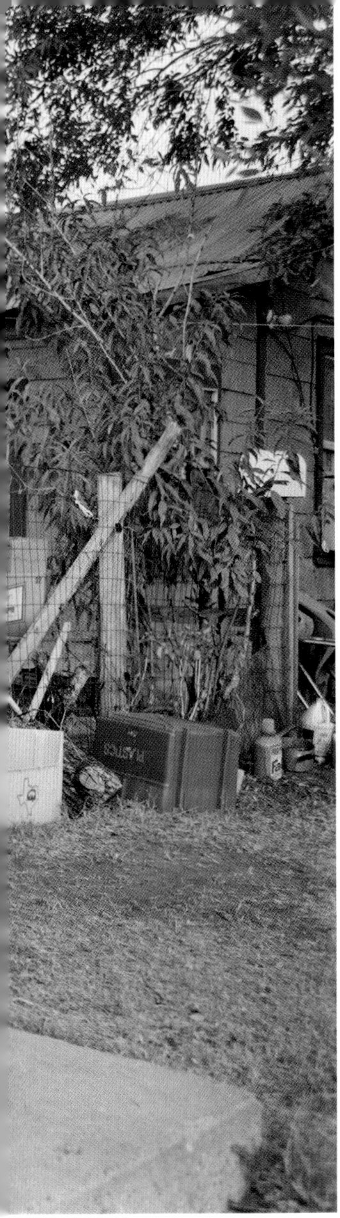

"Yeah," Rosie replied, "but he was no-'count. My daddy was *no-'count!* My Mama was scared of 'im. We stayed there, and my brother went to feedin' us and everythin'. We had Howard there, but Howard was just lookin' out for hisself. He would work some, but he looked out for hisself—he didn't care. Look here, my sisters—two of them was gettin' beat good—Geneva and Lucy. They was gettin' to be big girls. They were gettin' beat good, and my papa was so ugly, he tried to ravish my sister, and she had him arrested. She sent him to the penitentiary for thirty years. Thirty years!

"He said he wanted her to go down in the pasture with him. I was just about seven years old. And he told her he wanted her to go help him do somethin'. I was sittin' down on the ground, and way after a while, she come back runnin' and cryin'. I said, 'What's the matter?' She said, 'Papa tried to rape me,' and she run on into the house and told Mama. Mama tol' her don't be lyin' on her daddy. She just went on straight through the house, went on up there, and told our white friend, Miz Daisy Good. So they sent the law down there and got 'im, carried 'im away. Carried me to court to witness, and I was seven years old.

"And that day when they had the trial at the courthouse—you know it was segregation then. Everybody was in every window up there, and the courthouse was so full, you couldn't get in there." She guessed this was around 1935.

"Were you scared at the trial?" I asked her.

"Embarrassed," she answered. "I cried 'cause I was embarrassed. And my grandfather was there. My grandpa had some land, a lot of land—he had a farm. My grandpa lost his land, 'cause the lawyer told my grandpa that if he would put up his land for collateral for his lawyer fee, he wouldn't send Daddy to the pen. And Grandpa did. He was cryin'. When they sentenced papa to thirty years in prison, Papa tol' me to come there, and he hugged me: 'My little girl, I just love you.' And I was so embarrassed. Grandpa said, 'Oh, son, I hope you do well,' is what he called my daddy. Grandpa was cryin' and they was cryin'.

"I was cryin' because I was ashamed. Ain't that right?" she inquired. "You know, that's a hurt you never get over it. I'll never get over that. See, he meant well by huggin' me, but I said, 'What you doing huggin' me?' you know, by me being so little. He might be tryin' to bother me too, you know.

“Papa stayed in the pen so long. And one day, we was comin’ from school and we saw a man comin’ way down in the bed of the creek. And we were goin’ to break and run. He said, ‘Hey there, wait up.’ I said, ‘Who is you?’ I didn’t even know who he was. He said, ‘This is your daddy.’ Them other children took off. But the girl that he tried to rape, she left home right away and went on to San Antonio. She couldn’t go to school ’cause they was talkin’ about her. She caught a truck on the highway and went to San Antonio. And she didn’t come back to Mama but ’bout two times.

“He come on that night to the house. And we pulled Mama’s coat. Mama was workin’, but we made doggone sure she didn’t come to that house while he was there, without knowin’ he had got out of prison. So we sent a sister up the street to tell her, pull her coat. Mama come on to the house and she spoke to him. She said, ‘How you doin’?’ He said, ‘Oh, I’m all right.’ She said, ‘You can’t stay here—you can’t stay here.’ He said, ‘I don’t want to stay here, but can I spend the night?’ She said, ‘Yes, you can stay all night here if you want to, if you ain’t got nowhere else to stay.’ And Mama put every one of us in the bed with her. She put every one of us in the bed. The next mornin’, he got up and told her, ‘Well, Pearl, I’ll see you.’ She said, ‘Okay.’ Then he went on to East Bernard.”

Rosie told about being a little girl left home by her mother, completely alone, for weeks on end, with only her two younger siblings: “See, Mama wasn’t there. Mama was off in the cotton pick. She stayed at the cotton pick for about two, three months—left me at home by myself with my other sister and brother. She went way up there in Lubbock, or somewhere, and left us, left me with the chil’ren, and we didn’t have no food. And we had to go lookin’ [for food].

“We had a li’l dog that caught some li’l rabbits. It was a hollow, and the rabbits would go in the hollow. Then we would go there when we heard the dog’s barkin’—go over there, and take a stick with forks on it, and twist it in the rabbit’s hidey-hole and pull ’im. We were catchin’ hold to his feet, jerk ’im real quick, and hit ’im up ’gainst the tree and kill it. That is how we eat for about a month, boil the rabbit and put salt on it. I wrote Mama a letter and told her, ‘Send us some money, please,’ ’cause we was starvin’!”

Wasn’t there anyone to help look after them—grandparents or an aunt? “Our grandpa and them was dead,” Rosie said. “Our auntie tried to help us in the best way she could. But Mama tol’ us, ‘Don’t go there a-beggin’ her for no food’ while she was gone. She tol’ us she gonna beat us up if we go down there. Mama was *slow*—she didn’t *know* no better. The little stuff she left there, she thought it was gonna last.”

Rosie said she did any kind of work she could get from the white neighbors, in exchange for scraps of food and a few cents. “Then I went over to a white lady’s house, name Miz German, asked her let me clean her chicken house out for some meat rinds and some bacon grease and stuff out of her garden. And the woman let me clean it out, and she give me fifty cents, and she give me some cabbage and onions and sweet potatoes to eat. Then I’d go over there every week and do that.

"Bacon grease," Rosie pondered. "People don't eat that no more. We eat it when we was little because we was glad to get it. And I just *loved* that lady, Miz German. I was always glad to catch up with her, find out where she was, but I never did. I would always inquire about her, but I never did get a chance to go see her. Yes, she was nice. I appreciated what she did."

Rosie explained some of the side effects of cleaning a chicken coop: "You know, I'd get so full of them chicken mites. They are some just *crawl* on you. When I get down to the creek, that little old branch creek what I had to go through, I had to wash head and everythin' down there at the creek—get in that little creek and I'd wash myself off, get those things offa me. Get in there with my clothes on, cleanin' the chicken house."

Marie Williams said that Rosie's mother, Pearl, would regularly walk seven or eight miles on foot, carrying bags of groceries from the store in Glidden to her home in Borden. She had no car and was badly handicapped in her legs with some kind of severe swelling like elephantiasis, which made walking terribly hard and painful.

"Another thing," Rosie continued. "When Mama would get sick, I had to go do all her washin' for Mr. Tom Taylor. There was an old white guy named Tom Taylor—Mama was washing for him all the time. When she got sick—she had a bad leg, had a *big* leg; she'd get sick with that leg 'cause it got fever in it—I'd always go with her to wash. And when she got sick, I knowed what I had to do. I wasn't nothin' but a little girl. *Ain't that somethin'*? Go over there and wash for that man. He give me fifty cents. He wore blue striped overalls, and I had to boil 'em in a pot. When I got through, he gave me fifty cents, and I went to the store and buy food for Mama.

"Mama said, 'Buy some food, buy some sugar, buy some lard, some meal, some beans.' And you know what I do? I'd steal me ten cents out of it. I'd buy me a nickel worth of candy. Then I bought me a can of sardines. And I asked the lady to give me a few crackers. When I got down to the creek, I opened my can of sardines and eat 'em. Mama didn't know it—she didn't know I cut me ten cents out of that fifty cents. I said I'm gonna get me two nickels 'cause I worked hard for this money—I'm gonna get what I want. I bought me a can of sardines for a nickel, a nickel worth of candy. One time I found a nickel and lost it. I think I looked for it till dark. I looked for that nickel till dark—still didn't find it. I musta didn't lose it right where I thought I did. I sure did dig up the grass and dirt and everything lookin' to find that nickel!"

Rosie quit school in the sixth grade. "I got tired of bein' hungry," she explained. "I said, 'I'm gonna move away from here. I'm gonna leave.'"

Thankfully, there were happy times as well. "Lots of colored people down there in Borden," she said. "At night they used to get together, honey, and had suppers down in the bottoms. *Whoo-eee,* you talk about *fun!*"

Rosie told happy stories about "house suppers." The older folks would get together at each other's houses and share meals. "They'd be cookin' fried chicken, goats and sheeps, all *kinds* of food, back over there by Osage, down in the bottom over there," she recalled. "What happened, they'd take all the furniture out the room when they knowed they gonna have a supper. Get rid o' the chil'ren. Then they be cookin' and barbecuin'." Someone would bring a guitar, and they would dance and sing and mightily enjoy themselves. "I didn't dance, 'cause I knew better," Rosie noted. "I was too young. But when I learned to dance? Lawdy Miz Claudie! I would *really* dance! They used to do the 'Snake Hip' too. That's a *bad* dance, right there! They put their hand on they hip and go down and come back up—look like a snake—*snake hips!*" she repeated, laughing. "I was *wild* when I could dance!"

She added, "They don't have the suppers no more, 'cause people don't get along like they used to."

There was one special older man who used to show up at the house suppers when Rosie was in her early teens, a man named Buddy Lee. "Had a mouth full of gold and his coat over his shoulder. And his guitar—ummmm, mmmmm," she reminisced, smiling dreamily decades later. "He was *so good-lookin'* when he young. I was stuck on him. I was *stuck* on him—wasn't nothin' but a li'l ole girl. If Mama and them a-knowed that, they'da beat me to death. He'd come in with his coat on his shoulder and his guitar, hmmm, mmmm, mmmm. Was sittin' round there lookin' at the man—wasn't nothin' but fifteen years old. He could *sang the blues!*" He would sing "Corinna, Corinna" while Rosie gazed at him with longing—and her mama was trying to get her young girl back home.

"I was *fast,* like little girls are—wanted to dance with the mens *bad!* I wanted to dance with the mens *so bad!* And Mama come and get me home."

Rosie admitted to having had several husbands and a bunch of romances. "Menfolks? Oh, I had one or two. I had one, one time, beat the crap out of me.

"I had my first man on layaway. He whupped the mess out of me, fightin' me on every corner. He died, though. He was jealous of me too, and he drank pretty heavy. You know how they can be, drinkin'. We stayed together quite a while, but we'd get to 'bout half-drunk fightin'. Then later on in life I hit the mark and married a Mexican man. He don't live here no more. He wasn't too hot. He wasn't nothin' much. Then I had some more mens—I ain't gonna tell you 'bout *that!*" She smiled naughtily. "I won't give that lowdown. I ain't nowhere now," she said, laughing.

"Then, my sister, Willie Mae—I raised all her chil'ren," Rosie continued. "She was the mother of ten—lost five, raised five. Her mother-in-law raised one of the boys, and I helped raise the others. She told 'im that my sister give 'im away 'cause she didn't want 'im. It wasn't that. She wanted to run around, my sister.

"I was a single woman, workin' hard. I had this café over here next door, and I cleaned chitlins and tripe for my daily. That's how I made my livin', chitlins and tripe. I'd sell a bucket of chitlins like this here back then for forty and fifty dollars, cleaned five or six buckets every evenin'." Rosie said she bought them "out at that slaughter pen, till in 1965, they stopped lettin' people have 'em—they said it was against the health rules." Rosie noted, "It was right next door here, Rosie's Diner. We sold food, beer, soda water, cookies, pickles, chitlins, tripe, sweetbreads, and fish. We made money." She closed the café in 1970. "I tried to make it with the other stuff," she said, "but it didn't do as good as it did as when we had the chitlins."

Then Rosie launched into another subject: "Did I tell you why I ain't had no chil'ren? When I was young, I got pregnant and had an abortion, and never had got pregnant again. And I tell all my nieces, don't do that. Get pregnant? Have 'em. Because you think you have some when you get ready? You might not ever be ready. Ain't that good advice? I went to the doctor—somebody told me later on in life, say he was drunk. Probably damaged me inside.

"And my nieces, what I raised, they laugh about the differ'nt things what they didn't know! I tells them things, you know, that they don't know, and that tickle them to death. Know what they said the other day? Two of the girls was here the other day from Plano, and they say, 'Rosie, you know what? It was a *blessin'* for us to be 'round you, 'cause you taught us things our mama didn't teach us.' Ain't that somethin'? They say, 'You're just a wonderful auntie. You just teach and tell us so many li'l things we don't understand.' I'm glad. They said, 'We were never afraid of you, to talk with you about things.' I said, 'Well, I am glad you all feel that way about it.' Said they'd never get another Aunt Rosie. I always had sense."

Hosie "Sonny" Hasty

I first saw Sonny Hasty on the sidewalk in front of Bill's Five and Dime Store in Weimar. It was the time of the Weimar "Gedenke!" Parade, and Sonny was sitting on the sidewalk in his wheelchair, watching the passing floats and school bands. I was struck by the necklace he wore, which displayed a Cadillac emblem, and also with the way he held himself—tall and erect, looking distinguished as he sat there in the crowd. We talked. Sonny said he wheeled himself all over town and felt safe doing it—there was little traffic and most of it was slow, slow, slow.

Sonny was a man of few words. I got these pieces of his story from Rosie Lee Hasty.

He was born Hosie Hasty Jr. in 1932, on a farm in the Borden area where his family was working and living. He was the youngest child, with an absent father, a hard-working mother, and a responsible older sister, Rosie, who helped care for Sonny and all the other little ones. The other children were Burton, Elmore ("Little"), Mollie V. ("Veay"), Sherman ("Man"), Howard ("Baby"), Lucy Lee, Geneva ("Tutie"), Pearlie V., and Willie Mae.

Rosie Lee had this to say about growing up in Borden, a hamlet between Columbus and Weimar: "We were livin' near my aunts, Mollie Nelson and Empress Stevenson. *Lots* of colored people lived out there. We had a *good time*."

Sonny worked as a truck driver in Houston for thirty-seven years, delivering frozen foods. He later had two stays in the Texas Department of Corrections, as had his father before him ("stole some sugar out of a boxcar with some more mens," according to Rosie). Sonny moved several times back and forth between Houston and Weimar, working various jobs along the way. The first time he was in the penitentiary, "his wife left him and her grandfather raised their son," Rosie told me.

The second time, Sonny was in prison was for five years. When he got out, "he done pretty good, stayed at my house and worked," Rosie said. "Got married to another lady. Then he lost his oldest son at 'bout five months. Then he was fightin' his wife, and she went away." Sonny went back to Houston, where "he got to be a drunk and got down sick," in Rosie's words. She added, "I had to go get him to Weimar and take care of him." There he stayed.

In early 2001, Sonny was suffering from a return of throat cancer complicated by poor circulation; the doctors could do little for him. Sonny's health was in decline, but he continued to wheel himself through town. "My brother Sonny goes up the streets every day. He goes to visit his friend, and he go get him some wine too. And

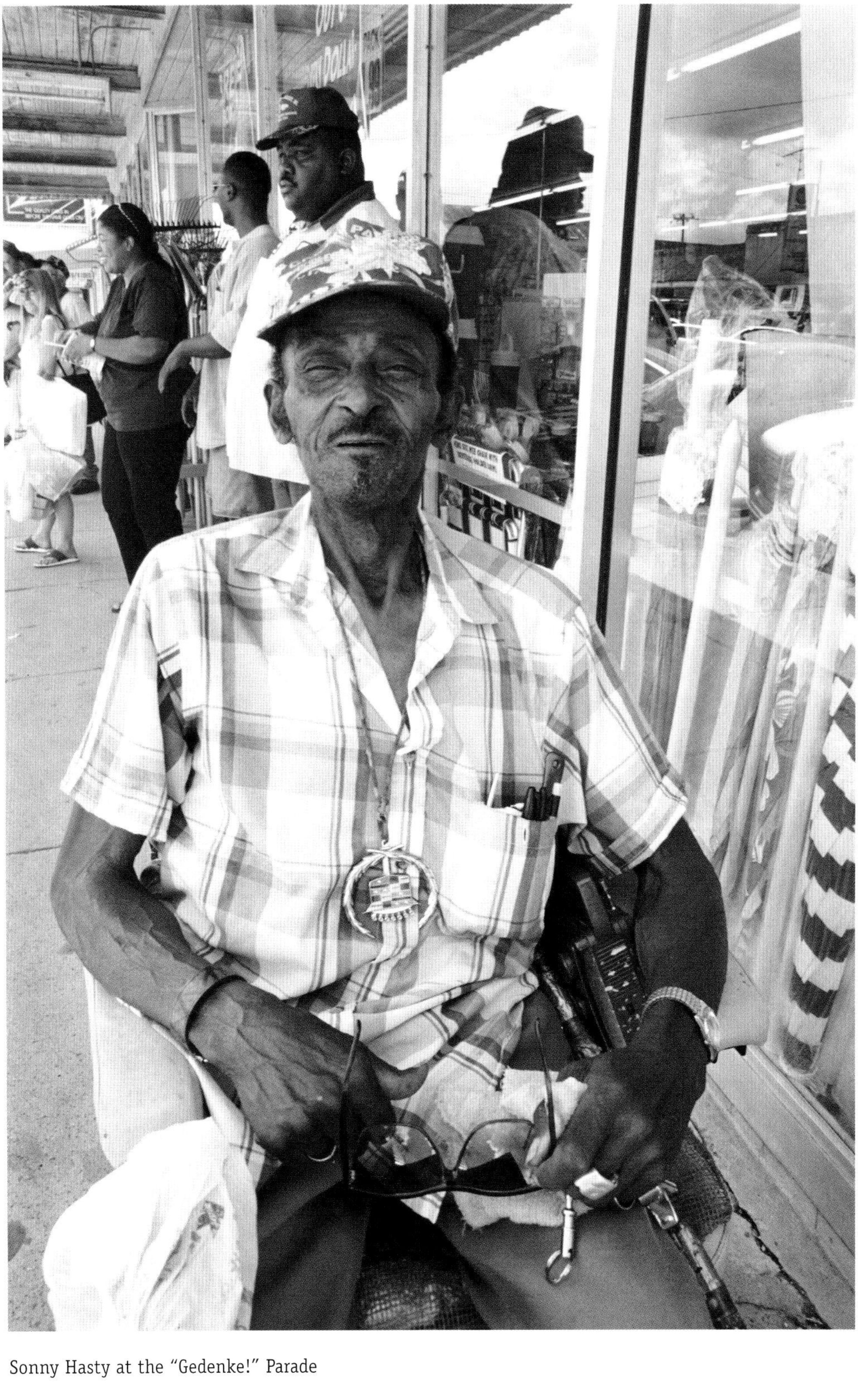

Sonny Hasty at the "Gedenke!" Parade

the other boy, Howard [Rosie's other brother], he visit some people, but some days he goes early in the morning and get his 'water.' He was wantin' me to wait on him, but I said, 'No, I'm old as you is! Ain't many difference in our years, and I'm not gonna wait on you. You have to do it for yourself. If not, go to the nursin' home!' I'm not gonna kill myself behind my brother."

Rosie talked about when they were young: "Mama would whup me when I tried to admonish those other chil'ren. That's why Willie Mae and Sonny are in the same condition, bein' so disobedient, 'cause they wasn't taught. I knew right from wrong, and I tried to discipline 'em. Mama would say, 'You ain't got no chil'ren. Don't be whuppin' on 'em!' *She* didn't know."

Howard too was living at Rosie's, the two men in separate rooms tacked on to the back of her house. Howard was the first Hasty family member I ever ran into, and I remember well how chilling the experience was.

Years ago, I was walking toward my aunt's farm, down a remote dirt road with my camera. Then a man came up behind me, out of nowhere, carrying a gun. "Get out!" he ordered me. In a stern and menacing voice, he said, "You don't belong here. Get out of here right now, or you'll get into trouble!" I left, nervous and afraid, even though it was a public road. When I told Lacey Henry, a black neighbor friend, about it, she just laughed and said that Howard's gun was a fake and Howard was harmless. She said he had had a war injury that affected his mind, but he was gentle by nature.

"You should have called 'the man.' He didn't have no business doin' it! I'd have called the man. Don't matter *who* doin' me like that—I call the law! He kind of got shell shock, but it ain't *that* bad. He be talkin' nice to me if he want to."

Rosie laughed and said that Howard called his little room behind her house "the chicken coop." "He don't drink," she added, "but he got a 'mental streak' 'cause he was in the army in Africa, what you call it, World War II. He's gettin' so mean and hateful, the 'veteran Man' gonna send him somewhere. He told me to call the law on Howard, but I don't want to—don't know, they might hurt him or somethin'."

Said Rosie of her two brothers, "They gettin' so mean, I'm about ready to leave 'em alone. I do cookin' for Sonny, my baby brother. I wash his clothes, do his housecleanin'. But I don't know—he gettin' Alzheimer's or just getting' mean, 'cause he drawed a plank on me the other day. I had to call the police. They been here and give him a good talkin'-to. At least, he stay away from me awhile, act like he got some sense."

Rosie finished up her story by indirectly comparing herself with her brothers: "I always had sense. I was pretty smart. I never stole nothin'. I never hurt nobody. I tried to be nice to people. I didn't go to no pen. I had too much sense to go to the penitentiary. I wasn't gonna do that."

Hosie (Sonny) died in August 2001. Rosie prepared a lovely tribute to him, a lengthy and detailed printed order of service for his funeral. It was several pages long and included photographs of Sonny, his deceased son, his grandchildren, and his daughters.

Odie D. Townsend

Odie D. Townsend had an outstanding vegetable garden, one of the most luxuriant in Weimar. She lived on a large piece of land inside the city limits, set back on a dirt road, out of view, a pleasant secret. Her wide-porched house sat in the center of her neatly mowed lawn, mowed by Odie herself, with stands of roses scattered here and there and her huge garden off to one side. The roses were tall and full. They bloomed throughout the year. In her vegetable garden, fenced on four sides, she grew corn, okra, tomatoes, squash, turnips, black-eyed peas, mustard greens, collards, cream peas, cabbage, onions, beets, purple hulls, peanuts, bell peppers, peas, and green beans, which she planted at two different times of year, for two crops, as she carefully explained. Like most of my acquaintances in Weimar, Odie D. depended on the rain to water and nourish her garden. She personally watered very little, with a hand-held hose, and only her roses. And yet she still managed to have a successful harvest much of the time.

Odie told dramatic and horrific stories about all the chicken snakes she had killed in her yard—in the trees, in her flowerpots, and even on her front porch. She said she was trying to keep the snakes from eating the wild birds out of their nests. Despite her snake vendetta, Odie seemed to be a quiet, gentle woman. She never seemed rushed, and yet she did get a lot accomplished. Her yard, house, and garden were immaculate. How did she do it all?

Odie D. prided herself on her honesty. "I'm *always* honest," she said. And in response to a joking inquiry, "Do you really mean it, Odie?" she replied emphatically, "Yes, I do."

Odie was born in Weimar. Her father was Arthur Brown, a farmer and railroad man, "like a flagman, you know." Her mother was Pie Steward's first cousin, Sarah Steward Brown. "Uncle Lewis, Harvey Steward's father, and my mother's daddy were brothers," Odie said. The Stewards seemed to be related to just about everybody in the county.

Odie D.'s first school was Pleasant Union, out near her cousin Pie's house, in a church building in the country. Her teacher was the beloved Empress Stevenson. "She taught me, then she turned around and taught all my chil'ren," Odie said with a smile. She later attended the Weimar Colored School in town, where Lillie Atkinson was her teacher.

Odie had "four chil'ren, three boys, one girl." She bragged, "I have some sweet chil'ren."

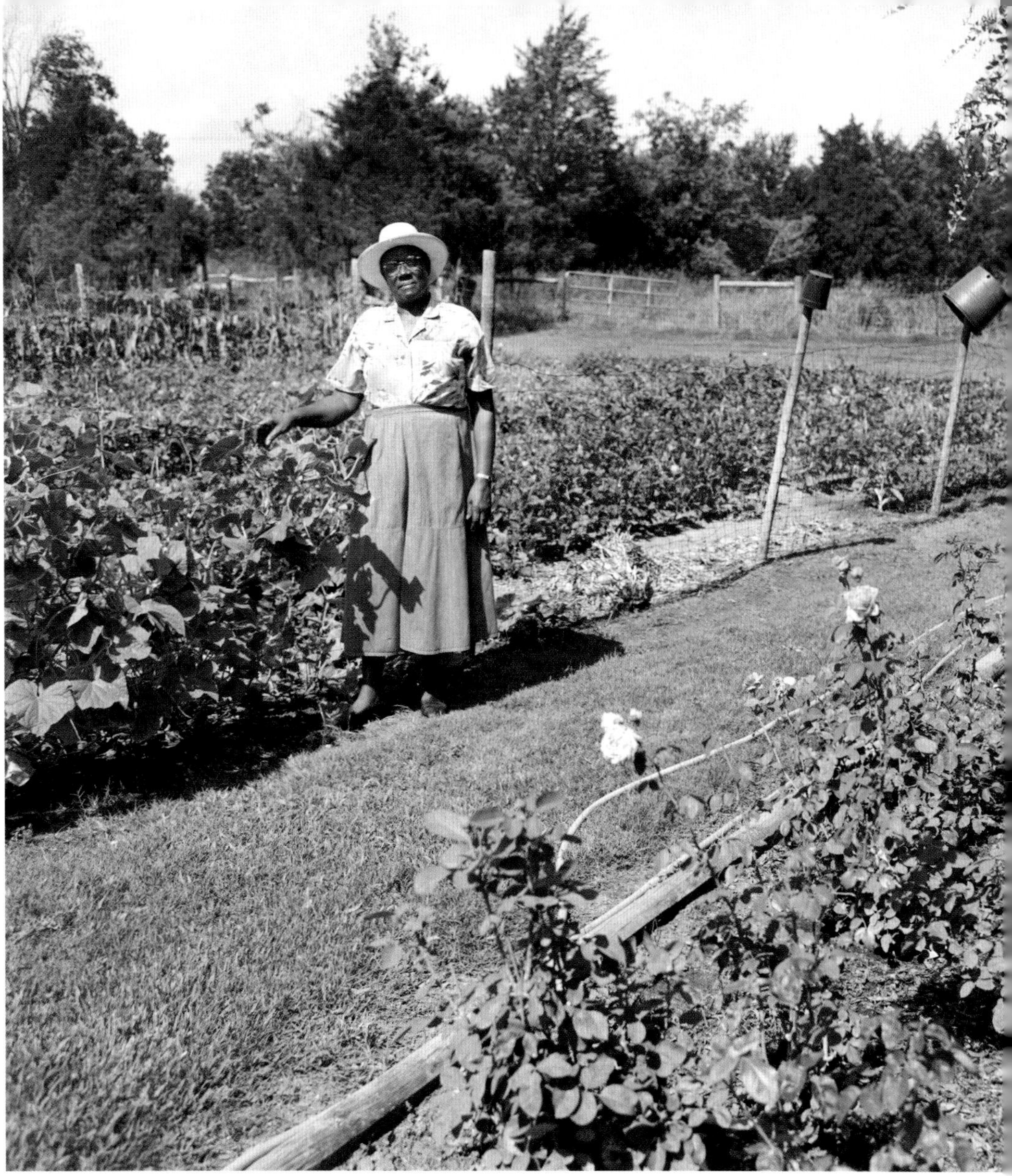

Odie D. Townsend in her garden

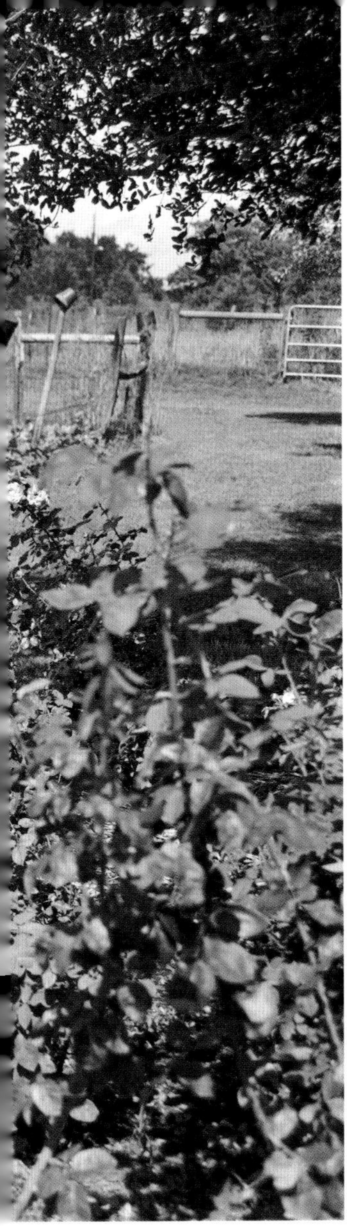

Odie sometimes showed a humorous side, evident in her description of an aging friend. "She sit up on the couch an' go to sleep like a' ole chicken," she said, laughing merrily.

In 2002, Odie D. startled everyone by having an unexpected heart attack, as she approached age seventy-three. A short time later, when she got back home from the hospital, she said, "My phone has ringed all day long. My friends who love me have showed me," and she smiled, adding, "I been prayin' a lot—main thing is that prayer feel upliftin'. My mother had heart problems and my sister. I wouldn't be su'prised if I didn't have heart problems. But the Lord has something for me to do—didn't take me yet. I thank God for letting me live this long."

Lillie & Richard Freis

Lillie and Richard Freis had been married for over fifty years when she said, "We've had good times and hard times, losing crops, losing parents, but we can't say we were ever lonesome or don't know what to do with ourselves. There's always somethin'." And Richard added, "We've never been bored. We're always busy."

"The hardest times, I guess, must have been around '36 and '37," Lillie continued, matter-of-factly. "That's the time when we always had to depend on our cotton crop to make some money, and that's the time we lost our cotton crop. The river got it. And then we didn't have *no* kind of money, no way, 'cept things to sell, and you couldn't get no job nowhere—there was *no job to get*. No way to make money. So you just had to live the best you can, best you could. But we always had somethin' to sell, and that way we got by.

"There was no jobs to get, so people worked on the road. Richard worked on that road too—they have ya a job they call the TWA. You could go and work down there in the gravel pit or somethin'. Well, golly! When you done worked half a year with them ole plows and mules, then go shovel gravel, that was like bein' in the pen. That was *hard*. But we survived."

"Man, I tell you!" added Richard. "We lost three cotton crops on the river, washed away. One time, 1936, we had a big crop—it was just time to pick cotton, the cotton was comin' open, the corn was gettin' mighty ripe, and then them suckers in Austin, they turned the water loose on us." He spoke with exasperation, "They gonna have a big boat race. They had that dam, and it rained, so they had to open the gate—and they *flood us*. They said they's gonna pay us, but we s'posed to get our money today yet!"

Richard and Lillie Freis had lived together for over sixty years when this photograph was taken. They did most everything together during their marriage and seemed to truly enjoy it. They had farmed; raised dogs, chickens, and doves together; attended church and church feasts together; grocery shopped; collected 'things'; ran a museum of Indian artifacts; kept a large vegetable garden; entertained friends; and just hung out together. He was talkative, she was quiet, he was bouncy, she was calm, so they balanced one another. Richard did note, with a laugh, that Lillie had "kicked him out of the bed" after they had slept together for many, long years.

Richard had some more thoughts about their compatibility: "We were both born poor, so we were well matched. And we both love to look for 'things.' When we were married, we both picked arrowheads. When the rain came, we quit, but soon as the

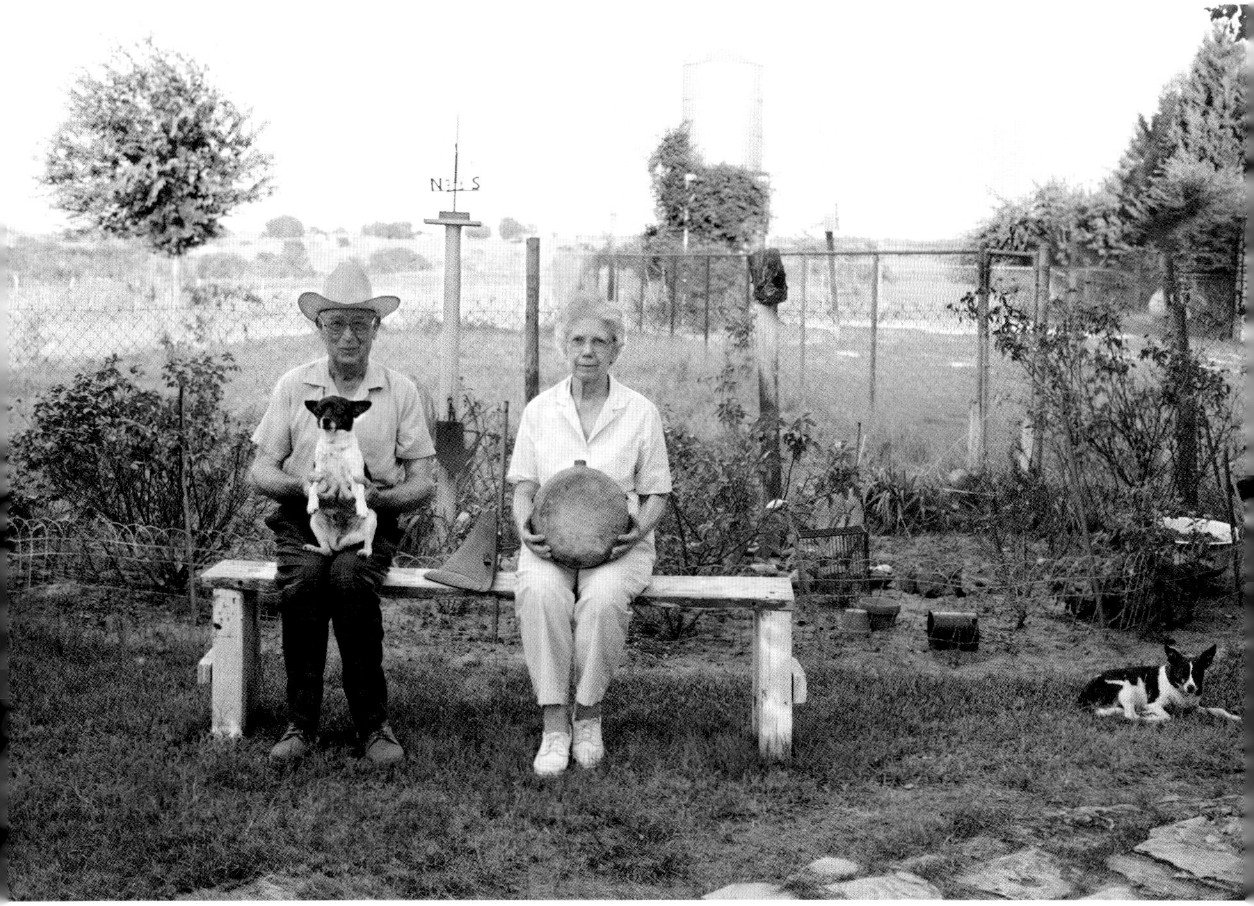

Lillie and Richard Freis with their dogs, Spotty and Missy

last drop hit, my wife and I, we went out lookin' again. On Sundays after church, and in the winter, nothin' much to do—we went out lookin' again." They eventually gathered an extensive collection of arrowheads, spear points, greeting cards, Civil War relics, painted signs, old photographs, snakeskins, odd rocks, iron pieces, glass bottles, barbed wire—you name it, they saved it.

They knew each other from childhood because they were both from the same small community of Wildwood a few miles from Weimar. The day Richard cut Lillie's hair was the day he began to court her. He was the neighborhood barber, the 'official barber' for Wildwood, since he was its only barber, cutting hair from a tree stump in his front yard. "All the people in the country come on Friday nights and get a haircut," explained Lillie. Richard preferred accepting "contributions" over making formal charges for his services—Indian points were favored as payment, no doubt. Most folks paid ten or fifteen cents. One boy brought a rock for his haircut. "Sometimes they didn't have the fifteen cents. They would find a arrowhead and they'd trade it for the haircut," said Lillie, laughing.

"I guess, livin' around here, we all just knew everyone," she continued. "One knew the other one and each other. And besides, he was the barber. Then when we went to a dance, well, he asked me to dance with him. And then it went on and on and on." They married in 1935.

Collecting things, visiting, and farming pretty much describe how the Freises have spent their days together. As children, it was Cracker Jack prizes, arrowheads, and toys they saved. When Richard met Lillie, he found that she too had collections. "So they put their collections together," the local newspaper once wrote. "You have to be a little crazy to do this!" was one of Richard's favorite sayings—good crazy, one might add.

Richard began his passion for collecting as a child when his daddy would take him fishing down along the river and, bored with fishing, the boy would wander off and 'look around.' "I started pickin' arrowheads, and I got started more and more. And I just never stopped." The newspaper story, written in 1990, when he was honored as the oldest living student from the Wildwood school, went on to say, "If a neighbor boy waved at him to show Richard a rock or arrow, he would drop his hoe and check it out. His father was impulsive too. If, before a rain, he thought fish would bite, he'd drop his hoe. So would his sons, to the amusement of the neighbors, who would keep on chopping cotton or corn. Their neighbors would look up and say, 'Gone fishin'!'"

Lillie explained that she came from a family of eleven children, so she, logically, "was always outside, walkin' the woods, things like that, lookin' around." Together, she and Richard amassed such an extensive collection of Indian points that it became known around the state. They opened a museum in La Grange and managed it for five years, until protecting their collection became too burdensome and restrictive for these two free spirits. They decided to sell out and regain their freedom. "We was there day and night, 'cause if you wouldn't stay there, they'd break in there, somebody. And I don't *like* to be penned up inside," said Richard. One day he told her, "Lillie, do you realize we missed two weddings this week? I believe we quit this job." And they went home.

"The onliest time I quit collectin' is when they put me in that box," laughed Richard. "And I don't want that box now!"

Lillie added, "I told him, if I go first, I want him to get the cheapest coffin and the cheapest funeral he can get. Why put all that stuff in the ground there just for nothin'? You could use it for some other thing. If I would have a good pine lumber, I would make mine too, how I want it, ya know?"

She continued on the same topic: "We usually have, it's like a party—when someone dies, well, everybody gets invited to—it's called 'refreshments.' Ya know, we go to a hall and have all kinds of refreshments, tea and cakes and coffee. Everybody's already thirsty, especially if they make a long sermon. And that's the only time kinfolks or friends get together is at a funeral or a wake. So it's mighty nice. You're s'posed to be happy when someone dies, and when a baby is born, you're s'posed to be sad, 'cause they done come into the world to suffer. And once you die, well, you really got it easy and you can go to heaven." She smiled.

Returning to the theme of their hard times during the thirties, the time of the Great Depression, Lillie said, "I tell ya, at that time, you never went to town empty-handed like we do now. You had either some eggs, you had some cream, or you had a couple of fryers. Or maybe you had a couple old hens. And you'd sell 'em and buy your groceries." Added Richard, "See, and another thing, you didn't get no *money* for that—you got chips. It was just like coal miners. See, they *had* you. You couldn't go nowhere else and buy somethin' cheaper." Lillie added, "You have to go back to the same merchants and buy again. Couldn't go to another store with them chips. Had to trade where you sold." The chips were small disks made of wood, metal, or pressed paper, imprinted with a value: "Good for one turkey gobbler," "Red Goose Shoes," "Good for one 12½ cents drink," "Good for one five-cent cigar," "Buckhorn Bar," and "Good for one dinner at Beineke's." Richard especially treasured a chip called a hard-time token, from the time of the Civil War. "After the war, people didn't have no money, so they had to make some tokens they could trade with," he said.

What if they needed a winter coat or some other essential item? "Well, you'd raise a few turkeys," Lillie said, "and you'd sell that—you'd have Christmas money. We'd buy clothes with that. Turkeys brought more money than chickens did. We got by like that."

Like all farmers, they worked hard. "I used to work with four big mules and a turnin' plow, and them was *big* old mules. Big fat four mules. When you lay down, got through at night, you ain't gonna go *nowhere*. You gonna go to bed!" declared Richard good-naturedly. Lillie related, "We worked *hard* in those days already. We had that walkin' planter. Some of 'em had that big ridin' planter where you could sit on, but we just had one of them walkin' planters with two handles like this, and one mule or a horse in front of it. And then you had to go behind it and hold this one mule along that row and plant. Richard would open up the row, and I would plant. Every time we got to the end, when it got around four o'clock, that mule always wanted to go home. He pulled me all the way down, and I had a *time* pullin' him back." She laughed. "That mule would go right on that row just as pretty! We had one mule that never would step off. He would stay right on top. It was *hard* work."

Richard said, "We had a neighbor n——. His name was Concho Lee. He was an old slave, used to be a slave. He used to live by us. He could catch a wild steer out in the pasture, and in two months time, he had the *best* ox. He would catch that wild steer, hitch him to a tame ox, and, man, that tame ox would pull him just where he want to, where he's s'posed to go. And then in about two months, that wild steer, he'd be an ox. That n—— was six feet six, and he was strong. He's say, 'Hooiee! You better walk like I want you to!' He'd be talkin', 'Hooiee!'" And Lillie added, "They'd talk different to an ox. With a horse or a mule, you say, 'Whoa!' And a ox, they'd say, 'Hooiee, hooiee!' See, when they say, 'Hooiee,' that ox knew already how to go. And when they shout, 'Turn,' they'd say, 'Eiikk! Eiikk!'"

Richard loved to talk, and he had a huge storehouse of stories in his head. He loved to tell about his Austrian grandfather, Anton Freis, who had been a soldier in the king's army and left his homeland in 1866 to avoid fighting the Prussians. Anton came to Texas and settled in Colorado County, in Sedan, to be near other Austrian refugees. "We're from Austria," Richard said. "Our ancestors all came from Vienna, Austria. And my grandfather from my dad's side, he was a guard for the king of Austria. He was a sharpshooter.

"My grandpa, on my mother's side—Frank Kainer was his name—he lived out there 'bout three miles, and they just had a li'l old one-room log house—one room just—they had no floor. He used to crawl up there, and he would shingle, you know, just shingle. He was a shingler—he would cover roofs, what they call 'em, shingles."

Sometimes Grandpa Kainer had to leave his wife alone at home for a couple of days in their one-room cabin in Sedan, while he took the wagon and oxen to Columbus, fifteen miles away as a bird flies. Grandma Kainer was a tiny but stouthearted woman. "These Indians was stealin'," Richard said. "They'd slip up at night and git anythin' you had. One time Grandpa Kainer and his neighbor, Bittner, went for provisions to Columbus. One day down and one day back, 'cause they went with oxen. Grandma was left alone. It was a bright moonlight night, and she hears that horse a-nickerin' and a-nickerin' down there, and she look, and she see somebody tryin' to catch that pretty black horse, and she hollered, 'Frank! Frank!' And that Indian jumped out and ran, and she caught that horse and tied him near the log house, and she was sittin' all night with that muzzle loader and that six-shooter, watching." When her young grandson asked, years later, "Would you have shot him?" she replied, "*Sure,* I'd have shot him!" Richard bragged of the petite old lady, "Like Annie Oakley she was, tough as she had to be." And Lillie added, "*Had* to be tough to survive."

Richard's grandfather advised him about staying healthy: "He said, when you work, you work that off, but if you set down and you set, that's the worstest thing you can do, when you quit workin'—that's when you get all the trouble. See, my grandfather Freis told me that. And he was the sharpshooter on my dad's side. He said you got to work. If you work, the more you work, the less trouble you gonna have."

Lillie's family came from Germany. Her immigrant grandfather, Henry Brune, fought in the Civil War. When he tired of fighting, he walked home to Texas from Alabama, got caught, and was forced to return and fight again. It is his army canteen Lillie holds in the photograph.

Said Lillie, "We didn't speak German at all." And Richard said, "It was German and English all mixed up together at home, when we were kids. When we went to school, we couldn't barely talk English." Yet he found it easy to speak two languages as a child.

In 1942, Richard's mother's parents, the Frank Kainers, were invited to Austin by Governor James Allred, to receive the first pension check ever given in Texas. He was 103 years old, and she was 95. They were driven there in a Model T Ford by a friend, Johnny Walker, the owner of a local lumberyard. The event was recorded by official photographs and noted in many newspapers. "One hundred and five, nine months, nine days, when he died," Richard said. "And he never had a pair of glasses. He could read that little print till the last three weeks. He could read in three languages, Austrian, Czech and English. He lived with us a long time."

As a couple, the Freises collected as many friends as they did objects. They were loved by many for their warmth and good humor. Lillie was a woman who showed that she genuinely liked and cared about all people: "I talk to everyone and trust everyone—they're all as good as I am.

"That's the way I feel about it. We lived between colored people. They just as good as I am—just another person to us. That's the way I was raised. I talk to everybody. We were good neighbors with them. We raised hogs or pigs, then turned 'em out; we never fussed or fight over 'em. We raised turkeys, and they'd go over to the neighbors. The neighbors' [turkeys] come over here. Never no problem, you know. Lot of people wouldn't let nothin' come on their place."

The Freises usually had a full garden. "Was just two of us," Lillie said, "and them colored people over there, they couldn't understand that. They said, 'Ummm, ummm, just two people and *so* much to eat!'" She laughed. "And we'd let 'em come and get a pick of whatever how much they wanted." Added her husband, "Them little colored boys, they'd come here, 'Can we get a watermelon?' and I said, 'Go ahead and get ya one,' and then they'd pick the biggest one—they could almost not carry it home."

The couple's hardest times were in the 1930s, when they faced the drought and floods that stole their crops. But they agree that their life has been good. "Interesting things happen to us," Lillie said.

Lillie made another statement that beautifully summed up their life: "We've had good times and hard times, losing crops, losing parents, but we can't say we were ever lonesome or don't know what to do with ourselves. There's always somethin'!"

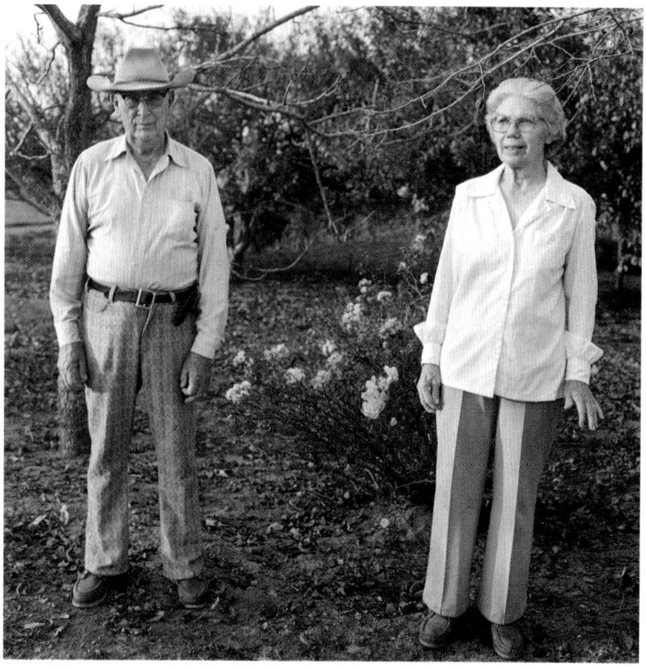

Lillie and Richard Freis

Lillie was born Lillie Brune in 1913 in Wildwood. "I was borned October the eights, 1905," said Richard. His parents were Joe and Pauline Kainer Freis. He had four brothers—Joe, Adolph, Fred, and Felix—and one sister, Regina. His parents were farmers who raised cotton, corn, sugarcane, cattle, horses, chickens, turkeys, geese, and ducks. Richard and Lillie both attended Wildwood School.

Since Richard's paternal grandparents lived to be 95 and 103, it seemed likely he and Lillie had a good many years left to spend together, enjoying life and collecting things—if there is anything left in Colorado County to collect.

In 2004, both Lillie and Richard were living in a nursing home in Weimar, their dogs given away, their house empty. Richard was suffering from Alzheimer's disease. Lillie was fragile, sad, and missing her old life, asking for prayers from her friends. In 2005, she said she had cancer in her jaw and that she feared the pain but not the dying. She said she felt like a prisoner in the nursing home, saying, "I'll never leave here. They won't let me leave here, not let me go home. The place is good, but . . ." And since she was unable to live her life as she wanted, free and outdoors, she said, "I'm ready to move on. I'm not scared to go on." She had told Richard that she would soon not be able to come see him as was her daily routine. She seemed calm and accepting of the future. She died in early summer.

Elizabeth "Lillie" Lemons Atkinson

Elizabeth Lemons Atkinson was born in 1900, the youngest of eight children. She wanted to begin by talking first about her mother, whom she described as "wonderful," a woman who worked hard and lovingly to raise her large brood. "My mother was a *very* beautiful person, humble, and she loved all of her children," she said. Lillie showed a photograph of her mother, taken in 1916 in Houston. It showed Mrs. Lemon sitting in a starched domestic uniform, holding a white baby. She had left Weimar and gone to Houston to care for the children of a family who lived on Pierce Street, near downtown. She had to leave home to be able to earn the money she needed for Lillie's college tuition, since jobs were few and poor-paying in Weimar.

Thanks to her mother, Lillie did get to go to college. She attended Prairie View State Normal and Industrial College for one school year, 1916–1917, and received a first-grade teacher's certificate. After that, she said, "in the summer, for six summers I attended Prairie View because I couldn't go during the regular session—I was teaching." Lillie received her bachelor of science degree in 1930. "But in the meantime, I bought my house, paid for it, attended school, and was helping my mother," she noted. In 1949, she began work on a master's degree, which she completed in five years.

Lillie said she chose to become a schoolteacher in honor of, and in gratitude to, her much-loved mother. Luckily, Mrs. Lemons lived until 1930, long enough to know of her daughter's academic success. Lillie was described as a fine, dedicated teacher whose pupils remembered and revered her still, fifty years later. She was a woman who said about her students, "The children were so *lovely*."

With great pride, she spoke of "all the children I've taught and touched." She added, "They come by and call and send cards and tell me of the influence I had on their lives. I was tough and a hardship on them. But I was a part of their lives that they appreciate now they're grown. Some were inspired by me and became doctors and teachers. Some are just ordinary workers—but they hold good positions." Many have passed on, but the children still think about me. They tell me their accomplishments."

Lillie bragged that she had "missed only three days" in fifty years of teaching, from 1917 to 1967, first in one-room country schools for fourteen years. She taught thirty to forty children at a time in the same room, all together and all working at different levels. Individual students worked according on their abilities and depending on how much school they were able to attend. Some came only occasionally, when they were allowed to leave their farm chores. In the fall and spring especially,

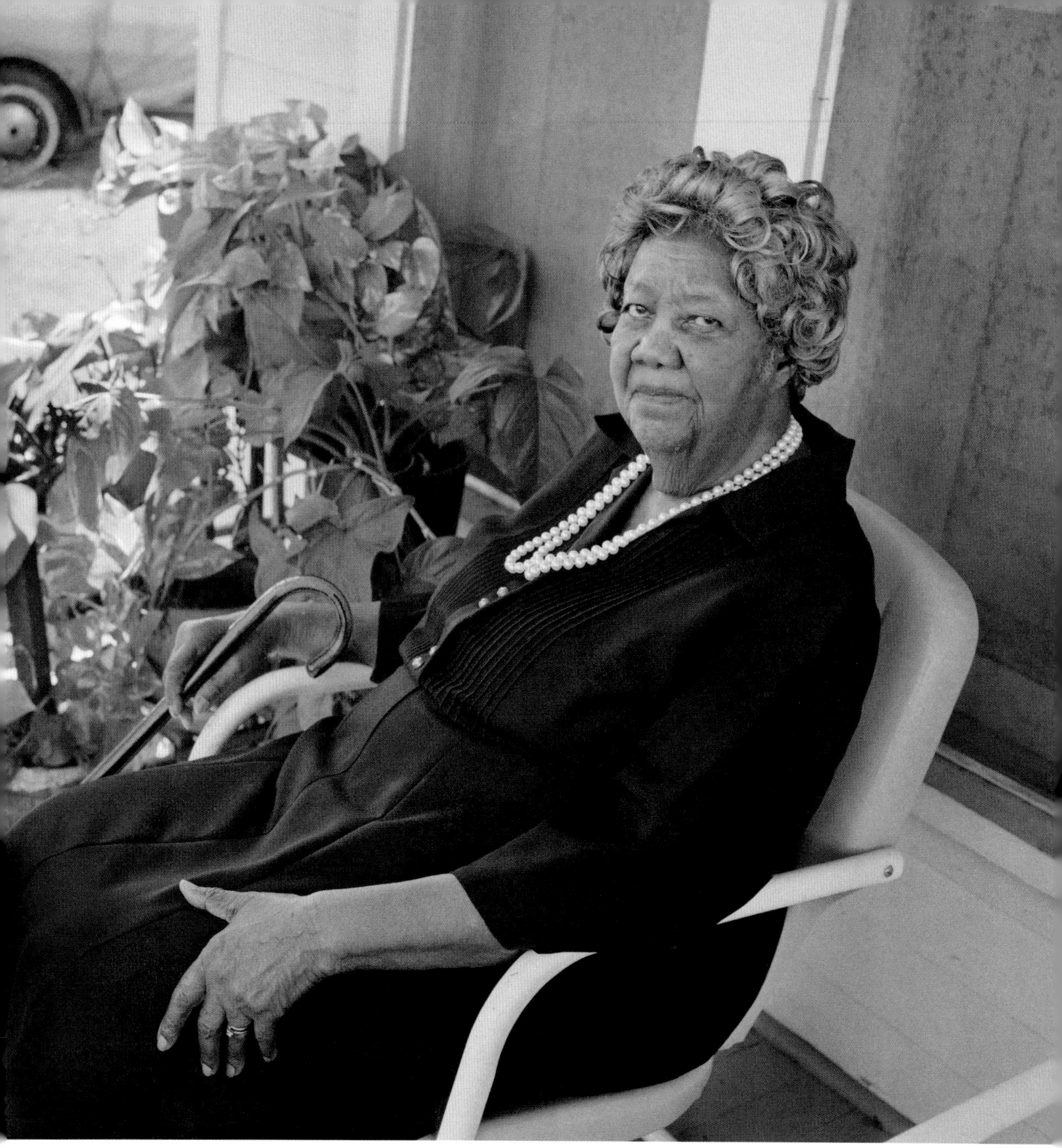

Lillie Atkinson on her front porch

many had to stay home from school and work in the fields, so the school year was "short term" for them, six or seven months at most. When the farm families required their children's help, they simply took them out of school for as long as they were needed at home.

When Lillie first began teaching, she was only seventeen, which made her but three or four years older than some of her charges. "The children I taught were as old as I, or just nearly," she said with a laugh. She had to work very hard to act self-assured and in control so the children would not guess her youth and inexperience and take advantage of her. She said she had to "rap *hard* on the desk sometimes" to get them quiet, and she knew how this still tickled some of them years later. She smiled as she said, "They mimic me, but they love me."

Lillie taught in both Fayette and Colorado counties, at Dry Branch, Clear Creek, Holman, and Osage schools.* "My first school was in Aurora, Dry Branch, out of Weimar," she recalled. Sometimes the rural black school classes were held in church buildings, using improvised desks and always with secondhand, well-worn textbooks. "The church let us use the building, and we used wood for burning [for warmth]." Lillie said. "Pleasant Hill, Dry Branch, and Clear Creek, they were church buildings. Sometime it would be so cold, and sometimes it would be a month or so before I could afford to go home"—even though home was only a few miles away. Lillie later taught in town, from 1930 to 1967, and had the pleasure of teaching in a real schoolhouse, "but never in an integrated school," she pointed out.

"I have always had friends from both races," she emphasized, her voice firm and clear. "And I never considered myself above or below any class of people.

"Integration is helpful in a way, very helpful; it has many advantages. But on the other hand, we still don't have the same privileges we had when we were segregated." She, like others, told how the white academic establishment had thrown out or burned all the memorabilia from the black schools at the time of integration—yearbooks, sport certificates, team photographs, and other such cherished objects.

Lillie married a school principal in 1930, the same year her mother died. The marriage produced one son, her beloved Robert. She sighed and said mournfully, "He lived on the wild side of life. But he never hurt anyone but himself. The hardest time, I think, was when my son called and told me he had been diagnosed with lung cancer, and it was incurable. It upset me real hard. And then I realized how he was taking it, and his attitude, and then that brought me out of that spell, and I was able to go along and accept what was inevitable and do what had to be done. But my son's going was the darkest part of my life."

When he knew that he had lung cancer, Robert prepared himself for dying. He made changes in his life and also made arrangements for his mother, by asking three

*Osage is where Jack Johnson, whose story appears later in this book, was her student. It was he who led me to "Miz Ak'son," saying that she was the best teacher and the finest woman he'd ever known.

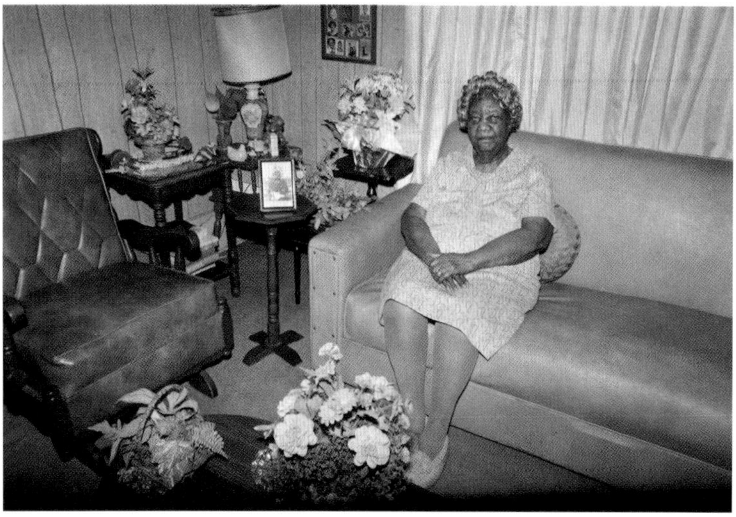

Lillie Atkinson
in her living room

of his closest friends to look out for her. "He made a wonderful change in his life, spiritually, physically, and financially," Lillie said. "Everything was in God's hands, and he was happier than he had ever been."

Lillie's face was veiled with sadness, and her voice dropped when she talked about her adored Robert. His picture stood on top of her television set, next to the picture of her mother holding the baby she tended on her job.

"People expected more from him than he could give," Lillie said. "But in the end, he paid back all. He was a *beautiful* person, and he loved Mother." Robert died in 1986 in Dallas.

Lillie summed up her life and work like this: "I had inspiration and aspirations to do something to help myself and to help Mother. She gave her life and soul to keep me in school. She was the mother of eight, and I always wanted to help her have a better life for herself than she had been used to—she had always worked 'out.'

"I am now ninety-one years old and have much to think back about, many happy days. And there were some days that were not happy or pleasant, but God was with me, and he brought me out of the shadows all the times there were depressions, sadness, or unhappiness. The Lord has helped me out to live through my mother and my son, which was my heart. He didn't come up to expectations in life as I had hoped he would have done, but God was with him, and in his last years he made me happy. And I am happy being his mother.

"My neighbors, close here and around me, white and colored, are all nice to me, and that I enjoy. If I passed away, I would have nothing to regret, because I have lived a full life and I have many friends. God has blessed me to be this age. I don't know what the future holds for me, but I do know I have my hand in God's hand, and I will be ready to go."

Lillie died on Friday, May 8, 1992, ten days after entering the hospital with cancer. "She has closed the great textbook of life," said the minister at her funeral.

Jaynice & Jodie Feyrer

Jodie (Joseph) Feyrer loved to talk and loved to tell stories about growing up in Colorado County. To hear him tell it, he ran barefoot through the countryside in all kinds of weather—"We didn't have no shoes"—and spent his childhood fishing, hunting, looking for treasure, and exploring the woods and creeks with friends. He tells his stories with gusto and excitement, just bouncing in his chair as he talks.

He told stories of people hunting for gold, digging "holes so big your house might fall in 'em," of five-cent homemade beer and dance halls in the woods. He remembered tornadoes that blew the henhouses into the trees and rolled the chickens in the mud, and "house dances" when folks would open their houses on Saturday evenings and dance to accordions, washboards, and fiddles. He had seen the aftermath of an atomic bomb ("only dust for miles and miles") and had lots more tales, funny and sad.

"When I went into the army," Jodie said, "that was my first time I owned me a pair of shoes, when I was eighteen years old. Lot of 'em might think I'm tellin' a story, but that's the truth. I couldn't stand shoes much. I used to go huntin', all the way down the Colorado River from right here, barefooted. I mean, we'd go huntin' at night, rabbit huntin'. Them days, you could go huntin' anywhere with a flashlight, and nobody would bother you.

"I walked barefoot *all* the time. We'd walk to town, to Weimar there, and there used to be this boneyard, but it was a junkyard, on this side of Weimar, and one day I had me a good pair of shoes, and I had my rubber boots on, and I couldn't stand neither one. So I put them boogers in a bucket over there in the junkyard where nobody could find them. When I come back, somebody done stole the bucket with all my shoes. Both pair of my shoes! From that day on, when I went to Weimar, I went with my shoes under my arm, and when I got to town, I washed my feet there somewhere and put the shoes on, and when I got ready to come back home, I'd take my shoes off. My feet got soft after I went into the army, and I got a shoe on."

His wife, Jaynice Ulbricht, was born in New Bielau, a few miles away. "It's blackland, muddy. It's real sticky." The mud "would pull my boots right off." Her family home was located "just across the road from the New Bielau dance hall."

Jodie was born in Osage, where the couple were still living, which he described as "sandy land." His daddy was Stanley L. Feyrer. The Feyrers were German born—"Mama's name was Martha Manofsky." Her parents were Joe and Annie Manofsky, Czech immigrants who came to America in the 1870s and purchased the land in Osage.

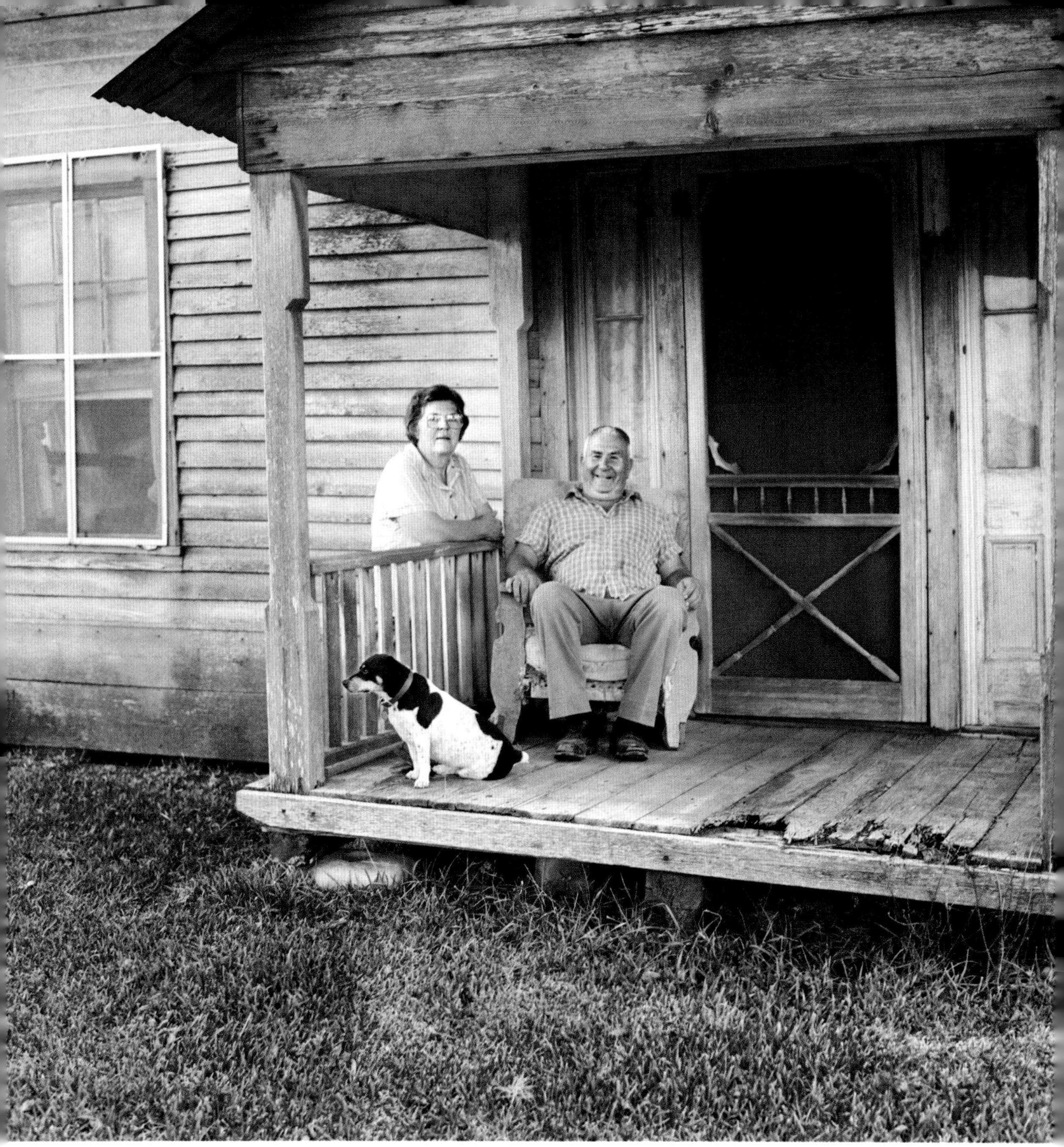

Jaynice and Jodie Feyrer

Jodie pronounced their name "man of sky" and added, "They are all originally from overseas. And I had two sisters, Dayla and Marie.

"My grandpa and my grandma, they bought this place, I think it was in 1880, or somewhere along in there—they bought this farm," Jodie continued. "And they raised nine children over here in this house. There's two sisters livin' now, yet. I was born and raised on this farm in 1927, January the twenty-second, but not in this house. We had a house over by the tank there, and then, in 1935, my grandma and grandpa both died the same year, and we moved over to their house with my folks. Grandma died first, and Grandpa didn't want to live without her, so he just didn't care," Jodie explained gravely.

"And I stayed here till I was drafted into the army in 1942, myself. And stayed in the army for around close to two years. That's too long ago already. They didn't get me over there, so I came back home and I got married and moved to Houston in 1955. It had got so dry up here that all the grass died and all the fence posts dried up around the place, so we had to leave."

He said that this was his and Jaynice's biggest mistake, moving to Houston. They found nothing there but stress and misery. "I worked at the Carnation Milk Company for twenty-seven years," Jodie said. "Had a kind of nervous breakdown there, and then I decided to retire. So I retired at age fifty-five, and I moved back up here and that's where I'm at now."

When they returned home, Jodie told Jaynice, "If I don't make it in the country, I'm gonna chase rabbits and bark at the moon!" Happily, that was not necessary. The two looked cheerfully settled in their trailer house next to the old family home, which was falling apart bit by bit. In the rainy times, Jodie cultivated a large field between the house and the road, where he planted as many kinds of vegetables and fruits as he could fit: beans, lettuce, greens, peas, Brazos blackberries, peppers, peaches, squash, cabbage, broccoli, onions, and carrots. At the same time, he battled with the deer and birds for first rights to the garden pickings. Jaynice was creating and selling crocheted items, making preserves, and praying for rain for Jodie's garden.

Jodie reminisced, "Must've been in '38 or '39, somewhere along there, a tornado come through here and rearranged everythin'! It picked up everythin' over here and put it down over there. That's when it picked the old house up and over about four inches. That's when the fireplace fell down, see?" Jaynice asked, "Is that when the white chickens were black the next morning?" and Jodie replied, "Yeah, see they slept in the tree. They had about eight hundred of 'em ole white leghorns. The next morning, we got up, and there were chickens all over the road and lookin' in the windows over there. Blowed 'em outta the tree, rolled 'em around in the dirt, twisted 'em in the mud. That was a mess that time! Whoooooee! I tell you, I never seen *nothin'* like that in my life! We had a hog pen over there, and the roof was sixteen feet long and eight foot wide, and it took that roof off the pen and hung it up, laid it up on the top of an ole post oak tree, a *big ol' tree* over there. And thing laid up there for years and years and years, till that ole tree started dyin', and it fell outta that tree."

"Across over here is the Hubbard Place," he once said, talking about hunting for treasure. "They dug up that place so bad down there, if you walk through that place at night, you liable to not get back, them holes so big! People lookin' for money. They say there's gold around here that they lookin' for. See, that gold disappeared when General Sam Houston and that Spanish general had that big battle. This used to be the Old Spanish Trail, used to go through here somewhere. But I can remember back in the thirties, our government men used to come through here, lookin' for that stuff.

"Daddy, he smoked cigars *all* the time. He'd never throw it away, I mean, he smoked the *whole* cigar. When he'd smoke that cigar—when it got this short—he'd stick the rest of that in his pipe and light it. He never threw away nothin. See, he used to raise tobacco years ago and, see, he'd roll them cigars. Man, you had to be a *man* to smoke that tobacco!"

On a very different note, there was the time Baby Marie, at nine years old, took sick and died. "My sister Baby Marie, she died," Jodie recounted. "She got sick—it was in January. She got sick, and in those years, you had to take some kind of medicine, I don't know what it was—quinine or somethin' like that, yeah, quinine they give you. Somewhere or another, they got the quinine and the strychnine mixed up, some kind of way which nobody could ever figure out how it was done. And so, when she got sick, Mama went out and looked in the cabinet and moved somethin' around and she found them doggone pills. So she gave her one of them, and in about two hours she was dead. You couldn't get out here with no doctors or nothin', because the road was so muddy. It was rainin', and you couldn't travel with no cars, so our neighbor went for the doctor, and she was already passed when he got here.

"Well, it was a real bad feelin', 'cause I can remember—I think about it every once in a while 'cause it was hard, somethin' like that to happen. I know to all of us it was terrible, but those years, people had a funny way of doin' things. You had your turkeys runnin' loose, and they would lay, and people would crack the egg a little bit and put that strychnine in the egg a little bit and put a piece of tape over it, and kill varmints like that. I got the idea that's the way it happened, you know, some of that stuff in the medicine cabinet.

"We laid her out on the kitchen table. Hubbard [of Hubbard's Funeral Home in Weimar], he took her into town and embalmed her. She was over here in this room in a casket, and they had the funeral from this house and buried her in the Osage Cemetery down here. "It was hard on everybody," he said, his voice trailing off.

In time, he continued: "Daddy got sick after that. He got the pneumonia, and he liked to have died. He went from over two hundred pounds to a hundred sixteen. And after that, he got the hiccups. And talk about hiccups! They tried curin' those hiccups with everything under the sun. Man! You oughta've heard the remedies that people brought in. People wrote letters from Fort Worth and Dallas. Mama cooked a bunch of cornmeal hot and laid it on that man's stomach. And lard—they tried everything. They couldn't cure them hiccups. Had doctors come from San Antonio and try. And he hiccuped for, I don't know, it must have been a month, all night, all day long, just hiccuped. One night he started cryin'—oooohhh, he was cryin'! And he went to sleep. We thought that was gonna be it. And he woke up, and it was gone. All the money they spent, all the medicine they tried—when he cried, woke up next mornin' and hiccups was gone."

Of the Depression, Jodie said, "Yeah, we used to raise vegetables here. Onions and carrots and turnips and stuff like that and take 'em to town. And they had Grady Shaver and Harlene—that's the only ones I can remember. They used to give you fifty cents, thirty-five cents, or a dollar—it was like tokens—like paper, you know. But that's what they were worth. But if they sell your vegetables and stuff like that, you come back and they pay you in that, you know. And you had to spend that money at that store, you know—when you come back, you would buy groceries for it. Most of those years, that's what most of the people lived on, from one crop to another, on credit. That's why a lot of those stores in town went broke, a lot of 'em. The years come along where you couldn't raise nothin'! See, it rained so much back in them years. It rained so much—you have no idea how much it rained. I've seen water over here knee-deep. Them days, it was like a sea. The poor farmers, in wet years, they lived on credit till the next year. See that's when a lot of these people went broke, lost their land and all that stuff. A lot of 'em moved in with other farmers. Well, we didn't have any shoes—had no money to buy any shoes! I remember workin' in the fields—and it was filled with ice—barefooted.

"They were *hard times*. Your times didn't start out getting' good till after '41, '42. Then it started goin' up. But it was *rough* back in those days. Back in '36, '37, '38, '39, when you couldn't get *nothin'*—eggs was a nickel a dozen. You go to town with thirty dozen, they might not buy them, you might bring 'em all back. Daddy brought a lot of 'em back home. We'd had to just throw them in the creek 'cause we couldn't eat that many eggs. In them days, there were boiled eggs, fried eggs, scrambled eggs, poached eggs, all kinds of eggs. That's all you had left was eggs and a big fryin' pan of bacon. Always bacon and eggs. That's all you seen for years. It was just *hard*. You couldn't make any money *no kind of way*. I used to pick cotton, chop cotton. I used to walk from here down to Brandts' or Trefnys', down there, and I'd chop cotton. Fifteen cents a day—that's all they'd pay.

"Electricity didn't come in here until '38 or '39, somewhere along in there. Electric bills now, a hundred and fifty or two hundred dollars a month. Then they were two dollars a month or a dollar and a half, and Mama and Daddy would scream, 'Lord, have mercy! They're pricin' us off the market at a dollar and a half a month!' We had coal oil lamps. They had graduated from coal oil to gasoline lamps, which you had to kind of stay awake with 'cause I seen a lot of 'em blow up around here."

Jodie remembered gleefully when his father bought the neighborhood's first radio, which ran on thousand-hour batteries: "We had a Philco. Daddy went to town and bought that battery radio. Must have been somewhere along about 1932. I guess we must have been the first ones had this radio, because Sunday evenings at five o'clock, Gene Autry would come on. I guess you heard of Gene Autry. 'When I'm back in the saddle again,' you know? That was *way* back there. You're too young, you prob'ly don't remember that. But that was the goin' thing. The neighbors would all walk over. And Mama would make kolaches and cakes and pies, and there'd be people comin' down that road, look like gonna have a party down here. Come down to listen to that radio for that one hour. Durin' the week, they'd only listen to the news, nothin' in between. That's all they'd listen to, fifteen minutes at dinnertime. We couldn't listen to nothin' but the six o'clock news come on from San Antone. Us children, we couldn't touch that button or we get buttoned up! On account of the battery wore down.

"And you had to put an aerial on it, a wire on it for an antenna—it wouldn't pick up real good. So Daddy got the idea of tyin' a doggone wire onto that stovepipe in there. He run it out the stovepipe, out the side of the house, and down to the ground there. But that didn't bring in enough reception. So they decided to put it on the stovepipe and run it out the window and put it on the metal clothesline, and run it *way* down in the garden where a big pecan tree was a-settin'. They had a *big* ole pecan tree out there in the middle of the garden, and there was the clothesline onto that pecan tree. So Daddy said, 'Well, we gonna get some good reception now!' So they tied that wire onto that clothesline. It worked *real good.* I mean, you pick up stations a long ways.

"Now comes Sunday evenin'. Everybody in the neighborhood would come and see us. And one night we had a big front in here from the northwest, like those fronts come in. It was kinda cool, and they had a fire built in that stove. And we had a big t'understorm come up, lightnin' and hailin' and a t'underin'. And that cotton-pickin' lightnin' struck that pecan tree down there and runned up inside the house. It come up that wire—that lightnin' come all the way up that line, come in the house, come down that stovepipe, and blew that lid offa that stove! Blew that stove wide open. Busted the bottom of the stove. We was all sittin' in front of the stove—we sure woke up! Scared the daylights out of everybody. I don't know how far we jumped. I mean we was all fulla ashes. And Daddy was sittin' in front of the stove, smokin' a cigar. It blew the cigar right out of his mouth. It just shook up the whole place. Coals everywhere. Just imagine sittin' in front of a stove, and all of a sudden—BLOOM!—the whole thing blows up. We were so busy pickin' up coals with shovels and throwin' it back in there.

"But we took that wire off that stovepipe then," Jodie mourned. "The sad thing is we had got really good reception on that stove!"

Jodie continued his reminiscing: "Used to have house dances. People come over and one of 'em play accordion. My mother use to play accordion. One of her broth-

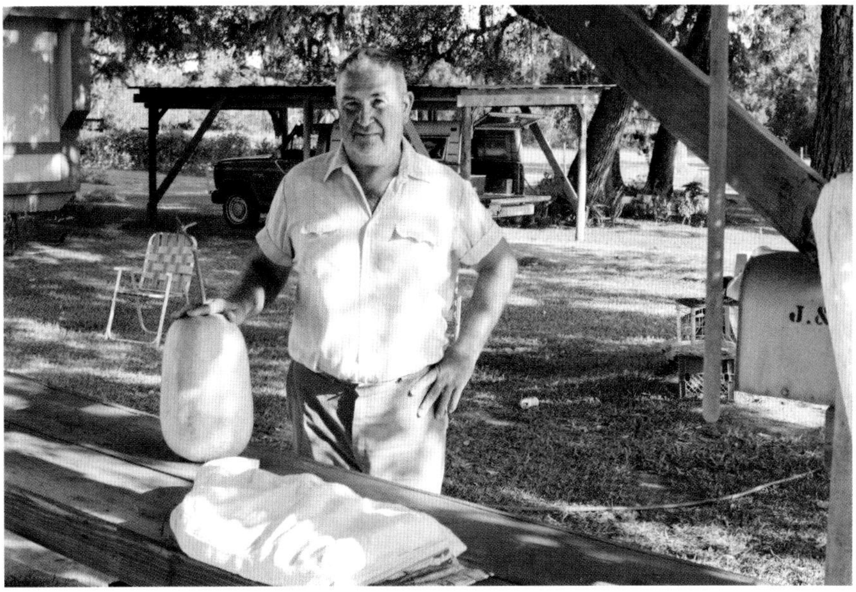

Jodie Feyrer and his prize squash

ers played a fiddle, and one of 'em played a guitar. They'd all dance. They used to have a dance hall back in them woods, called Manofsky Dance Hall. But that got tore down. That's where they built that big barn and all them chicken houses from the dance hall wood.

"Mama, she was tough. She had to be. My sisters Dayla, Marie, and myself, we was playin' in the backyard. We got mad at one another, and I chucked a rock at one of 'em. But anyway, Mama saw that and she come out there, and she said, "If there's gonna be any hittin' done around here, *I* do the hittin'! *I* gonna do that!" And she got a peach switch, and she whipped us. And one night, we stayed under the house till about ten o'clock. You know, we thought we were gonna get away, so we wouldn't get spanked, you know? Well, we come out and we still got spanked, 'cause it got too bad under there. It got dark; we got scared.

"And years ago, they used to have an old sayin' around here too—you see a strange car comin' down the road, you better run, 'cause they might steal you, take you along, you know. And I tell you, I sit under that house many a time till it was dark. People would come over here—I wouldn't come out from under this house till they left. I had kinfolks, we'd go visitin' them, and there was six or seven boys. Them buggers, when they seen you comin', the car comin' down the road, they'd be fallin' out them windows, headin' for the woods. They'd hide. They wouldn't come back till we were leavin' to go back to Weimar. We get to the gate, and we could look back and they was all a-marchin', comin' out of the woods, comin' up to the house." And he smiled his familiar happy smile.

Jaynice died quickly and unexpectedly of cancer in 1996, leaving Jodie alone and mournful.

Rosezena Woodson

"I'm eighty-two. I'll be eighty-three on the fifteenth of October. Yes'm, hmm, hmm, and I'm preparin' for another home, 'cause you cain't have two. I'm eighty-two, and I thank the Lord I've lived such a long time, ha, ha, yes!" exclaimed Rosezena in a happy voice, "I *thank* the Lord for my past days. And I'm preparin' every day for a better home. Yes'm, and it's time to tell my story."

These were Rosezena Woodson's words on the day we first met in 1991, when I dropped by. It was time for Rosezena to talk, and she was ready.

Rosezena was one of those rare persons who seems so comfortable with herself and others that nothing seemed to ruffle her, not a camera, not a stranger. Perhaps this serenity was one reason she had outlived her two adult daughters, one grandson, and so many of her friends.

"I have three chil'ren," she said, proudly. "My oldest child was a boy. And when my son lost their chil'ren's mother, I had *those* three chil'ren too, which was a boy and two girls. So I've had the chance to raise six chil'ren!" Asked how she felt about raising two families, Rosezena replied in her melodious, singsong way, "Oh, I feel *fine*. I'm just so *glad* of 'em. I'm just so *proud* of them chil'ren, I don't know *what* to do! It's a lot to be proud of."

Her youngest daughter, Romona Cheeks chimed in, saying, "She was a good mother. She was a Christian-goin' woman and she was home, and we all worked hard, and she showed us *how* to work. We don't know what else to do *but* work."

"You didn't bother Mama, or she had *somethin'* for you to do," continued Romona. And Rosezena added, "When my chil'ren were growin' up, when it was cold and rainin', well, I would get them in the house around me, and I would tell 'em stories and tell 'em speeches and things, to keep their minds on somethin' what I thought would be *worthwhile* to them. Then I would be tellin' 'em, 'Whatever y'all do when you grow up, don't pick up somethin' what you can't put down.' I always told 'em, I say, 'You have to stay out of trouble, 'cause I don't know how to get *nobody* out of trouble!'

"I'd tell 'em, I'd say, 'Whatever habit you get—that that's hard to put down, don't pick it up. Then you don't *have* to put it down.' I don't smoke, I don't drink, I don't chew, I never did dip, no snuff or nothin'. My mother was a snuff dipper, but I didn't take to that."

Rosezena clearly remembered a grammar school recitation from seventy-some years earlier, which she loved to recite—to her family's great amusement. She had learned

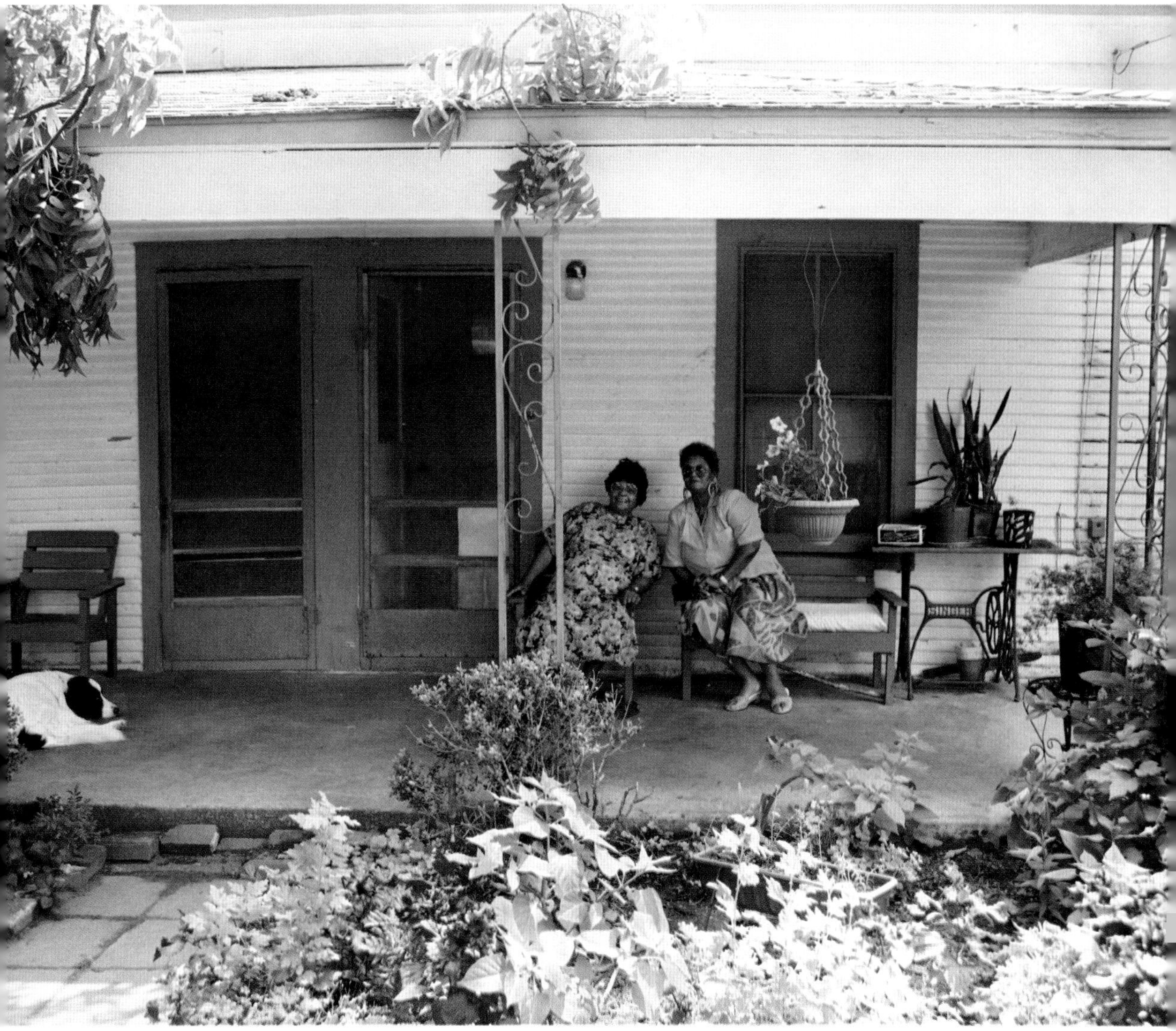

Rosezena Woodson and Romona Cheeks

it from her father, but no one remembered where he had found it—Rosezena thought maybe from the newspaper. I call it the "Snuffin' and Puffin'" poem:

> Let us cleanse ourselves from all filthiness of the flesh and spirit, perfect holiness in the fear of God.
> If any man defile the temple of God, him shall God destroy. For the temple of God is holy, which temple ye art.
> There are fathers and mothers all over this land, chewing tobacco as hard as they can,
> While their children are scolded and pushed off the bed, all dirty and ragged and cryin' for bread.
> The filthy old snuff fair ladies will dip, and spoil their great beauty by fillin' their lip.
> A very small baby sittin' on mother's knee—smokin' a cigarette, a sad sight to see.
> So my father once said with his eyes full of tears, "I cannot quit smoking—I have tried it for years,"
> While a dyin' young man said he sadly regrets that he ever did learn to smoke cigarettes.
> Are you snuffin' and puffin' for the glory of God? Are you treading the pathway our Savior once trod?
> Oh, snuffer and puffer, ye slave of the weed, is your path clear to heaven? Is your hope sure indeed?
> You'll confess that you're angry and cross and all wrong, when you're craving a cigarette and your pack is all gone.
> Oh, slave of the weed, heed the word that I say—lay down your tobacco, no longer delay.
> For Jesus is calling to you and to me. He'll save you. He'll cleanse you and let you go free.
> Now surely you'll confess that my story is true. So how can you continue to smoke, dip, and chew?
> Stop snuffing and puffing, and be wise evermore. And seek for a home in Kingdom's bright shore.

Rosezena recited the poem, and as her grown children burst into laughter, she continued seriously, "You have to pick what you want to be in life. And so, if you pick the right thing, you'll be proud of your life as you grow older. And I want to say that I'm proud of my chil'ren. I've never had to get them out of jail. I've never had the law to come after them for drugs and stuff like that. So I'm proud. And I think I've lived a nice life, and I thank God for that. It's a lot to be proud of!"

Born in 1908 in nearby Lavaca County, Rosezena moved as a child to Oakland, in Colorado County, with her parents, Molly and Ambrose Adams, and her three sisters, Perlaner, Mabel, and Willie. "Daddy had two fifty-acre plots. I was reared there in Oakland. My husband [Grady Woodson], he got me from Oakland and I married him.

"And I'm proud to tell what I know, because one of these days I will go to a new home. And when I go, I want to leave a testimony, and that is that I've done my best.

"I'm prayin' that the Lord lets me live until I cain't do nothin' for myself. My eyes is growin' dim now—I cain't see well. My happiness is goin' to church. That's the happiest thing I can see in my life now, is just goin' to church and comin' back. An old car, an old dog, one old cat, and me"—she laughed—"yeah, and we all live here together."

Not long after this conversation, Rosezena moved to Houston to a nursing home near her son, Grady, and her two ill daughters. After the two daughters' premature deaths, their mother stayed on in the nursing home. She was there in 1999 when we visited, still spirited, still happy, still talking and telling stories—she could probably have run the place if she had wanted.

Rosezena summed up her life like this: "I don't have no enemies. I've never been called to go to jail. I've lived the best I could and been considerable to everybody. I've had no trouble with nobody as I know of. Everybody's my friend—that's all I can say. So I think it's been a very nice life to live."

Romona Woodson Cheeks

Romona was Rosezena's beautiful youngest daughter. She had left Weimar and was living in Houston, working as a nurse when we met. She was visiting her mother on weekends.

"There was five of us in the family," she began. "And I remember one year we picked eight bales of cotton through the five of us and harvested it all ourselves. But I want to say this, and I tell everybody today: We worked hard, but I tell you what, Mama never stayed home! When she got up in the morning—it brings tears to me, I don't like to talk about it too much because I get tears—I get emotional. Because she'd have breakfast ready before daybreak, and she'd have dinner already cooked for us when we got home, at lunchtime, from the fields.

"And when we picked up our haul, our sack, and whatever it was, she didn't stay back and say, 'Well, I'm gonna cook dinner.' There's a lot of people tell me, say: 'We went to the field, and our mother cooked, and then she'd come out here after cookin'." But that never was like that here. Mama was ready to go with us.

"And I know now, a lot of times when I have to be at work at six in the morning, I know if I'm gonna get dinner, I have to get up at four or five, if I'm gonna have a whole lot of cookin' done. She was cookin' on a woodstove, see. And when we got ready to go to the fields, she was leadin' out. She didn't say, 'Y'all go ahead on and I'll come on.' She went, and I mean it. And I get very emotional because I look at her and I know how hard she has worked." Tears came into Romona's eyes as she said, "And the good Lord have left her here and I am thankful.

"But my mother taught me to work. I *had* to work as a child. There was never a dull moment. If you worried Mama," Romona reiterated, "she had *somethin'* for you to do." She laughed. "So you don't worry her too much! But I don't regret it.

"And I tell other people, workin' is something this family here have done. We didn't have *time* to get in trouble. We didn't have the time!

"We raised everything except the flour we used and very little other things that we had to buy. And we had to work to help get it. No one had a free day. We all worked forward to that. I can remember picking cotton in a little ten-pound sugar sack—that was the size I was. Because there was no one to stay home with me—everybody had to be in the field. So I had to go too. So Mama made me a sack out of a ten-pound sack of sugar, and that was my sack. And from then on, I always had a sack. Picked off everybody else's row. But I would be out there.

"And I've had a job all my life. I don't know how to not have a job. I don't even look forward to not having a job until I can't go.

"Picking cotton was hard work, *hard* work. But it was gratifying work, because that was all we knew. You know, you hurt your fingers. And we had to harvest shucks and corn and everything else. We did all our work ourselves. We hired no help.

"We rented our land until we get here to town. It was somethin' like sharecroppin', called 'third and fourth'—that's all I remember. One place we worked, we lived on a gentleman's property called Winkins. It was a joy to live there. I loved to fish, and Mama'd give me time to do a little fishin' in the creek, and I always think about that. I was much younger than my brothers and sister, and I liked to play. My sister was *not* a person who liked to play—she studied and read and was doing all those things. My play was dolls, and I had me a little dollhouse on the other side of the creek under a big tree where I could go and cook and pretend I was havin' my own home. Mama give me some old cookin' things, and I'd take a little pot and I'd make my fire over there. That was my fun. That's what it was like in the country." She smiled.

"Mama didn't keep us out of school," Romona continued. "One year we went to school, and we walked a long way. We would walk a *long* way. Try to say it was thirteen miles, but it seemed like it was farther than that. And we got to school on time. And my mother let us know—well, my brother was the oldest, and when he put his foot on the first step, be ready to put *yours* on the bottom one, and the next one. That meant we come together, and we leave together. And that is how we did. And lot of times, I would get so tired until he'd have to carry me on his back, 'cause it was so far for me to walk. Or either my shoes would get so muddy. But we had galoshes. We had the things that helped protect us. We'd get to school, and we'd be just frozen almost.

"We had the clothes. Mama could sew, and Mama worked for a lot of people that give her good things, but Mama could sew, and with her knowin' how to sew, we never was cold. We never was hungry; we raised everything. We never were without food. We didn't have hamburgers like some people. We didn't have fruit like you—say, bananas—'cause we didn't raise 'em, but we had pears, we had peaches, and Mama canned. We had year-round food. We killed three hogs, and we put it down in the lard—don't talk about it much, but that would cure until time to kill hogs again. We had a big barrel where we made syrup, and we had syrup. We never was hungry. It was hard work, but, believe me, we had aplenty.

"I've always worked. It's the only thing I know. I couldn't depend on a husband—I didn't know how to. See, so that was always the way. So we've had it good, I bought a home in San Antonio. I've been married, but most of my life I've been single. I'm married now, but I have lived most of my life and raised my daughter alone, I sure did. I have one daughter and those three grandchildren—that little one stays with me.

"I went to beauty school and I did hair for seventeen years, and then I went to school for nursing. And now I'm in that field now, and I work every day."

When she was in her early sixties, Romona got cancer and entered Methodist Hospital in Houston. She died soon afterwards, at sixty-four years of age, far too young for such a healthy woman to die. She left behind her daughter, Patricia Anderson, her mother, and several grandchildren.

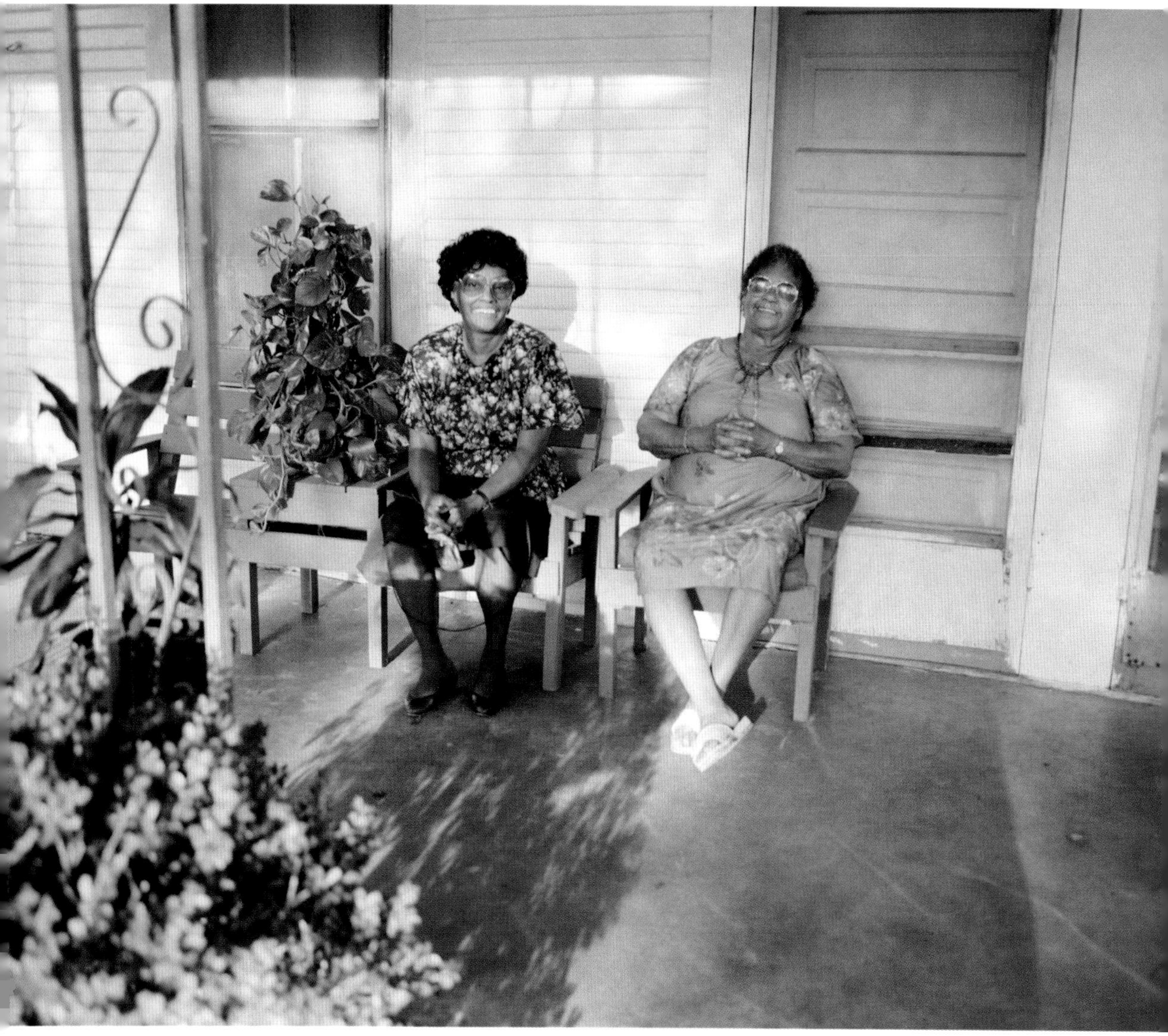

Cassie McGrew and Rosezena Woodson

Cassie Woodson McGrew

Cassie McGrew was Rosezena's oldest daughter. She too was born in the country and moved into Weimar as a youngster. When she married, she went to San Antonio with her husband, had two sons, divorced, and came back to live in her birth town. When she returned to Weimar, her pleasures there were her sons, Quillen Rex and Audren Kent, her clothes making, and her jobs as music director and pianist at two local churches, Greater Macedonia Baptist Church and St. Paul's Baptist.

Cassie, always tasteful in her clothes and jewelry, acted as the observer each time I was around, watching silently in the background while others talked. So she surprised me when she asked to talk on camera one day and tell some of her life experiences, which she did in a very clear, straightforward way, having obviously thought a lot about racial divisiveness.

"I think the big drawback in the relationships with the races is that we don't know people," she began, in a quiet, steady voice. "And a lot of times, people just look at you and they think, you know, that you are so much different. But when I was in San Antonio, I was confined to the state hospital, and I had never been in close proximity with white people before. But when I was there, they put us all in one big room, and I slept in the same room with white folk, and I learned. I would sit and observe, and I said, 'These people are no different from me—it's just their color. Beneath the skin, we are very much the same.'

"And we got up and we talked, and whatever we did, we did, you know, as one. There was nothin' to separate us there. And I learned. And when I first went there, being brought up in a small town where we were always separate, I had never been close to anyone of a different race. You get kind of queasy 'cause you think they're so much different. But they really are not!

"I learned through observation that they have the same pain and the same feelings that we have. Beneath the skin, we are very much the same. Their emotions are a lot the same as ours. They have the same pain, the same suffering. But I didn't realize that before. And I felt different, you know.

"Ever since then, I'm not intimidated by color. What intimidates me is people with a lot of knowledge. You know, people that's real smart. To feel terribly inferior, that's bad for us. And if we feel that we are superior, we can't get along. So, if we would get to know each other, you know, we could communicate better, I think there would be a lot more peace in the world. I think there wouldn't be so much fear like we have."

Cassie died in a nursing home, after a relatively simple surgery that cut an important spinal nerve, leaving her paralyzed. Cassie handled this situation with grace and faith, a sad ending to her life. Friends remembered Cassie healthy and happy, as she was playing the piano at Greater Macedonia Baptist on Sundays, her red nails tapping and moving deftly over the keys, her earrings swinging as she kept time, hair and clothes immaculate, a smile on her face.

Mary Hausner

Mary Hausner began to talk about her life: "I am ninety-one. Eighteen ninety-nine I was born, August 16, 1899. I'm birthed in Columbus. I'm just a country woman.

"My daddy died when I was two years old. Mama never did got married again. I had three brothers and one sister. They all gone. The brothers' wives are all gone. They none of 'em liked me, you know, because Albert, my husband, and I got along so good. They were lazy, and I wasn't.

"When Daddy died, we was on the farm. And the broker man down there tol' Mama, he says, 'You got to sell that place, because, you see, you cannot work.' My brother was four or five months old. So Mama took that money, you know, and then, in Glidden, she bought two acres of land, built a house down there. And then she got a job. There was a old, whatcha call 'roundhouse,' you know, where the train switches. And Mama got a job down there.

"Those days, there wasn't no automobiles like now. You know that. Automobiles didn't come in—I think I was about fifteen, sixteen years old before they come to Columbus.

"I had no high school education. Third grade! Don't look—I went only to third grade. What Mama did, I watched her all the time. See we had only Mama, no aunt and no uncle. We didn't like none of them. I was big enough to do the work. Mama needed help, and Mama had lots of trouble, you know, sickness.

"And we were already big enough then, you know. I could make kolaches and bake bread when I was eight years old. I watched her, you know, I did. She was making kolaches, you know. And I said, 'Mama, can I help you?' She said, 'Every step.' Mama used to use them goose feathers—you know? them long ones?—and strip 'em and made her a little brush out of it, you know? And dip it in butter and then she put prunes—she put prunes inside and on top. Oohhh, they were delicious.

"They didn't have where you go and turn on the stove. Those days we had woodstoves. Mama had five kids at home, you know, and the elder one has to go help. Mama said, 'Mary, you think you can bake that bread?' I tol' Mama, 'I don't know if I can do it.' She said, 'Oh yes you can.' So I did."

When I told Mary how I admired her spirit, she only said, "Anybody can have it. They just have to make up they mind and do it." It sounded simple as she said it.

"I'm Bohemian," she continued. "My husband was a German. My daddy came from the old country, Czechoslovakia, eighteen years old." Of her husband, Albert Hausner, she said, "I call him Albert. He's my husband. Albert was a little boy, only four years

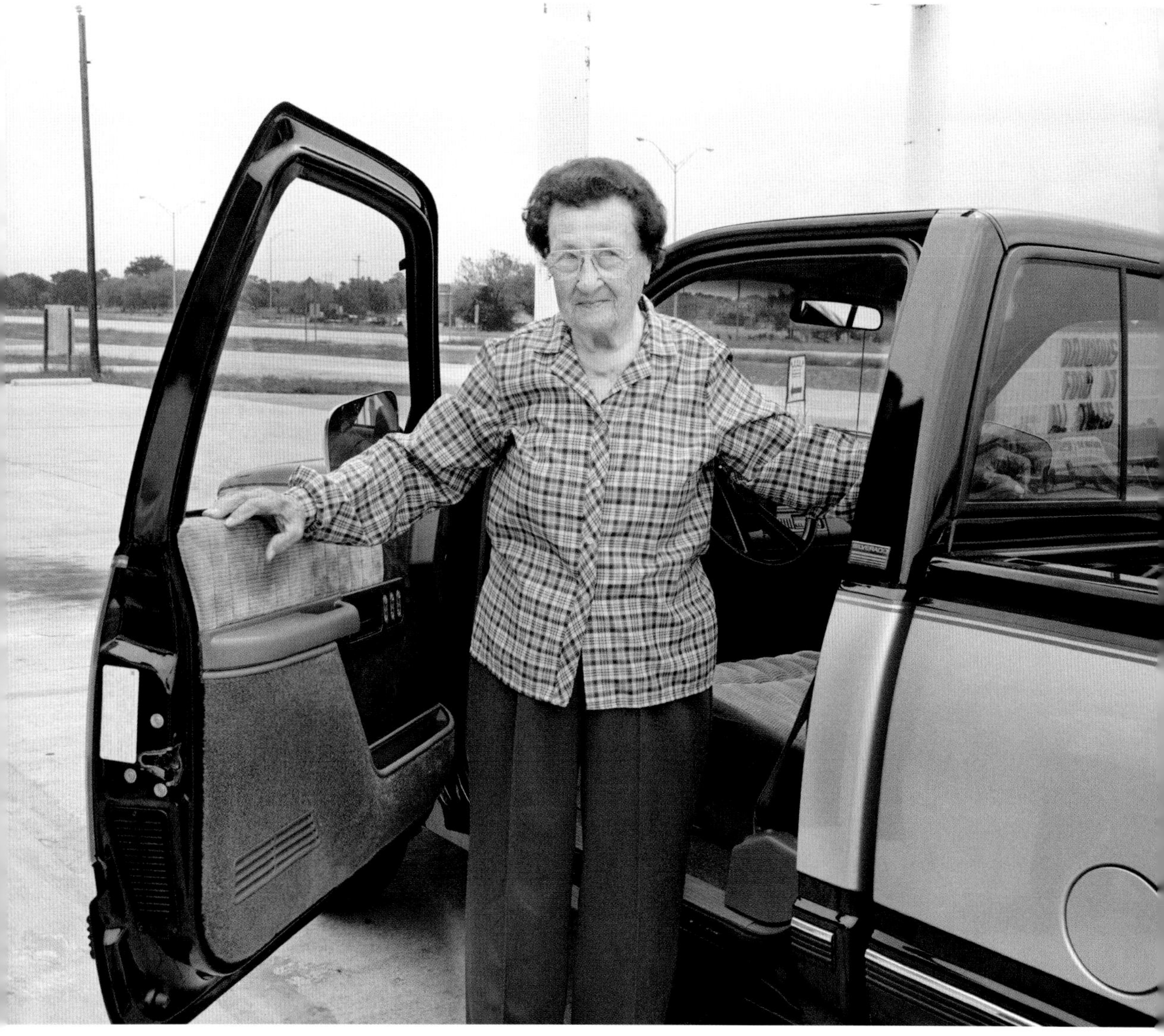

Mary Hausner with her new pickup truck

old, when his daddy left the old Germany, or Czechoslovakia, right on the border of Germany. And it was getting down there bad."

Albert himself didn't leave Germany until he was seventeen. "When he was leaving the old country was when Hitler was pickin' them boys up wherever he could pick up a boy, you know, that could carry a gun. He took a lot of them boys that was with Albert in that school. They went down there one day, and the third day, they brought the bodies back. The boss told Albert—he was tailoring, you know, then in school—and he said, 'You're just a youngster. Get outta here!' he said. 'Don't stay here, you know. Hitler's going to pick you up. You too good.'

"So Albert walk at night and slept at daytime. He got to the port, and the officer told 'im, 'Don't you get on that street. The ship is leaving tomorrow mornin'. I got friends down there, I am goin' to tell them to hide you.' And so they hid 'im. One fellow told 'im, he said, 'Don't you leave here. I'll bring you eats down here.' He brought him water and eats down there, you know. And he said, 'Tomorrow mornin' we gonna be in the port. When you get on the soil, run like hell to get away from the policeman.' So he came to Wisconsin, where his daddy worked in a grocery."

Albert learned his trade and ended up in Fort Worth. "You see, my husband was a clothin' designer, what they call tailor, you know. He could take a cloth here, you know, lay it down, and cut the whole suit out. Take the measure of a man. He was good. His boss didn't want 'im to quit, you know. But he said he liked to go out and be elbow room."

Albert traveled with his job, and that's how he met Mary. "When Albert started coming down, well, I met 'im already about a year, you know," Mary recounted. 'And he said, 'Let's go steady.' So next time he come down there, he brought me a engagement ring. They didn't believe me. He fell in love with me, he said, when he first ate a meal down there. He said, 'You had a real good meal,' he said. 'Wherever I went, even the mamas cooked a sloppy meal. I don't like sloppy meals,' he said. 'That's what I eat in restaurants.' And so, in time I tol' Mama I was gonna get married, you know, and she says, 'No you don't. I don't want 'im.' I said, 'Mama, you not the one that gonna live with 'im. It's me that's gonna live with him!'

"Mama wanted this one and that one for me, and I said, 'Mama, I don't like him—he holds a beer bottle by the neck.' Was already big enough to know the difference! And I tol' my Ma, I said, 'Mama, I wouldn't have a man that drink his beer.' My daddy didn't drink, and Mama didn't drink, you know, and we all got like Mama was—no drinkin'. So when I was going to get married—you know, I knew Albert four years—and I told Mama, 'You know, it's springtime.' She tol' me, she said, 'Is Albert coming to marry you? I hope he don't marry you,' she said. 'I don't like 'im.' I said, 'Mama you're not the one that's going to live with 'im—it's me. But Albert I'm gonna marry! I'm gonna get married this fall.'

"I tol' 'im, 'Meet me in Temple. We gonna go down there to the church and ask the priest.' It was Father O'Reilly, and he said, 'Sure, I'll marry you.' I was twenty-eight years old, and he was thirty-four. When we got married, we were sweethearts. I asked him on the seventh day of November. On the twenty-first day, that's two weeks later, we got married with the priest, in 1927.

"When I was leavin' home, my folks tol' me, 'You don't have to come home.' I said, 'That's fine. I'm twenty-eight years old. I can take care of myself.' They said, 'He ain't gonna stay with you. He gonna leave you.' I said, 'No, he's never gonna leave me.' Now, I tell you, they didn't want us to marry, but we married fifty-three years before he passed away, you know. And we never had a argument! You tell me who's gonna do that!

"Yeah, but a nickel was hard to make. Wages was only thirty-two dollars, but we work overtime. Every week he got paid thirty-two dollars. We bought this place in 1938, and we paid for it in four years—during the hard times! We didn't run around or anythin'. We put our money, all what we had, in the land, and we gonna pay it as soon as we can. 'Ma!' I said, 'If we can't pay for it in eight years, I don't want it.' And she said, 'You can't pay for it in eight years.' We pay for it in four years! But I tell you, we slaved. You can see my hands. My hands ain't no thing to look at.

"*Hard work*. Creek got us, washed everythin'. You couldn't hire hands in those days. Nobody wanted to work. So we did ninety percent of the work ourselves."

Albert died in 1981. "It's gonna be ten years pretty soon that my husband is gone. Well, I get used to it. You have to, you have to," Mary said sadly, looking down at the floor.

Mary was living alone when we met, with two fox terriers and a few stray cats. She said of her dog Tiny, "You oughta' see how lovin' she is when I'm by myself. That's better than having a woman down here with me."

A friend of her husband, a man named Jerry, visited Mary most every day. "I got Jerry to help," Mary said. "The reason he does this, you know—when my husband was in Weimar hospital, and when he was pretty sick, he was holdin' my hand, and last words he said was, 'Jerry, would you take care of Mary,' he said, 'till I come home?' And they were the last words that the man said!

"Because Jerry come down here, that's no sin, is it? People may talk, but I don't care. I've lived my life, and they're gonna live theirs. I'm ninety-one years old, you know—already passed, you know—and I said, 'I've made it!'

"We been through our years. My mother, I seen her die. I lost Albert, and I seen him die. I was happy with Albert. I had a good husband, you know. If he had lived, we would have been this year married sixty-four years. We never argued—that's the funniest thing.

"None of my blood kin have anythin' to do with me. Do you know they don't speak to me? They didn't want me to have anythin'. I got me a lawyer. I wasn't gonna be without one. And, well, I got the land, you know. They don't talk to me now. You know somethin'? I don't give a damn!

"My brother and his wife—you know, no use to talk about 'em. They both dead. She didn't like me, because I could do sewin', I could do hay balin', you know, I could milk, I could churn butter, I could feed the hogs, I could feed chickens. She didn't like no chickens, no hogs, no dogs, no cats, no nothin'. Layin' in the bed all the time. But you know, I'm like this, and I don't care. I've lived my life, and they're gonna live theirs. I don't care."

Mary was driving a shiny new silver-and-black pickup with red stripes when I knew her. She said she bought it because "I got two bits. It's burnin' in my pocket. I don't want nothing left behind when I leave."

When we parted, she walked, oh, so slowly to her truck, using her walker. Then she picked up her walker with one hand, tossed it into the truck bed, and climbed aboard. "See many women do this?" she challenged. I asked if she was going to catch a fellow with that sexy truck. "No, they're like fish—they be around, but they ain't gonna bite! And I don't need nobody. I can take care of myself with Jerry to help me."

She said, "I broke my knee, and the doctor wanta take a one-hundred-dollar X-ray. I said, 'What you gonna do wit' a one-hundred-dollar X-ray? I'm gonna limp anyway!' So I'm goin' around wit' a walker. Some people don't like it. Well, I say if they don't like it, they don't have to look.

"I didn't expect to live that long like I'm livin', 'cause I worked hard, you know."

Mary was nearly impossible to persuade to be photographed. "Not even for a million dollars!" she said more than once, "I know I'm ugly, and it's all right—I'm old." She was wrong. She looked great, and she clearly had "made it."

Lillie Williams

"My grandmother was a slave in slavery times. She was a young girl," said Lillie, at ninety-seven years of age. "But, see, when they heard tell of the war—that freedom was goin' on, freein' the slaves—well, a lot of the people bought up these here younger people and brought 'em over to Texas, where they thought they'd never be free.

"And my grandmother said she remembered they brought 'em all from there—they got 'em all like you do calves, separatin' calves. They got 'em all separated and loaded up. And she could remember her mother, standin' on the fence gate, wavin' at 'em. All that they could see, her wavin' at 'em. Far as she could see, she was just a-wavin' and a-tearin', and a-wavin' and a-tearin'.

"It was awful sad, but they had to come on and leave her. Broke up slavery over here, but she never *did* see her mother no more . . ." Lillie's voice echoed sadly in the room.

So spoke Lillie, in a quiet, serious way that was unusual for her playful nature. She told her daughter-in-law Marie afterwards that she had talked on tape about her grandmother, "'cause no one who come before her had ever had her story known."

"My name is Lillie Steward Williams, born in eighteen and ninety-five, March the twenty-first. I was reared in Colorado County, born in Colorado County. I wasn't born here in town, but I was born out in the 'rurals,' place they call Harvey's Creek. I never did like no town! I'd like to be still there, live out in the rurals. All that good fresh breeze.

"I confessed religion when I was eleven years old, and from that time till now, that's where my membership is. Joined the Pleasant Hill Baptist Church, and I been there ever since. I am ninety-seven years old and still remain in Pleasant Hill Baptist Church. And if the good Lord say so, when I leave this world, that's where I wanna go from, Pleasant Hill Baptist Church." In fact, sadly, she was buried out of another church, one that suited her family better.

Lillie Williams seemed never to be very clear about her age, which would vary from time to time in her statements. She surprised me one day, by saying, "You want my age? Sure, I tell it! Sixty-nine," she cackled. "If you turn that around, ninety-six—I'm ninety-six." "How about a plane ride to celebrate turning one hundred?" I asked. "No, *ma'am*!" she answered. "You won't take me on no airplane ride. If I make a hundred, you can take me on a car ride." "Then how about a younger man?" I asked. Lillie said,

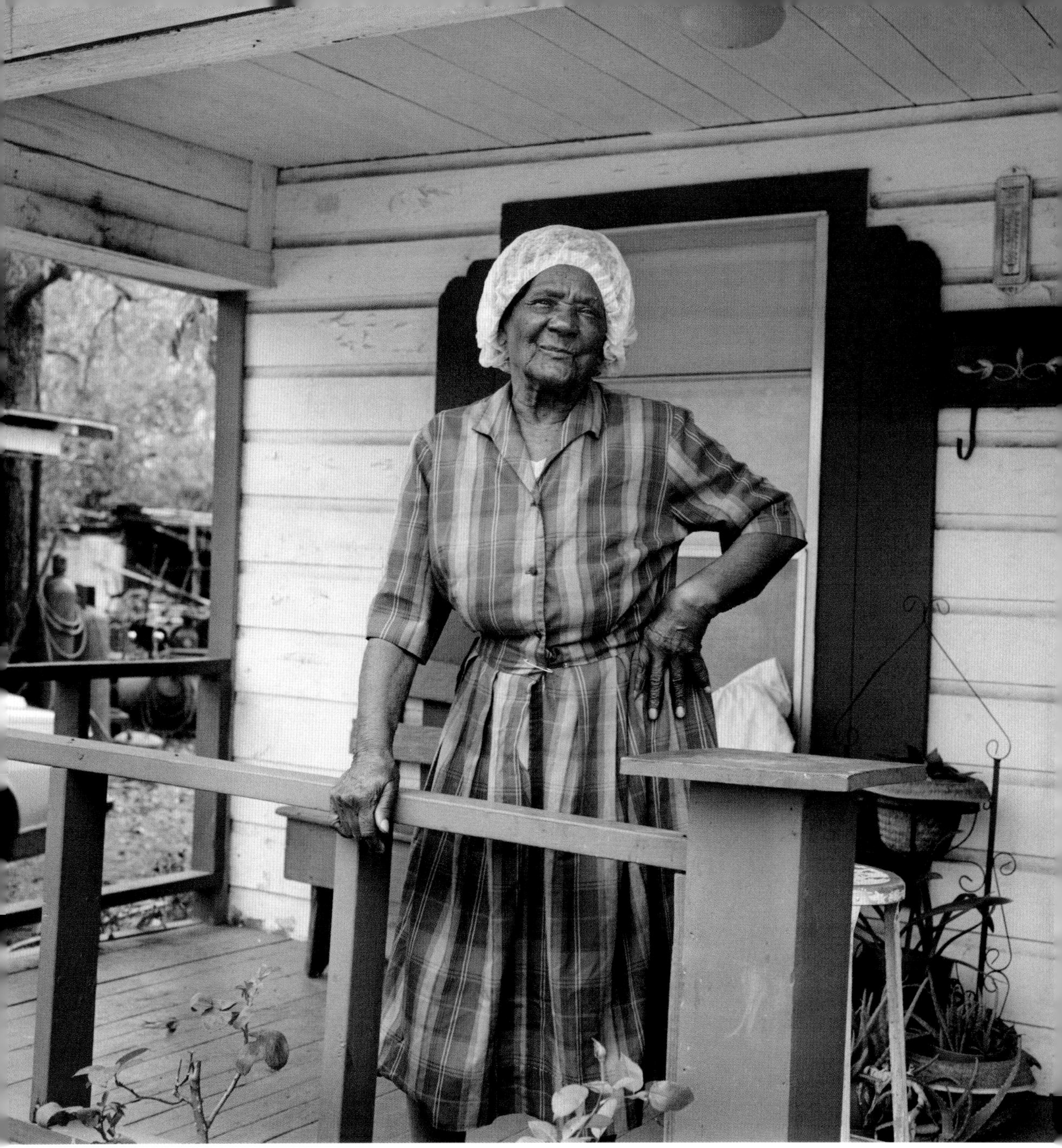

Lillie Williams, acting sassy

"You can get me one about eighty-nine, if I make a hundred!" She laughed, then added, "It sure would be suicide to get one younger."

Whatever the truth of her birth date, her looks and her mind belied her age. She was lively, as sharp as glass, and as tough as two big guys. She loved to bluff and bully. She knew how to set you straight and wouldn't hesitate a second to do it. She called herself "the boss of the family," saying, "I tell 'em they cain't boss me! 'This ain't your house!' I say. 'The house and everythin' else belong to me! I'm the oldest one, and I take care of it.' Everyone in this house got to bide by my command, from the old to the young on up. I'm the real boss! *Everythin'* go by my command. Whenever I speak, they *gotta* move!"

When Lillie wanted to show how she used to catch a man, she struck this pose, and here she is in the photograph in her mid-nineties, hand on hip, 'struttin' her stuff,' acting sassy in her usual way.

Although Lillie lost the lower half of both legs when she got older, this seemed not to dull her spirits or temper her strong will. The first leg she lost, her left, was amputated below the knee in 1990—"The hardest time of my life," she declared. "I don't like to depend on *nobody.*" But in typical fashion, she quickly learned to use a prosthetic leg, going to the hospital in Victoria for therapy. I joked that she would probably be out dancing before long—that when everybody was asleep, a good-looking younger man in a big Cadillac would drive up, wheel her silently out of the house, and take her to the Jungle Hut, a local hangout, to dance. She giggled into her hands, like a schoolgirl.

The favorite family joke was that Lillie was going to kick her grandchildren with her wooden leg if they acted up. "Sometime," said Marie, "she be sittin' there and she'll say, 'Well, I tell you, it feels kinda like I wanta kick somethin'.' And my son said, 'Well, I tell you, you better watch out because an ax will take that foot right off.' Like Pinocchio, she's a hunk of wood," said Marie, laughing while Lillie hid her face in her hands and shook with the giggles.

When I first asked her for a photograph, nothing could persuade her to do it. First she refused, then she complained, and finally she agreed, looking me straight in the eye and saying, "You must be a Jew!" Too startled to respond, I finally asked what she meant by that, and she said, "'Cause you could talk anybody into doin' anythin'," chuckling at her own wit.

Another time, as I was pursuing her for yet one more photograph, she turned and blocked the way with her tiny body, saying, "Now I want to ask *you* for something. I want you and your family to make a donation to my church, and I want you to come to church on Friends and Family Day and bring your donation." I felt a strong sense of relief that that was all she wanted, because knowing Lillie, it could have been anything, and there was next to no way to get around this strong-willed old matriarch.

So I made my first visit to Pleasant Hill Missionary Baptist Church on a Sunday afternoon and was made welcome. There was a wonderful feeling of community in their little church, a narrow wooden building set up on cement blocks with contact-paper "stained-glass" windows. The members couldn't have been any more cordial. We listened to the eloquent guest preacher and the visiting choirs from small towns nearby. I found out that in the smaller towns the preacher visits only every other week, alternating between churches.

Pleasant Hill, before it moved into Weimar, was situated in the "rurals," on a place that was bought by my two aunts, a farm they called the Grace Place. I'd been in the deserted church building many times, empty except for two homemade wooden pews, tilting precariously, a few mouse droppings, and the old lectern. On the wall was a small blackboard with a chalk-written lesson barely visible. "We study to serve," it read, giving the space a sense of expectancy that was unsettling. It was as though the congregation was there, ready to begin the service, and the building was holding its breath, waiting for the first spoken word.

The abandoned cemetery in front of the church was in serious decay, overgrown with cedars and thorny greenbrier vines. Most of the graves had fallen in. One lady whose family is buried there said that few of the graves had ever had real markers, only handwritten paper cards, so most of the grave sites have been lost for years. It was all fast disappearing. And friends in Weimar said they were still making regular visits to the cemetery until the late 1980s to tend graves and visit their dead relatives. An old, old wagon road had passed right by the church in former days, and traces of it were still visible in shallow ruts in the ground.

In *Coming Through Hard Times,* Marie Williams, Lillie's daughter-in-law, talked about how they used to bring wagons full of church members and food out to the rural Pleasant Hill church for daylong picnics. "But I tell you, we used to have a *grand* time," Marie said. "And the people would come from all directions. And when they started hearin' the singin', they'd get in a hurry to get here.

"How we used to put wagons together out there and spread lunches on it! Everybody brought a basket of food, a *whole lot* of food, not just a little food. We just had wagons stretched end to end. You talk about good eats! Those older people could cook. And the children—they were so happy 'cause they knew they were gonna eat. I don't know if they were so interested in church activities, but they were interested in that food. They loved those eats. And they had a *good* time.

"Mama Sing" [Lillie's favored nickname] always came here, where her husband was the minister and her father-in-law was also a minister. And they used to come regular 'cause this is where the membership was, from a child up. They spent their childhood days comin' here. Up until about '40 or '50 or somethin' like that."

Lillie was married to the Reverend Gathenia Williams for over seventy years. "I knew him 'cause his people and my people, we all belonged to the same church, Pleasant Union," said Lillie. "Praise to Mary!

"You didn't go to college. You couldn't stay single long enough to go to no college. And at sweet sixteen, I thought I was growed. Went on and married." Lillie didn't know then that she had eighty more years to live. "No, I didn't know that," she said. "And I wasn't takin' *no* chances."

Lillie talked about her married life: "I tell you one thing, the hardest job for me was housework. I didn't like no housework. I always liked the outdoors. My son, when he married his wife, they stayed with me for about two years, and after she got in the family, well, I'd always put the cookin' off on her. I'd do the outside work myself—go to the field, go to the well, git the wood—that wasn't hard on me. Choppin' and pickin' cotton—I *liked* it.

"In the spring of the year, when the cotton was comin' up, why, that time I'd get to bust middles. Take a mule or a horse and put him to the plow, and go down that middle and bust that middle. And after a while, and always like that, it'd come a-poppin' open, the bolls. It'd be just like you see popcorn. Open, open, open— then my time had done come. Oooohh—I'd be so glad when I'd see that cotton openin' up, I wouldn't know *what* to do. Then my time had done come. Git my sack, and I'd go to that field, and at dinnertime, if I didn't got my two hundred [pounds], I thought I hadn't did nothin'. When that sun got ready to go down, I'd have four hundred. Two in the mornin', two in the evenin'. Leila [Steward] and I. That lady, she could get hers! That Leila could go! And I'd be right with her. Get them big old long sacks. Be so full till I couldn't, you know, pack it. I'd have to pull it, drag it back again."

Lillie was always a tough one. As a girl, she loved to play rough with the boys. "I stood my ground with the boys, rasslin' and playin' ball," she said. "And rapjack. We'd cut switches out of young dogwoods and hit all round the shoulders and round the hips. Tear 'em up again. Tough! That's the way I come up. I was the toughest. I wasn't scared of no boys." She laughed. Asked if she hit the boys back, she replied, "Sho' I did. Never *did* back down. We'd be out there, fightin' and tusslin', wrasslin'. Tear 'em up again! I wasn't scared of no boys. They better be scared of *me*. I'm tellin' it like it is." Marie added, "She says she's a little weed, but a bitter seed!"

The family's favorite nickname for Lillie was "Mama Sang" or "Mama Sing." "Sing" was a name given to her as a little girl. "They nicknamed me Sing, I reckon, keepin' on with so much racket, goin' in singin' and a-goin' dancin'," Lillie said. Her best childhood friends were "Flute" and Cordelia.

"I wanted to be a musician—that's what I wanted. I had a lady was a schoolteacher and musician. She wanted to send me up there to Schulenburg to go take music. Before I finished school in Pleasant Hill [where the church building served double duty as the local schoolhouse], they bought us an organ to be practicin' on. Well, I tried playin' it pretty good, but they came and took it back before we paid for it. I sure did want to be a musician. Like I say, reckon I always singin' so much."

At age ninety-nine, Lillie was still singing with gusto, sitting on her couch, having lost both her legs by then, but enjoying her favorite hymn, "This Little Light of Mine."

Lillie loved to dance when she was young. "Mostly," she said in a naughty voice, "it was waltzin', two-steppin', and doin' the Sassy Wiggle." And she giggled like crazy. "Shake that body *all over!* Take it down to the floor and come on up. Ohhhhh, bring it on up. Brrrriiiinngg it on up!" she moaned, using her hand to make a slow, spiraling motion, lifting it gradually up from the floor. What a dance that must have been!

"I tell you one thing, the hardest time is *right now*. In the old times, in the hardest times, I was always healthy. Never sickly. Nothin' like that. We ready to 'go and do' when I was young. And them babies didn't bother me. Went on and did what I could. Yes, ma'am. I never did shirk work."

Lillie celebrated her one-hundredth birthday in 1995, with a big party at the park. She died later that year, at one-hundred years, eight months. The selections for the hymns at her funeral included "This Little Light of Mine," of course, and "I'll Fly Away."

What a wonderful, feisty old dame she was, one of those rare individuals who seem too full of life to actually die. And one could only imagine what trouble she was stirring up in the heavens, bossing everyone around and dancing the Sassy Wiggle.

Lillie was a lifelong member of Pleasant Hill Missionary Baptist Church and the Smith's Pride Chapter 388, Order of the Eastern Star. She left six grandchildren, sixteen great-grandchildren, and thirteen great-great-grandchildren.

She was born Lillie Sivilla Steward on March 21, 1895, it is believed. Her parents were Parthenia and Al Steward.

Marie Williams

Marie Williams was Lillie Williams's daughter-in-law and Lacey Henry's oldest and dearest friend. Lacey and her husband, Oscar, lived at my parents' farm and worked for them for years. "I calls Lacey Henry a sister," said Marie with tenderness in her voice.

This was not because the two friends were blood related but because they loved one another like sisters. They had been the closest of friends in the country for many years, beginning as newlyweds, when they lived side by side in the rurals. When folks lived in the country those days, they were pretty much stuck there. Roads were dirt or mud and often impassable, cars were rare, the workload was endless. So friends were chosen from whoever lived nearby, and friendships were treasured. "When we were in the country, we visited most every day, quilted together, went to church, had a *good* time." They shared common lives—marriage, housework, church, choir, quilting, the social bonds that built friendships that lasted for decades.

Many years later, Marie, her husband, Oliver, and the widowed Lacey all moved into Weimar, to be across-the-street neighbors. The two women complemented and balanced each other: Lacey was the quiet one, retiring and steady; Marie was the more talkative, vivacious, and active. She raised six children to Lacey's one and kept several of them, plus her mother-in-law, living in her house with her even into the children's adulthood.

Marie said, "I was born in Seguin, in Guadalupe County, on April 7, 1915, to Irene Cain and Sidney Miller. I remember my grandparents weren't slaves, but if he was asked if he was a slave, he would tell 'em, no—but he 'was close enough to smell the smoke.'

"And my daddy came down here when I was four years old, to work, and he caught that influenza and died. He left my mother with three children, me and my sister two years old and my baby sister nine months old, Albertina and Nadine. That hit me like a ton of bricks. I was like Chicken Little when an acorn fell out of a tree on her head. Well, I thought the world had fallen in on me and my sisters. So my mother went to San Antonio to work so she could help support us, and we stayed with my grandmother and grandpa."

Marie spent a happy childhood, living with her grandparents. The three youngsters learned to work as they helped the old lady with her chores. "And when we were about three or four years old, we had chores to do," Marie said. "We would follow around my grandma's apron strings, holdin' on to her apron strings, and she would

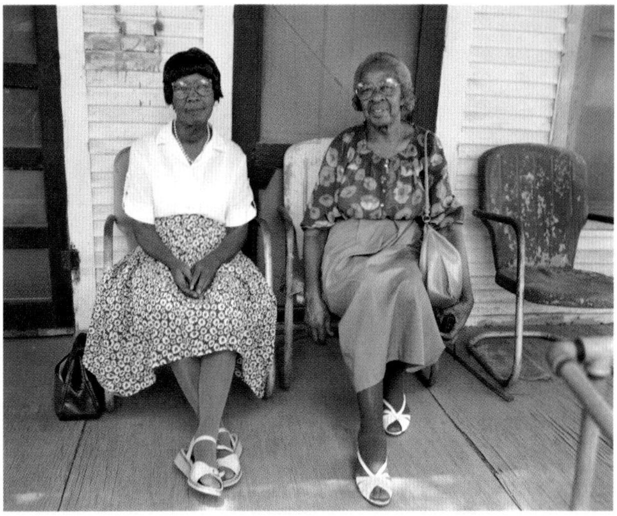

Marie Williams with her friend Lacey Henry

have us pickin' up chips and dried corn cobs to burn in the stove—you know, the cob, after you eat the corn off of it—and it was dry. And that would be the kindlin', to start the fire.

"And then, when we were about five or six, well, they used to get flour in forty-pound sacks, and when they emptied those sacks and cotton-pickin' time would come, they would start us out on little bitty sacks like that, and we would fill those sacks. Not that I was in love with pickin' cotton. But I had an enjoyable childhood."

When Irene Miller remarried, it was to a man named Marshall Green, and in 1922 she moved back to join her children with her new husband, who found work in Glidden with the railroad.

Marie recalled being very fond of her elementary schoolteacher in Glidden, Empress Stevenson, a woman whose name came up in several people's memories as an exceptional woman and educator. "We had such dedicated teachers, and we loved those teachers like parents.

"I graduated from school there in Glidden. I played basketball—rather play basketball almost than eat," she joked. "We played rapjack too, played with the boys. We played basketball against the boys, just any game they wanted to play. Shoot marbles with them. We had a good time together."

Marie met her husband to be, Oliver Williams, in 1935 at a park, playing basketball. "I met Lillie Williams' son," she said, "and that's why I'm here in Weimar. And I been here ever since. Then after I married, I got children, and that kind of slowed things down for me. I always said I didn't want to marry a farmer or a preacher, so I ended up with the farmer. But he was so nice and everything. And I loved him. I had a good life. However, every day wasn't Sunday—we had our ups and downs, but we had a good time."

When they married, they moved onto his family farm. "I was never too hot on farming," said Marie with a grimace, "but I had to do it. But I thank God for blessing us with *something* to do. And I thank God that he blessed us with the cotton and the pecans we picked. Whatever we could do to make an honest living, we did it, and I thank God for that. We just had a good time.

"I didn't like field work. Mama Lillie liked field work. And we had to go back every summer to help our grandparents gather their crops."

Life on the farm had other hardships. Water had to be collected from a spring a good way from the house. "We had a place dug out, had rock underneath, and we would set a bucket." It was good water, but fetching it meant a long walk back home with a heavy load. "I remember I've seen my mother and grandmother with a bucket on her head and one in each hand.

"How'd we get work? Well, I remember my husband went in the fall and gathered rice, down around Eagle Lake, and they would go and stay all week. I kept the babies most of the time. I remember we lived once off of three dollars and about eighty cents a week with three children. But we raised chickens, we had eggs, we raised hogs and had our bacon. We had milk and would raise corn and bring it to town here and have it ground into meal. So we made it.

"Every day wasn't Sunday out there, I tell you. But we had good times. We were young. To tell you the truth, we have more worry now. We could leave our houses unlocked—we can't hardly do that now. I've just enjoyed life, I reckon.

"We would buy blankets to keep warm, 'cause the homes we were in were 'well ventilated,' in summer and in the winter," she said with a laugh. "We didn't have heat all over the house. We had a wood heater in one room, and I would roll those kids up in a blanket and maybe warm some irons up and put it at their feet. And we made it! It was water down at the spring. On Wednesday night would be prayer meeting and youth meeting, and that's where we would learn, like, to pray and to sing and to help in the order of the service.

"To tell you the truth, that was some of our happiest days! We weren't afraid to leave our doors open. We would lay there with the window open and the doors open and catch all of that good cool breeze. We were happy-go-lucky in a way. I enjoyed life. And even in our hardships, life was lucky. Whatever life was like, we went through with it.

"We didn't dance or drink," Marie noted. The fun was centered around the church and church activities. The men and women had a singing group at church and practiced their music together. "We did piece-quilting in each other's homes," Marie said. "Neighbors would all come together. We had a *lot of fun* doin' that.

"Oh, I *loved* church! I still do. We grew up in church, Olive Branch Church in Glidden. The Baptist Young People's Training Union was such a joy in our life. They taught us how to pray. I think the good Lord had answered my prayers. Just be sincere in what you prayin'. And I know my prayers are answered."

Marie and Oliver moved to Houston for a while to work "when cotton went low," to send money home for the family. Marie worked at the Shepherd Laundry. Eventu-

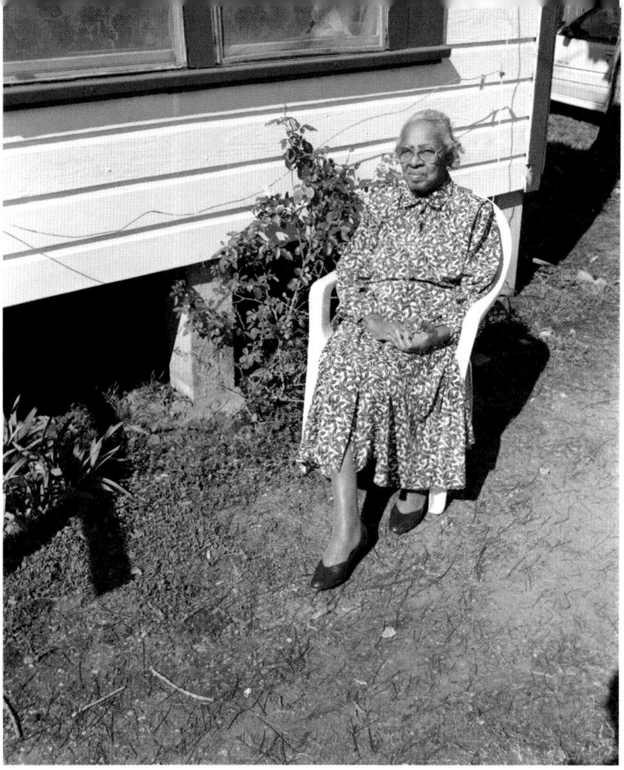
Marie Williams

ally they returned to the country. In 1948 when the country schools closed, Marie took her youngsters into Weimar to live, and Oliver followed. Her mother-in-law, Lillie, moved into town with them, and they shared a house, with the tough old matriarch mother-in-law at the helm. Said Lillie one day, laughing, "When I grab my stick, she runs! Tries to do me a lotta talk, sassy talk, you know. I'll grab my stick. 'Get outta my way! What I say go! I'm the boss here!'"

How hard it must have been for Marie. She was taking care of her wonderful, but demanding, mother-in-law, who lost both her lower legs and spent her last days on the couch, bossing everyone. Clearly, Marie loved and respected the old lady, and she handled the situation with grace.

Marie rarely said anything critical or negative about anyone, and it was impossible to get gossip out of her. But she did express a few cautious thoughts on the 1935 lynching nearby in Columbus: "We were all sorry and heartbroken for the families that were left behind. It was a sad, sad time, and our hearts were broken. And the only way we talked about it was in our family. It brought quite a bit of anger—it didn't change our lives though. It was somethin' we had no control over, but we all knew we were sad."

When her husband, Oliver, died on November 17, 1976, Marie was left with six grown offspring. Three of them continued living with her and their grandmother. Marie's daughter Lillie lived next door with her husband and children, the four generations amicable and close under the strong leadership of the two older women.

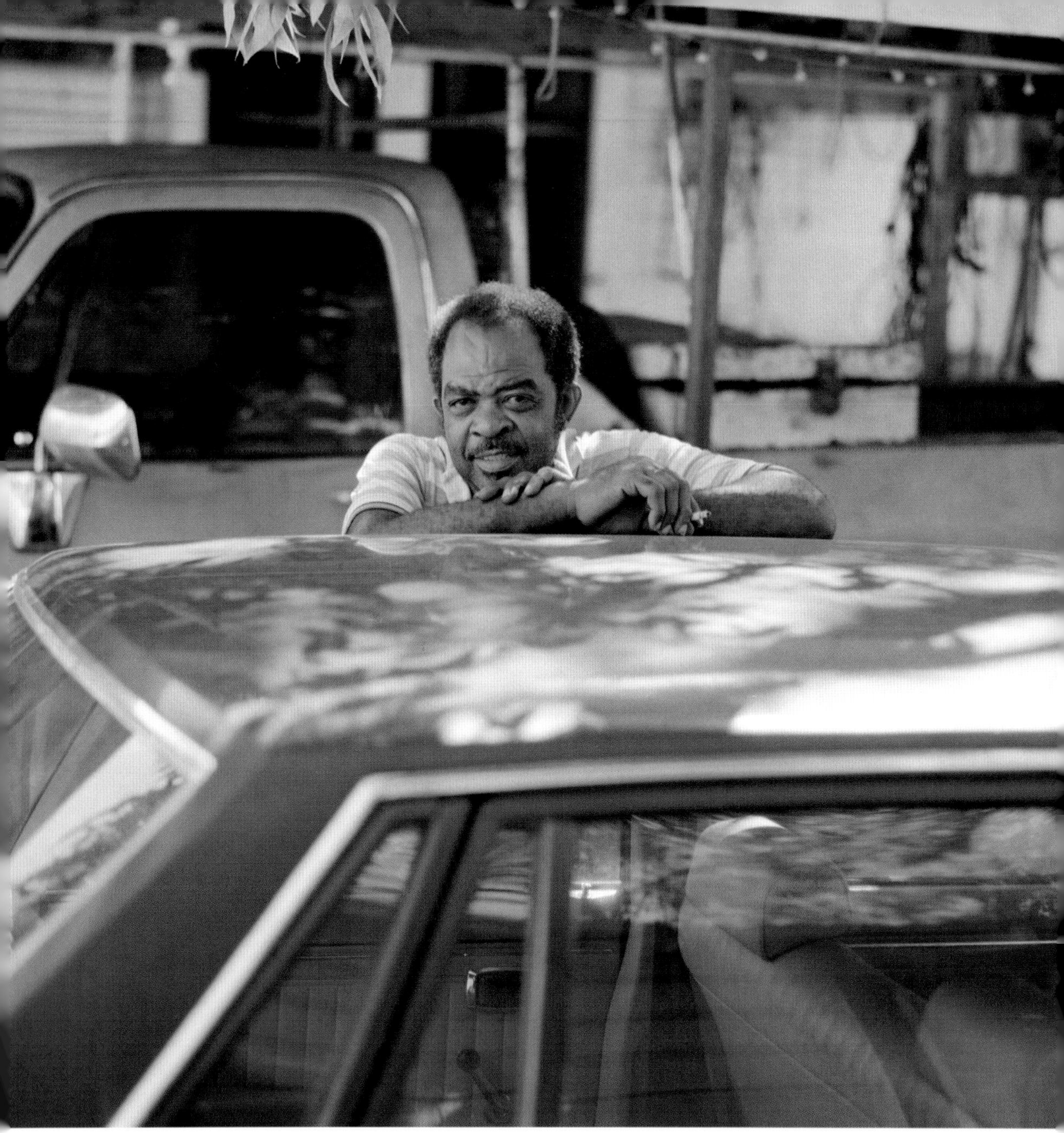

G.A. “Big Boy” Williams

G.A. "Big Boy" Williams

"My name is G.A. Williams. I was born here in Colorado County in 1937. They called me Big Boy, I guess 'cause I was such a fat baby. I stayed here until I finished high school. Got married and went to Houston. Lived there for a while, from 1956 to 1986. And I moved back home, and I'm livin' here," said he in a rather flat, abbreviated way.

G.A., christened Gathenia, was Marie Williams's son and the grandson of the tiny but indomitable Lillie Williams. He was living in Lillie's house the whole time I knew him and living there very quietly, rarely evident when I visited Lillie and Marie. It took some time to learn who this shadowy person was. And I was grateful to finally talk with him and begin a friendship. I found G.A. to be kind and friendly, in his own reserved, melancholy way.

G.A. and his brothers grew up in the country—the rurals, as Lillie always said—on their grandparents' farm. "Mama Lillie raised us from the time that we were small," G.A. said, "and kept us until—well, in fact, my mother and father went to Houston, and they lived down there a number of years. And also my grandfather was workin' down there too, and we children were livin' with Grandma until they decided to come back home." Knowing her forceful ways of running a family, I could easily imagine a very disciplined environment, with "spare the rod, spoil the child" being, no doubt, the rule in that household. "Our grandmother was strict with us" was all G.A. said about that.

About his father and grandfather, he said, "They was somebody I really did care for. Whatever they could do for us, they did it. They tried to raise us in a proper way that children should be raised, and they were strict. And I can just say that I appreciate the way they made an effort to try and teach us the right things in life. And that still sticks with me, what they had to teach us. I might stray from it, but I go back to it."

G.A. described his memories of life on the farm: "We had a spring we had to go to every evenin' after we got out of school and bring ourselves a supply of water to last until the next day. At that time we had no electricity—we had oil lamps. Sometimes that was hard to study by, but I guess we got used to it at that age.

"That was happiness. Mostly was runnin' up and down the hills, playin', bird huntin', and goin' to the river and lookin' over. I never did swim there; they told us it was too dangerous. Fact is, heard there were alligators and things there—we didn't want no part of that."

He had a few words on racism in Weimar: "I know when they changed the schools [during integration], the pictures and things we had taken while we were goin' to school, they destroyed 'em. That's what I was told. They wasn't even givin' it to the families, they *dumped it on out!*" This act brought lots of anger within the black community, this trashing of memorabilia from the black schools by the white authorities, an event related by several people. It was clearly a bitter and sad memory for them, losing their school history when getting an education had so much meaning and importance.

On relations between the races, G.A. said clearly, "I see the younger ones are close related. I see very little change in the older ones. Whatever they had buried in 'em is still there, and I don't think it will ever leave the older ones."

G.A. always seemed a little troubled. I found out later that he had problems with alcohol and cigarettes, two mean addictions. Once he said plaintively, "There's peace and happiness out there if you can afford it." The hope is that G.A. found this peace and happiness through Greater Macedonia Baptist Church. After many long years of absence from the church of his childhood, he joined and attended it in the very last year at of his life, when he was sick with throat cancer. He died at age sixty-one, at his brother Walter's house in Sweeny, Texas.

Walter Williams

Walter was Marie Williams's fourth child, in a lineup that went Junior, G.A., A.C., Walter, Lillie, and Lee Andrew. In 1961, when he'd finished school, Walter left home looking for work and ended up in Sweeny, Texas, working as a welder at Dow Chemical. "All the young people left, *had* to leave, to get work. There were no jobs here," lamented his mother. Walter remained in Sweeny with his wife, Cathy, from nearby Clute. Together they had one daughter, Pam.

Walter told a very funny story at "Mama Lillie's" one-hundredth birthday party. She was the person he and his siblings lived with when their parents left home to work in Houston. The story made a huge hit, but Walter refused to ever retell the story on tape. Here is what I remember of it. He stood in front of the hall, which was filled with his family and friends, and began to describe how sad he was as a little bitty boy when, year after year, his family left to go pick cotton (led by the enthusiastic Mama Lillie)—and he was always left home. Every year they said he was too young to go, and every year Walter cried and begged to be included. "My brother told me I didn't really want to go," Walter confided, smiling. He had heard Mama Lillie rhapsodize about the joys of picking cotton, which she considered to be the highlight of her year—and he wanted to go too. Poor young Walter was so forlorn watching the others leave for their "fun in the fields," until finally came the day he was old enough to go. Mama Lillie gave him his very own miniature cotton sack and led the way into the fields. "Ta-dum!," he thought to himself, triumphant and happy. "At last I get to go too!" And then reality hit him. It was hot, it was painful on his fingers, it hurt his back, it was miserable in every way, and "I wanted to *go home!*" remembered the adult Walter. But Mama Lillie said no, simply and finally. He could *not* go home—he was old enough to work, and work he would—end of sentence.

Everyone at the party knew Lillie's love of cotton picking as well as the hardships of the work, and there was much laughter and hilarity. In this photograph, Walter is once again refusing to tell his story on tape.

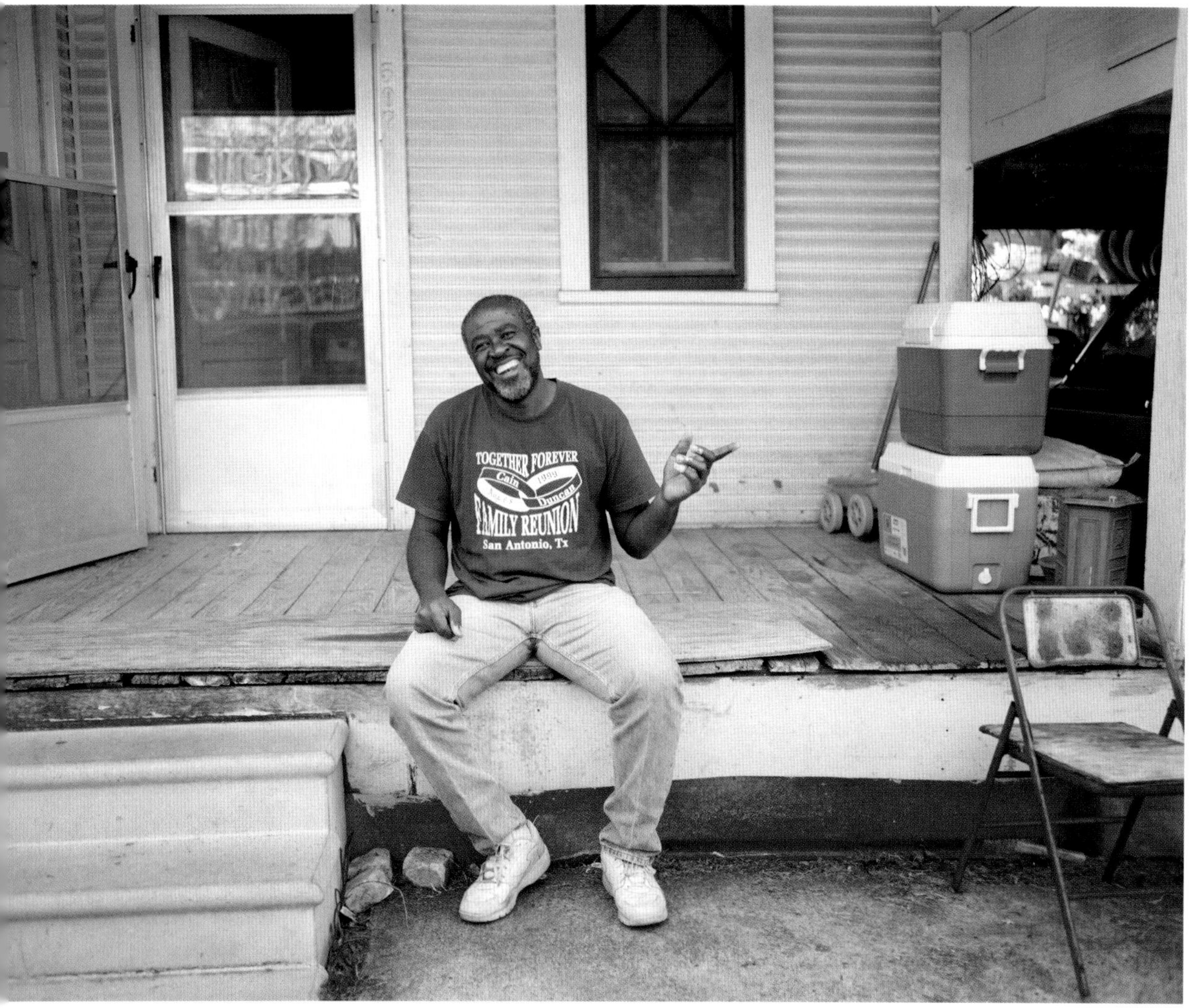

Walter Williams

Lee Andrew Williams

Lee Andrew was Marie Williams's son. He was born in 1952, gifted with a lovely singing voice. In 2001 he was a member of a men's gospel group, called the Gospel Crusaders, in Schulenburg, Texas, and they were producing their first CD.

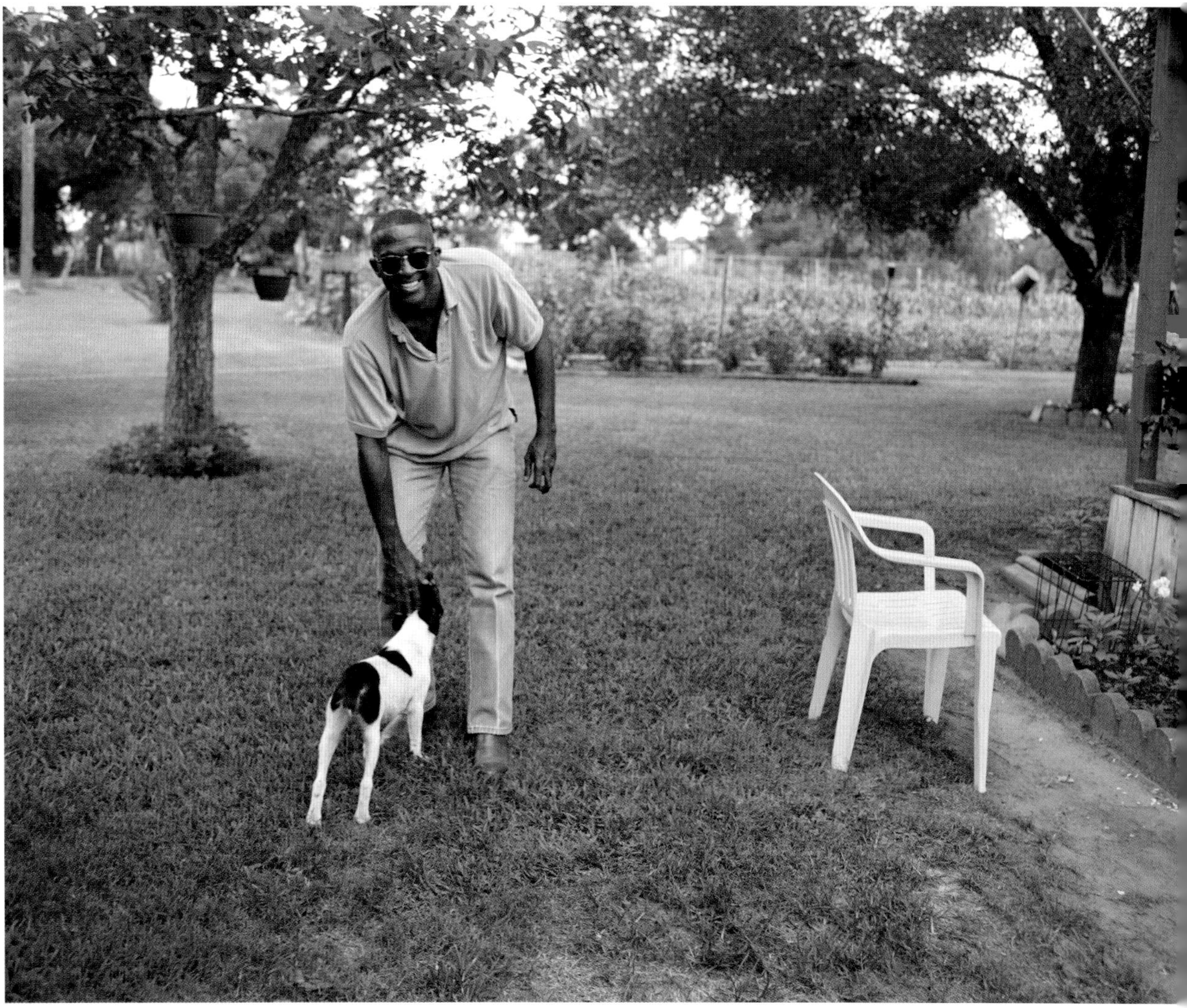

Lee Andrew Williams

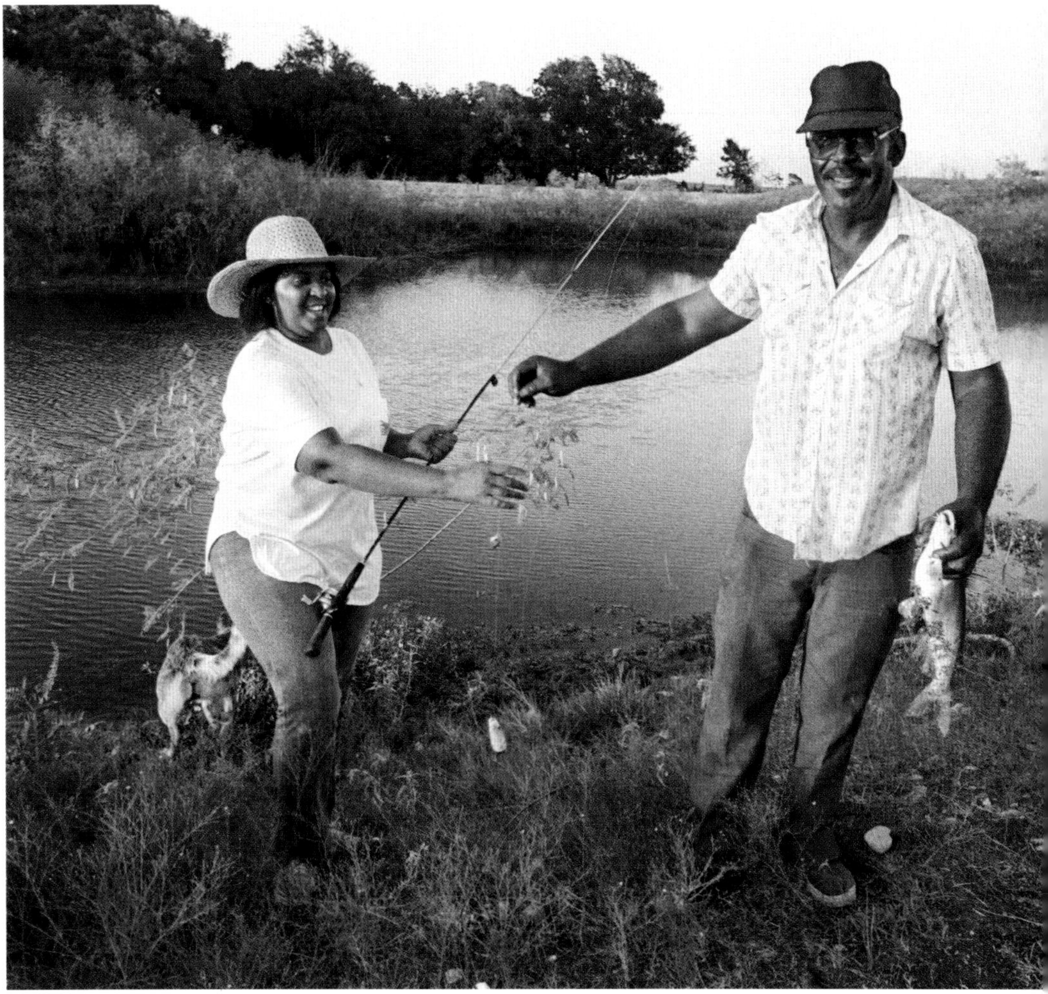

Lillie Williams Barnes and her husband, Wilbert

Lillie Williams Barnes & Wilbert Barnes

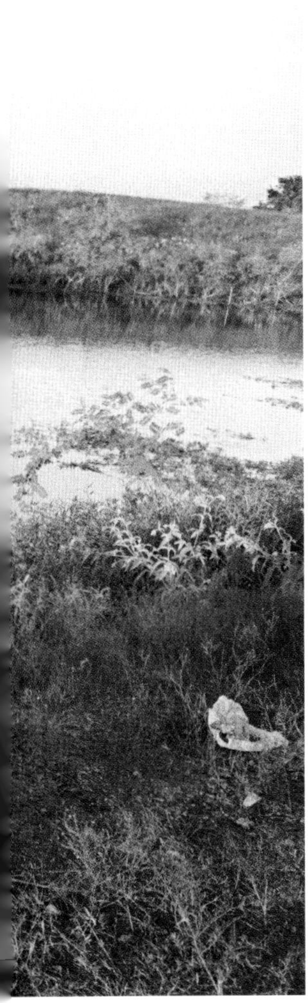

What fun Lillie and Wilbert were having together on the day this picture was taken, fishing, enjoying their grown children, working side by side on the family farm where they raised cattle and hogs. They had begun spending more good times together after Wilbert became ill with serious heart problems and had to quit his job. Then he suffered a stroke in 1983, one that forced him into an even more sedentary lifestyle. He struggled with his new life, having always been a very active man. Lillie kept her job at a Schulenburg nursing home but spent her free time with Wilbert, as he became more and more ill and dependent. By early 2000, it became clear that only a heart transplant would save Wilbert's life, so he and Lillie spent several months in a Houston hospital, waiting and hoping for a heart donor.

Lillie showed tremendous calm and serenity as she sat with Wilbert, day after day, sleeping in his hospital room, seldom leaving his side. It was remarkable to see how she maintained her strength and faith during this time, waiting with him for the heart that never came.

Wilbert was always serious and reserved with me, but he did talk some about his life and health. "Had a stroke in about '83, and then I had to go have brain surgery. Went out like a light, don't remember a *thing*. Stayed unconscious for six weeks," he said in a distressed voice. "Have to take a lot of medicine. My balance is off. And I don't wanta get completely down. You know, I ain't too much for the house! I like to be outdoors mostly, if I can. And it's good to be here alive, I tell you!" Wilbert still appeared healthy then, except for having to lean on his walking cane.

"I didn't get to finish school," he continued. "My daddy got sick, and I had to do most of the farmin'. When I got big enough to work, I worked every day mostly." He had always felt very close to his mother, who lived fifteen to twenty miles from Weimar, in Hallettsville. "Mama's livin'. When I'm down, she's usually right there by me. If she's down, I stay around by her bedside. So we're kind of real close to one another. I goes to see her every other day."

He was born Wilbert Loraine Barnes in 1940 in Hallettsville. He worked in construction jobs for years and later raised hogs, even though he had given up eating pork himself: "I don't fool around with no pork or nothin'. I don't eat beef. I scared of pork now since I got high blood pressure. I wonder sometimes why I raise hogs. I don't eat pork."

Years ago, my youngest son had the most gentle dog, a yellow Lab named Chamois, who had never hurt any creature and who would always go with us to the farm. To my dismay, Chamois began sneaking off and going next door to Wilbert's place to chase his piglets. The little creatures turned out to be quite fragile, and a couple of them died from Chamois's rough play. I did not know Wilbert in those days, but I still remember seeing him for the first time, this large, solemn stranger walking across the field to our farm, carrying a tiny lifeless piglet, to give me the bad news. How tenderly he carried the little dead creature, and how bad we felt. Chamois was kept leashed from then on.

Lillie and Wilbert first met each other through friends in Hallettsville and married in 1971. They had two children, Reggie and Lisa, and lived next door to Lillie's birth family: Mama Lillie, Ma Marie, G.A., and Junior Williams. They stayed in close touch and shared responsibilities for the care of each other, from the oldest, grandmother Lillie, to Brendan, Reggie's young son and Mama Lillie's great-great-grandson—five generations, side by side.

Wilbert died in 2000 at sixty years of age. Lillie, left alone, had the good fortune to have her family close around her in that painful time. She continued with her life. She worked in a Weimar nursing home, cared for her baby grandson, visited with friends, and attended church regularly. In time, her smile and her sense of fun returned.

Oliver "Junior" Williams

Oliver Williams Jr. was born March 15, 1936. "The springtime came in and so did I," said he, with a shy smile.

"Junior" always lived in his mother's home. Once, we were told, when he was in his teens, he went out of the house and came back immediately, scared by something or someone—and he never went far from home again, living the remainder of his life there with his birth family.

He told me that he once tried to enter the army but was designated 4-F and sent back home. His mother, Marie, explained that Junior was diagnosed as schizophrenic when he was in his teens and had to live in and out of treatment his whole life, never marrying or holding a job.

My own daddy also said, years earlier, that he had once gotten a call from Junior's father, Oliver Senior, who said he was worried about something and needed to come to Houston to talk to Daddy. It sounded like a serious matter. So he came with his minister and explained that Junior had been found in our farmhouse, which he had broken into. The poor father had been expecting the worst from Daddy, who turned out to be neither angry nor upset. The matter was easily resolved, and all was well.

Junior seemed to be quiet and gentle, rather like a child in some ways, but a big, tobacco-chewing child. For a long while, I barely noticed him, because although he was always around the house, he sort of folded himself into the background. Then one day he asked me to take his picture. Junior liked the copy when it was done and grinned happily. As he left the room, he stopped, came back, and handed the photograph to Marie, saying, "You keep it for me, Mama."

Junior never did leave home much, not even for church, not even for Cousin Lacey's ninety-first birthday party. And I still wondered what had happened to him on the street all those many years ago, when he came home so frightened that he never again went far from home.

In 2000, Junior entered a nursing home in Weimar because of some health problems. He missed Marie terribly at first but then found several of his old high school friends working there, as well as his sister Lillie. He grew to like the company and the contact with people and to be happy there. Maybe he had been lonely all those years at home, so his hospitalization became something of a blessing for him. He died peacefully in the nursing home.

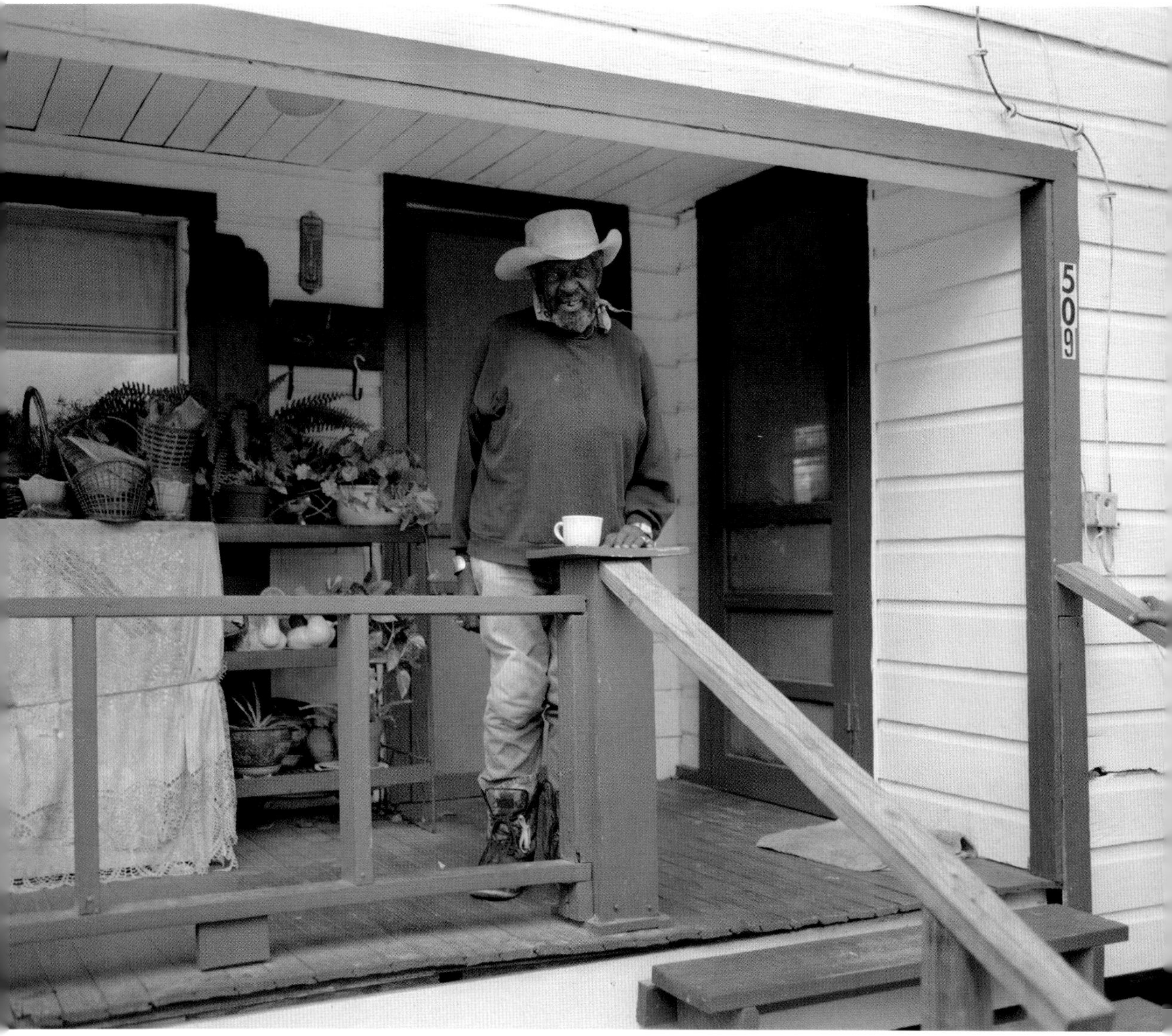

Oliver "Junior" Williams

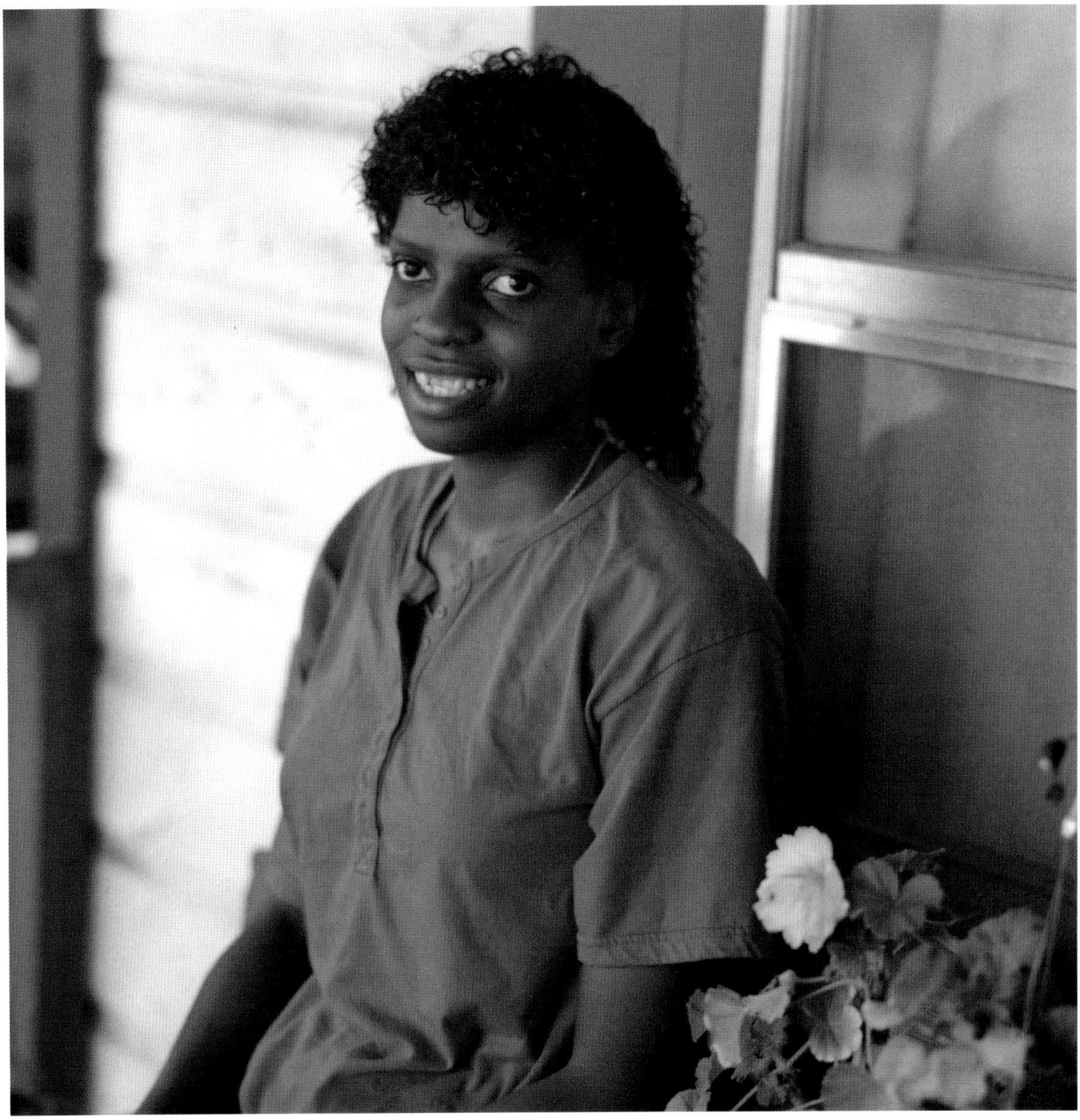

Lisa Williams

Lisa Williams

Pretty Lisa Williams came from a long line of strong, loving, matriarchal women. Her great-grandmother was Lillie Williams, her grandmother Marie Williams, and her mother Lillie Barnes. Lisa appeared to be a shy young woman who went to church regularly and enjoyed spending quiet times with her family. Her ambition was to go to a small college, take computer courses, get married, find a good job, and start a family "like they did," her female relatives.

Lisa became engaged to a man from Weimar who was living in California. To the horror of her grandmother Marie, Lisa flew alone to the West Coast to visit her fiancé. Marie said cautiously, "In August he went out to California to work—so that they could make money and stuff for the wedding. If he hasn't changed since he's been out there, he's a loving character himself. They worked together before he went out there. But now he wants to take her out there, so I don't know. It would be an adventure if she could get acquainted, but you know, she's just a little ole country girl. I just hate for her to get in a big city and anything go wrong. But you have to give 'em a chance. If she doesn't like it, then they'll come back on home. I'm keeping my fingers crossed." Lisa made it back home safely and their wedding was in 1991.

Lisa adored her grandmother and great-grandmother, who lived next door. She spent a lot of time with "Ma Marie" and "Mama Sang." They said they would sorely miss her when she left Weimar with her husband, James Jarmon, to live in the next town, Schulenburg. Thankfully they were near enough to come home often for visits, and Marie was happy.

Alex Williams, Tycie Williams, & Tennille Almeida

Tycie, Alex, and Tennille were neighbors on North Saint Andrews Street in Weimar and closest friends when they were teenagers. Here they are seen on Alex's great-grandmother's front porch, hanging out on a summer afternoon.

They usually talked almost in unison as they echoed each other's thoughts: "Weimar is okay, but you have to go to school. In Houston or another city, you meet a lot of people and do more things than here, but Weimar doesn't have as much killin'. You can walk around without gettin' messed with or gettin' hurt. Not much goin' on here! There's sports, basketball, school, eating, hunting, and fishing. Not many drugs here. No drugs in school." A familiar refrain followed: "But it's hard to find work in this town. There just *aren't* jobs."

Tycie's dream was to go to beauty school or study law, then find work in another town, where she could make money, and live in Weimar again later. The boys wanted to get scholarships in track, football, or basketball and so be able to go to college.

By 2001 the three were in their late twenties, and still there were almost no jobs in town. Tycie was lucky to have gotten a nursing job at an excellent hospital in Houston, a job she left after a few years to return to Weimar so that she could be closer to her mother and grandmother. And Tycie was fortunate once again to find a job in Colorado County as a hospice nurse. She seemed happy and had some ambitions for furthering her nursing career. Alex was married, with a baby boy, and living with his grandmother Marie. He was a newly appointed Baptist minister. Tennille—"Dede" to his father, Gabriel—was twenty-five, married, and living in Weimar with his wife and their two sons. Jobs for young men remained very limited in their town.

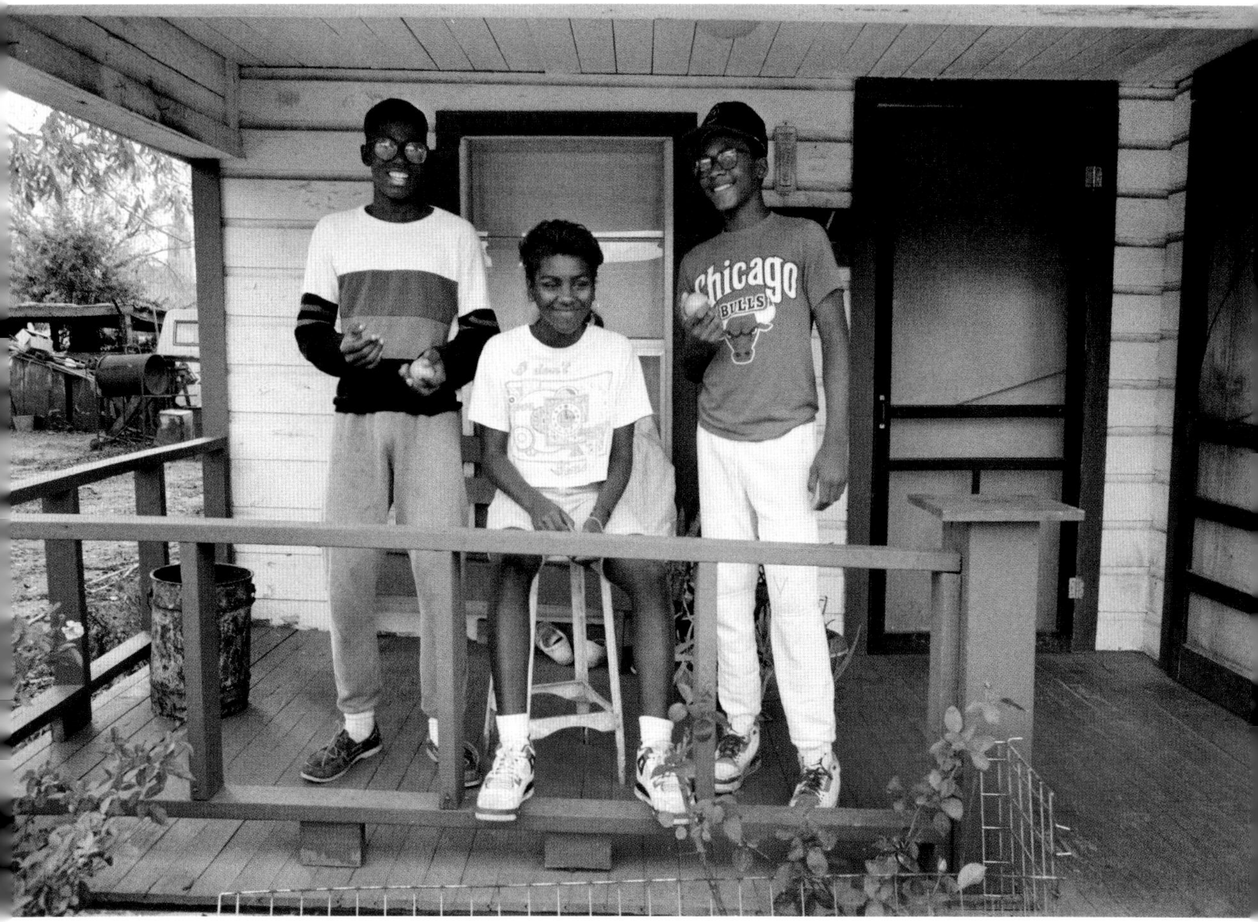

Alex Williams, Tycie Williams, and Tennille Almeida

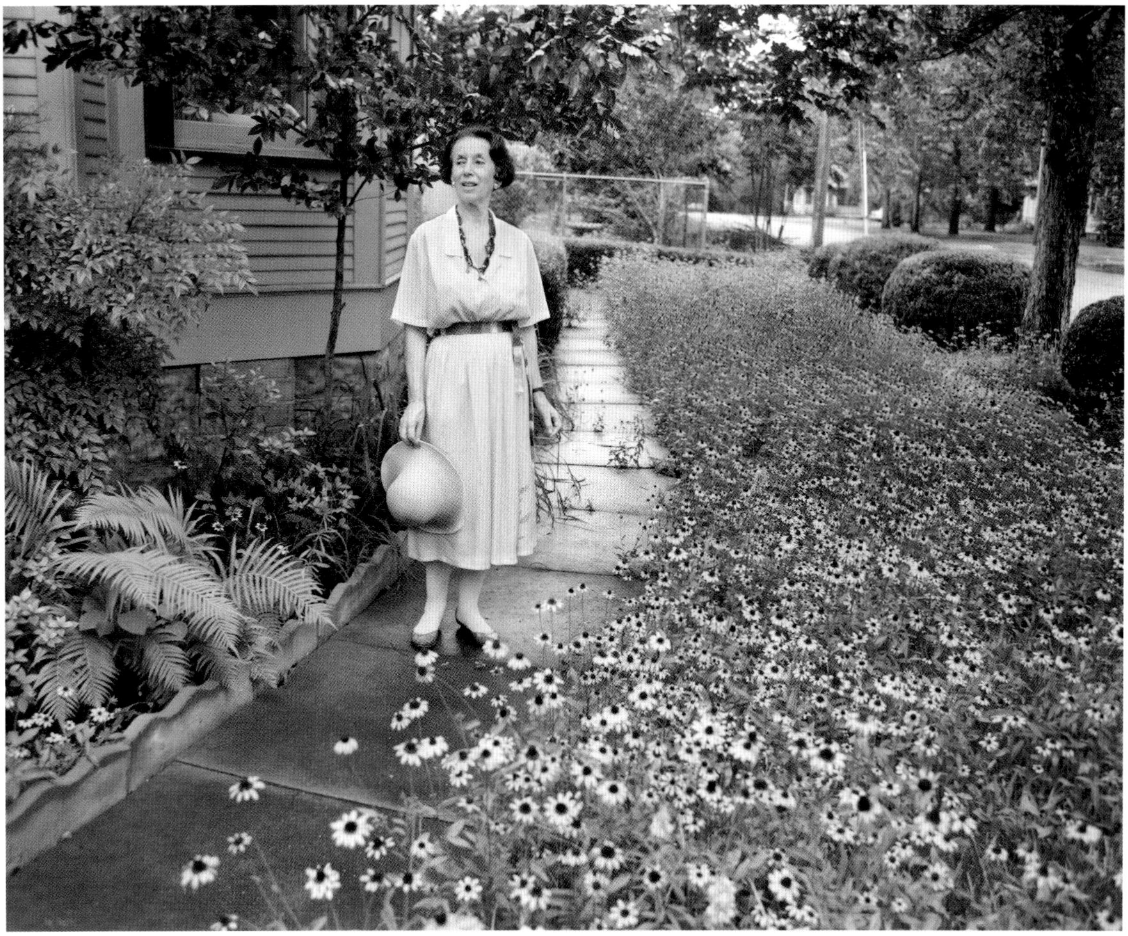

Quentin Steitz

Quentin Steitz

"I'm known as the Weed Lady," said Quentin Steitz, gaily.

When Quentin and her husband, Frank, first moved to the Texas Panhandle from their home in the Northeast in the 1970s, she was delighted to discover "the magnificent weeds and grasses that grow in this state." She observed, "Then they were classified as weeds, and I suppose that's why my nickname started, as being 'the Weed Lady.' Now you don't call them weeds; you call them ornamentals, grasses, or decorative vegetation."

New Jersey–born Quentin built herself quite a name as an expert on native Texas plants and grasses, or the "aesthetics of grasses," as she writes. She loved her work. She adored her own wildflower garden and showed great pleasure in creating the arrangements of native vegetation that earned her a widespread, solid reputation as an imaginative and creative designer. As a testimony to her artistry, she was chosen to create arrangements for the opening of the prestigious Menil Museum in Houston. She was also the author of the book *Grasses, Pods, Vines, and Weeds: Decorating with Texas Naturals* and has spoken, "wild grasses in hand," to many plant and garden societies and at the Lady Bird Johnson Wildflower Center.

In this photograph, as she stands in her elegant clothes in front of her immaculate, turn-of-the-century house—with its iron fence, neatly mowed front yard, and spotless walkway—it is easy to imagine Quentin as a visitor to Texas from her home in the Northeast. Yet she is very clear about her admiration and enjoyment of Texas, its plants, and her life here. Proof of this can be seen in her own exuberantly blooming beds of native flowers.

Quentin's Eastern reserve vanished when she talked gardens. "To me, a garden is like a painting—a place in which to express oneself," she said. "As a little girl, roaming the banks of the Delaware River was my preparation for my love and lust for plants. I grow mostly Texas native plants that I believe in. Rewards are many for the eyes, in watching the play of birds, the butterflies, and the little creatures that find this haven.

"Perhaps they call me the forerunner in this field because I was dedicated. I could see quality, and I knew how these plants would become recognized. And like I say, many times, they go to the *most* beautiful places, and they do—I mean the Menil Museum, on opening night . . ." She smiled dreamily, remembering the event.

"I'm not trying to flatter myself, but, you know, if you're dedicated in your work and you've got your nose directed into one line of work, something nice happens—if you believe in what you're doing. In a review of my book was the phrase 'botany and art.' That gives you an idea it is an art medium."

Truman McMahan

Truman McMahan was the coeditor of a Columbus newspaper, the *Colorado County Citizen,* along with his wife, Elizabeth McLeary McMahan. Together, Truman and Liza ran the paper for twenty-two years, from 1946 till 1969. Truman was born in Madisonville, Texas,* and arrived at Columbus after working on the *Houston Post,* where he honed his journalism skills.

Along with managing the *Colorado County Citizen,* Truman wrote a column called "Mulling It Over." As his friend Tex Rogers said admiringly, years later, "Truman wrote over the head of most of his readers. And I really enjoyed reading his stuff. He's absolutely a true Democrat. He predicted Harry Truman's win over Dewey, in 1948. *And* he's a great guy!" "He truly inspired thought," wrote Tana Ross, of the *Columbus Citizen,* after his death.

After Truman and Liza sold the paper, they remained in the Columbus area, in the nearby community of Glidden, about two miles west on Highway 90. Liza ran an antique shop out of their house while Truman read voluminously and wrote occasional articles for various journals, such as the *Southwestern Quarterly*. Liza died in 1993, leaving Truman bereft and lonely. He ate little and exercised less, met friends at the City Cafe in Columbus for coffee, drank more alcohol than was good for him, and read, alone in his little house. His mind was good and his curiosity lively, but he was saddened and depressed by the loss of Liza, his declining health, and the shaking of his hands. In time his handwriting became so shaky it was nearly illegible, and he became more and more frustrated by this, being a person who loved to write. When typing also became hard, Truman gave up writing at all, the pastime he had so treasured. "The reason I do not write more, I tell myself, is that the typewriter keys move and shake beyond belief when my fingers try to punch them," he wrote in a letter.

By 2000, his health had deteriorated so badly, he entered a nursing home in Gonzales, near Liza's nephew, his closest family member. He hated the place he was in and sounded dispirited over the phone.

In November 2000 he wrote by typewriter:

> I am ensconced in this 'assisted living' (halfway house to hell) place with 14 elderly women and two old (Allhimered) men. I know that I risked losing you, along with two or three others whom I treasure, with my silence which is not of my making. I've had no control of my being since the doctor wouldn't let me

*North Zulch was listed as his birthplace in the Columbus paper's obituary.

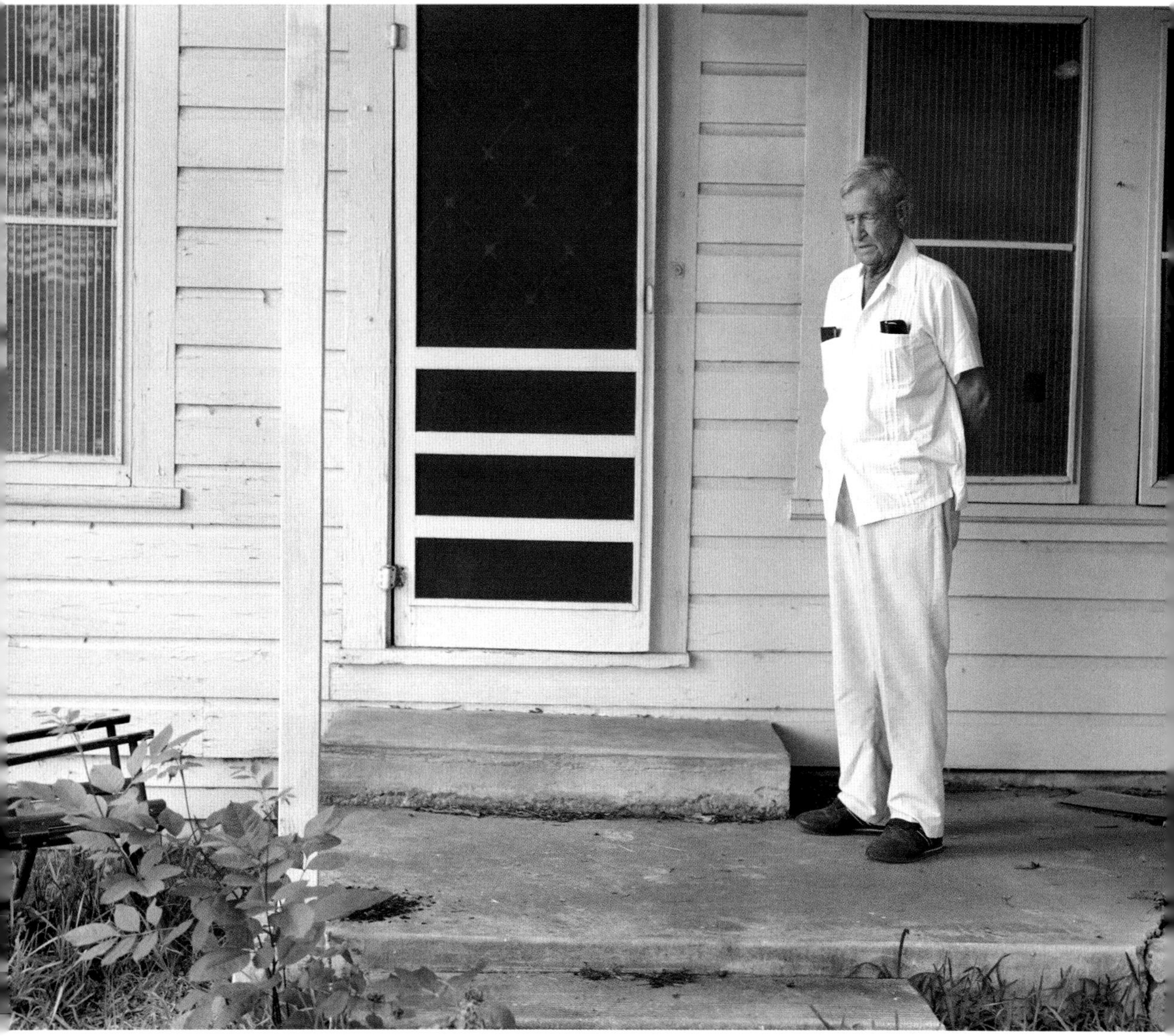

Truman McMahan

go home from the hospital. . . . Be of good cheer. TM [accompanied by a very shaky, handwritten "TM"]

He added, during a rare phone call, that his room was cheerless and bare and that he felt weak, out of breath, and out of spirits too.

This is Truman, in another letter:

> If you portray me in my own words I will deny everything. At best I jest. I am honored that you think I could add anything to your book. Hurry it up because I'd like to see it. Cordially, TM

And here are some passages from other letters:

> You made me feel goodest (note command of language) for wanting to read one of my pieces in *Southwestern Quarterly*. And here is one, the best. Another is a two-page piece about dinner with J. Frank Dobie, and the other is boring to everyone but the author. It's "The Fight Against the Pink Bollworm in Texas."
>
> These carbons come from a pile which I kept at my moldering place in Osage, and I'm glad to say that some well-cultured wrens cavort inside there. The mere white spot you see at the bottom of one page is only expression of editorial opinion of one of those birds. Ignore it. Thank you for much. Vaya con Dios, TM

> Forgive the typewriter for it knowth not what it does.
>
> Your thoughtfulness has really almost destroyed my facade; for kindness is something I do not handle gracefully.

> If the dogwood are blooming, you ought to go on the Todd's ranch to what I call the "Mewhinney Place."** The beauty—acres of it—will astound you. I have seen the blooms many times and even yet "they flash upon the inward eye which is the bliss of solitude."

The following excerpts are from a story Truman wrote for the Columbus newspaper many years ago:

> What I'm trying to do is to back into doing a little piece on becoming educated in the art of cursing, or, to put it another way, the inability of some people

**The Mewhinney Place was named for Hubert Mewhinney, a journalist at the *Houston Post,* and it was actually my aunts' farm that Mewhinney used to visit and write on in his column. He jokingly called it the Wray Wolf and Wildlife Farm.

> to talk without cursing. And it is my contention that that ought to be spelled "cussing," because that is a more pleasing word. . . .
>
> In the early days of newspapering, cussing was seldom practiced by my associates while they were on their jobs, but as I became more accepted by my peers, I learned that many newspapermen, while off duty and telling tales, were accomplished cussers. Only a few were original, creative cussers. Very few cussers are; for, let's face it, all cuss words have been used many times. . . .
>
> One thing for sure, army life was an education in the use of cussing. In those days, the army didn't insist that you be all that you can be—although some did—unless it was to be the most stupid cusser in your company.

One of the best qualities in Truman was his interest in and caring for people. He was one of the very few white individuals who were around Columbus near the time of the 1935 lynchings who would discuss them, and he spoke honestly on how he felt about them—horrified. He was one of three men who told me they knew members of the Columbus white community who had never believed the young boys were guilty but believed they were simply set up. He described, chillingly, how loudspeakers where put in the streets the afternoon before, to call attention to the coming event and to warn the black citizens to stay home the next day. One can only imagine how the parents of the two teenage boys felt when they heard the announcement and knew it was *their* young sons who were going to be killed. Truman said that the black undertaker, Ben Davis, was told to leave the boys' bodies hanging from the tree for a day, for everyone to see.

Truman spoke of the ignorance and fear he saw in the white community around people of color, and he spoke sadly of the inhumanity in our society, comparing it with Nazi Germany. Truman could be stubborn and negative, but he also was a man of true conviction.

Truman died in January 2002 in Gonzales. His breathing had become difficult, and he simply stopped eating and let himself pass on. His services were graveside in the rural Osage Cemetery. He was buried, as he wished, next to beloved Liza.

Lonzo Dorn

"My name is Lonzo Dorn, and I was in church this mornin'—and we really enjoyed ourselves this mornin'. The pastor was talkin' 'bout how we should live together in peace and harmony and try to help each other about our burdens." Thus Lonzo began his story.

"That's how to live, in order to help someone that need help," Lonzo continued. "And I've always been thatta way—you know, try to help someone that need help, try to live right and nice, and between different ones, don't care what color it is. I try to get along with everyone. That's been my motto, yes, ma'am!

"I was born in nineteen and eight, and I'm eighty-three years old, and I count it a blessin' that the Lord have let me stay here this long. And I wanta say that so many people are not able to say what I'm a-sayin'. And so many have come along with me, and at this time they have gone to another world. And I wanta say that I thank the Lord for the many blessings he have bestowed upon my soul."

Lonzo and his brother, Leo, were the twins in their birth family, different one from the other and yet very close. "It was a Spanish lady named us," Lonzo said. "My twin died about six years ago. When our mother was fixin' to get ready to die, she called us chil'ren to her bedside—she called us *together* 'cause we was twins. We were as one, you know, and she said, 'All of you try to be good chil'ren, and serve the Lord, and do the right thing. Work and try to live so that no one will hate you.' And she said, 'Lonzo, I know he gonna do his part. He gonna stay with the other chil'ren. He gonna help his sister to try to take care of all of y'all. But Leo, he ain't gonna stay. He gonna leave pretty soon—goin' on off.'" And sure enough, Leo did leave home and move to Houston.

Lonzo continued: "And she said, 'Your father's gonna do all that he can to help y'all, but there's gonna be times when he ain't gonna be there, but Lonzo will be there.' And sure 'nough, it come out like she said. 'Try to live so people will like you. Because of the way you live, they gonna have to love you.'"

So Lonzo followed his mama's advice and stayed home. He acted responsibly, as a loving brother, husband, and father, looking out for other people and living a church- and family-oriented life.

"I went to the rural school," he said. "They didn't go no higher than seventh grade. I was brought up the hard way. Didn't have nothin'. My mother and father never did have to scold me—me and my sister was two in the family they could depend on. We was the two best workers they had. I was plowin' when I was nine years old with

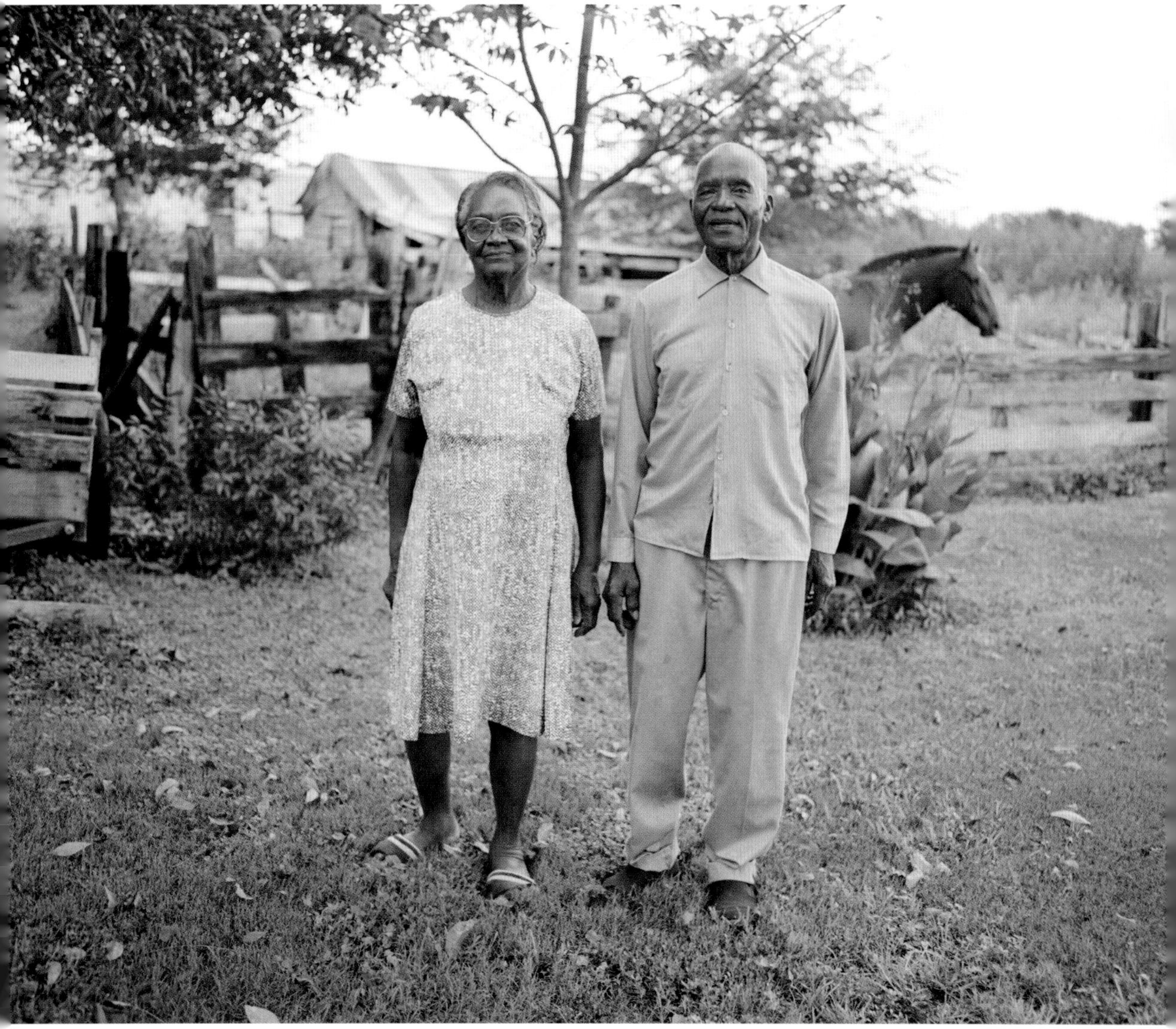

Beulah and Lonzo Dorn

four mules—*just* could stand up high enough for the plow! And *always* was a good farmer."

Lonzo worked most of his life as a sharecropper, as had his father before him. When he and Beulah married, "We lived on a white fellow's place, same man where my father was livin'. And I went on halves. We was raised on that place—Brandt's. We really got along with 'em."

He explained, "Sharecroppin' means that you get three-fourth, and the boss man get one-fourth. But after all, you have to furnish *everythin'.* You see, your boss man don't have to furnish *nothin'.* If you sharecroppin', you know you have to do that all yourself, and if you don't make anythin'—why, you just up against it, 'cause you done *lost out,* way I see it!

"We'd go to Osage, I reckon about seven miles, me and my wife. We would pick corn. That's where we made our money. Sometimes I would leave home before day, just in order to be there when daylight come, you know, so I would get my part of the corn. And it was a wonder if I hadn't got bit by a rattlesnake—I tell you, it be so dark, I'd be *feelin'* ahead of me! We'd pack them corns out of that bottom in a sack. You had 'em tied up and thrown across your back, and pack 'em out. If you could make seventy-five cents a day, you thought you had seven or eight dollars. I've worked for fifty cents a day from sunup to sundown. We come through some hard times!

"I know what hard times is, 'cause I have been through. But the hardest time was—well, I used to grub a lot. Grubbin' trees and stuff like that can be *tough*. And times was tight then. Like I said, I have grubbed up stumps, and the boss man give me *just enough* to make some money out of, and also we could have some Christmas money out of, so I could buy sugar and stuff to have cakes and pies for the little 'uns. My daughter, she said lots of times, 'Daddy, we may not have all we want, but you done all you could to try to take care of us.' And I said, 'Well, I'm glad y'all feel that way, yes, ma'am!'

"My grandfather used to get me to plant all his crops. I'd get the seed up so nice and everythin'. And right out here, below Weimar, we farmed nineteen years. And we had some hard days here. Nothin' but nut grass and johnsongrass. I'm tellin' you, that was tough! But we made it through. Then it just got so we couldn't make nothin', so I just decided to quit and come over here to Weimar." He showed an old torn photograph of himself, taken on his Weimar job, pushing a wheelbarrow full of egg cartons.

Lonzo often thought about his grandfather Holman, who was born into slavery. "My mama came from the Holman side," he said. "They went by their boss man' name, Holman—their master's name. I used to go around my grandfather a whole lot, and he would talk to me 'bout slavery. My grandmother, she was too young to work in slavery. And I want to say that he told me that some of 'em were real nice to 'em, real good to the people that they were possessed of, and some were mean. They didn't have hardly anythin' to eat—they had to go out in corn patches, potato patches, and fields and steal to try and feed their family."

He spoke of how the slave children were divided up by their owners, sold off, and shipped away from their parents, to be sent off to other states. Recalling his grandfather's words, "Just loaded 'em up, shipped 'em on off like cattle. The mothers be cryin' for their chil'ren, runnin' around, cryin' for their little 'uns, tryin' to hold their chil'ren—didn't want to see 'em go. Like cows cryin', like calves taken from their mothers—just take 'em away from their mothers and load 'em on up in freight trains and ship 'em on off! Just like you see cows runnin' around, cryin' for their little 'uns, women wantin' to save 'em but they shook 'em on off, kick 'em away, and just carry 'em on off!

"And that's why some were marryin' their kinfolk, didn't know they was related to 'em, half-brothers or half-sisters, 'cause they didn't know better. My grandfather said, 'We don't know our kinfolks—we don't know who kin to us and who ain't.' They didn't know what they were doin'. They had some *hard* times they went through.

"He taught me a lot of things. He told me how to do by my wife, how to raise my chil'ren. And he said he would never forget it, that at the time of freedom, when they freed the colored people, his grandma heard the white people say, 'All the coloreds are freed!' She said some of 'em didn't want to walk away—they had good boss masters, and they wanted to stay right on, and some of them were glad to go.

"Well, I feel mighty proud that I'm not in that position where I have to have people over me, get put under bondage like that. And I think it's a blessin' from God that we have all been freed of those things.

"Lots of times I have been afraid—different things have went on around me. And I felt for myself—you know, these things could happen to me. You know, people so sinful and doin' so many bad things—you feel like you can't hide. You might be one in a number, be somethin' wrong did to you. I had an older brother, and my mother used to send us to the store. And when they'd see us comin', the white boys, they'd come over here with big knives and everythin', and I couldn't run off and leave my brother. I had to stay there and try to help him. Yeah, I was afraid for my life, 'cause I didn't want to get hurt. And I didn't want to hurt *nobody*."

Lonzo expressed these thoughts on racial hatred and violence: "Well, I can't forgive 'em, you know—I leave that up to the Master. And he said all human beings belong to him. Let him do the punishin'. I try to forgive. It's up to the Lord to judge—it ain't up to us to judge. So I forgive, but I never will *forget* what been did to me. Like you cut your hand, get a scar on it. You look at that scar, you always know where that scar come from. But I forgive—I just don't forget." And he sat in thoughtful silence, looking serene and certain.

Lonzo made it clear he was a churchgoing man, and he described being seized by faith: "Nineteen hundred and twenty-five, I confessed religion, and that's the truth. You may not believe it, but I felt like a kite, flyin' in the air. I just felt so light, you know. [I] fell to the ground, and someone older said, 'Get up. You done got religion!' And I got up and told my religion, and I ain't departed it from that day till this!

"We used to have revivals, old-time revivals, and we would go to revivals in wagons. And would be sometimes a half a mile from the church and you could hear those sisters a-shoutin', and hear the deacons prayin' and tryin' to capture the candidates. And at that time they didn't just lay their hands on you—they made *sure* you got religion when you got up. You would feel somethin', feel like you want to fly or somethin'. When I got religion, I knew I got religion. And God have laid his hand on me, 'cause I have never changed and I don't never intend to go back on God's word. I know I have been born by the Holy Spirit."

Lonzo was also a deeply romantic man. "I always asked the Lord to give me a good wife," he said. "And when I was young, I would say within, 'Give me a good wife.'

"The first time my mother sent me over to a friend's house to have some dresses sewed, I laid eyes on my wife. I knowed her older sister, but I didn't know her mother had a baby girl like *her*. And first time I laid my eyes on her, I fell in love with her, and I said 'Lord, there's my wife, right there!' And I always prayed to the Lord to let me have her for my wife, and he did. I was about twelve years old. And from then on, I knew she was put in the world for me. Look like I fell in love with her that day when I laid eyes on her. And I've never regretted it from that day unto this," he said with a big smile, his affection palpable. They met as youngsters and were married for more than sixty years, until Lonzo's death.

"I find no fault in trying to serve God," he said. "And I know it will pay off. That's the thing—the life you live will *speak* for you. When you dead and in you' grave and you cain't say a word, your life will speak for you. That's all I want to say."

A troubling footnote to Lonzo's life is that his death was caused by his beloved Beulah, who hit him with his crutch; he died a short time afterward. Their daughter told this story and said that neither Lonzo nor Beulah had any memory of how he had been hurt. And Beulah was diagnosed soon afterward with early Alzheimer's disease. There was too much genuine affection and caring between them for it to have been a deliberate act of malice.

Beulah Dorn

"You serve the Lord and do his will, he will carry you through. And so I thank the Lord I'm still here. He carried me this far, brought me a mighty long ways, and I thank him for it." These are the words of Beulah Dorn.

The first time we talked, Beulah began her story like this: "My papa had three girls—I was the boy!" She gave a quiet laugh and went on. "I worked hard. Worked like a man, haulin' hay and all that. I hauled hay, I plowed, I grubbed, I done all of that. Drove a cultivator when I was young. My daddy went to town, I hitched up the mules and plowed every field round the house 'fore he got home," she said, chuckling.

"Like I said, was three girls—but *we* was 'boys,' 'cause Papa farmed," Beulah continued. "And I was nine years old when I started plowin' with mules—helped plow with a cultivator with four mules to it, a ridin' cultivator. I was the one stackin' the hay. I didn't mind that, I enjoyed doin' that. That's how I was brought up. That's why I don't mind workin' today. There was five of us in the family—well, we'd pick a bale a day, just us. We was raised to it, and we was raised to go to church.

"I never was a shirker. I just like to work. I'm proud the Lord helped me so I *could* work. Like I said, you serve the Lord and do his will, he will carry you through. So I thank the Lord. You know, a lot of people, they don't wanta get old, but I don't mind gettin' old, 'cause they ain't makin' me any younger. Some younger than I am can't get around like I can. And that's a blessin'."

Describing her married life, she said, "I worked *every day of the week*. Go to the bottom, to the cotton patch. Come home that Friday and do my house and wash, and back in the pecan bottom or cotton patch till sundown. And so I liked to work. I liked to work the garden. I liked to pick cotton. I liked to chop. And I still, thank the Lord, I still can do my work. I'll be eighty-three October seventh."

Lots of farm families without sons treated their daughters like boys and worked them in what would normally have been men's jobs. Beulah was one who thrived on it, declaring often and proudly how she had worked hard all her life and enjoyed it too. Born in 1909, to Pearl and Rufus Williams, Beulah was still working hard in her eighties, although she admitted the work was getting harder and she had begun to need help with some chores. This she didn't like. Still, you couldn't pass her house that you didn't see her out raking leaves or planting something, surrounded by kittens. The Dorns' corner lot was a joy to pass by. Beulah had flowers almost everywhere—in pots, in beds, in old tires, some grown from seeds, some from cuttings.

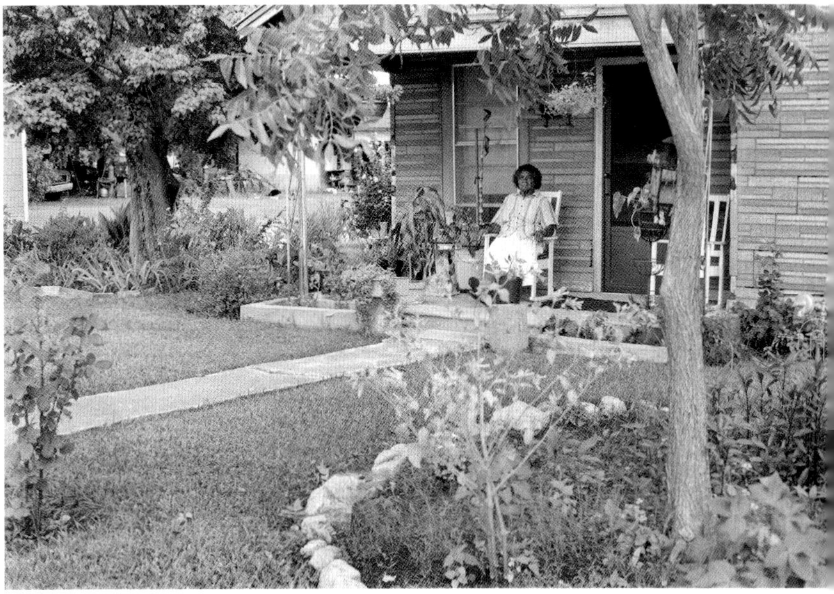

Beulah Dorn,
enjoying her garden

All of the pecan trees in the yard she had brought by hand, as saplings, dug by her from the river bottom years before, when she and Lonzo had moved into town from the rurals. She filled my car trunk with cuttings one day, generously sharing her garden wealth.

Beulah bore seven children with Lonzo. Six survived. The first three were born in the country and were carried by her into the fields every day so she could do her field work. "I'd work, and I'd carry 'em to the fields," she said, "and drag 'em on a sack behind, pickin' cotton. But that was all right. I don't mind."

All six Dorn children left Weimar when they were grown, moving to Houston and San Antonio, where job opportunities were better. One of the daughters, Vivian, spoke with frustration and anger over some of the things she and her parents had had to endure in Weimar. While she talked, Beulah softly protested in the background, emphasizing the gulf between the younger city dweller and her traditional, small-town mother.

"Just like slavery," Vivian called the wages they had been paid, while Beulah countered, "I worked here in town, you know, for lots of white womens, after I come here. Done their work and babysit—work in the day, babysit at night. I done all of that. I just wanta say I enjoyed everything. They were nice to me. We worked for fifty cents a day, but you could get a sack of flour for fifty cents. Payin' fifty cents for wages, well—" and she grew quiet and thoughtful as her words trailed off. "But slavery, I haven't ever been through that."

Vivian responded, frustration ringing in her voice: "Racism, it's still here. We have to be truthful—it's still here. See, I wouldn't hire *anybody* to work for me for no fifty cents, 'cause I'd feel awful, you know? You know what I'm sayin'? I send you in my house to do all of my ironin', cookin', washin', and babysittin', and you got through, I give you two dollars. They should pay you for the work you do by them hours! I started workin' when I was fourteen years old in houses, cleanin' and babysittin' with children. And when I leave, I get like a dollar and a half, two dollars, two-fifty, and *I* be doin' all the work!"

Beulah responded, "I just want to say, people they were nice to me. The same way, the Bible say, 'Revenge belong to me.' I don't care what they do to me—I still do not hate 'em. Do not hold it against anybody. That's what the Lord want us to do."

"White against black—well, we was brought over here as slaves," replied Vivian. "So that makes us the product of our foreparents' slavery. Although Abraham Lincoln signed the bill and set the blacks free, we still not free. We still up under racism and oppression. It's a different kind, but it's still there. I cannot erase that out of my mind—you live with it every day. It's gonna be there till the end of time. Hearts can change, you know, get better toward their fellow man. But racism is going to be there till this world ends."

Beulah summed up her life: "I learned to work. I never was lazy. My papa was smart. My mama was smart. And they taught us to work. By them, I know how to work. I'm proud I can work, and I'm proud the Lord have taken care of me and helped me so I *could* work."

And while one could admire Beulah's toughness and her elegant spirit, it seemed that at eighty-three it was okay for her to slow down. When Beulah died in 1998, another daughter, Lonnie Mae, moved from Houston to Weimar into her parents' house and began keeping her mother's garden for the enjoyment of all who passed their corner.

LaVon Simpson & Mary Ann Nicholson

LaVon and Mary Ann, sisters, grew up outside of Austin. In time, both women married and left home, each eventually divorcing. The two women moved physically away from each other, but their sisterly bonds remained strong—visible in the way they joked and laughed together, head to head, and in the way they corrected each other's stories and seemed to read each other's thoughts.

Before I met Mary Ann, I knew only LaVon, and I knew her as the "wonder woman" who helped run the Borden Country Club, also known as the Poor Man's Country Club or the Borden Store. She had come to Colorado County several years before and married Jimmy Simpson, a native of nearby Glidden. Together the couple managed the "Country Club," an establishment that acted as *the* local, rural meeting place. It was a wonderful, doors-open-to-all pool hall, beer hall, and restaurant of sorts on old Highway 90, set just at the turnoff to our farm, at the road marker "Borden"—no town remains, just a marker.* The store was housed in an old, two-story, wooden-plank building with a bunch of pickup trucks parked in front, day and night. It was friendly, welcoming, and relaxed. There were a few canned items on the shelf (that was the "store" part), beer and soft drinks at the bar, a pool table, a handful of plastic-covered chairs set around metal tables, and a few simple snacks—crackers, pickled pigs' feet, that sort of thing. LaVon and Jimmy had a gift of making each customer feel special and worthy of their time. LaVon was the one who made supper on Sunday evenings, free to everyone who showed up.

The Borden Store seemed to be the place that brought in the lonely and the solitary for a meal, a beer, a Coke, or simply a visit. Some were clearly regulars. One older man was there often with his young grandson. He would put the boy on a barstool, telling him in a gruff voice, "Sit down, boy!" Then he would order himself a beer, give the child a soft drink, and visit with his friends.

LaVon seemed to be a gatherer of people—not a "collector," which is a cold word, but a "gatherer." She had a way of pulling people around her by listening intently to their stories and truly enjoying them, like the man from Mexico who told her how

*Borden was named for the family of John P. Borden, born in 1812 in New York. He became Texas's first land commissioner and was a member of Stephen F. Austin's second colony and a participant in the battle of San Jacinto. He was the planner of Houston, along with his brother, Gail. Gail Borden patented Borden's condensed milk and in 1866 built a meat-packing plant and homes for himself, his sons, and his brother in Colorado County, at what was to become the community of Borden. John died there in 1890, the "last commissioned officer of the San Jacinto veterans."

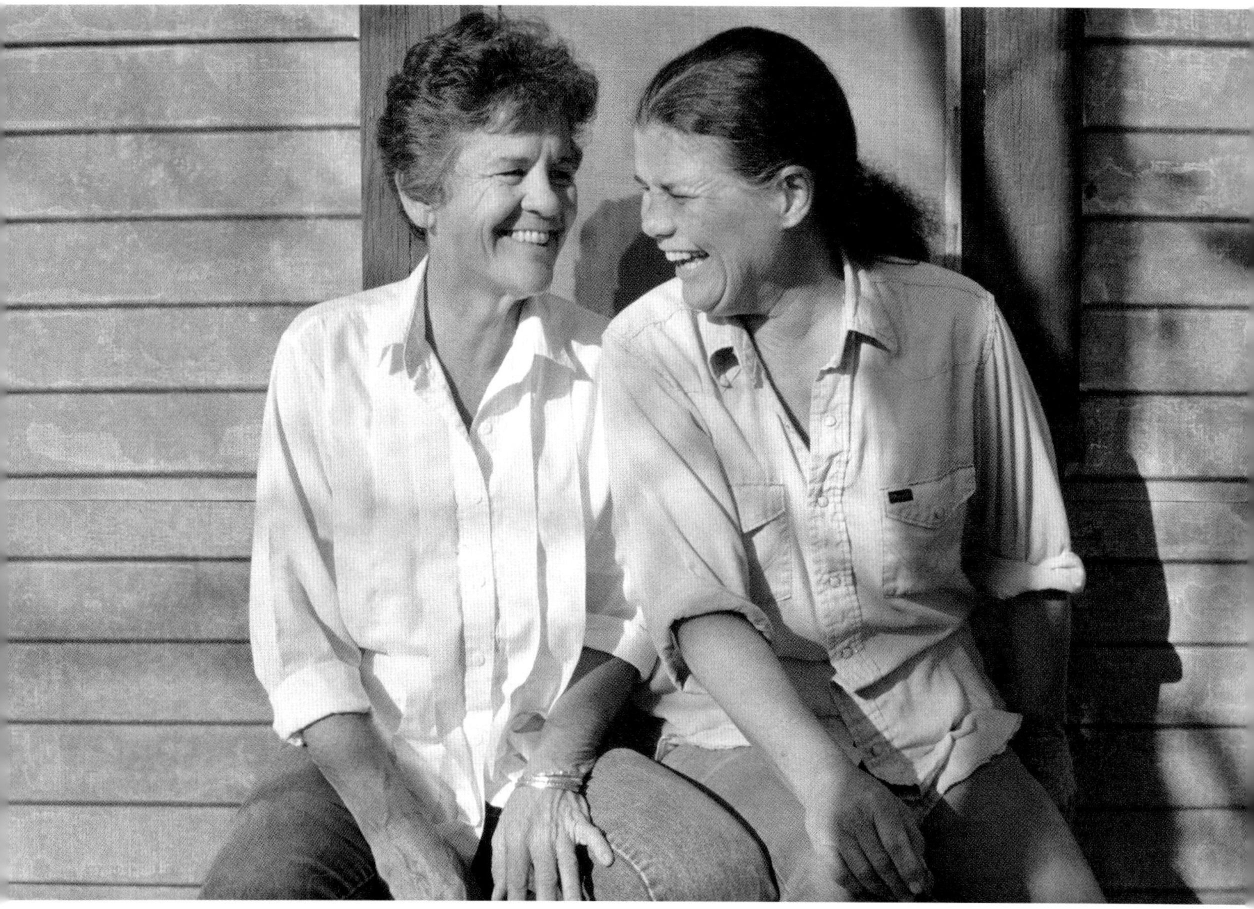

LaVon Simpson *(right)* and her sister, Mary Ann Nicholson

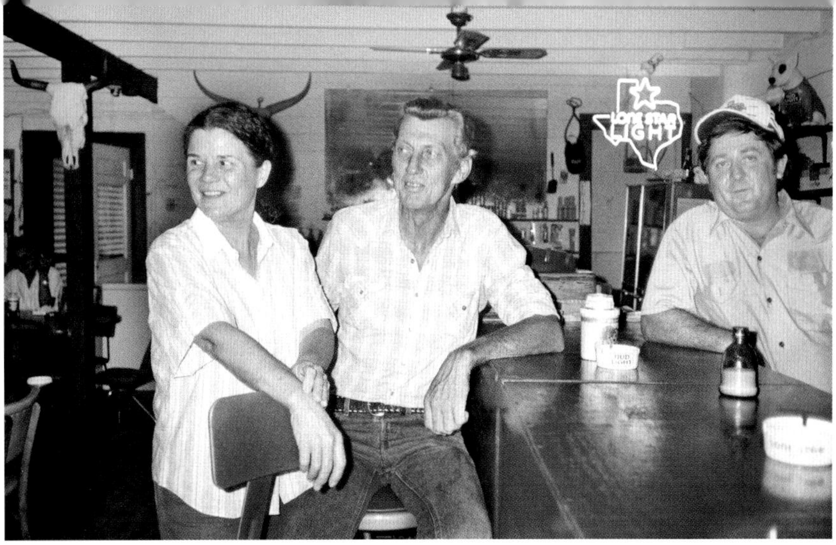

LaVon and Jimmy Simpson and bartender Willie Beyer at the Poor Man's Country Club

he had been stolen by gypsies as a child, or the woman whose doctor husband had her falsely hospitalized for insanity. Then there was Bud Greak, the loner, the man with a brain injury whom she befriended. Everyone seemed to like and trust LaVon. And she in turn treated them with respect.

One Fourth of July, LaVon planned a big party, with food, drinks, pool, and a fortune-teller from Austin—a first, surely, for Colorado County. That is when this picture of LaVon and Mary Ann was taken. These two lively women appeared to find a lot of fun in life. And they had a lot of personal history to share, no doubt about that. By then, LaVon had been married twice and Mary Ann three times. There were bound to be stories there, and maybe that's what they were laughing about.

It was years after the Simpsons had left and retired to Columbus that I discovered that warmth, hospitality, and good food were not LaVon's only talents. She also could paint well and was creating a series of "Jesus paintings," each with a different visage of the man, and a set of depictions of the original one-room schoolhouses from around the county. She and Jimmy were living in a cabin in the woods, east of Columbus. She was working part-time cleaning houses with her cousin. Jimmy was making cedar benches. Times seemed to be hard economically and, at the same time, good creatively. Jimmy died in 2004, and LaVon was hoping Mary Ann would come live with her.

LaVon described her birth family as complicated, intelligent, original, willful, strong, and almost all of them addicted to something: depression, alcohol, medicine—something. Her mother was "brilliant, always dressed up, looked wonderful, even at our poorest." And she was tough, "a steel fist in a velvet glove." Daddy was handsome, charming, debonair, and a manic-depressive.

LaVon said she had married at eighteen to get away from home, thinking "that was all there was." She seemed content and at peace when we talked in late 2004—mourning Jimmy, but at peace.

Willie Beyer

Willie Beyer was raised on a farm a few miles north of Weimar, one of eight children. His parents "didn't have no place," Willie said. "They just rented from another guy." All ten members of the Beyer family worked for their landlord, doing "whatever the boss needed done." Willie said, "The landlord raised cotton, and we just done the pickin' for him—we'd haul hay for him and all that." All eight kids went to school in Weimar: "We had to pay for the bus at that time, a quarter a day, I believe, twenty-five cents." Willie stayed in school till the sixth grade, when he had to quit "to help Mama and Daddy on the farm—and done that for twelve years anyway.

"My family didn't have hardly nothin'," Willie continued, "and I never did keep my money neither. It all went to Mama and Daddy all the time. They might give us a little out of it, but that was *it*. We very seldom went to town—we was workin' too hard." It was a really hard life, feeding ten people on meager earnings. "Once in a while I'd go to town, wash a car for a quarter. It was *hard* that way," Willie said.

Willie eventually married, started a family, had eight children, and "stayed in Weimar all my life." He bartended at the Borden Store (the Poor Man's Country Club) for several years. "I *liked* it over there," he said. "I just like the boss lady and the boss man [LaVon and Jimmy Simpson]. They treat me nice!" Willie, in his turn, treated the customers "nice." He was always smiling, friendly, and willing. Years after the Simpsons had left, Willie mourned that the place had lost its friendliness and warmth when it lost the Simpsons.

Willie disappeared from the Borden Store one ordinary spring day. When I asked where he'd gone, Jimmy said that a blonde in a convertible had driven up and "just gone off with him." Willie did reappear, but only after quite a long time.

I lost track of Willie for several years after the Borden Store changed hands, but I finally found him in 1999, searching through his old friend and former "boss man," Jimmy Simpson. I encountered Willie at the Weimar Tavern, a family-type beer hall, soda hall, and pool hall. He seemed to be his old self, as friendly as ever. He said he'd come back home when his wife died, and he was thoroughly busy parenting his teenage children. And, he said, he was tired, tired, tired—"takin' care of the little ones." What else was going on? "The same old shit," he replied laconically. And what he had learned from his adventure with the mysterious blonde? Willie smiled a weak smile, sighed, and answered with two words, "A lot." He looked tired as he said it.

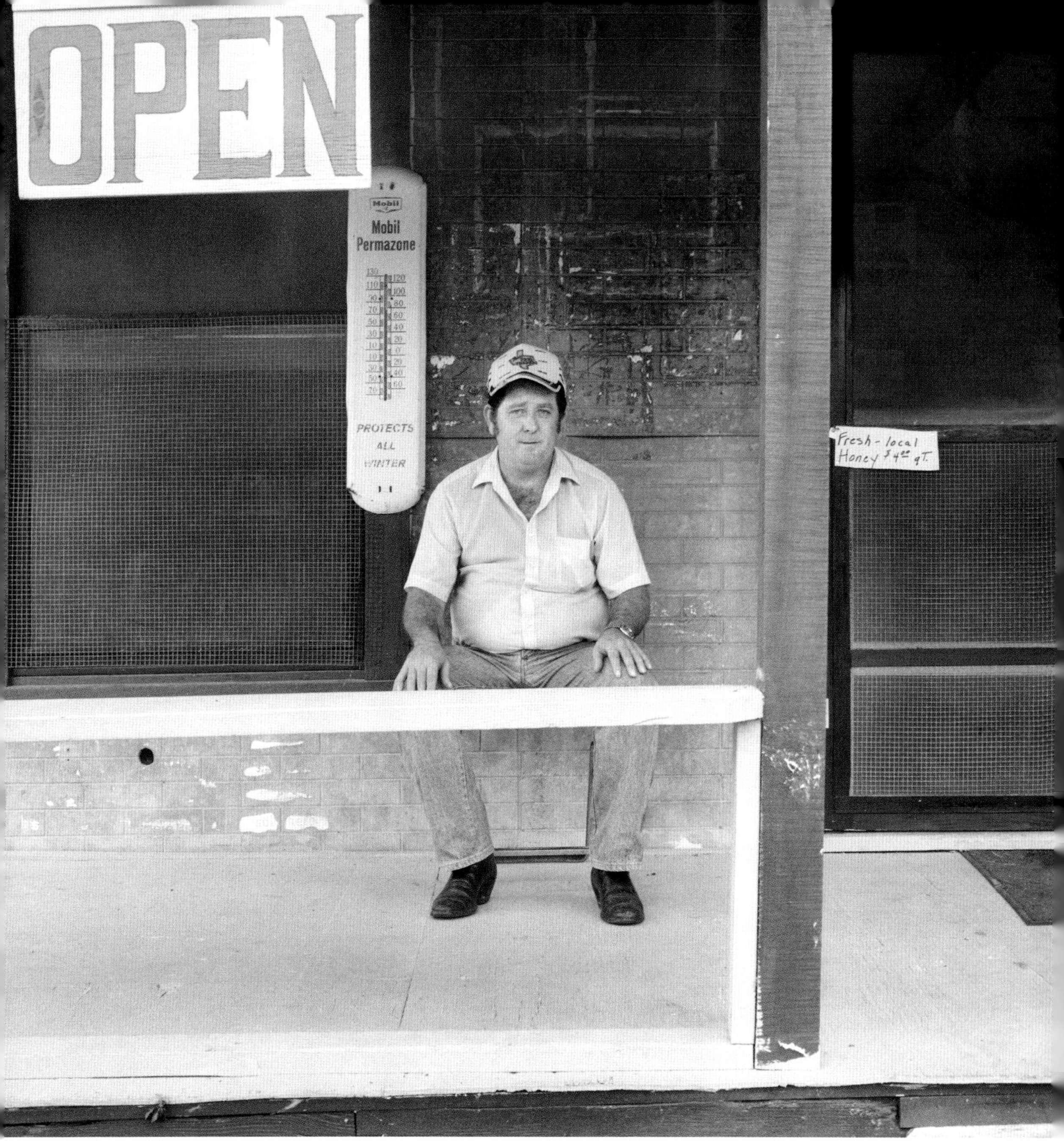

Willie Beyer at the Poor Man's Country Club

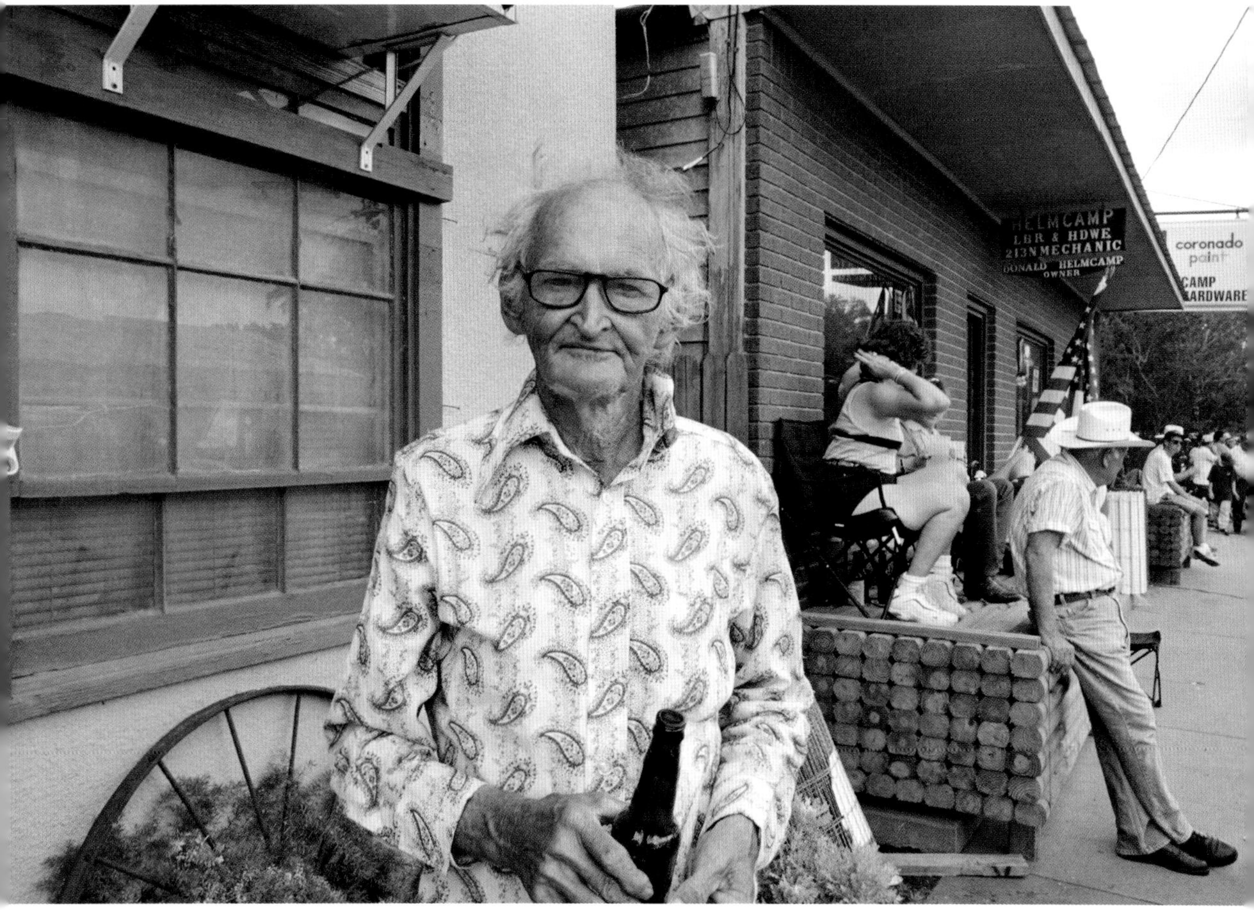

Willie Walchar at the Weimar Tavern

Willie Walchar

Right off after we met at the Poor Man's Country Club, Willie Walchar declared, "I'm not a talker. I'm not a man like to talk. I'm a worker, like to work. I'm Weimar, born this side of Weimar, right near roadside market. Moved all over the country, then finally I lived south side of Weimar."

"I'm sixty-one—I'll be sixty-two. Family from Weimar, all farmers." He was born February 10, 1930.

Willie ran Willie's Grocery for years. "Goin' on eleventh year, Willie's Grocery. Old-time store. Old store. Old-fashioned, right? I keep it original, right? Original place. I'm there six days, but sometime I come there early the next morning, work around, get things in order. Good worker. Right! Good worker. I worked in stores a lot. I worked in stores, had three bosses. Goin' out of business today. Competition too great—don't have the buyin' power—too competitive. And money's short. Gettin' shorter all the time.

"Stayed in school till eleventh grade. Went in the service for two years. 'Round 1951, '52, Korean conflict, Germany. I was in the artillery."

Asked if he would change any part of his life if he could he do it over, he replied, "I wouldn't change it for nothin' in the world. I learn step by step. I been around a lot of old people. The way I learn, I learn from old people. Step by step, not by leaps and bounds. I wouldn't change nothin'!"

When asked what was his best time, he said, in his own staccato, understated way, "Grocery store was all right. Gotta have teamwork. If you don't have teamwork, you're lost."

His worst time was "when the store burned—worked many days cleanin' it up." Willie's Grocery had been destroyed in a mysterious fire whose cause was never found.

Willie disappeared from sight when the Borden Store, his old hangout, changed hands and Jimmy Simpson left town. It was several years before Willie reappeared. Whenever I called the sister he lived with, she said he was at the Weimar Tavern. That was where he spent most of his time, and that was where I finally found him. That is where you can see him in this photograph, as he posed on the sidewalk in front of the tavern.

Bud Greak

Bud had a surname, Greak, but everyone called him "Bud," just "Bud"—no last name, no formal first name.

Bud lived alone somewhere between Weimar and Columbus, and he neither owned nor drove a car. He simply walked where he needed to go or depended on the kindness of friends for rides. To see people walking the back roads into town is not that unusual around Colorado County. There was another man from the same area who walked regularly between Borden and Weimar, a distance of ten or more miles.

Bud was standoffish at first—he just stared at me with a wary look. He refused to have his picture taken, but he later agreed, signaling his distaste for the process by a determined silence. Yet when I found that the negative was scratched and had to go back to him again, Bud shook his head no. So I gave up the idea of ever photographing him, until the day he followed me to the car, offered to carry the camera case, and said in a grouchy voice, "Okay! Go ahead, do it!" We became friends and, from that time on, got along fine. He called me his girlfriend.

Bud could be found most every day at the Borden Store. That's where Bud found friendship and kindness.

Bud entered a nursing home in 1994 and died in 2001. His funeral was held at a funeral home in Weimar. The preacher at the funeral admitted he had never met Bud, but he did have some stories from Bud's relatives. He knew that Bud was born in 1919 and named Leroy and that he had lived with his mother until she died in the 1970s. The preacher also knew that Bud had lived alone after that, until he broke his hip walking to Weimar and entered the nursing home. He had never married, never driven, and never held full-time work. He had only done occasional jobs for people, things like picking turnips. He had worked for Jimmy and LaVon Simpson over the years, at the Borden Store, doing various tasks for food, friendship, and some pay. His routine pleasure was visiting the Borden Store, Mary Barta's café in Weimar, or Kasper's Meat Market—all three popular hangouts—or he would visit the domino games at the Weimar Tavern. The preacher described Bud as "a generous soul that others sometimes took advantage of."

Many years later, a friend told a story that helped explain Bud's wariness and eccentricity. He said that when Bud was a youngster, his father had swung him by the heels and slammed the child's head into the barn wall in a fit of rage. The story may be unfounded, yet it would explain a lot if it were true.

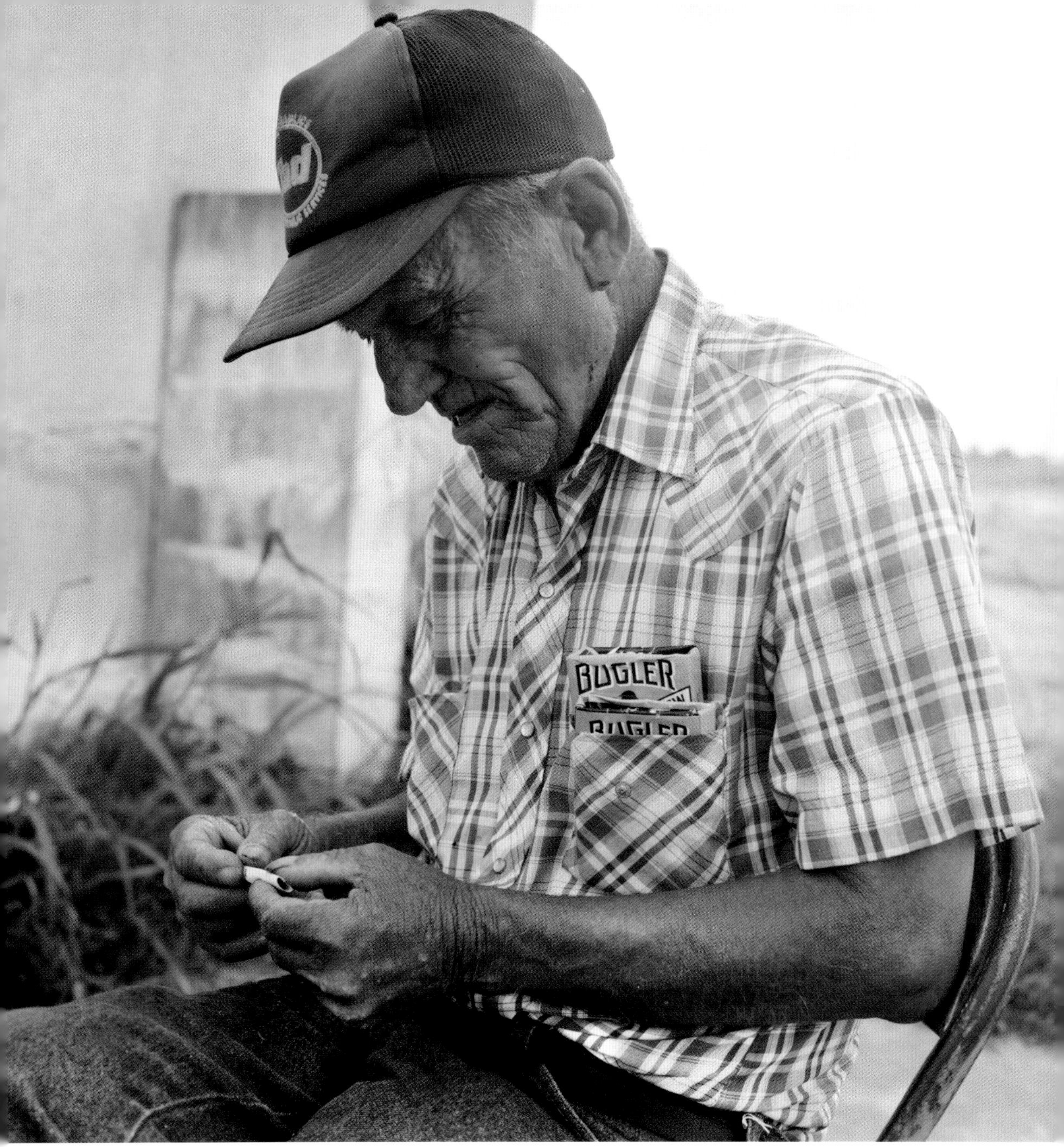

Bud Greak, rolling his own

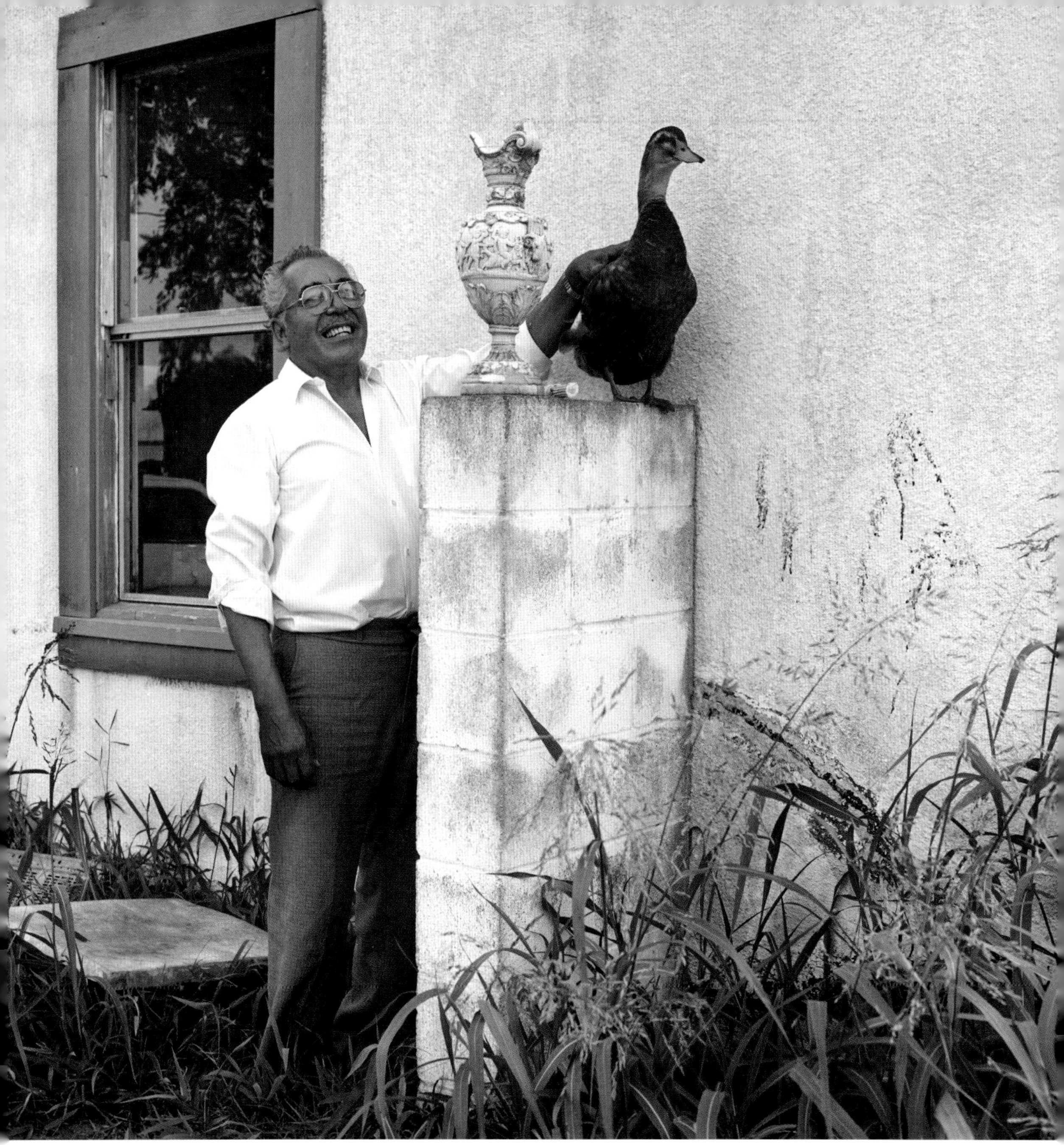

Isabel Garcia and his duck, Pasquale

Isabel M. Garcia

Isabel Garcia was born in 1920 in San Patricio County, near Mathis, Texas, down near the border with Mexico. His grandfather had been a policeman in his small hometown in Mexico, General Terán, in the state of Nuevo León. Isabel's father, Segundo, also was born there in 1880. In 1905, Segundo "come across the river in a little rowboat" to Texas. "It cost him one dime," said Isabel. In time, Segundo brought over his wife, his widowed mama, and his siblings and began a family of his own. His first wife died in childbirth, and in 1918 he married Isabel's mother. Segundo "began ramblin' around the cotton fields" as a migrant farmer until he settled down to sharecropping in 1931. "I only got through third grade," Isabel said, "cause Daddy was always movin' around, searchin' out work." Eventually, the family moved to McAllen, in South Texas, where the older man stayed and began work as a grocer.

What a familiar story this is, and how many times it has been repeated. Most of the older rural people never made it past third or fourth grade, because they were too important to their families working as extra hands in the fields, or their families were too poor to pay for the children's school clothes and textbooks.

When Isabel enlisted in the U.S. Army in 1940, he became a private first class in six months and served in the First Cavalry Division. He was good with horses, he said, and he was a good squad leader. He served with his division in Australia and the islands north of there, hunting for the Japanese in the New Guinea Campaign.

But he recalled that when promotions were awarded at the rest camp following the fighting, he was stunned to find himself overlooked and unrewarded. In his words, "thieves, deserters, and all kinds of bad types" were given promotions while he, who "never missed a day, never had a bad day" in the service, was excluded. "The commanding officers were prej'diced!" he said angrily. And he left the army with a nervous breakdown and a deep resentment.

"There was a *lot* of prej'dice round Texas, when I was growin' up—'no Mex'cans allowed,' you know? I heard my commandin' officer say he didn't want 'no Indian or goddamned Mex'cans for NCOs! How'd you like that?"

Isabel moved to Colorado County with his ex-wife (one could say "one of his exwives," since he had been married three times . . . and expressed the hope of marrying again). He was living in the former Lakeside Inn, a For Sale sign always taped to the front door, and two or three dead cars and a boat or two "adrift" in the front yard. His sister, Marcela Llaverino, lived a half-mile away in Borden, in a mustard yellow house by the railroad track. I know the house because my father used to tell me about a man who once lived there who was reputed to be a witch and who was said to cure any kind of sickness with his magic.

Pasquale, the duck Garcia was holding in the picture, was a mallard that lived wild in the lake next door and came to his human friend when called by name.

One of the special things about visiting Isabel Garcia—besides the fact he was almost always there and ready to visit—was his garden. With any rain at all, it was lush and brimming with roses, bananas, apples, tomatoes, peaches, pecans, beets, chile pequíns (tiny hot peppers), cactus plants, jalapeños, greens, and heaven knows what else. Much depends on the drought conditions, of course. For many local folks, water is in such short supply that when it rains they have a garden, and when it doesn't, they don't. And when it was there, Isabel's garden was special. He tended both his plants and his duck lovingly.

In early 2001, Isabel called me with two important facts. One was that he might move to Michigan to join his daughter, a sergeant in the army.* The other was that he had given Pasquale away to a friend (who probably ate him) because the little creature had begun to think that the lake, a public picnic site, was *his* lake, and he was getting mean with people who stopped there to fish or picnic. Isabel did move away in the early summer of 2001. The Lakeside Inn remained, the "For Sale" sign on the door. Unhappy in the city and lonely for his life in Colorado County, he came home in 2003.

*His daughter, Diane Garcia, featured in a story in the Weimar paper, was serving in Iraq in 2004.

Mamie Johnson

"Well, my name is Mamie, but some people call me Mother Mamie. I was born Mamie Small, and I been Mamie Johnson now for seventy-four years—I was married that long ago. And this is my hometown. I was born here in 1896, and I been here practically ever since. Ninety-five years and six months old now.

"My children and most people that don't call me Miss Mamie, calls me Mim. And all my closest friends call me Mim, and them that don't call me Mim, call me Mama or Mother Johnson. So I told 'em, I got so many children—like 'the old lady who lived in the shoe, had so many children, she didn't know what to do,'" and she laughed at the thought of this. "I'm the mother of Weimar almost because I don't think there's but mighty few people livin' that were born in Weimar like me, 'cause I was born in 1896, and Weimar just become in the nineteen hundreds."

Mamie Johnson told wonderful stories. She had a gift for drama, humor, and color—and her life held all three. At ninety-five, she still had total recall, a quick wit, and an eloquent tongue.

She lived alone for many years in a tiny house in Weimar, from 1937 till her death in late 1995, visited most weekends by her only living son, Clarence, who came from Houston on the bus. Her house had been rented to her by her employer for her use during her lifetime, "for the kindness I did toward his mother when he was gone, and his mother's house caught afire, and after they put out the fire, everybody left her there and wasn't nobody there. Well, I stayed there till he come back. I didn't leave her there by herself, because she had been very nice to me when I worked for them, always nice to me. I been workin' in their family since 1914. So when he bought the place I was livin', I went by his office and said, 'Well, you done bought me out of house and home.' Well, he said, 'No, I want to talk to you about it. Mamie, why don't you move up there to my house? That be your home long as you want to stay there,' and I said, 'Oh, you might charge too much rent.' And he said, 'How much rent here you payin'?' I was payin' four dollars a month—now, you know 'bout how long *that's* been! And he said, 'Well, you move on up there and we just keep a dollar off a week for your wash money, and then it won't seem like you payin' *no* rent!' So that's what I did. So I been here ever since '32.

"But there's a problem," she said, laughing. "It looks like to me I'm gonna outlive the house." As we sat in her living room talking one rainy day, water dripping onto our heads, I knew she was right—she might actually outlive the house. "They gonna have to put a roof on *me,* instead of the house!" she joked.

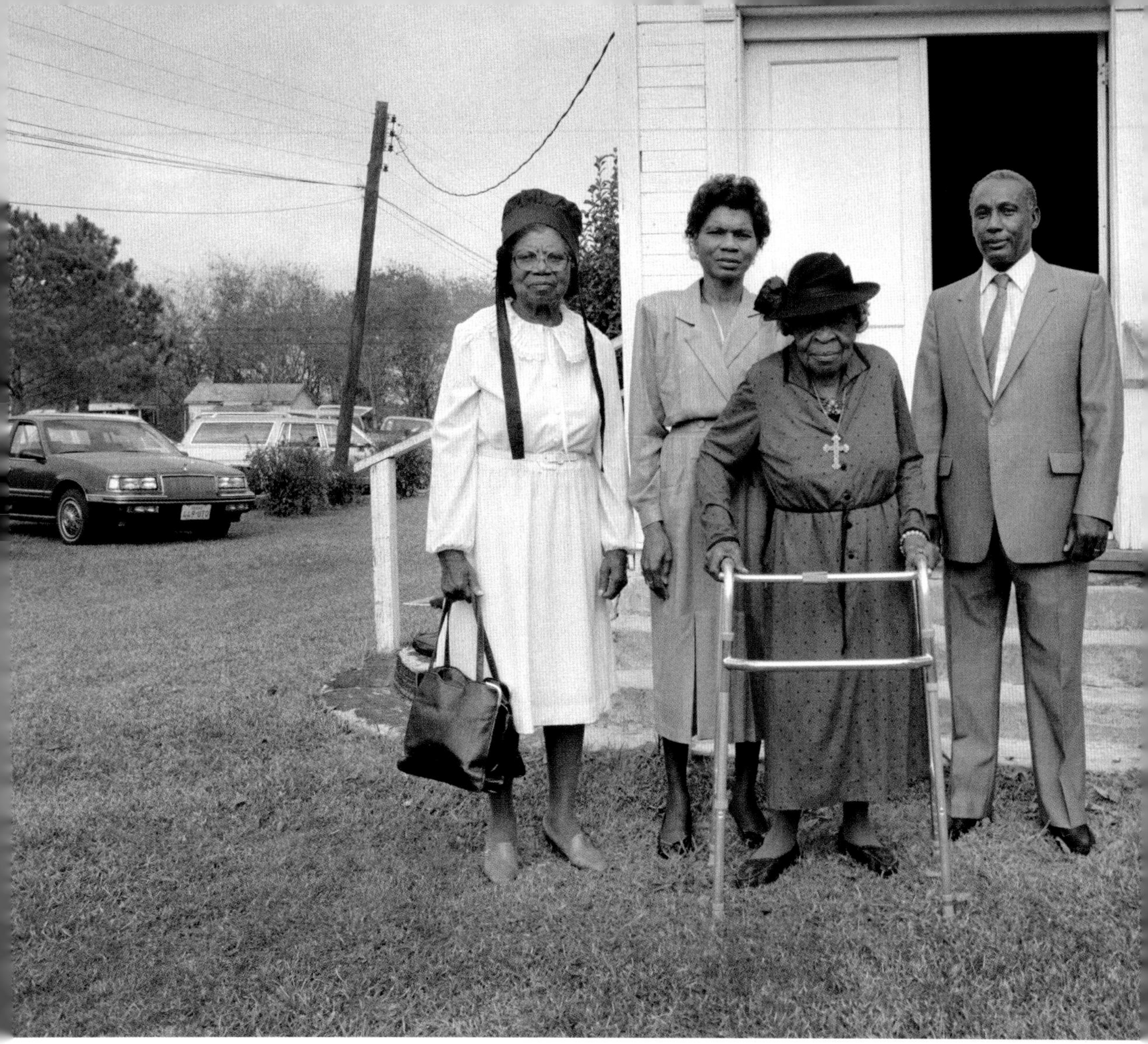

Mamie Johnson *(with walker)* and friends at St. James AME Church

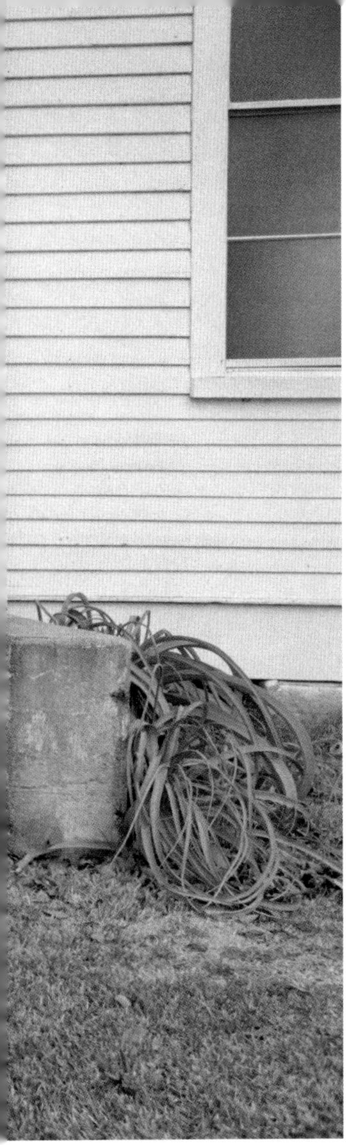

I first met Mamie at her home, led to her by her across-the-street neighbor, Lillie Atkinson (who had in turn been referred to me by Jack Johnson, her grade-school pupil from many years before). That first day, Mamie was dressed in her house robe and slippers, seated in her favorite spot, a huge ejecting chair, which dwarfed her small frame but served the purpose of tilting her up onto her feet when she needed to stand. She was in her mid-nineties.

To see her again on the way to church, dressed in an eye-catching crimson dress, with a broach, a broad-brimmed red hat, and a wig, I was struck dumb. She looked stunning. "Are you out to catch a man?" I asked suspiciously. "Now, what would *I* do with a man?" she replied, flashing the coquettish smile of a young girl.

Mamie was still active in her church, St. James AME (African Methodist Episcopal). She sang in the choir, in spite of her advanced age, and still received compliments on her voice. When she had been a member there for seventy-three years, St. James honored her with a program and a eulogy calling her "the Anchor of the Community and the Church." She had become the oldest member of the oldest church in Colorado County. What's more, she had made every church conference for sixty-three years. "So I'm pretty well known in the church, 'cause they made me the 'Mother of the Conference' that I belong to, Mother of the Southwest Conference. I'm the only layman that the bishop has to speak in the annual conference. And I speak just like I'm talkin'. I don't get up with no whole lot of what somebody else said and all like that. Just what comes to me. Daily, I make speeches to myself, and I made so many to myself until I go to bed at night, I dream that I'm at a place makin' a speech, and when I wake up, I don't have no shoes on and don't have no wig on! Just dreamin'," she said. "You're an inspiration to us," people would tell her. And she was an inspiration—through her spirit, her humor, and her devotion, resiliency, and faith.

"That's been my whole life—my church," Mamie said. "I tell people there are addicts to dope, and addicts to heroin, and addicts to whiskey—I'm a church addict. I go to church *any chance I get,*" she smiled.

"I belong to St. James African Methodist Episcopal Church, the first church that was ever built in Colorado County. I been knowin' it since 1904, but I been a member of it seventy-six years. I joined the church in 1916, and, of course I been there ever since. I started from Sexton. I rang the bell and cleaned the church. And after that, I served in every other office we've had—class leader, steward, stewardess. I'm the oldest steward there. President of the choir. And then I sang in the choir till I got sort of crippled like, so my pastor told me I didn't need to go in the choir anymore." She served as president of the senior choir, member of the steward board and the trustee board, class leader, church treasurer, and Sunday school superintendent at different times.

"That's my joy, is singin'," Mamie said. "I think I was *born* for that purpose, 'cause I remember singin' when I was about nine years old. My comfort at home is singin'. When I gets lonesome, then I sing to revive myself, and then I do all right. I just sing from one song to another until I get revived." And she sang, "I trust in God, wherever He may be . . ."

After singing, she said, "There are three things I don't get tired of—eat, sing, or talk. I sang once over the radio, but other than that, I just sing naturally with the congregation as a soloist. Or I just sing when I feel like singin'. And that's all the time!"

Mamie also talked about her family: "See, ole man Laas, they come to Texas after slavery, landed in Oakland. My grandmother was workin' for 'em as a slave, and she came with him. My grandmother was the slave mother of the boss man, the boss people that I worked for. His wife died, and my grandmother raised those children then, until he married a second time. So she was a slave mother, you see, the only mother he had till he married again. And I worked for them until they all dead. And there's just one in that family, and that's Miz Massey. My father worked for 'em, my son worked, my brother worked for 'em, my mother worked for 'em, and I started workin' in the family in 1914. Worked for the grandparents, then the parents, then for the granddaughter, then for the great-granddaughter. All the people I worked for is gone. One of them said one day, out at the cemetery, says, 'Mamie, you *always* with us.' Always sit with 'em at funerals, just like family. Been with 'em so long, so one of 'em says, 'Yes, and Mamie will bury us all.' And it seems like I have—I'm still here." She chuckled.

Mamie was orphaned as a young girl. Her father, John Small, died in 1900. Then her mother, Mattie Walder Small, died of pneumonia in 1905. Mattie was a laundress for the Brasher family, "people used to have the Buick company here," and she walked several miles to work each day. Mamie said that that one day "it come up a real cold spell, and come up a freeze, and the wash froze on the line." Her mother "got too cold up there" and got sick with pneumonia, "never did get over it," and died, leaving six small children. The youngsters were split up among relatives. Little Mamie was chosen to go to a childless cousin in Waelder, and there her troubles began.

"I was the Joseph in the family," she said. "Like Joseph, I was sent away.

"So my mother died in 1905. And when my cousin came down from Waelder, now, she didn't have any children and she wanted to take one of us. Well, I happened to be the Joseph in the family because I was too young to take care of my younger sister, and so I was the one they give away. So I went, and I stayed two years. She was a very 'temperfied' kind of person. She didn't know 'bout children, didn't know how to raise children. She raised children like she did stock in the yard or somethin'. I stayed with her two years. She had me to do everythin'—scrub floors, wash, and everythin'! And if I didn't do that she wanted done, then my little body had to pay for it. She used to whip me like she would whip a grown-up person. I don't know if she wasn't used to children—she'd never had children or knowed one, so she expected more of a child. So the least little thing, don't know nothin' else to do to a child when he didn't do what you said but whup 'em, I reckon. So that's what she would do to me. That was my worst years, after my mother died, the two years up there.

"I was raised by people who don't care about me. I hated it." It was hard work in a harsh world, something young Mamie had never known before. "That was the hardest time of my life," she said. "She'd whup me, she'd carry my dress over my head, with my arms in it, and then she would tie 'em up over my head, and that's the way she would whup me—just nothin' on me. She'd whup this body. Naked—just my panties on. With a quirt, like you quirt horses with. I was blindfolded—I couldn't see which way I was goin'. And I just bounced around on the floor. I couldn't see; I couldn't fight off the beats or nothin'. I still got a quirt mark on my leg where she hit me. Finally the last time she whipped me like that, I fell off the porch, all blindfolded and everything. I tumbled out of the door onto the back porch, and she pushed me offa the porch. But after that, I think she got scared. She never did whip me like that again.

"The hardest is I just didn't think that she should've had to hit me like that. 'Cause I was nothin' but a kid, eight or nine years old. What could a kid do so bad to get whupped like that?

"I was the one they give away," she repeated. "That's why I say I was the Joseph in the family. Like Joseph, I was sent away. Course, they *sold* Joseph. They didn't sell me. They just *give* me away," and she laughed.

"I joined the church at fifteen, where the older people took care of me, and so I made it up to now," she continued. "That's been my whole life—the church. See, I didn't have any parents, and the older people, they seen that, and they helped me. Looks like they knew that I wanted to make somethin' of my life. They were pretty good to me until I got to where I could help myself. The older people knew my parents, and when I joined the church, I stayed around older people most of the time, and they lifted me! They just put their arms around me—they knowed that I was tryin' to make good in church.

"I was very tenderhearted, but I had to get out of it. After I got grown, I decided I wasn't gonna cry no more—started prayin' instead of cryin'. So my life has been pretty rugged, the first of it, but the last sixty years I've had real experience in my life," she said as she smiled. "My nature is to never hit back, but I always come out in the lead. Never did want to hurt nobody. And if they did anything towards hurtin' me, well, I'd just cry—I was near growed before I stopped cryin'. After then, my life began to get shaped up better. So the last fifty years have been *beautiful*.

"I just went to school until I was a fifth-grade scholar. But after I got into the church, I learned from others, goin' among people who knowed more than I did. I would listen and associate with ministers and laypeople who were educated. That's how I got my education and my learnin'." At ninety-eight, Mamie still read the *Weimar Mercury* regularly, so she could know "who did what to who, and who got caught doin' it."

Mamie then described her married life: "I married in 1916. I had a little girl. My baby girl died. She was one year, four months, and sixteen days old, my little girl was. Just beginnin' to walk and talk," she sighed. "And then I had three sons. So after I had those three boys, I figured that was enough for Uncle Sam, so I told him I didn't want any more."

Her husband, Jesse Johnson, "was born in a place down there called Borden," Mamie said. "His mother and my mother was just like two sisters, and it was funny that I have to marry one of her sons, so they both have the same grandchildren. He was raised without his parents, raised 'from here to there.' So he always liked to be *somewhere*—couldn't get used to family life. And so we disagreed about that. We didn't lose our friendship—we just stayed apart. He just didn't have the idea of being a good husband. He just didn't know what it meant. So he was a good fellow, but he wasn't a husband type.

"His uncles, they were farmers, and once they come to visit us, and said, 'Jesse, you ought to come and farm with us.' He said, 'Well, Uncle, I tell you, I just couldn't do that because I think too much of the good Lord's soil to dig it up like that. I just couldn't do it!'" And Mamie laughed.

"And so we didn't have no up-to-do, but he wanted to go to San Antonio. When he died, I went up there and buried him and left him there. That's where he wanted to be, so I left him there.

"I loved him so much when I married him, I coulda eaten him—but three or four years after that, I wished I had! I didn't understand marriage, and he didn't understand family life. He didn't drink and carouse—a very peaceful kind of person, but he just couldn't get used to family life—said his constitution wasn't quite strong enough.

"I raised my three sons here alone. My husband, he decided he wanted to go to the city to live, but I figured the city wasn't no place for me with three children and no job, and I didn't go with him up there. After my husband said he wanted to go to San Antonio, that's the way I got rid of him. So we still was good friends with each other, but I just didn't go up there to stay. After that, I prayed and prayed.

"My minister talked to me, 'There's no need of you givin' up. You just pray.' And that's what I did. Come from work, got on my knees, and I prayed and prayed. And just like I'm talkin' to you now, seems like somebody says, 'Take this world as you find it, and do your prayin'. And from that day on, I've been goin' up the ladder. And I went 'bout as far as I could reach, and then the Lord brought me back down to earth. And so finally I just come to it in my life that I felt like I wasn't gonna be worried about nobody but me and my children.

"And I've worked for most all of the older citizens here, and they all about gone and left me here—still here. So I guess he leave me here for some purpose, I don't know. But I'm not in a hurry to leave, so I don't worry about it. I quit work when I was ninety years old. At that time I was sick. Bakin' pies for my church and sellin' the *San Antonio Register.* And a few months ago the *Register* was sixty years old. And I was the only one they could find on record that sold it when it started out. They had a big write-up in the paper about it, and all of that. Did laundry work for most people. I just done home laundry, men's shirts." Of the daughter of one family she washed for, she said, "I was the first colored face she seen."

Mamie always sat in the family pew at her employers' funerals—"They were *all* like family to me." When one of the older members of the Laas family died, the granddaughter came from Columbus to see Mamie. "Held hands and shed tears to think I'd been in the family so long, and we were the only ones left," Mamie said.

"All of my comrades, all of my schoolmates, all of my church mates that come up with me—all of 'em is gone but me," she said. "So I don't know whether there's somethin' he want me to do, or somethin' I haven't done, and he's probably givin' me time to do it. I don't know what it is. So I'm not questionin' nobody. I'm just leanin' on out for it!

"Taken pretty good care of myself when I was comin' up. Worked pretty hard, but I didn't drink, didn't care 'bout smokin'—only thing I used to love was dance and go to ball games and stuff like that. I used to rather dance and eat fried chicken.

"They ask me how I'm doin', I tell 'em, 'Well, I'm doin' fine. I don't have heart trouble, I don't have high blood pressure, I haven't never been on a diet.' I told 'em, 'I'm like an old car: the motor's tickin', the body's in good shape . . . just got bad axles and flat tires.'

"Yeah, I'm that old, but when I'm in church, I don't feel old. So if anybody asks you how I am, you just tell 'em I'm hoppin', but I ain't stoppin'. That's the way I amuse myself. See, I don't pity myself. That's the wrong thing to do when you get old—sit around and pity yourself and worry about what you used to do. 'Cause Lord knows, some things I used to have to do, I'm glad I don't have to do no more.

"I pray for myself and for the nation. Pray for everybody. And I thank the Lord for bringin' me this far, through all I had to go through by myself, because all my other people are dead. I've worked for most all of the older citizens here, and they all 'bout gone. So I guess they leave me here for some purpose, I don't know, but I'm not in a hurry to leave, so I don't worry about that.

"Church, children, and friends are what I lives for now. Like the old lady who lived in the shoe, they're *all* my children. If it hadn't been for the older people in church to bear me up when I was young and alone, I don't know what would have happened to me. Only them to bear me up." So Mamie was returning the gift in kind many years later.

"I tells people now, if you want to do somethin', first you have to want to be. You got to do somethin', know somethin', go somewhere, and you'll learn somethin' or get somethin'. So you have to determine that for yourself 'cause anybody hear me talk at an annual conference to two or three hundred people wouldn't think I just went no further than fifth grade in school. I never did get to go to school no more after 1912."

Mamie Johnson died in her sleep in early 1996, in a nursing home in nearby Schulenburg.

As I left Mamie in the nursing home in December 1995, having given her a copy of the video she was in, thoughts came up about her words when she had said, "The Lord still takin' care of me 'cause I still here by myself. He leavin' me here for somethin', I don't know what. So I told him, 'Whatever you've left me here to do, tell me,' and I was gonna do it." She didn't know why God had 'left her here so long,' and I wondered if talking in the video might be 'the thing she had left undone,' and perhaps her life would now feel complete. Clarence called three days later to say she had passed on.

"She was faithful to her church till the end," her funeral bulletin read. Her friends, the Nelsons, wrote in the Weimar paper that she was "spirit filled" and "among the Heroes of Faith." They described how she used to make such a grand entrance into church, wearing her vermilion outfit. Yes, indeed!

Wouldn't it be great to be like Mamie in old age and be able to say, "The last fifty years have been beautiful"?

Clarence Johnson

Clarence Johnson was Mamie Johnson's youngest son and was often at Mamie's house when I dropped by to see her. He came regularly to Weimar by bus from his home in Houston to check on Mamie. Yet it was some time before I got to know Clarence, separate and apart from Mamie. She was so dynamic and verbal that Clarence always gave her the floor—everyone gave Mamie the floor.

Clarence was one of three sons born to Mamie. And he was the only one to stay with her when their father moved to San Antonio, leaving part of his family in Weimar. "We was livin' in town," Clarence said, "where you came to. My mother and me, we got along. We had to get along—my father had left when I was seven or eight years old. Then my oldest brothers put their age up and went to San Antonio to work, leavin' me there. My mother did washin' and ironin', gettin' about a dollar and a half a day. I worked too and had to buy all my own school clothes—didn't have a suit for years."

Mamie said, "Me and those three sons, we stayed together, all for one and one for all. I never had no trouble with 'em. I taught 'em. I used a little strap on 'em, but I didn't abuse 'em. I'd tell 'em, I did it 'cause I love you, and other people won't love you if you're bad and contrary and getting' into somethin'."

She continued, "That's my prayer since then, for the Lord to let me live to see them grown. And he did. I was sick twice—said I was gonna die. I just told the Lord that if it was his will to take *me,* to just leave my chil'ren in the hands of someone that would take 'em and not have 'em to come up like I did. That's all I said to him—and I'm still here. So he let me live to see my chil'ren and gran'chil'ren grown and to see great-gran'chil'ren."

Clarence described his eventual, short-lived move to San Antonio: "I was about to get my diploma in Weimar, and I went to San Antonio, to Dad, to work. But my dad was takin' and cashin' my checks. I was workin' at a sort of stop-and-go, and then at Brackenridge Park, helpin' with the horses, bein' fed by a Spanish family. And my dad took my checks and I couldn't get back home—had no money. So I hitchhiked to Schulenburg. Had a big old suitcase—couldn't get another ride, so I walked from Schulenburg to Weimar. Had the feelin' my mother was sick or somethin'. I went home, and she had blood poisonin' from havin' a tooth pulled—was purty sick. So we stayed together.

"I got along with everybody, white and colored," Clarence said of his childhood. "We lived in that white neighborhood, and I was invited to the white kids' birthday parties and all that. They didn't treat me no different.

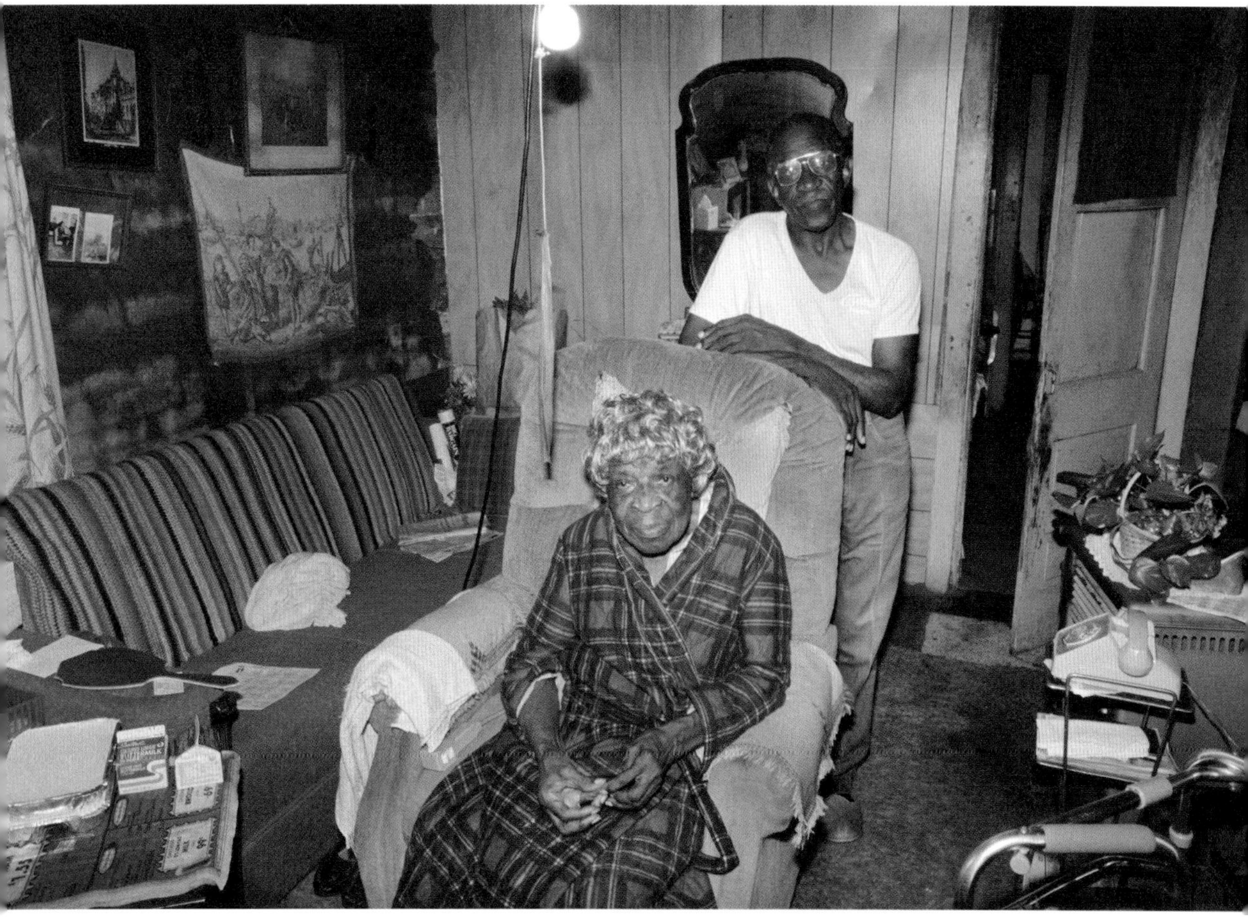

Clarence Johnson with his mother, Mamie

"Then I got married and lived in Weimar. Got sick with the ulcers, went to the VA Hospital down there in Houston. Been workin' for the Moodys. They had a Ford dealership in Weimar. They were real nice to me. I'd been makin' twenty-five or thirty dollars a week before, and they give my wife the check every week while I was laid up. Treated me *real* good."

Mamie said of Clarence, "He's a wonderful son to me. That's my whole life now, him and my oldest granddaughter. If it wasn't for them, I don't know whether my life would be as happy as it is. That's my youngest son, but he always stayed close around me, never stayed no further than Houston or San Antonio and said he could hitchhike here if I needed him."

Clarence worked at Mission Petroleum in Houston for over twenty years and was still going there to work odd jobs, years after his retirement. He remained friends with his former co-workers and one of his ex-bosses, Arch Kelly, who invited him back to work whenever he wanted. "I started back in 1969," Clarence noted. "I still work part-time for 'em. I was off 'bout two years. Then the vice-president of the company call' me to see did I want to work some. Said that I wouldn't have any bosses—I could pick what I wanted to do, leave when I want to. Whenever they have a party, they include me like a regular employee. They treat me so *nice*—tell me if I need anything to tell 'em. I'm the oldest employee there. It was a small company when I first went there. Now it goes up in Canada and all over anywhere else. At first I would work seven days a week, cleanin' the trailers; I even had to dispatch some nights. You know, when you retire and sit and do nothin', it'll get you down—you need to do *somethin'*. So I help him out and help me out too."

Clarence and his wife, Thelma, were both retired by the time we became friends, and they were struggling financially like most everyone in retirement. He kept going to Weimar now and then, even after his mother died, visiting friends.

One day he suggested I meet him at Ella's Café, a favorite haunt of his, near downtown Houston, "where the homeboys meet." The day came and Clarence was unwell, so I went alone to Ella's, housed in an unpainted, two-story wooden building, five or so blocks east of downtown—one of the type of wonderful old buildings that were being torn down in the name of "progress." Ella was totally surprised to see this stranger, until she learned I was a friend of Clarence's. Then she graciously gave me something to eat and invited me to join her for a bus trip to the casinos in Louisiana. Sadly, Ella's Café closed soon after this, before her trip to Louisiana.

Clarence told a nice story about Ella's Café. When my video, which featured Mamie, aired on Houston public television in 1996, he went to watch the program at Ella's. When the show began, the jukebox was unplugged and every person in the place turned and watched the program in rapt silence until it was over, no interruptions—an honor for Clarence that he was very proud of.

Dorothy Lain

"I'm a tough old turkey bird," said gentle Dorothy Lain, alight with a mischievous smile.

One day, several years earlier, my phone had rung and I'd heard a voice say, "You don't know me—we haven't met—but I'm calling you 'cause I saw your photographs in the Columbus library awhile ago, and I want to find out if you've done your book yet. I want to get one when it's done. And I'd also like to work with you on a project I have in mind, to get the African American and white communities together here in Columbus." This was my introduction to Dorothy Lain.

At the time, I had no intention of working on a book. Then came Dorothy's call, quickly followed by a call from another woman with the same idea. In good time, Dorothy and I met face to face, and it turned out we had a mutual friend and many interests in common. She became a treasured addition to my life. She challenged me, and other friends of Dorothy's have said she challenged them as well. In her own quiet way, both through her example and her commitment to living life with zest and spiritual energy, Dorothy asked us to act and change our lives.

One friend, who knew Dorothy for years and was once her priest, described her as genuine, loving, wise, serene, and 'godly'—"in the sense," he said, "that God is love, and she is loving." He saw her as being "tied up in the love of God" and said he admired her for "being reflective and for having allowed her mind to evolve over the years." He told about the time when Dorothy disagreed with him over the principle of "an eye for an eye." Dorothy "corrected me like a good mother," he said with a laugh, and he wondered "if God was using her as a prophet with me." Neither preachy nor self-righteous, Dorothy was instead fun, lively, and occasionally irreverent.

Born on February 2, 1925, in Detroit, Dorothy arrived in Houston as an infant. "I am a *real* Texan," she declared. She moved from Houston to Columbus in 1985, with her husband, Ernie, and their six children. By the year 2001, a slew of grandchildren plus four great-grandchildren kept Dorothy happily busy. "I wouldn't want to live anywhere else *but* in Texas and in Columbus. The people in Columbus are very, very diverse, and they're also very generous. In Columbus, if you state a need, you'll have one hundred people on your doorstep tomorrow morning to help you. The people here may fight, but they'll do anything for you."

The project she had spoken of—to help unite the black and white communities in Columbus—was never begun, as Dorothy developed serious health problems and became too weak to take on anything more. She kept busy with "whatever God put

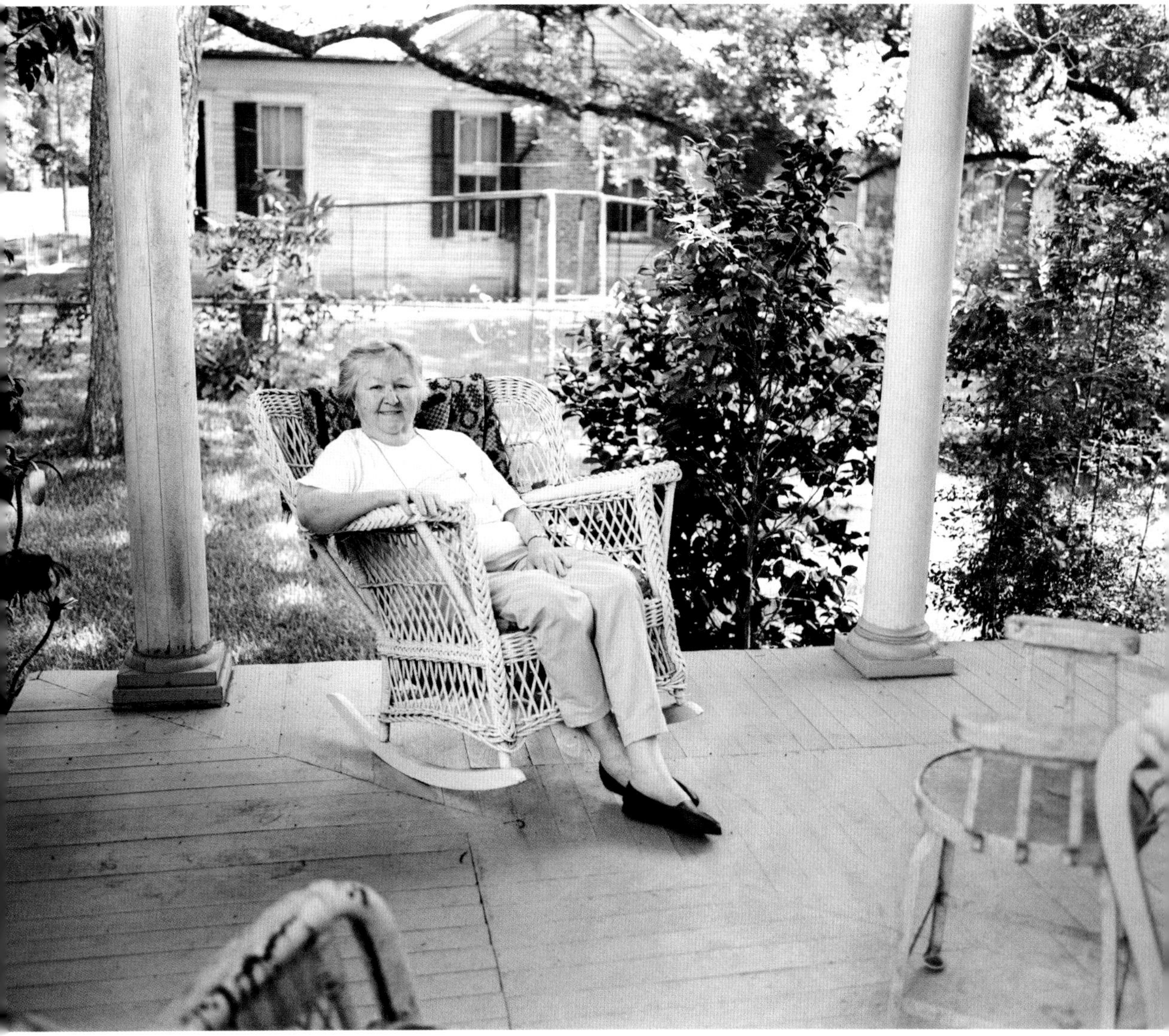

Dorothy Lain

in my path," such as participating in the Columbus Live Oak Art Center and with RATS (the Readers and Thinkers Society); visiting with friends from Houston, the "outlaws," who came to Columbus every month to spend time with her; taking care of family concerns; and reading voraciously on spiritual topics.

Her husband, Ernie Lain, had been a Rice University graduate, a member of the Cotton Bowl Hall of Fame, and a professional football player for the Washington Redskins. Dorothy could never remember the name of the team he played for, saying simply, "I'm not much for football." Ernie died in 1987, soon after their move to Columbus and right before Dorothy lost her mother. Dorothy missed Ernie deeply, yet she remained cheerfully optimistic about life. "The world is evolving, change is inevitable, and it is God-blessed," she said calmly one day, in response to the sad state of world affairs and referring also to troubles in the Catholic Church, her church for many years past, and noting its resistance to needed changes. Yet she always hoped for and anticipated positive change, even where resistance seemed greatest.

"I had to make *all* new friends here in Columbus after Ernie died. Now we're all growing old and decrepit together," she said, laughing, "but there's nothing I can't handle—I'm a tough old turkey bird!" She certainly displayed great courage during her illness. In 2001, she was in and out of a Houston hospital, until she put an end to that and came home to Columbus to take care of herself. "I fight hard for my independence," she said—another way of saying, "Leave me be!"

In mid-2002, Dorothy had a serious stroke and seemed to have little time left in her life. Yet, a few days later, she woke one morning asking for a cold drink and declaring she was not ready to die, because she still had things to do. Weeks later at her funeral, her son Wayne told of a frantic call to his sister Sarah Wiebold after their mother's stroke. Sarah, who lived nearby, rushed to Columbus, only to find her mother sitting on the couch, eating barbecue and "having a great day." A short time later, there was a second crisis. Sarah was called again and came to find Dorothy sitting up in bed and telling stories, "rejuvenated by her children's presence." Dorothy lived on, until the third stroke, when Wayne called Sarah yet again, hesitantly, saying, "I don't know—but the nurse said to call you." Dorothy died shortly thereafter. She told her kids that she was both ready to die and not ready to, that she too did not understand dying, and yet she was not afraid.

Her funeral service, which was definitely nontraditional and quite personal, was planned in large part by Dorothy herself, including the choice of the music and the musician. Robert Sanders, an African American teacher at Prairie View A&M, came to town with his keyboard, out of caring for his friend Dorothy. He told me that Dorothy had gotten his wife placed on the board of the local arts center and about how grateful they were to her for that respectful gesture.

Three of her closest friends, all former Catholic priests, spoke at the service. They described her "disregard for decorum," her wry humor, her intellect, her curiosity, and her charisma. They portrayed her as "strong and formidable," mannerly, gregarious, a lover of life, someone "firm in tradition but ready to learn from other traditions," fun-loving, godly yet "understanding of atheism," exciting, "a great friend" who was often "exalting and encouraging the other," a fighter, a "wondrous lady," and in love with Ernie, with whom "she had a harmony of thought." They called her a teacher, "theologically twelve months or more ahead" of her priest friends, a disciple, a visionary, a free thinker, and someone far ahead of her time.

One man told of losing his beloved son when the son was only in his twenties and how he went into the deepest grief. Then, he said, "Dorothy offered to carry my pain for me for a while," and when he accepted, he found himself feeling a welcome relief and a new sense of peace for that period of time. "How extraordinary," wrote her daughter Sarah of this loving gesture Dorothy had made. Sarah also wrote that Dorothy had a "special gift," in that she "really saw people as they were" and could not be fooled—a special woman indeed.

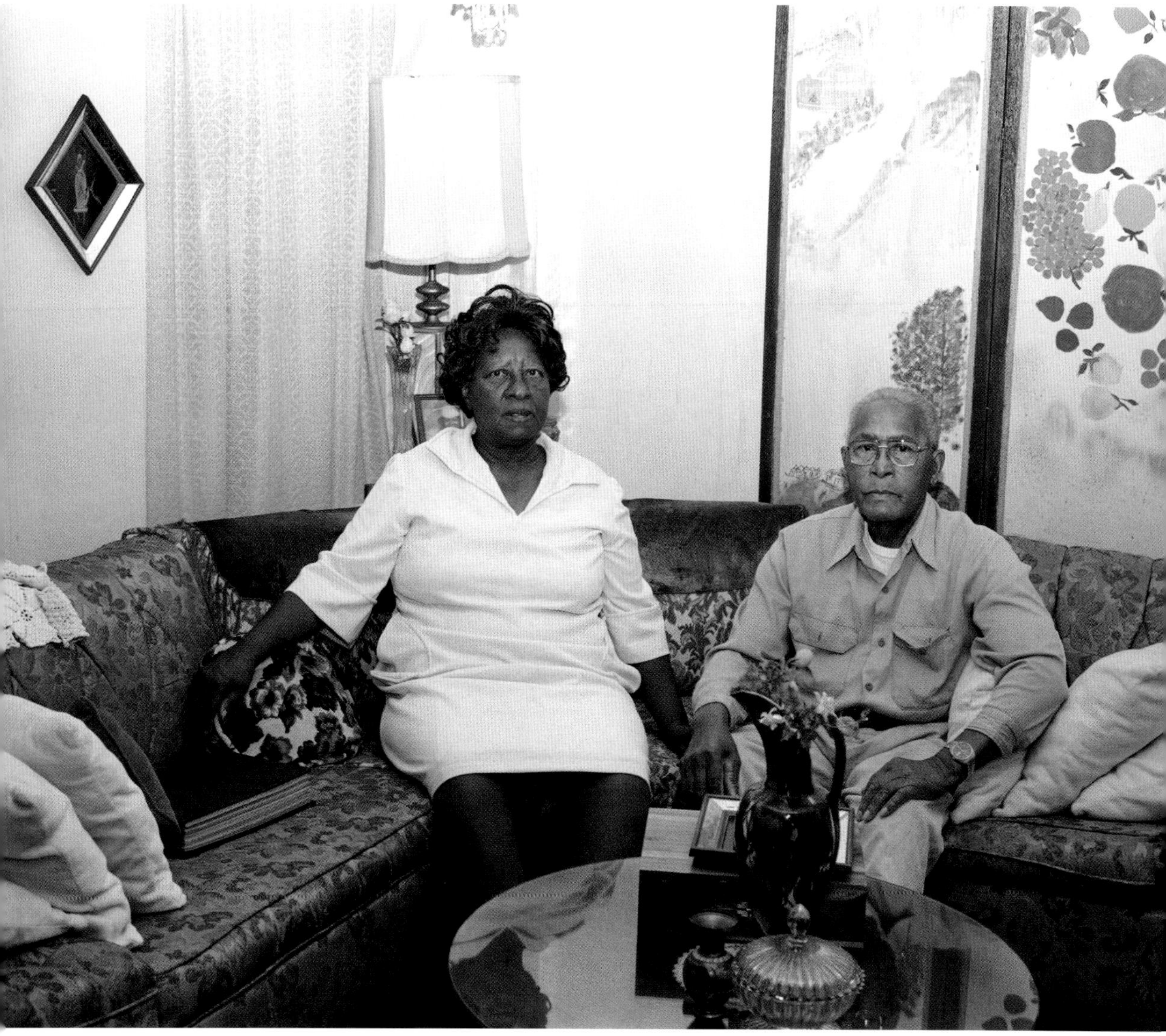

Leora and Louis Henry

Leora & Louis "Bug" Henry

I paid my first visit to Leora Henry one spring day, introducing myself and receiving a friendly welcome from her. After we'd talked a while, it was clear that Leora loved to talk. And she had her own special way of talking: dramatic, melodious, and flowing. When her husband came into the room, Leora introduced us. "He's here!" she exclaimed, her voice rising and falling musically. "This is Louis, Louis Henry. This is Oscar's brother! You heard talk about him, so and so, and so and so—well, this is *him*!" And she smiled broadly at the two of us, like a proud magician producing a dove from her sleeve.

Together, Leora and "Him" talked about their three sons, handsome and straight in the photographs that lined their living room wall. They were Louis Junior, born in 1932; Ross Herbert, 1936; and Frederick Douglas, "Fred D.," 1945. All three were working as very successful educators, as teacher, counselor, and school principal. One son was in Galveston, the other two in California.

How did the Henrys raise such accomplished and motivated sons? "Well," Leora replied, "they just *wanted* to go. They worked *hard* to go to college. And I worked *all my life*, every day. This second one here, he be a-eatin' his breakfast, sittin' there with a book beside him and readin', readin', readin' *all* the time, uuhh-huh."

Added Louis, "And my oldest one, when he was young, he'd get him a job. It was a highway going in. He was too little, and he said, 'Daddy, I'm gonna work.' I say, 'You know you ain't goin' to work on that highway. You're too small!' So he fooled around here and picked up some stuff. He sure worked—he *sure* worked!

"They finished school right here in Weimar. And then they went to Prairie View A&M. They would work in the summertime. They'd take up a broom and go earn money. They'd go there, and then be goin' in the evenin', and then take off and study. Just take a broom and get a dust cloth, and go ahead and earn you' money. And that way they could work and go to school. It *sure* did help!"

Leora continued, "But now some people say, 'Don't spank your children.' We spanked ours if they *needed* to be spanked. And I always said, 'I really spanked mine so when they're grown, nobody'd have to beat 'em.' My mama said this—she said, 'If you spank 'em yourself, when they get grown, the law and everybody won't be beatin' on 'em. You do that yourself.' Uh-huh." These words recalled a familiar refrain in the community on raising good children.

Louis, called Bug by some, was born in Port Arthur in 1911 but moved as a youngster to Colorado County. His mother was Bessie Steward, sister to Pie Steward's father.

"We had good times in the country," Lewis said. "Good water from the spring. Yes, Lord, I'm tellin' you! Got bass from the river. I was like Mama Sang's boy," he said of Lillie Williams, whose farm his family's place adjoined.

When Louis Henry was grown, he served in the navy for "one year, seven months, and three days," working as a mechanic on airplanes. After World War II, he was employed by Gulf Oil in Port Arthur and by a rubber plant in Beaumont—"hard times!" he allowed. The Henrys eventually retired to Weimar.

Louis and Leora had quite similar backgrounds as children. Leora explained it this way: "Everything went on at their house—seemed like we had the same story. And I was the youngest in my family, and he was the youngest in his mama's first family. And so and so . . . And you know how the older children—the things that he said they done to him—my sisters done the same thing to me. Uh-huh. Louis teased me sometime. He said, 'Y'all could have come over there, where we were.' See, he didn't have no brothers. And I said, 'Louis, you could've come over and seen *me* sometime, and played a brother.' We didn't know little more about one another till we started going to the high school, you know.

"Louis has made a good husband. When a child was raised without a father [as Louis was], sometime I think they make a better father their self. Because he know the things he would've liked to have had in a father, and yet they were separated."

Leora's family had no sons. "All girls," she said. "My mama had seven daughters she raised to get grown. Uh-huh. She just loved her family, her children. Loved people. He did too. The names were Marvella, Sevader, Odessa, Rodie, Dorothy, Marjorie, Leora—I'm Leora.

"I was raised right out here on the farm. It was my daddy's own farm then. It was his place, but it was Maury's property—and Daddy had bad luck. Daddy said he paid all but ninety dollars, but they took the place away from him. It was the *saddest* thing you *ever* heard of. They *took it away* from him . . ." Her voice faltered as she spoke, and she looked stricken. "I was just getting' married," she went on. "I remember, Daddy he just moved on out! He was *sad*. It was *so pitiful*. It was so pitiful 'cause he put that home first of *everything*. He never did buy a car 'cause he was payin' for his home. And it was just . . ." Her words dropped off.

"Yes, that's the hardest thing that ever did grieve me," she continued, "'cause he had told us from babies we was goin' to die and all like that, and so and so, and we had to give account of our own sins. That sometimes comes on me now, uh-huh. But I had a special father. And my mother stayed with him till death. But he was just straight and plain and stayed close by us. You *got* to stay close to these daughters—so much *development* goin' on!"

Leora told about a renter of theirs who wouldn't pay his rent and how she handled him: "I told 'im, I said, 'I'm glad to see you have a nice comfortable place here and buy you some nice chairs, but if you don't pay you' rent, you won't have nowhere to put it! Uh-uh.' I just *hate* not to talk to 'im nice. And I doesn't like to be puttin' people outdoors, 'cause I haven't had a home all my life either. You don't run 'im out, because the next one you get is worse than the next one. Isn't that funny? You just train the one you got. He's gettin' to be better. And I have to teach 'im like he's a boy! I say, my goodness!"

Leora and Louis' middle son, Ross Herbert, died in early 1991 in California, when he was only fifty-five. His parents were deeply sad and mournful whenever they talked about him—as though their grief was right on the surface. Leora had to miss his funeral because she was unwell and could not travel that far. She said softly, "It's just nice to have a man I sure did love. It's nice to say that I had a husband, and that's what my daughter-in-laws tell me. She didn't know he would pass on. And she said that was the only husband she had. She lost Ross, but she just didn't know—and that's so sad."

The Henrys lost a second son, Louis Junior, in 1998. His obituary said he had a master's degree in elementary education and had been a respected teacher and administrator for thirty-five years in the same school district, Alum Rock Union. He was also the first African American principal in that district. I never met the two men, but knowing the Henry parents and hearing their descriptions of them, I grieved too.

I asked Leora to talk about relations between the races and about the accounts I had heard of the 1935 lynching in Columbus. She readily replied, "I don't talk about *nothin'.* But I sure listen.

"I listen to what went on there," she continued. "Now, there's been some things that wasn't right, things that I heard went on, and maybe it was in Columbus. And that was more ignorance than it was being mean! And—now listen what I'm gonna tell you. Like in your home, your parents taught you things you thought was right, didn't you? Well, mine taught me. Other people, they didn't know no way for a person to be punished without hangin' 'em and killin' 'em. And now they're sorry."

She whispered softly, bending closer, "And I don't like to bring it up. I don't like talkin' about it 'cause I have lived long enough, and I will work with some of the people they said was in there [at the lynching]. But I never complained, 'cause we wasn't supposed to talk out of our home.

"But you know I lived face-to-face with some of those people that was in those rackets? And I didn't tell 'em. I wasn't ever supposed to work for 'em. I made out, but I make an honest livin'. And you don't hold nothin' against nobody you don't know nothin about. You can't. And they have talked to me concernin' the things, concernin' what happened. They *grieved* about it. They worried about it. They took that to their grave.

"For doing that thing, they grieved about it, but they didn't know any better, uh-uh. And they sure did treat me nice. They was better to me than *anybody,* because they know. They have learned, and they changed. It was tough, but when they changed, they know so much better how to treat me, better than the ones was talkin' about 'em! There's just *so much,* if we keep on livin'," she concluded quietly.

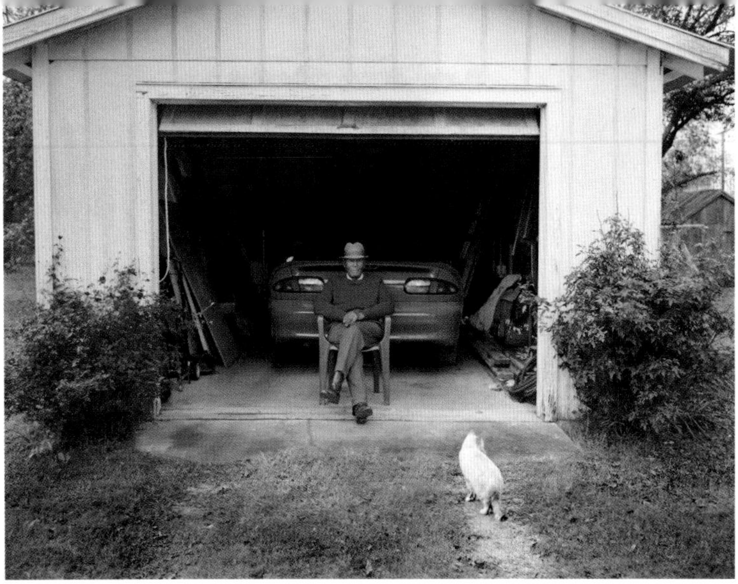

Louis "Bug" Henry with his red convertible

Leora expressed her hatred for the First Gulf War, which our country was engaged in at that time: "It's like this, Desert Storm—I can't get my head up. I can't talk it. Uh-uh! No, ma'am, uh-uh." Her voice was low, as she leaned forward and said, "I might get in trouble. I had a husband in the service. I had two sons in there. They didn't ask to go in there. They were bein' obedient to their country. These people what's over there fightin', they're innocent people. They got to do it—they're taught to do that. Maybe it might make a better country, but there's *somebody* shot—somebody's husband, somebody's son. Uh-uh, hmm, hmm, hmm." She shook her head.

Leora spoke for many women and men everywhere by saying this, but she said it softly and with caution, as though she was afraid she might be overheard.

When Leora died in 1994, she and Louis had been married for sixty-three years. She turned out to have been modest about herself, never having mentioned that she was a lifelong member of St. James AME Church; a founding member of Smith's Pride Chapter 388, Order of the Eastern Star; president of Stewardess Board No. 1 for over forty years; a life member of the Missionary Board; and a longtime Sunday school teacher. The Weimar newspaper said she had received many awards for arts and crafts, and I remembered seeing some attractive crocheted items around her house, made by her hands, no doubt.

After a period of grieving for Leora, Louis bought himself a sports car, a dashing red convertible, which he drove slowly and carefully the few blocks from his house to the Weimar town center and back home. He looked happy, relaxed, and debonair, in a yellow sweater and a snap-brim hat, one elbow resting on the windowsill of the car. He said he was definitely *not* in the market for another wife. And I told him he had better be careful because, in that red car and yellow sweater, he looked pretty appealing. He just smiled.

Ruby Hicks

I knew Ruby Hicks for years, as a reliable presence at Pleasant Hill Missionary Baptist Church. She was the secretary of the congregation, the person who stood in front of the church and read the announcements each Sunday. She had an air of confidence and efficiency about her, always neat and handsome in a business-type suit, quite citified in some respects, unusual for Weimar. One could imagine her as an executive secretary or a businesswoman. It turned out she had been neither, though she had lived in the big city.

The day we talked on the phone, Ruby was busy "tryin' to clean up the old park and keep it goin', try to rent it out." She meant Weimar Community Park, where the black citizens held Juneteenth celebrations and other special events such as Lillie Williams's one-hundredth birthday party. For years, this had been the only park that the black residents of Weimar used, a lovely site with generous shade-giving oak trees, an outhouse, swing sets, and a decent-sized building for seated events. And there was no abundance of money in the black community, so maintaining the park was hard at best. It was not surprising that Ruby was involved in this endeavor. She was a doer and a concerned member of the community.

"I was the mother hen," she said before going off to her park duties, "was like a mother hen for my family. I was the oldest, and a mother hen after my mother passed away in 1957. I took over and helped my sister with her twelve children—she had a husband that didn't provide—plus two more my other sister had, and I raised them up." When I expressed happiness that these children had Aunt Ruby as a resource, she simply said, "Well, I guess that the Lord put me here for some reason.

"We were born in Colorado County, in the town of Oakland, Texas. Back then, people in Oakland farmed all over. There were cotton gins there and two or three stores and a bank. Used to be a little place called the Friendly Inn. Now the town is dead—everybody moved away, started going to Weimar, made Oakland fall apart. Everybody left 'cause there was no way to make a living—*had* to move away. Used to be called Grand Prairie. Not anymore."

Ruby herself moved to Houston for a while after she married and worked there for years in the wealthy Memorial area, for an older widower in his home. Her husband, Tommy Ray, had a job at a lumberyard on Lawndale Avenue. They lived two years in San Antonio, while he opened a lumberyard for his employers in Houston, clearly a trusted employee. When they retired, they moved back to Weimar. Tommy Ray died in 1989, and Ruby lived alone after that, alone but busily occupied with church, friends, the sixteen-year-old daughter of her dead sister, and her dog, Snowball, as well as an array of community activities.

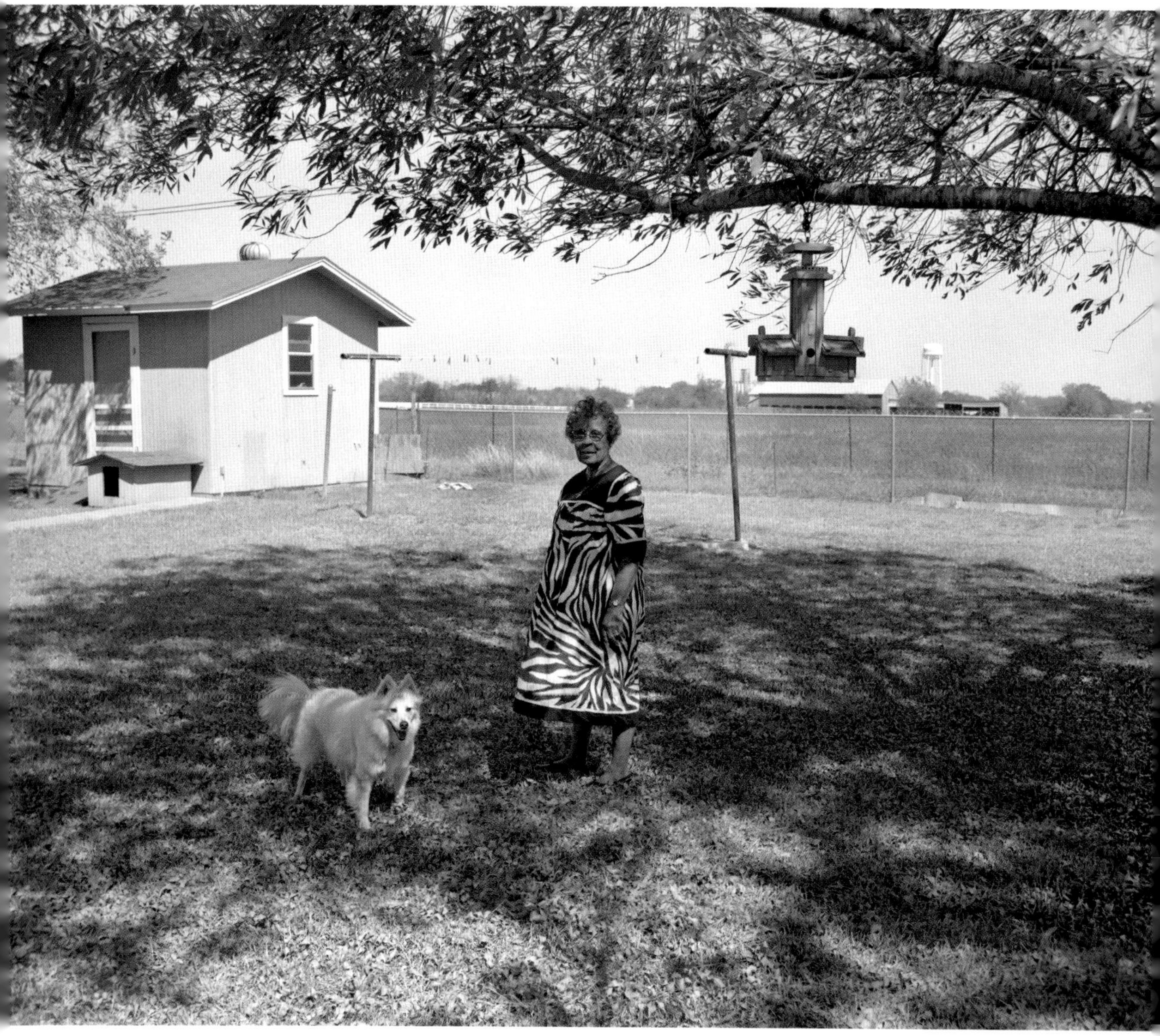

Ruby Hicks and her dog, Snowball

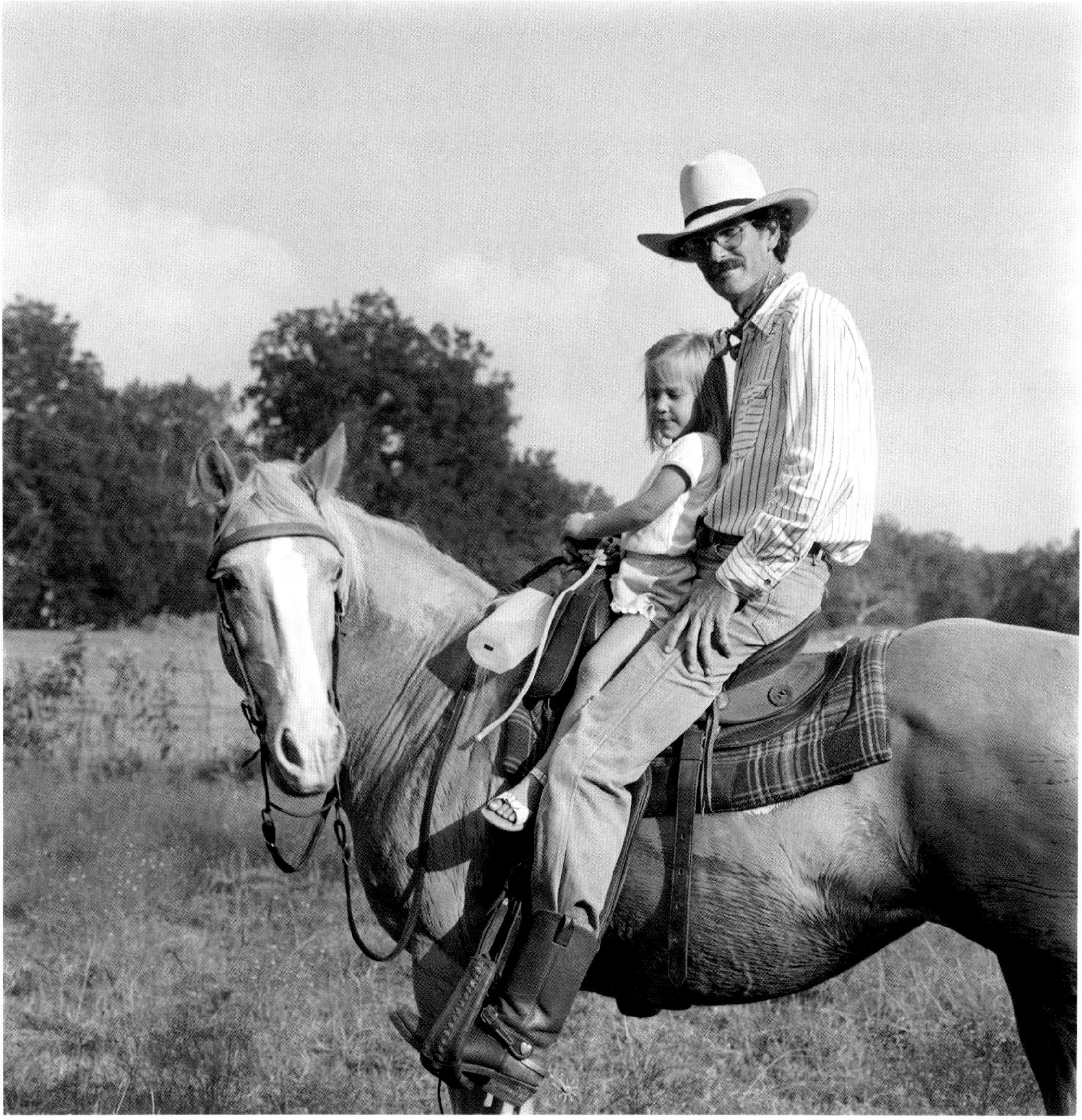

Jim Kearney, with his daughter, Sarah

Jim Kearney

Jim Kearney was born into a ranching family in Columbus. He grew up on the family ranch, where he learned to ride and work cattle as a youngster. His said his ongoing love of the outdoors developed there on the ranch. Jim later attended Texas A&M University and then graduated from the University of Texas at Austin in 1969, with a double major in history and German. Soon after starting graduate school, Jim was drafted into the army, where he served as a commissioned officer. All COs became combat medics, so he "served in Vietnam as a Dustoff medic in the First Air Cavalry." Dustoff medics used military helicopters to evacuate injured soldiers. Wounded on a volunteer mission in January 1971, with six days remaining in his tour of duty and only fourteen days in his entire army service, Jim was awarded a Purple Heart and the Distinguished Flying Cross. He had already received a Bronze Star with a V, three air medals, and six army commendation medals. He spent three months in hospitals and was discharged, only to experience unexpected difficulties transitioning back into civilian life.

Jim resumed graduate school at UT, but majoring in German only. He successfully completed most of the work on his degree, but he never finished his dissertation. During graduate school he married Paulina van Bavel, a fellow student and an artist. There were few jobs in the liberal arts at that time, and it became reasonable for them to move back to the ranch in Columbus. Jim's father was retiring from ranching, and Jim decided it would be wise to go back to his roots to raise his family there, close to the land he so loved. He said he never regretted this decision.

He and Paulina became active in the local community and there developed many strong friendships. In 1998, Jim ran for county judge, narrowly losing but learning a lot about Colorado County and its many communities in a way that he found valuable. He said that, despite losing, "it was a wonderful experience." He kept a lively interest in public service and served as the Democratic county chair, a Scout leader, an educator in the local high school, and a member in many local organizations. In 2002, he once again entered the race for county judge as a Democrat, a race he lost.

Paulina van Bavel Kearney

Paulina Kearney was an artist who called herself a potter. Many others called her an artist, because while lots of people can throw pots, few individualize and refine their technique the way Paulina had. And little other pottery has the grace, originality, and delicacy of Paulina's work. Her pots' strong colors came not from the glaze, she said, but from the firing. The "pod" shapes she often used seemed to be unique to her eye.

Paulina had been showing and selling her pieces for years, and her work was represented in galleries around the country, from Philadelphia to Houston and Santa Fe. In the 1990s, Paulina was developing new forms in her pots, female and Cycladic in concept. She was still exhibiting in 2005.

She and Jim met when they were in college together at the University of Texas, where she was majoring in art. They married in 1972. She taught school while Jim was studying for his degree. When Paulina was awarded an artist's grant to work at Paisano Ranch, outside Austin, the two moved there, had a baby they named Sarah, and afterwards decided to go back to Columbus to ranch with Jim's father.

In time they had two more children, both sons. When the children were old enough that Paulina could be freer, she became involved with local affairs in town, such as the Columbus library board, the PTA, the art center, and local politics. Paulina tried to work daily in her studio behind the Kearney house, but it was not always easy being an artist, a mother, a wife, a housekeeper, a community worker, and an occasional teacher.

Yet she said clearly she had a good life and was glad to be in Colorado County. "They know I'm different," she said, "but we fit in fine, Jim and I, and we have many friends. We're very happy here."

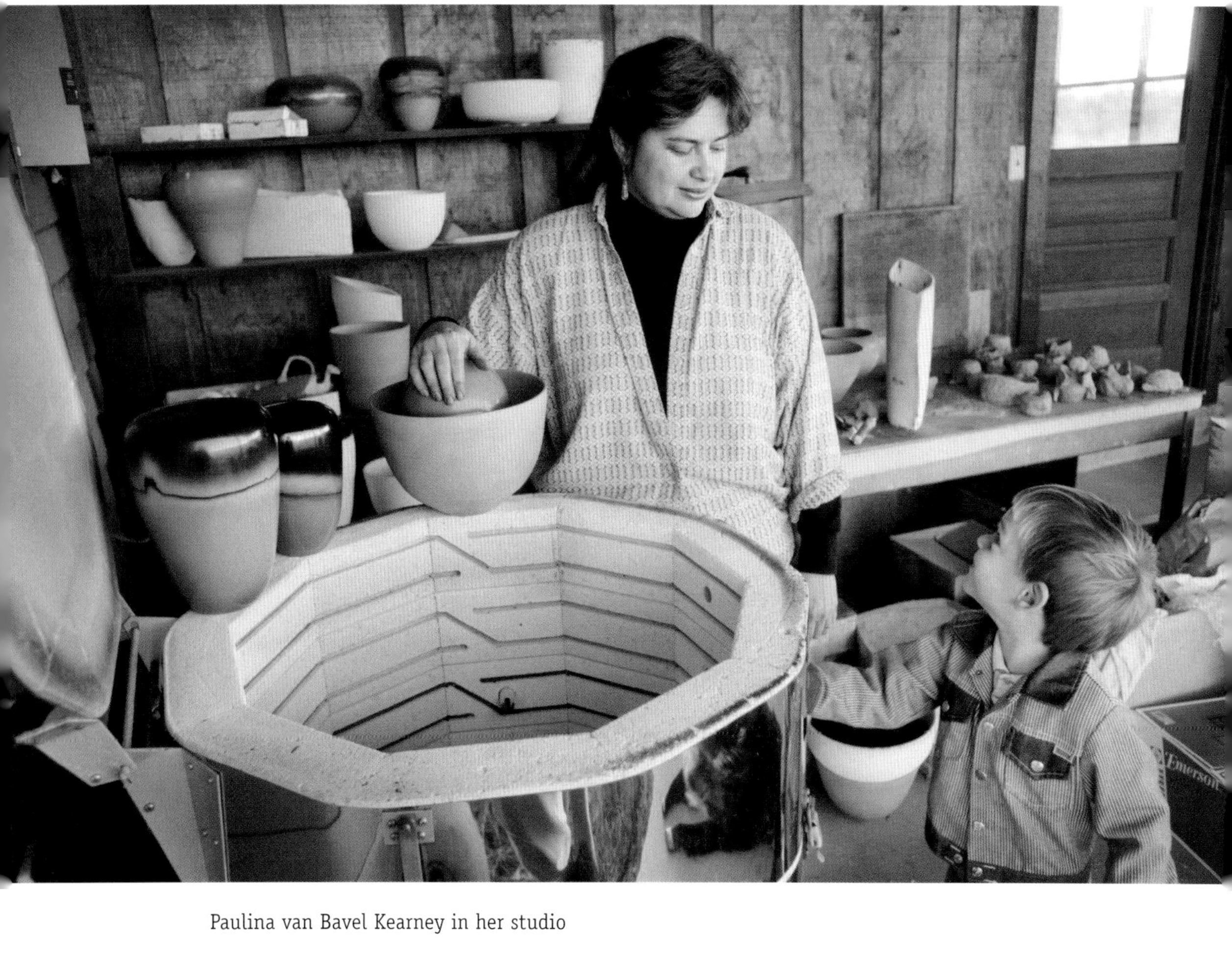

Paulina van Bavel Kearney in her studio

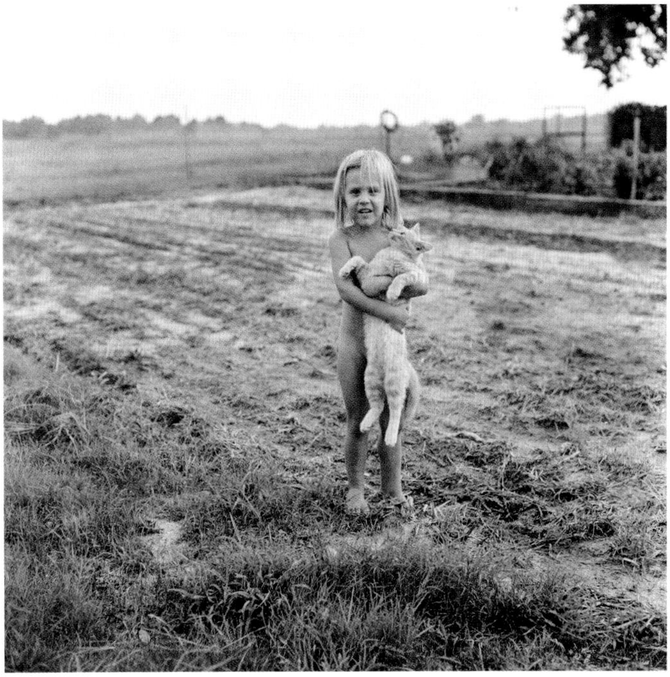

Sarah Elaine Kearney
in the garden

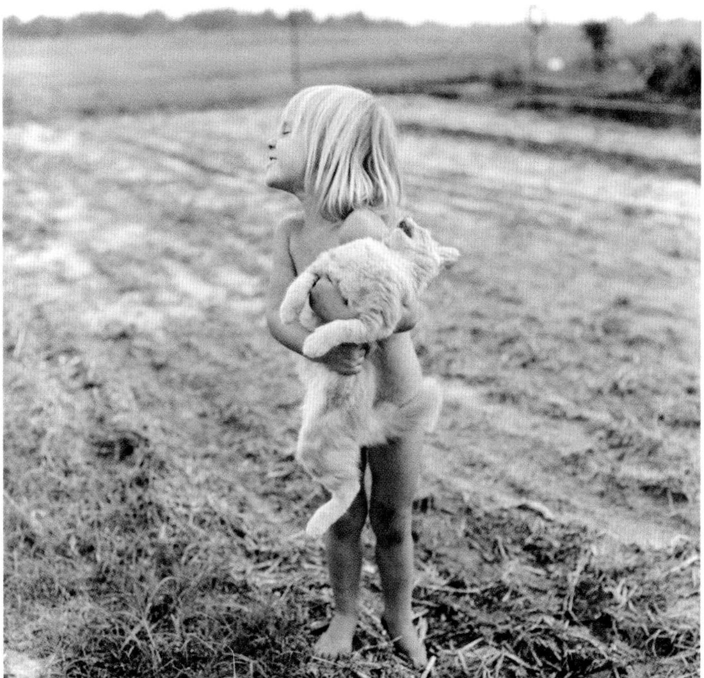

Sarah Elaine Kearney

Sarah must have been about three and a half years old when these photographs were taken, on the day I found her playing in the garden where her mother was hoeing and preparing the soil for a garden. It was clear that Sarah had other, more important, things on her mind than working in the garden.

It was eighteen years later, and Sarah was that many years older, when this story was written. She was by then a magna cum laude college graduate and an accomplished young woman on her way to advanced studies in landscape design at Harvard University. It seemed only fair to call Sarah and get her thoughts about this photograph before including her darling little body in a book. Sarah, who had by then changed her name to Elaine, was unworried about the picture and happy to talk some about her future.

With a bachelor of arts degree from Trinity University and a minor in German, a new name, and a junior year spent in Freiburg, Germany, behind her, she said of her coming studies at Harvard, "I'm *very glad* to be on the track of doing something I've always loved." She talked about being raised on the farm and about her lifelong love of the land, adding, "I also love getting back to my artistic roots with my mom [the potter of rare talent]."

Paulina related her and Jim's thoughts on their remarkable daughter's choice of careers. She talked about how Sarah grew up on the Colorado River and Harvey's Creek (which crossed the farm where they were living), spending happy times watching her father work on the land, fishing, picnicking, exploring, and riding horseback. Sarah recognized later in her life how much these childhood experiences in the country had shaped her. "And her bond with her dad was always special," Paulina emphasized, remembering a trip the two made down the Middle Salmon River, in Idaho, when Sarah was sixteen. Paulina said that her daughter "couldn't have been any happier" than on the farm, where Sarah/Elaine's love of nature was formed.

Evidently the Harvard student was finding new concepts of working with nature in her studies at the university—"Naturalism is out," Paulina quoted her as saying, suggesting that the approach there was more cerebral and of a more intellectual aesthetic than Sarah had experienced before, a "design of space rather than plants."

Lacey Henry

"My name is Lacey Henry, and I'm eighty-three years old. I'll be eighty-four this comin' May, if I live. And I was born up there to Holman at that ole hackberry tree—is dyin' now. And my parents were named Mace Williams and Mattie Williams."

Lacey Henry was still youthful in looks, mind, and spirit when she talked on tape at age eighty-three. Lacey was notorious among her friends for her silence, for the way she sat, smiling and listening, quietly agreeing with whatever the others said. So when she finally talked openly on record, these friends were amazed. Marie Williams asked many times, "How'd you get Cousin Lacey to talk?" The truth was that no one got Lacey to talk. Lacey simply let it be known that she was ready to talk, and we showed up, out of politeness, expecting little from her. To our amazement, Lacey was very forthright and direct. She may have realized she had only few years left to live and did not want to pass on without describing the most painful and significant event of her life: the beating of her husband, Oscar, by their white neighbor.

Lacey had been born in 1908, in Fayette County, just over the Colorado County line. "Behind the live oak tree on the road near Holman, that's where I was born," as though anyone would know exactly what she was talking about.

She was one of the fourteen children born to Mace (Mason) and Mattie Williams. Mace himself was born a slave somewhere in the Deep South—Lacey didn't know where. Mattie was born free. Lacey, the youngest child, didn't recall her father ever discussing his past, so she knew no details of his early life. Lacey's mother was buried at the now abandoned Pleasant Hill Missionary Baptist Church in the country, her grave lost along with many others in a thicket of yaupon, brush, and brambles. Mace's gravesite was unknown.

The Williams children had some wonderfully euphonious names: Lovely (a boy), Irena, Lacey, Mace, Ponetter, and Parthenia—as if one of Lacey's parents had a rare ear for musical sounds.

"We was a *load* to feed," Lacey said of her large family. "We had a time, I'll tell you, a hard, *hard* time. But the Lord helped us, brought us on through."

One of her most painful memories was of the time her father lost the farm he was trying to buy. "My daddy, see, he was just farmin' and wasn't makin' no crops hardly in those years, and he got way behind in the payments, and they closed the note on him, just for ninety-some dollars. As I say, he didn't make no bales some years; he make one or two bales and that didn't bring too much money to pay on, so he just lost out. Oh, yeah, he lost *all* the money he put into it [his land]. He had put in a

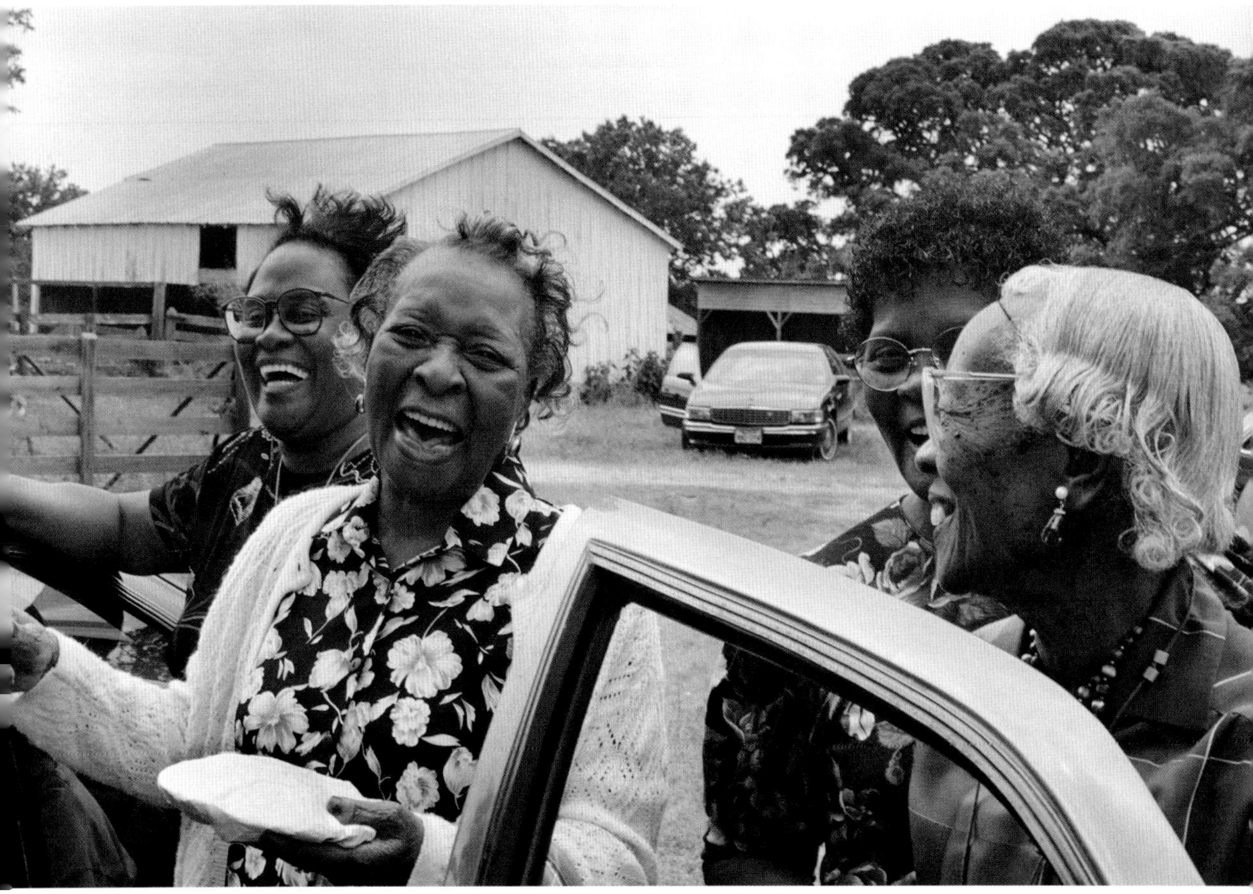

Lacey Henry *(left)* with her friends on her ninetieth birthday

good bunch of money, but he lost it all. He owed just ninety dollars, but they closed the note. That made my daddy feel *real* bad. He lost that place. He farmed on after that, but he never could make it," Lacey said in a tearful voice. "Couldn't make no money, couldn't make no money *no kind of way*."

When Lacey was a young girl, she met her husband-to-be, Oscar (O. Henry, as my father affectionately called him). "His name was Oscar Henry, and we went to school together," she said. "And that's where we started our courtship. And so we growed on up, till I married at seventeen years old. He was eighteen; I was seventeen. So that's how we met, at school. Just little ole children, little bitty kids." She smiled warmly. They married in December 1925, "a dry year." And they were married almost fifty-eight years, until Oscar's death. She smiled again as she said, "We stayed together. He died in '83. From '25 to '83, you know, that's a long time. Must have been good, 'cause—we'd have our little, you know, ups and downs, fussin' now like that—but we stayed together."

Oscar's nickname was Bro, for "Brother," and he became a preacher. "He was called to preach in his prayers. The Lord called him," Lacey said matter-of-factly. "Well, he was a deacon first, in the church. And he said when the Lord called him, he went to preachin'. He said he prayed for the Lord to let him hear thunder at twelve o'clock. And it was a clear day, just like yesterday was, and it thundered at twelve o'clock." Oscar attended Guadalupe College in San Antonio by mail and received his degree from there. "He pastored at St. Paul—it was out in the rural land," Lacey noted. "And he had it moved to Weimar here after his health was failin' 'im."

Lacey and Oscar lived most of their years in the same house, in the Osage community, keeping Oscar's mother with them. They rented farmland from their neighbors, the Trefnys. "We started farmin' with Mr. Charles Trefny there on halves," working corn and cotton, she said. "See, we made two bales—they get one, we get one. But if we only make one bale, they get half of that bale, and we only get half. Times was mighty tough in '25!

"We were *soooo* poor," she said with a sigh. "We paid on credit, you know. Get our groceries on credit and pay up at the end of the year after you get through with the crop. That was a *hard time*. Then we had to start back over, tradin' on credit for the next year." Was there ever cash money? "No. We done paid all that to the grocery man," Lacey said. "Sometimes you couldn't pay him up. Some years we made only six bales and give half to the Trefnys. We traded on credit—*everything*. Paid at the end of the year, at one time, and then—nothin' left.

"Yeah, yeah, we been through some times, I tell you. It was always hard," she said. Then, Mary and Rorick Cravens came from Houston, bought a weekend farm by the Henrys' place, and hired Lacey and Oscar to work for them. "When Miz Cravens come in, that was our blessing. Yes, that's when our blessin's started, when the Cravens come in—started havin' a little change to put up. 'Cause before, we'd spend all what we'd make. The Lord sent you by here. I prayed and prayed, and he heard my prayers."

There had never before been anything left for Christmas presents or any other sort of luxury. Their happiest Christmas, she said, was when the Cravens brought them both presents for Christmas—Lacey's first wrapped presents ever. "They were so *pretty,* little ribbons and all!" she remembered.

"It's better today, a whole lot better than it was. But the first was when your mother and daddy come in here. Looked like after they come in here, what was when here got better.

"You couldn't come in people's house—just had to eat outdoors when you workin' for 'em, just like cats and dogs. But after Miz Cravens and them come in, it got better. And they were so nice folks. They were just so *friendly*. And we just couldn't understand why they were so friendly and the others wasn't. And she'd come in the house, and I'd make coffee for her. She even brought some cups for me to make the coffee and put it in.

"But at first we was afraid of them, 'cause, see, we was afraid of white folks because they treated us so bad. They just didn't like Negroes, the black folks. They just didn't like 'em. I don't know why they didn't like 'em, but they just didn't.

"And then, one day we was sittin' at the table eatin', and Mr. Cravens come by, and he sit down, and we had a bench behind the table. He sit down on that and he was sittin', quiet as a rat runnin' across the floor"—she giggled—"'cause he was sittin' down with us. And so he said, 'Them cabbage look pretty good!' You know, he *loved* cabbage. And Miz Cravens told me after that, she said if I hadda asked him could he have some, he'd have ate some. But, you know, I couldn't do that, 'cause white folks didn't believe in eatin' what colored folks cooked. So I didn't never ask him that."

There was one story that, above all others, Lacey wanted recorded and saved. And this was it: "And so, after that, one thing that hurt me *so bad* was when Lillie Fries' brother hit my husband in Weimar with a ax handle, on the head. That hurt me so *bad*. He was a white man. And the girl I raised, Cassie V., we didn't go to town. We'd probably go to town ev'ry Saturday with Oscar. But that Saturday, we didn't leave and go to town. I said, 'I'm gonna stay here and wash and iron.' 'Cause he was a minister, and I had to get his shirts to bein' ready for church. And so I did. And so he went to town by hisself.

"And him and Ivory, we called Pie, and another man we called Rob Lee was sittin' on the sidewalk on the street there, you know, and this man come up with a ax handle and hit him on the head. But if I'd a'been there, I'd been *dead today,* 'cause I know that girl and me—we would have jumped on 'im, right then. Well, you know—nothin' we could do with men folk! I know that girl would have jumped on 'im and *I would too*—on that man, right *then*. I know that man would've killed me and also Cassie, that girl I was raisin', 'cause she was crazy about—she called Oscar 'Daddy,' but he was her uncle. Shoot, I know that man would've killed me! So the Lord just fixed it so I didn't go to town.

"So we looked for 'im. It's getting' late—so long, you know—I began to worry. I said, 'I wonder what's done happened. Oscar ain't come home.' Then, finally, here come someone bringin' 'im home. They say after the man hit 'im, he carried 'im on round to the doctor's, 'cause see, blood was just *runnin'* out. And he sewed his head up. And I believe today that's some of Oscar's trouble. His mind went bad, 'cause that affected his brain."

Stories differ on why this happened. Lacey explained it this way: "We was workin' for Mr. Trefny, choppin' cotton, and this man, he had a crop. And he went up about a nickel from what Trefny was payin', and asked Oscar, would he chop for 'im. Oscar told 'im, 'Well, I done promise' Mr. Trefny I'd be back, and I'd stick to my word.' But he just waited till he caught 'im in town, and that's when he hit 'im." Another version of the story is that Oscar walked across the Kahlden land, shortcutting from work, which was considered a serious offense by some farmers.

"But after that, Oscar forgave him. Because we would go into town, Oscar would stop and ask him to ride, ask did he want to ride? He didn't have a way to ride, you know. Every time he seen that man, he try to talk with 'im, catch up with 'im, and ask 'im to ride. And he said, 'No, I don't wanta ride.' He wasn't gonna get in that car with me.

"You know, I didn't like it 'cause he hit Oscar for *nothin',* just 'cause we wouldn't chop for 'im. He did it for *nothin'.* Just walked up, come up behind Oscar, and hit him there on the head with that ax handle. They say blood just come out. I did get angry! But I forgave him. I prayed to the Lord, yeah, and Oscar did too—he seen 'im in town, good while after that, and Oscar standin' upside a post in town, and he told 'im he had prayed to the Lord and would forgive 'im, Mr. Kahlden.

"But he [Mr. Kahlden] did that just for *meanness*. And so that *grieved* me, I tell you."

But, she said, "you got to forgive the person what done somethin' to you first—then the Lord will forgive you. If you be prayin' honest, he be forgivin'. But you can't just *hold it in your heart* all the time. No, I didn't hate 'im. I prayed for 'im. Ask' the Lord to forgive that man, 'cause he didn't know what he was doin'. That grieved me, I tell you!

"Oscar was a good man, I have to say that. He was a good man," she affirmed lovingly.

Oscar was a gentle man and kind, but he was never the same after this incident. He ended his life in a nursing home, "his mind gone bad." The assailant was never prosecuted. "Yeah, they arrested the man," Lacey said, "but they didn't keep 'im long."

Lacey was uncomfortable talking about the 1935 lynching in nearby Columbus, but she did offer a few thoughts about it: "After I heard about the lynching, it sure affected our lives, 'cause we was afraid they were gonna do us the same way. Because the way they hated black folks, they *would*. We'd go to the store, but we'd hurry back, wouldn't stay out too long, 'cause, when it got late, that's when they'd do it to you. Most of them were on the same accord with black folks. Some were a little better, but I don't know none I would trust."

She continued, in her gentle, soft-spoken way, "When we would be at church, we would tell 'em we was 'fraid for our lives. 'Cause they didn't like us. I don't know why, but somethin' about us. They didn't like no black folk. But God made us all," she stated firmly. "But they sayin' like we wasn't—I just don't *know* what's wrong. Wasn't nothin' we could do 'bout it, just be 'fraid, and stay out of their way much as possible. It was just awful! Oh, they treated us so bad!

"But God made us all, and if I cut you and come over here and cut me, red blood would come out of us," she said, then sighed. "But we'd talk about it and couldn't do nothin', couldn't do nothin' about it—just be afraid and stay out of their way as much as possible.

"Some of the white folk have changed toward us, but we couldn't go in their houses. If we work for them, they gonna give us somethin' to eat, they bring it out the back door and hand it out to you. That's the way they would treat us, like we was cats and dogs.

"I say the Lord, he brought us through, nothin' but the Lord. 'Cause, it wasn't for him, I don't know what would become of us."

In late 1990, Lacey had to bear another grief, the loss of her adopted daughter, Cassie V., from cancer. Cassie V. (for Victoria) came to live with Lacey and Oscar when she was three. "See, her Mama died and I taken her, and another lady taken her baby brother. There was just one girl, and I taken the girl," Lacey said with a warm smile. "She was satisfied with me, just like a mama."

She continued, "My first church was named Good Hope. After it got burned down, I moved my membership to Pleasant Hill. I been there about ten or eleven years." Lacey left her country home and moved to town at a time when there were rumors that it was unsafe for black folks to stay alone in the country. She settled in Weimar, near her friend Marie and her new church, where she sang in the choir until her hearing deteriorated. "My church means a lot to me," she affirmed. "We all get together, and we all look like we love one another.

"We had a time, I'll tell you—and the Lord helped us—a hard, hard time. The Lord sent you all by here. The onliest time I done lived like people should is through the help of you all, through the Lord."

When Lacey Henry died in 2000, she was buried out of Greater Macedonia Baptist Church. Pleasant Hill had gone through some major changes she didn't like. She had bought and paid for both her grave and her coffin. She was missed by her many friends, who loved her for her gentleness and good nature.

Pearl Ray Bremby

The two ladies pictured here stopped to talk to me on the street one day, in front of Marie Williams's house, as they were on their way home from a funeral, dressed in their finest and declaring they were ready for a photograph. Pearl later said, in wide-eyed dismay, looking at the photograph, "I hadn't *knowed* I was so *big*—I just fill up the picture!"

My experience in Weimar and Columbus is that everyone knows just where you are and what you're up to at any given time. "I seen your car at Cousin Lacey's house—knowed you was in town," they'd say, adding, "and you ain't come by my house yet." So Pearl would know just where to find me on the day she was dressed up and ready for her picture to be taken. There were few secrets in that small town.

Pearl was born Pearl Jackson in 1921, near the community of New Bielau, on the farm where her father, Harman, was working and living—"near the Sam Houston Cemetery," she said. Her mother, Laura Lee Wilson, died when Pearl was six. "There was three of us first chil'rens. We first, us three, were poor—that's Rosalie, Pearl, and Clarence. Harman Jackson, our daddy, he was a nice Christian man—tried to treat everyone right and never had no trouble out of nobody. Everybody knowed him," said Pearl proudly. Harman remarried and produced five more children to join his original three.

Pearl described her childhood on the farm as happy, even though her mother had passed away so early in Pearl's life: "My mother died when I was six years old, and we lived on the farm, and my daddy, he married again when I was 'bout eight, and we had to work hard. We went to school and come home in the evenin' and we *worked*! I had to quit school when I was in the fifth grade, to help at home. My stepmother, she had got purgnant, and I had to quit and do the cookin', the housecleanin', and all. And when I got through with the house, I had to go to the fields. I worked hard *all my days,"* she said with emphasis.

"Yes, it was good land where we was—it was good land. My daddy and my mama worked hard. My stepmama worked hard too. And when we was little, and Papa was workin', he had an old round wooden box he'd built to put us in, in the field. And had a dog, and that dog would stay there. And we'd go to cryin', and the dog would bark. And they'd be *way* out in the field, and one of 'em would come see 'bout us. And they would always tell us, 'Y'all don't cry now, don't cry. If you cry and the dog bark, one of us gonna have to walk way up here to see 'bout you!' And they'd put some bread and water where we could get it, and we'd stay in that big ol' box."

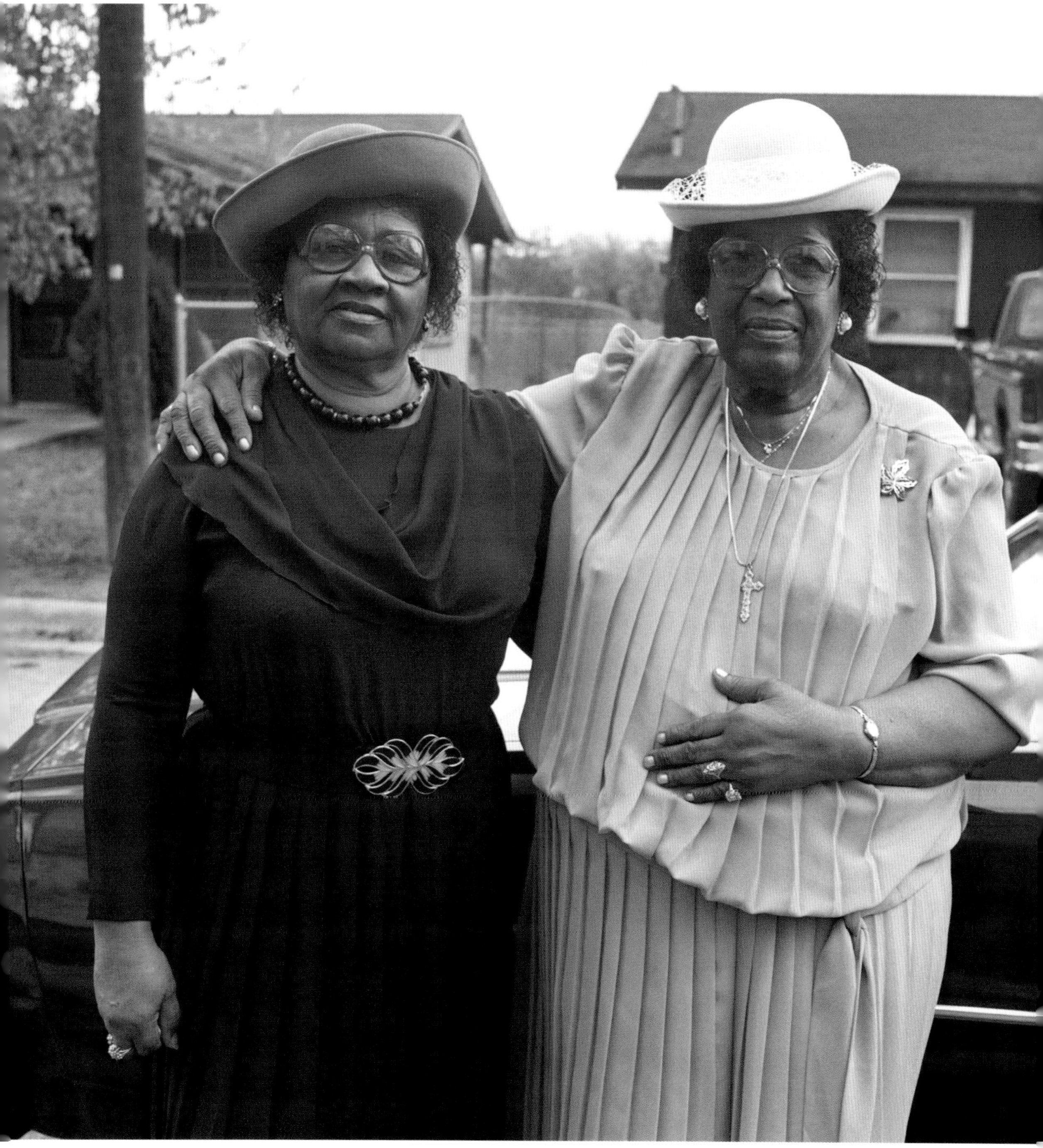

Bessie Mae Williams and Pearl Ray Bremby

It's hard, as a city dweller, to imagine carrying the children to the field every day to care for them while working the cotton. A friend from Alabama told a story similar to Pearl's, describing how she and her siblings were put in a washtub in the field and spanked if they left the tub even for a second. Their parents, too, left a dog with their babies, to alert them if the little ones left the safety of the tub. Beulah Dorn said she used to pull her children around the field behind her on a cotton sack she dragged, as she worked down the rows.

Pearl continued, "I went to school at Dry Branch School, a little one-room—wasn't no bigger than this room. And I had a teacher—well, she teached us, and we learnt. We'd have nice school clothes and programs. I'd like that 'cause they'd make us some pretty organdy dresses, and we would dress that evenin' and go to the school and have a *nice* program. We walked five miles to school, back and forwards, every day."

Pearl studied some at home after quitting school. "Daddy would give me a figure and stuff at home, and I knowed how to read," she said. "I can figure pretty good now—you can't beat me figurin' less you get way up in them thousands and things. Then I get confused, but other than that I can figure good. And I can read.

"We lived on the Albert Koehn place. My daddy raised sweet potatoes, corn, cotton, cane—you name it, he raised it—peanuts and *all that stuff*. We had watermelon, we had tomatoes in the field, we had okra, rows of okra. We had aplenty, aplenty!

"Used to be, when we would kill hogs, all the neighbors would come around to help you kill hogs. And we'd kill hogs, and everybody would get some meat. Today, you kill hogs, nobody knows *nothin'* about it. You see the hog a-hangin' up in the tree, and that's all. Papa used to give away so much meat when he killed hogs—'Papa, we ain't gonna have none left!' 'Y'all gonna have aplenty!'" he'd say. "He would kill three, four hogs, great *big* old hogs, and would give all the neighbors some. *Them* were the good times.

"I always worked hard. I mean hard! I cut cordwood, I sawed logs, I farmed cotton. One year, with Pete Bremby [one of her three husbands], we made fourteen bales of cotton; I weighed every one of them sacks, helped lift and weigh every one of 'em. Emptied 'em. Load and unload the corn in the barn.

"I been married three times," Pearl said—once happily, once disastrously, and once—well, who knows. Mr. Cook was first, when Pearl was seventeen. Her assessment of him was short and to the point, "Was *no-'count*! He was a *lazy*! Didn't like to provide, didn't like to work. We were farmin' on a place out there. And he'd work a day or two or three, and then he was sick or somethin'. I had to work by myself. I had to carry it on myself. I don't have but one son, Perry Leon Cook. His father never done *nothin'* for the boy. When the boy was born, he left, left 'bout two or three days after, with another woman." Good-bye, Mr. Cook.

"And I never heard no more till 'bout six months after. He come writin' me a letter and wantin' me back. I tol' him I didn't want *no parts* of him!" Pearl cried a tear as she said this and admitted, "I'm still grievin'."

The next husband was Jesse (Pete) Bremby. "He was a'right. He worked and provided. He was smart, but he'd always work. You know, he had a job with the Bekens, and he wouldn't help me with the crops.

"And the last'un I married, he was a preacher, Paul Lewis Ray. He wasn't no good either, so jealous—*ohhh,* he was jealous! Jealous of me and my own folks. He was from Bryan, Texas. Yes'm, that's where I found him, and that's where I left him!" She smiled wryly.

"I went to Bryan and married him, and they say I was his—he's a preacher, now—they say I was his *fifth* wife, and he never got no divorce from *neither* wife! He would always go to 'nother county and marry. If he stay in that county where he married, he'd put in for the divorce and then he'd go to 'nother county and marry the next lady. He was some preacher!"

That was Pearl's hardest time. "He didn't want me to go nowhere," she said. "I left my home here, and I wasn't through payin' for it. He made like he was gonna help me finish payin' for it, and he never would give me *nothin'.* And so I was gettin' behind and everythin', so I come on back here and finish payin'. He didn't 'low them neighbor folks to come over here and talk to me. Oh, he was somethin' else! I put up with it as long as I could. One mornin' I grabbed him upside the head, up the chest, side of that 'frigerator and called him a preachin' so-and-so!' and beat his head good, up against that 'frigerator!" She laughed.

"I was workin' for Mr. Charlie Allen. I turned it over to him. He said, 'Pearl, do you want to go back?' So I told him, 'No, sir, I don't want to go back.' 'Now I don't mind helpin' you if you don't want to go back,' he said. 'You just leave it to me.' And so he got in touch with the law up there and asked did they know Paul Ray. They told him yeah, they say they knowed him well 'cause they'd had trouble with him and his other wives."

So, with Mr. Allen's help, the police went with Pearl and her son, Perry (a big man nicknamed Poodle), to get her things out of Rev. Ray's house. "Great big old black man go out there with us and followed me everywhere I went, till I got all my things. I had already picked a lot of dewberries, and I had put up a lot of jelly and stuff, and I went to get that and he said, the old Reverend Ray said, 'Don't bother that jelly! Just leave that jelly there!' I said I had bought the sugar and put it up, and I said 'That's all right. You don't want me to have it, I don't *want* it!' And the lawman said, 'If you want it, you take half of it.' I said 'No! If he that needy, he want it, let *him* have it!' And I left it there."

"And he died hard too. When he died, he was married to me, but he was engaged to another woman. He was goin' to marry that one next—I was his fifth wife—and he was goin' to marry his sixth wife the next month or two. And he got in a car wreck goin' over to see her—and he died like a *dawg* when he died," she said, a sense of satisfaction in her voice.

"I stayed with him six months—and that was five and a half months too long. Should have quit him after thirty days!" She laughed.

"Since I been single, I've profited more than I did when I was married, 'cause this home, I built it up from the ground in 1962." Her boss, Mr. Allen, loaned her money, and "I worked and paid him back that fourteen hundred dollars. I paid fifty-nine dollars a month till I paid this house out—took me sixteen years. And no one helped me," she said firmly and proudly.

Pearl kept her severely handicapped granddaughter, Joyce, for most of the girl's life. "She can't do nothin' for herself but feed herself. You wouldn't believe she's twenty-six," said Pearl the first time Joyce and I met. I use the word "met" with qualifications, because Joyce was so frightened of strangers, especially white ones, that she only peeked around the door, squealed, and disappeared. "She's scared of people," Pearl assured me. "Can't talk. She call me Mama and jabber a little, but I don't know the rest. She call my name and her sister, Betty." Joyce was so afraid of strangers, she would get hysterical. "It's got to be somebody with her all the time," Pearl said. "Can't get her to no doctor or nothin', no time.

"Yeah, I always had to look out for myself, always. Now I'm lookin' out for myself and Joyce. And my son, 'cause I cooks for him all the time. He's married, but his wife, she don't cook but once a year, and that's New Year," Pearl joked. "Once a year. But she didn't cook this year 'cause they was sellin' some food down at the church, told her buy down there this year, so didn't have to cook this year. So I guess it'll be two years 'fore she cook now." Pearl was laughing merrily as she said this.

"I goes to church. That's mostly all I do, goes to church, to town when I have to," Pearl observed. She neglected to say that she also looked out for her friend Lacey Henry, as Lacey got older and more housebound. Pearl called Lacey daily and drove her places. She drove Lacey to La Grange in 1995, to a funeral home, so Lacey could plan and prepay for her own funeral service. Lacey died five years later. Pearl told me a month or two after Lacey's death that she still would forget and call Lacey, not able to accept that her old friend was gone. Real devotion is what Pearl showed toward her friends.

Asked if she wanted another man, her reply was quick and firm, "*No!* I'm just lookin' out for myself and Joyce."

In 2000, Pearl's health worsened, and her friends grew concerned. Her spirits flagged, and she was not her usual energized, feisty self. The question was what would become of Joyce without Pearl? To their relief, Pearl would rally after each scary episode and kept on going for far longer than anyone expected, with less bounce but with her sharp tongue, her spirit, and her humor still in evidence.

She said once, "Speakin' is the cheapest thing you can give anybody, 'Good mornin',' a good hello. Everybody I see—'Hi,' 'Hello,' 'Good evenin'.' Lots of times folks is so prej'diced you can walk down the street and speak to 'em, and they won't even open they mouth. Not only the differ'nt races, your own color do you like that. Up in the store the other day, I spied some little girls up there. I spoke to one of 'em, and she didn't speak. I spoke to the sister, and she didn't speak. Well, I asked the man in the store, 'What's the matter with 'em they couldn't speak to nobody?' [The girl] said she didn't have to speak if she didn't want to, and I said, 'No, you're just ignor'nt—that's what it is'!

"That's my prayer—every day I say my prayers—let me treat people and love people like I want them to love me, and I don't have no hatred in my heart against nobody, *nobody*."

Pearl died in 2003. Joyce was cared for by her half-sister and her father.

Bessie Mae Williams

Pearl's friend, Bessie Mae, was a resident of Oakland, a small town a few miles from Weimar, yet she seemed more like a resident of Weimar because she spent so much time there. Bessie's daughter and most of her friends lived in Weimar, and Bessie Mae regularly drove the fifteen or so miles to shop and visit there.

Oakland itself had a very small population and no store of any kind in the years I knew Bessie Mae. It was hard to drive into Oakland and imagine that it had ever been a thriving community, with a population of over three hundred at its height. There was no post office, no school, no market—only a handful of houses gave even a hint of the town's past glory, with their graceful architecture and tended gardens. One such structure was the Hutchins-Strunk House, as it was named on a historical marker (built in 1905 by a Confederate veteran and owned for a hundred years by the Strunk family). It was a lovely white Victorian-style dwelling. Otherwise, Oakland was only a couple of paved roads edging a grassy square, some falling-down outbuildings, about twenty scattered houses, three small churches, one fire truck, a pavilion, and an abandoned Mini-Mart. One woman who had lived in Oakland for several years around 1925 described it as having had a drugstore, a blacksmith, a rodeo arena, a bank, several cotton gins, and a café. No evidence of these was visible any longer. After the railroad and Interstate 10 went through Weimar and bypassed Oakland, the traffic and the commerce that Oakland had hoped to enjoy were diverted, and the town languished.*

By the time I knew Bessie, Oakland was pretty darned empty. She said, "There's really nobody left much—they all moved to Weimar. Nothin' here but field work. My church here was Methodist, but everybody died out—we closed it down. There are only two black churches left here, a Baptist and a kind of Holiness Church."

Bessie May described herself as "born *way* down in the country, in the community of Allan Quarter, born to Boyd and Lillian Lemons." She continued, "My parents didn't have a home of their own, so they rented from diff'rent white people. We would move around a lot—didn't get to go to school much. I said to myself, 'Someday I'm gonna get me a home of my own.' And I don't have the best. But," she added

*The book *Colorado County Chronicles* points out that Oakland was situated on land originally granted to James Bowie and was called Prairie Point. The stage line passed through, and Oakland had a store in 1844 that was a stage stop, on the route from Columbus to Gonzales. By 1947, Oakland was "little more than a ghost town."

proudly, "I have one, and I take care of it, keep it clean, keep it nice, have a yard." She smiled as she said this.

Bessie spoke about her life after the move into Oakland from her parents' rural home: "I did have house jobs. Everybody wanted me to work, said I was a good worker. I helped a woman across the street, raised her children, and now I don't hear from them *at all*. When they need you . . ." She grew quiet as her thoughts trailed off into silence.

"I miss Miss Lacey," she added in a sad voice. "I loved her—and Miss Marie and Miss Cleon. I come over and visit them." She expressed deep concern for her friend Pearl, who was in poor health then. Bessie sounded low but not defeated. When last we talked, Pearl had died and Bessie's brother had died in a car accident. Bessie Mae was grieving for them both. She was also gravely worried about her son, a soldier fighting in Iraq. She asked for prayers for him.

Irizola Wilson

I met Irizola Wilson in 1989 at Pleasant Hill Missionary Baptist Church in Weimar, with Marie Williams, a friend from Irizola's childhood days in Glidden. That is when this photograph was taken, after the service. Ten years later, I called Irizola in Glidden and found out that she was ill and housebound along with her husband. She sounded weak and breathless over the phone but said, in friendly fashion, to "come on by."

Although she had sounded awful over the phone, I always found Irizola in the same spot on each visit, seeming content and well. She was always sitting in a comfortable chair, facing the television, talking on her portable phone, looking happy, cheerful, and quite alive, in spite of all her gloomy words. Her family came by often, and her youngest grandson, a beautiful baby boy, obviously loved to snuggle on his grandmother's ample bosom while she sang to him. She said she had always loved singing. "My first solo was [at] only nine years old, in Mount Arie Church in Weimar." Irizola had been president of the District Choir, which was made up of more than forty choirs from nearby towns, with Giddings, Columbus, and Eagle Lake among them. She proudly displayed a plaque for her forty years of service to the La Grange District Association of the Baptist Church.

On the third visit, when the light was brighter and I got a good look at Irizola, it was startling to see that she had blue hair—not lightly tinted gray-blue hair but *truly* blue hair—indigo blue, bright, eye-smashing blue hair. "Oh, it's been blue for years," she explained nonchalantly. "It was covered with a hat the day you saw me at church, so you couldn't tell." She probably was behatted that day to spare the preacher and the congregation distraction.

Irizola used to own and run a small café around the corner from her house, on old highway 90, once a well-traveled road. The café was named the Do Drop Inn. "An RC Cola water man put a *big* sign in front of it, saying 'Do Drop Inn' in big letters," Irizola recalled. "The juke box is still over there." It might be a great place for a small party.

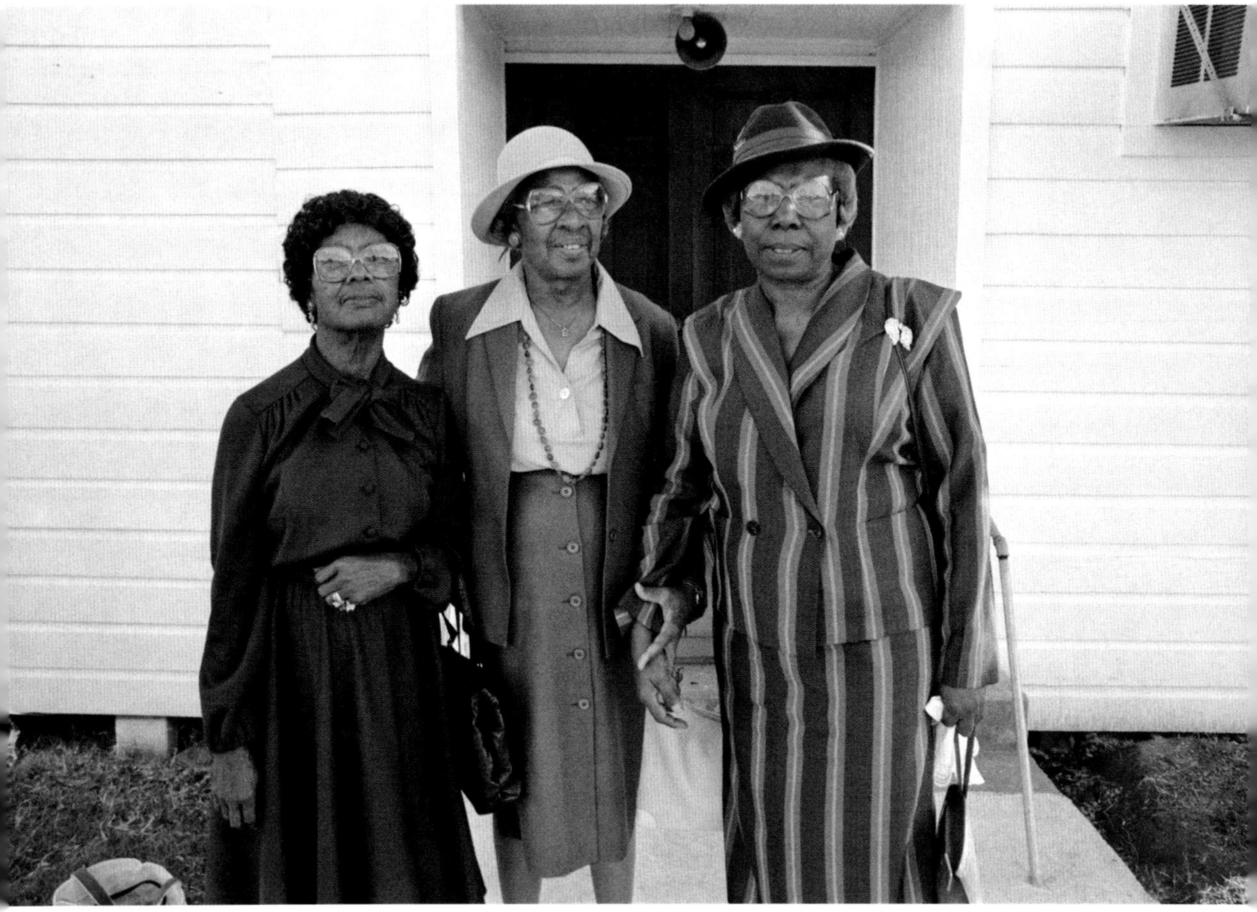

Lacey Henry, Marie Williams, and Irizola Wilson at Pleasant Hill Missionary Baptist Church

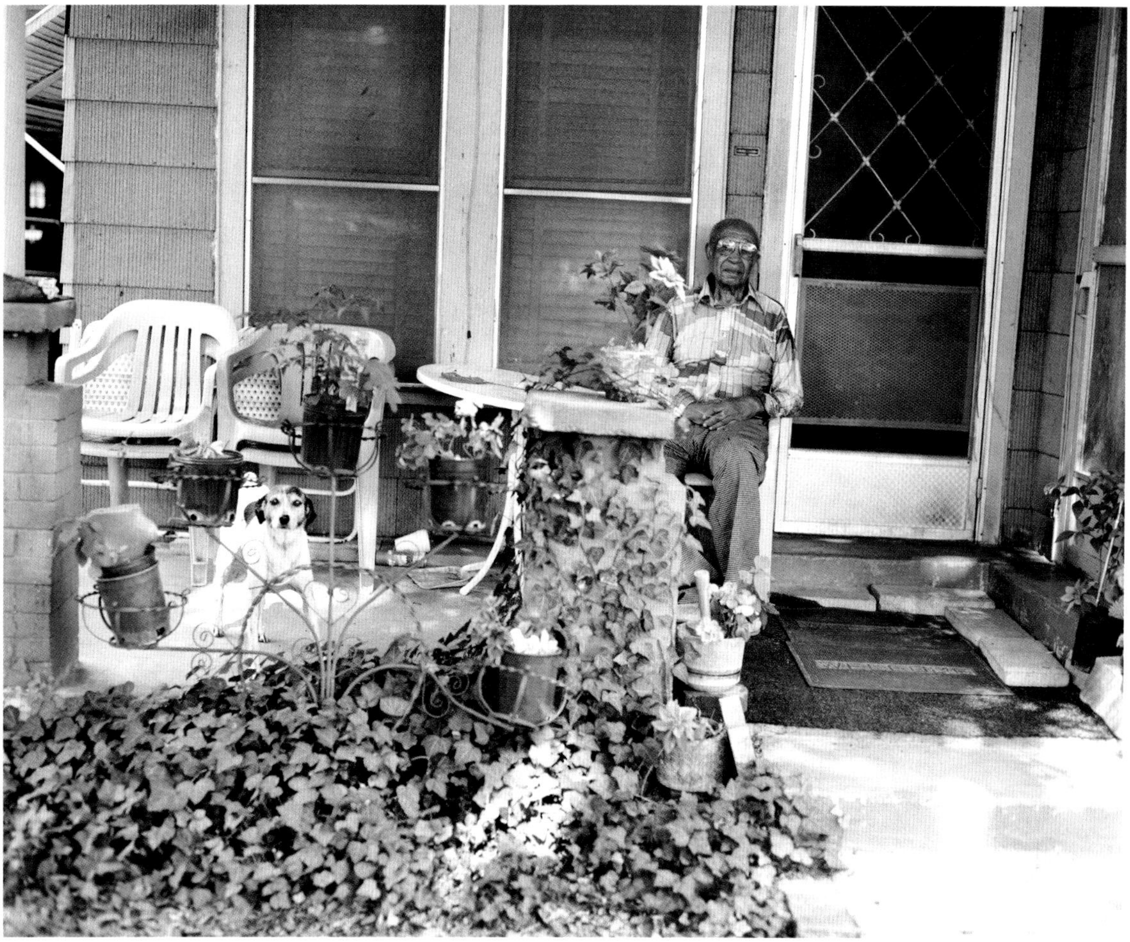

Early Wilson

Early Wilson

"Are you Early Wilson?" I asked the first time I went to the Wilson house. As I approached, I saw an elderly man sitting on the porch and looking out at the empty lane in the small community of Glidden, where little seemed to happen. "What's left of him" was his laconic reply, said without a smile.

At that time, Early and his wife, Irizola, were in poor health, according to what she had said over the phone. Early had heart trouble, and she suffered a bevy of other problems. Things were rough for them in terms of health. Still, they felt fortunate for their grown offspring who lived nearby and gave them loving attention.

Early was born on August 18, 1917, in the Borden community, near Glidden. His parents were Laura Brown and Early Wilson Sr. "Daddy worked on a section," said Early, meaning a railroad section. "Mama worked for people. We had a little plot of land." That is about all he had to say about himself. He married Irizola in 1938, which meant that he and she had been together sixty-one years when we met. Irizola gave more of their story, saying the two of them had gone through the Glidden schools together (along with Marie Williams, who remained their dear friend still, sixty years later and many miles apart). Early quit school in the ninth grade and went to work for the railroad, like most everybody else in the town of Glidden, where the railroad was "it" for work opportunities. His job was in the roundhouse.

Irizola declared, with a smile, that Early was the cutest boy in their entire school, not to ignore that he was also the winner of the state interscholastic meet. And he was a good public speaker. So she determined to catch Early, and catch him she did. Many years and many offspring later they were still together.

Sadie & George Dorn

The reason I stopped for the first time at the Dorn house was to meet and compliment whoever was living there, to tell them how much we all appreciated their place. Every time we drove by going into Weimar, it was a joy to see, the house looking freshly painted with brilliant white walls and blue trim, the flowerbeds brimming with colorful flowers. It was the best of all Weimar yards. In a neighborhood that was usually somewhat bedraggled, the Dorns' place stood out with its bold statement of love lavished and returned in kind by nature. Who were these people who tended their place so lovingly?

Luckily, George and Sadie were sitting on their front porch, relaxed and comfortable in bare feet and house slippers, an endearing fact. They responded modestly to the compliments. George turned his head and smiled, allowing that he just enjoyed working outdoors, now that he was retired and had the time to do it. Sadie said nothing, letting her husband receive all the glory.

Happily, they felt comfortable for the photograph, although Sadie did discreetly hide her cigarette behind her hand, away from the camera's eye.

When I next looked for them, the Dorns were gone, moved to another town. The house was empty, and the garden had lost its luster, looking sadder and sadder, clearly missing George's tender attentions.

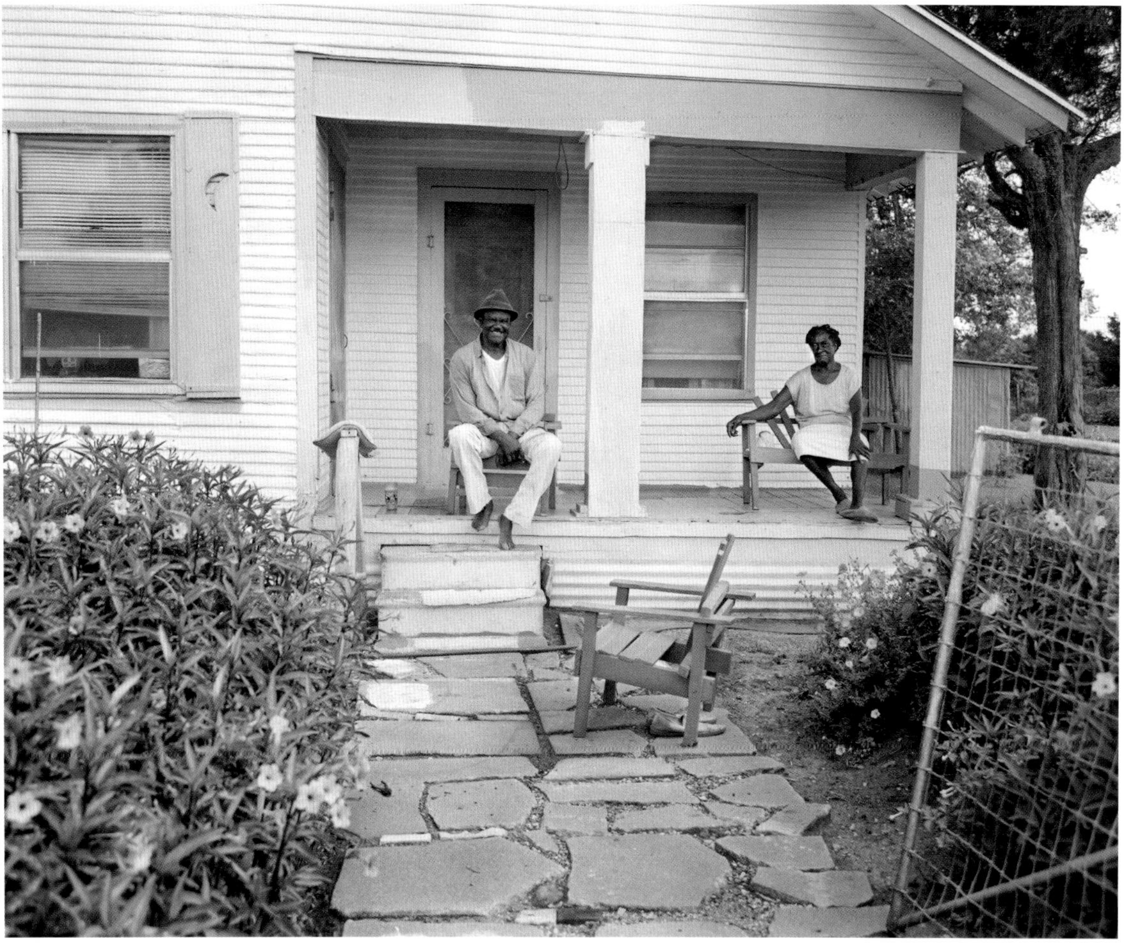

George and Sadie Dorn

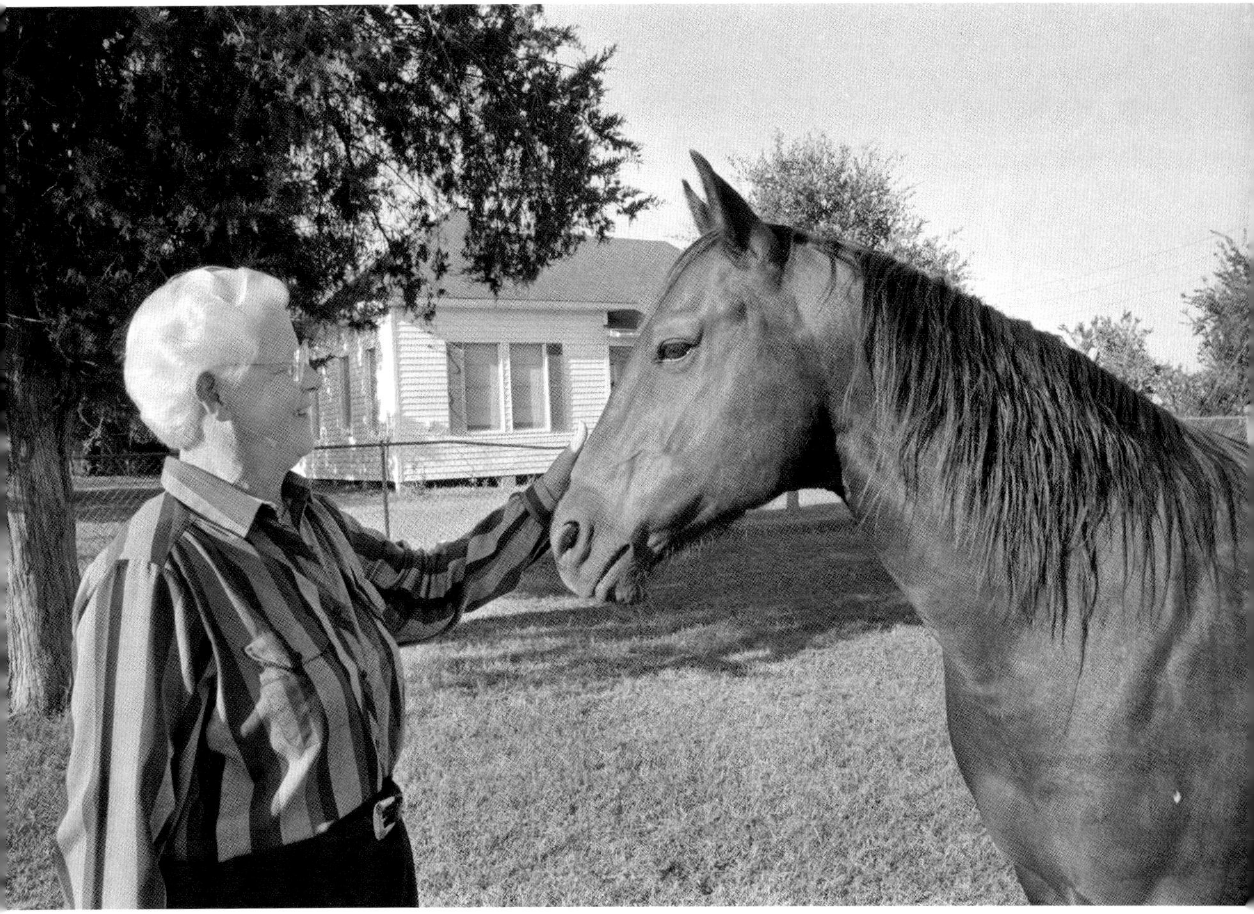

Lillie Kahlden Freis with her horse

Lillie Kahlden Freis

Lillie Freis showed in her face the kind of person she was—feminine, direct, strong, and modest.

Her family farm was just next door to ours, and before we ever met, I used to watch her at a distance over the fence, admiring her ways. She seemed independent, lovely, and strong. She could often be seen driving across her land, slowly checking the cattle from her battered and fading rusty-red pickup, her hound dog nearby, her arm resting on the window, her white hair soft and free, a dreamy look on her face. I found out later that she was grieving then for her deceased husband, Joe. "You *sure* would have liked him if you'd a'known him," she said with certainty, making one wonder if the expression on her face had not held an unrecognized sadness.

Lillie's tall, gangly black hound dog was always with her, keeping her company, loping alongside in his loose-limbed way or sitting regally in the truck bed behind her, staring off in the same direction as she, in imitation of his composed mistress. Like two close friends they seemed. He lived a long time, and before he died, he became crippled, so Lillie had to lift him up into his place on the truck. When he was gone, she asked for my photograph of him as a memento.

Lillie was born Lillie Kahlden, on the land where she was still living. It had once been the site of the old Adkins Plantation, as everyone said, part of a large farm dating from the mid-nineteenth century. The old Adkins cemetery could still be found there, headstones crumbling away, behind a low iron fence under large oak trees near Lillie's house, some words still readable in the weatherworn stone.

"I remember them building this house," Lillie said. "I was about five years old. I know I had a little bicycle, and a carpenter was here, and I had a little hammer, and he had vile language, you know, and I'd follow him everywhere whether he'd talk or not. But I thought I was helpin' him. And yet, I can remember the building of this house and that it rained and rained and rained and rained, and those carpenters, they brought the lumber in on the wagons 'cause it was so muddy. But I can't remember the tearing down of that old Adkins house.

"We were eleven in the family. Them days it looked like they all had large families. Like all the Brandts—my mother was a Brandt. It was quite a slew of 'em.

"You know, when you're young, you think nothin' gonna leave us. I've wished a many a time I'd've wrote down what my mother, Minna, told me." Minna Brandt Kahlden was born in 1876 and died in 1974. She came to America from Germany with her parents, Eilert Gerhard Brandt and Sophie F. Wilhemina Westing, and her brother

Theodore. The senior Brandts were married in 1865 and produced fourteen children. They celebrated their fiftieth wedding anniversary in 1915.

"I recall her saying she came over when she was twelve years old from Germany. They settled in the Holman area, then moved to the Osage community, then called Adkins." According to a news clipping, the Adkins farm was bought first and other tracts were bought later until they had acquired over three thousand acres of farmland.

"The older Brandt boys [Minna's brothers] came alone," Lillie said. "Emil, the oldest, was first to come, followed by his brother George in 1888. They came with work promised to them. And then later the rest of the family came.

"They were on the North Sea. And she would always tell me about how they had a big dike there and that the water would go *way* up. And she loved her grandma very much, and so she said they'd just wait for the water to go *way* down, and then they could walk across that dike and walk to Grandma's home."

Lillie's mother died at the age of ninety-eight. Lillie laughed when asked her own age and said, "I'm just glad I'm still here." She was born June 27, 1919.

Lonnie Coleman

"I worked with many historicals," Lonnie Coleman declared, describing his life.

His first job, at eight, earned him a meager five cents. But it gave him the chance to learn the skills that he then used for the rest of his life: cooking, catering, being a butler, and serving, often in the best houses of Columbus. Along the way, they say, he made many friends and gained the respect and trust of his employers. He also worked for the post office for forty-seven years and for Coastal Banc SSB (as it's called in 2005), retiring in 1991 after twenty-seven years. The bank honored him with a retirement party to recognize his "many years of valuable service."

Lonnie was born in 1918 in Columbus. He said he played as a child with a host of neighborhood white children with whom he remained friends—an amazing feat for Columbus, where the lives of the two communities, black and white, seemed almost totally separate. All of these childhood playmates had since died. In fact, Lonnie was coming home from the funeral of his last surviving childhood friend, Mary Youens Hopkins, when we first met. Mary was the great-niece of Josiah Shaw, the man for whom Shaw's Bend community is named and whose grave is on our family farm. I had been trying for quite a while to meet Mary Hopkins and, sadly, had failed.

"When I was little," Lonnie said, "I was good. People said, 'He's gonna get into somethin' 'fore the day is gone.' And I said, 'I'm not! I'm gon' be *nice*!' And so I was, I was always nice. I was always quiet. I always got credit from my teacher 'cause I was quiet. They used to leave me, go out the room and leave me in charge of the class. And I would be sayin', 'Y'all hush, got to hush now, 'cause *I'm* the teacher today.' And all my teachers used to laugh—she out in the hall, killin' herself laughing. 'Lonnie?' 'Yes ma'am.' 'Come on, now, you're in charge of the class.' And that was so cute—I laugh about that still."

Lonnie was a rarity. He had a softcover book written about him, with a copy in Columbus's Nesbitt Memorial Library. He was a Mason and the treasurer of his lodge. He was a deacon and usher at the Greater Smith Chapel Baptist Church and an officer on several church-related boards. He served in the army during World War II as a first sergeant and fought in Saigon, Okinawa, New Guinea, and Guadalcanal. He was awarded the Victory Medal, Overseas Service Bars, the American Campaign Medal, and two Bronze Stars. All of this, plus holding one job for almost fifty years, was pretty special.

Yet the most admirable thing about Lonnie may have been his daily visits to the nursing homes to see his former employers and the friends. He said he loved going

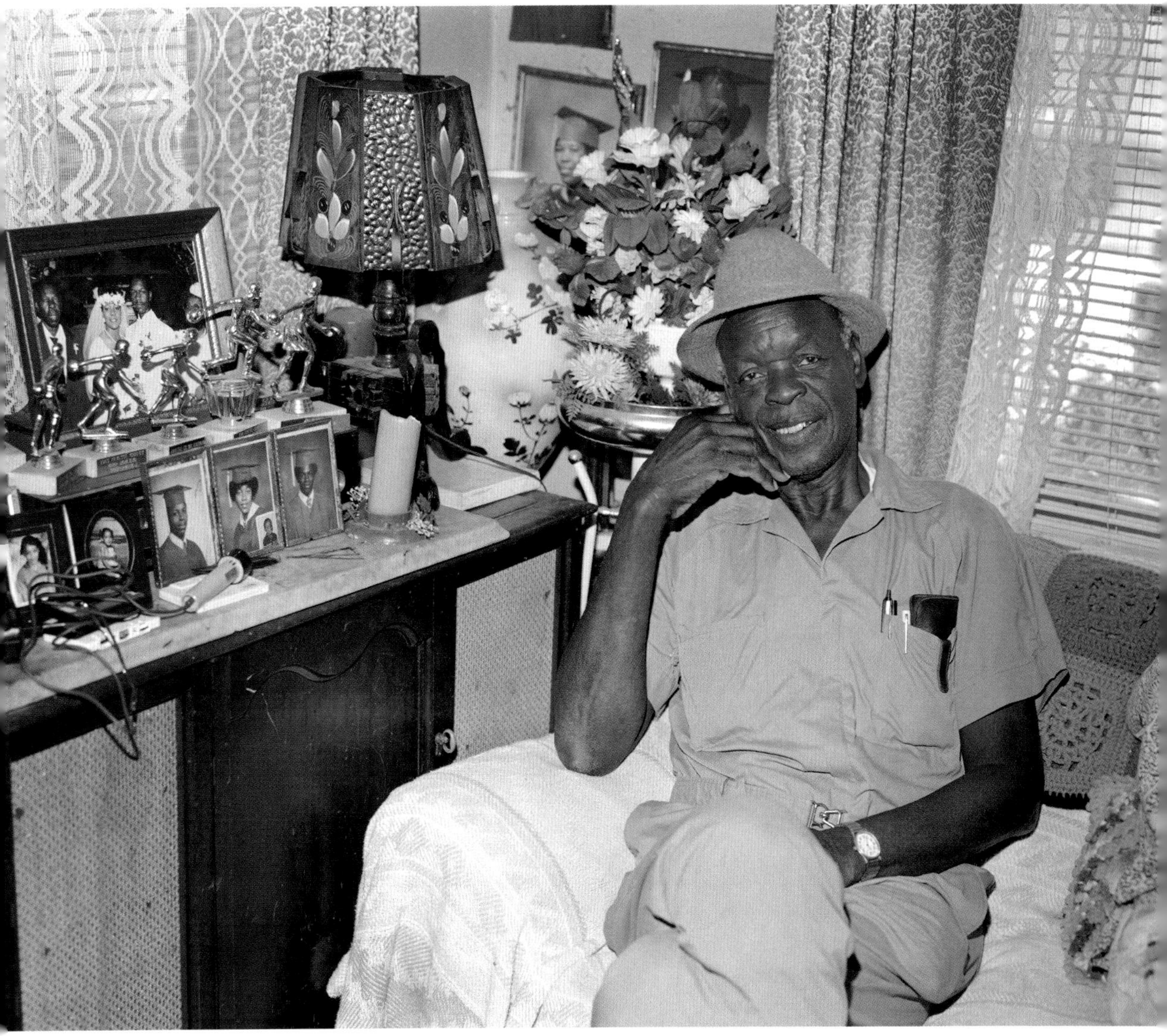

Lonnie Coleman

and that, far from saddening him, it made him happy to be there, cheering up the older folks in their confinement at the rest home. "I just go *all* the time. Runnin' here, runnin' there. To the doctor, carry 'em to the doctor. Nursin' home. Go to the nursin' home every day. Visit nursin' homes. Kind of like, I tell you, go, go, go with me. I *loves* to go! I'm just busy doin' things for people. I *never* stay home." And that was Lonnie Coleman.

Lonnie was living with his sister and numerous younger people of unknown relationship when we met, still busy, still "go, go, go," his house full of objects and mementoes of his life, rich with personal history.

Roy Lee Coleman

Roy Lee liked to write, saying, "I writes *all the time*." And truthfully, he was carrying paper and pencil every time we met—ready to write at any moment it seemed. He said he'd rather write than talk. And he wrote well, having made it to the ninth grade in school.

When he quit school at seventeen, Roy went to work on the railroad—"*hard* work," he said. He ended up doing "all kinds of work" in his lifetime: in gravel pits, on railroads, in highway construction, and in trucking. He was not working anymore when we met, but he was receiving living money from the government, $477 a month, $50 of which he sent regularly to his son, Christopher Wade, incarcerated in a Texas prison.

When it was time for his son to get out of prison, Roy said he was going to tell him "*not* to come home to Columbus!" He added firmly, "'Cause this is a *hard* town, a bad place." Two of Roy's sons had been in prison. His only daughter was a law officer, "with two kids, big and fat—they're *bad*!" he said with a smile.

Of Christopher Wade, Roy said, "He knowed he was wrong. He's a young man—all he has to do is go out and cut yards, rake leaves. 'As soon as I get my pension money, I'm gonna buy you a pickup. You go 'round and cut yards. Stay out of trouble.'

"See, the pen—I've been in there twice. I know. They *rough* on you. They really rough on you for dope and rape and stealin'—rougher on you for that than they is for killin' four or five people. When I first went— you might know the place—they call it Tennessee Tower, call it 'cold fields.' And it *stay* cold. These dawgs kept on whuppin' me, and I wrote Marvin Zindler [a Houston investigative reporter]. The last time, I was a turnkey."

Roy was once a fighter. "Somebody mess with me—*trouble!* That's why I stays at home. I ain't gonna take no foolishness. See, I used to drink a heap, but now a half-pint last me five days. But I got to have a bunch of soda water with it."

The last time I saw Roy Lee, he was sitting on a stool in the dirt road, the charred ruins of his house still smoldering behind him. He had fallen asleep with a lighted cigarette and burned his place to the ground. Notice the cigarette pack rolled in his pant cuff in the photo. The next time I called, Roy Lee was in a nursing home, and that's where he died. It was sad that he died without getting the home in the country he had wanted, "surrounded by pyracantha bushes with thorns, to keep people out."

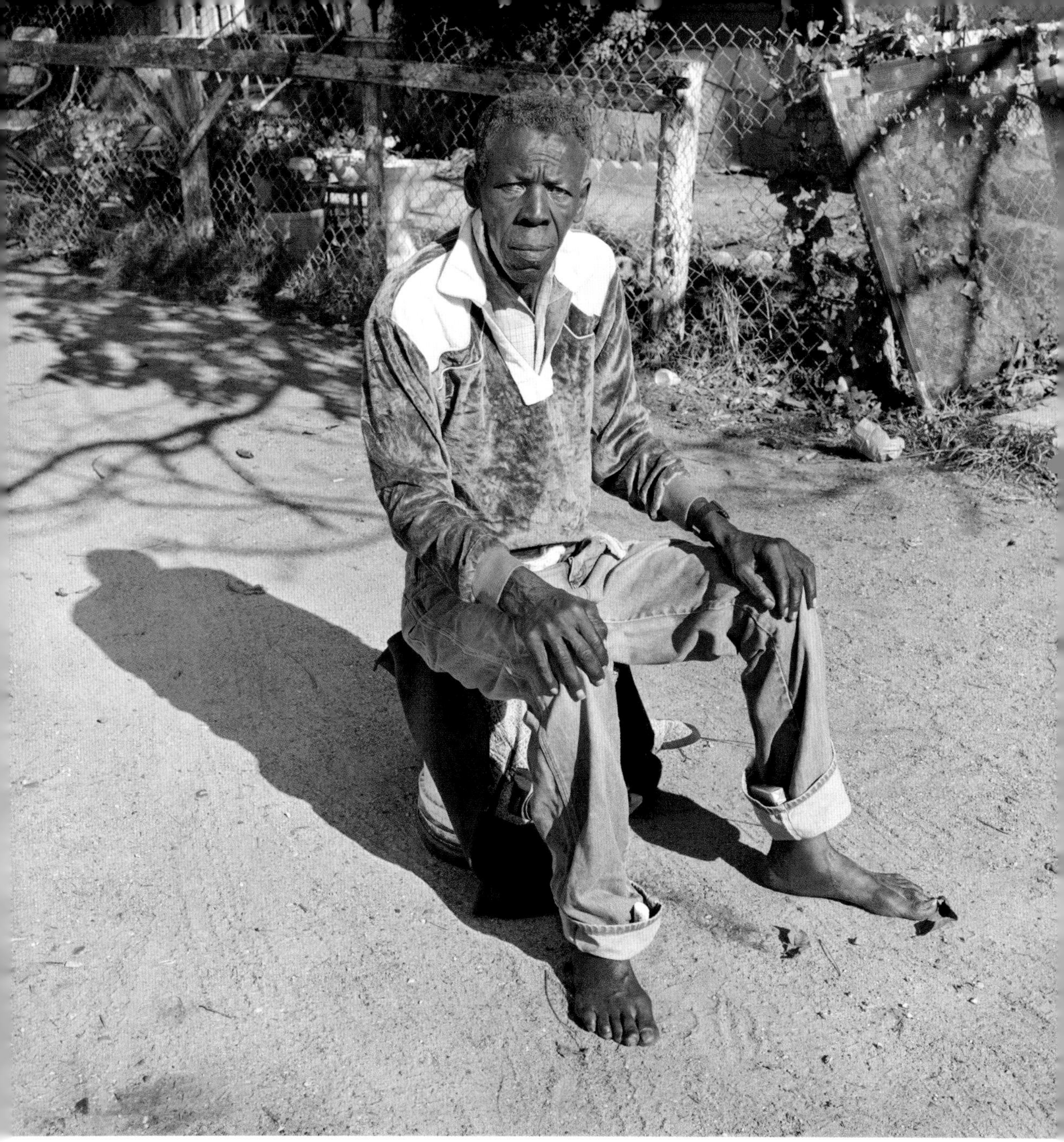

Roy Lee Coleman, sitting in front of his burned-out home

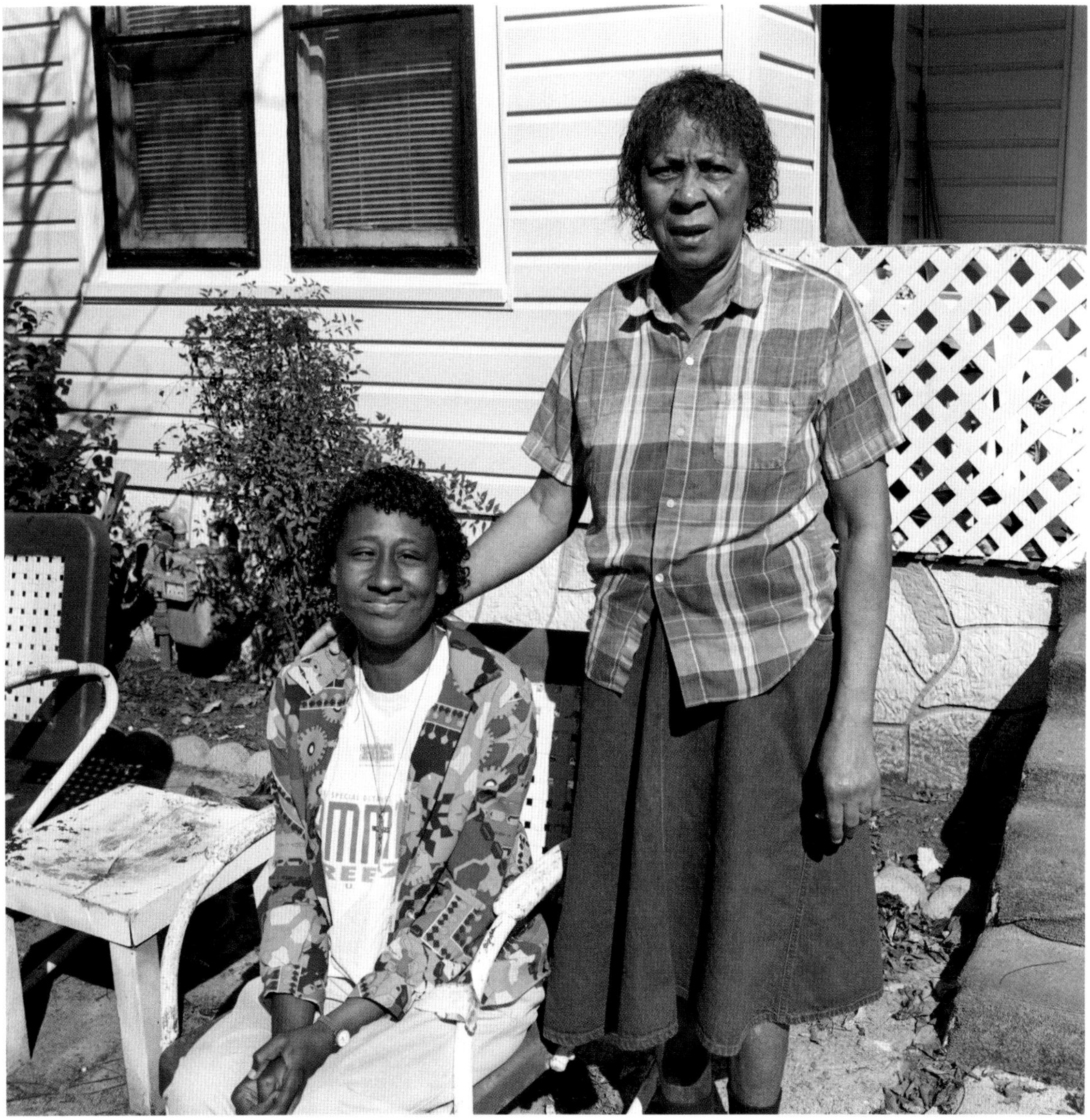

Willie Mae Denley and her daughter, Pandora

Willie Mae Denley

Willie Mae Denley, age seventy, didn't have much to say since, she stated matter-of-factly, her life "didn't had much to tell about."

Willie Mae was born in 1930, a half-sister to Lonnie and Roy Lee Coleman. They shared a common mother. "My mother was named Mattie Coleman, and my daddy was Will Denley," Willie Mae said. "No, he wasn't no farmer. I think he say he worked on some kind of weldin' outfit, and that's why, you know, by him weldin', that's when he lost his eyesight.

"And then I had a brother too. He worked in a gravel pit. And he went blind in both of his eyes, 'cause that's what he did—he did weldin' job. He just retired up until he died. Then his wife, you know, taken care of him. And my daddy, you know, he could feel and tell different things. He tried to raise chickens, and he had sheeps and li'l things like that. He know how to go out and feed 'em, how to cut wood and bring in the water. So, that 'bout all I know!"

Willie Mae said her life had been uneventful, yet she conceded that she was truly fortunate, more fortunate than her schoolmates, because she had had the good luck to finish all twelve grades of school, a rarity in her day. "Whole twelve years!" she exclaimed proudly.

She began to work when she was thirteen and said she was lucky there too, because her employers taught her all they could about cooking and housekeeping, enabling Willie Mae to get good jobs the rest of her life.

She worked many years for one family, the Isgrigs, who treated her "like part of their family." Ruby Isgrig, the only survivor at that time, gratefully declared Willie Mae "a wonderful woman, who cared lovingly" for Ruby's mother until the day the old lady died. "I worked for 'em forty-three years," Willie Mae said, "an' then after I retired, I worked for Miz McAnally. Then, after I retired from Miz McAnally, I had worked for her for twenty-three years. Then before then, I worked for Miz Sybill Knight Pristell for ten years. So I have did a lot in my life that I knows of."

As a youngster, "I went after school, and then I helped, you know, wash the supper dishes. And then after that, then Miz Isgrig started me doin' things—well, she was learnin' me, teachin' me different things, how to cook an' all. An' after then, I just started cookin' on my own.

"I just did what I had to do, you know, after school. I went after school at 4:30, and I worked till about 7:30 in the ev'nin'. Then after then, I had to come home and get my lesson. At the time, you know, they didn't want to pay me fair wage. I was just makin' like a dolla' an' a half a week. That was all. And then after, the prices went up a li'l bit—I went from there to two-fifty, you know.

"Well, my parents, they used to teach me right from wrong, you know, and teach me how to obey peoples, and teach me, you know, how to don't sass peoples out, things like that, you know. But that's most the thing—they always did try to bring me up right, you know. They always said obey old folks. So I tried to do that. But far as learnin', you know, my others, I learned that from the peoples that I worked for, like cookin'. And I did washin' and ironin' on the jobs, you know, like that.

"Yeah, I learned a lot, you know? From 'round the people, you know, that I worked for. So therefore, that's what I know in my childhood.

"Oh, my happiest time when I was 'long 'bout sixteen, goin' out and havin' a good time! Oh, yeah. Well, we had a place down here we used to call it the Rhythm Inn. And we used to go down there on the weekend. It open up on Friday for the teenagers. For Friday, Saturday, and Sunday—that was just for the teenagers, you know. And for the café, they wouldn't allow us in the cafés, but they had a teen hall for us to go to, yes, and a jukebox. We used to have a really good time.

"Well, so far, everythin' was a good time when I was young, and now everythin' is workin' out good. I haven't had no real hard times, you know, in my adult's life. Yes, I do very well."

When asked what was especially important to her to have in her story, she replied, "Well, whatever you wanna put. One or two words down there, you know, whatever. You can put down, you know, like when I was comin' up, like I was doin' work and workin' for the Isgrigs and them."

Pandora, forty-two, is Willie Mae's youngest daughter, one of four children. Pan, as she is known, has also been fortunate, said her mother. Pandora has been able to attend the Waldvogel Opportunity Center in Columbus where she was learning some crafts, and she was lucky enough to travel to the Special Olympics in Austin, something she really enjoyed. Pandora, of the lovely name and sweet nature, was living with her mother and Uncle Lonnie.

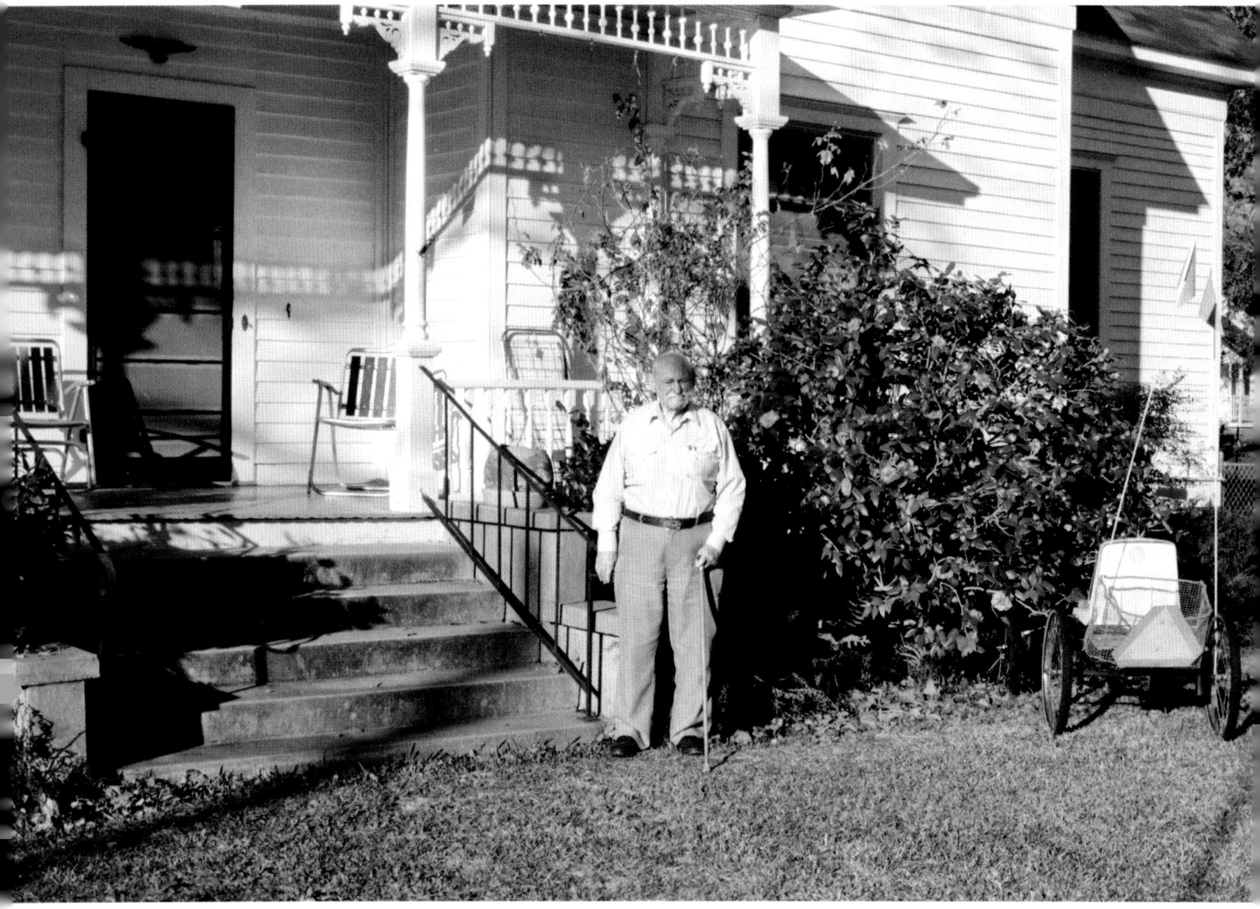

Bennie Isgrig

W.B. "Bennie" Isgrig

I first heard of Bennie Isgrig from Willie Mae Denley, who had worked for the Isgrig family for years in their home in Columbus. She described Bennie as a special man whose story needed to be included in this book.

I had seen Bennie several times around town, riding his three-wheeled bike. Little did I know that this cherubic-looking "Santa Claus" of a man on the tricycle would turn out to be a war hero, a respected local figure, a former high school football star, and a well-known trail rider. He was living in his family home, a lovely gingerbread house with a historic marker declaring the house to be noteworthy for its architecture and stating that it had been built in 1898 and bought by Bennie's family in 1916. Another plaque told a little of Bennie's personal history in World War II.

Taking Bennie's photograph was easy, but his story had to be gathered from his family and friends. His niece sent a newspaper clipping that described his participation in more than one thousand trail rides during his lifetime. It reported that he had broken his shoulder during one trip and was sidelined for a while, but it quoted him as saying, "I was mended in time for the next ride. Nothin's gonna keep me from going on a trail ride. Nothin'! I'm not gonna stay home, not when there's still a trail to ride." Bennie had a plaque commemorating his fortieth year as an original rider on the Old Spanish Trail, a weeklong ride to San Antonio. In 1976 he rode in a Centennial Trail Ride across the country from Texas to Philadelphia, when he was already an older man. The newspaper story continued, "When my mother was eleven years old, she drove a covered wagon from Kentucky to Texas. Nothing we do today can compare to that."

Regarding his war service, his niece said that Bennie served in the Third Armored Division in Europe and North Africa in World War II. After North Africa, he was quoted as saying that General Rommel was "a good enemy." Bennie also participated in the 1944–1945 Spearhead into Germany. A lifelong friend and admirer of Bennie's filled in more details on his war years, saying that Bennie was considered a real hero by many of the men he served with. Another man declared Bennie to be one of the greatest men he had ever known. "I wouldn't be here today," the man said, "if wasn't for Sergeant Isgrig. He saved my life after two tanks were shot out from under me." And there is another heroic story of Bennie having befriended an older soldier who was hospitalized with very serious wounds and a nervous breakdown. He was the despair of the hospital staff, until finally Bennie told the troubled man he would do "anything possible" to get him home to the States, and Bennie did just that.

One time Bennie's tank was surrounded by the Germans, and the tank's crew were forced to live inside their vehicle for more than a week; Bennie's job was to keep up the men's morale until they were freed.

Bennie was described as a person who liked most everybody and someone who had innumerable friends. He was called "a helper," someone "who would come fix a mile of fence" for a friend in need. Bennie was "not a braggin' man," one friend said, "but he wouldn't lie to you," even though he might tell you something you didn't want to hear. He was a man who could be "a fierce opponent," a most loyal friend, and someone who "had no fear in his life." "You could go to the bank with what he told you," a friend declared of Bennie.

Born Nathan Isgrig in Columbus, Bennie was a football hero in high school and "quite a beer drinker" in his later years. He never married and seemed to prefer walking and biking to driving a car. He lived in the family home until his death.

Ernest Brown

For several years, when driving through Columbus in the summertime on the way to the farm, I would see an old pickup truck parked on the side of Highway 90 just as the road left town. It sat at the top of a rise, after the golf course and before the Department of Public Safety, and it displayed tempting samples of fresh fruits and vegetables for sale. The proprietor sat in the shade—whatever shade he could find—waiting for customers. He seemed to be a man of great patience, because I saw few folks ever stop and buy anything from him, and still he came and sat and waited. I was usually too rushed to stop, hurrying to get to the farm after an hour's drive from Houston. Yet I felt a sense of sadness the day the man was no longer there in his usual place—he had become a familiar part of the landscape. I was glad to have stopped once or twice to buy something from him and glad to have gotten his picture. And I missed him and wondered where he'd gone.

It was a welcome surprise to find him again years later, through the help of the Columbus library, when I called searching for the name of the man in the picture, "the Vegetable Man," as I called him. The word from the library was that someone who'd come in thought she knew his daughter, maybe. Such is the blessing of small towns. And there he was, Ernest Brown—"the Man on the Hill," as others called him—retired and contentedly settled in Sublime, a minuscule town near Hallettsville. "You'll miss it if you blink," Ernest said, inviting me over to visit and telling how to find his tiny community.

In the way of many people I met, Ernest seemed unsurprised by my call and began right off to tell his life story over the phone. He told about being born in a place called Fullers' Element, close to where he was still living. He told about making fifty cents for each cord of wood he chopped as a young man, this being the main reason he left town and went to work in the oil fields, where he could make a whole ten dollars a day. He told about hauling cattle from Edna to Houston and San Antonio and how he had traveled "from here to yonder, *even* to *Louisiana*." And how, after all that, "I come back to where I left from," to his mobile home in Sublime.

We met again, face-to-face, in late 2000 and sat on the porch with his wife, Naomi, as their dogs and cats played happily together below us on the ground.

He began, "Well, I was born right back down here, I guess, about twelve miles back down here on the farm of Ernest Neuhaus. That is what my daddy named me, after him—he was one heck of a good feller, and my daddy was so proud of him.

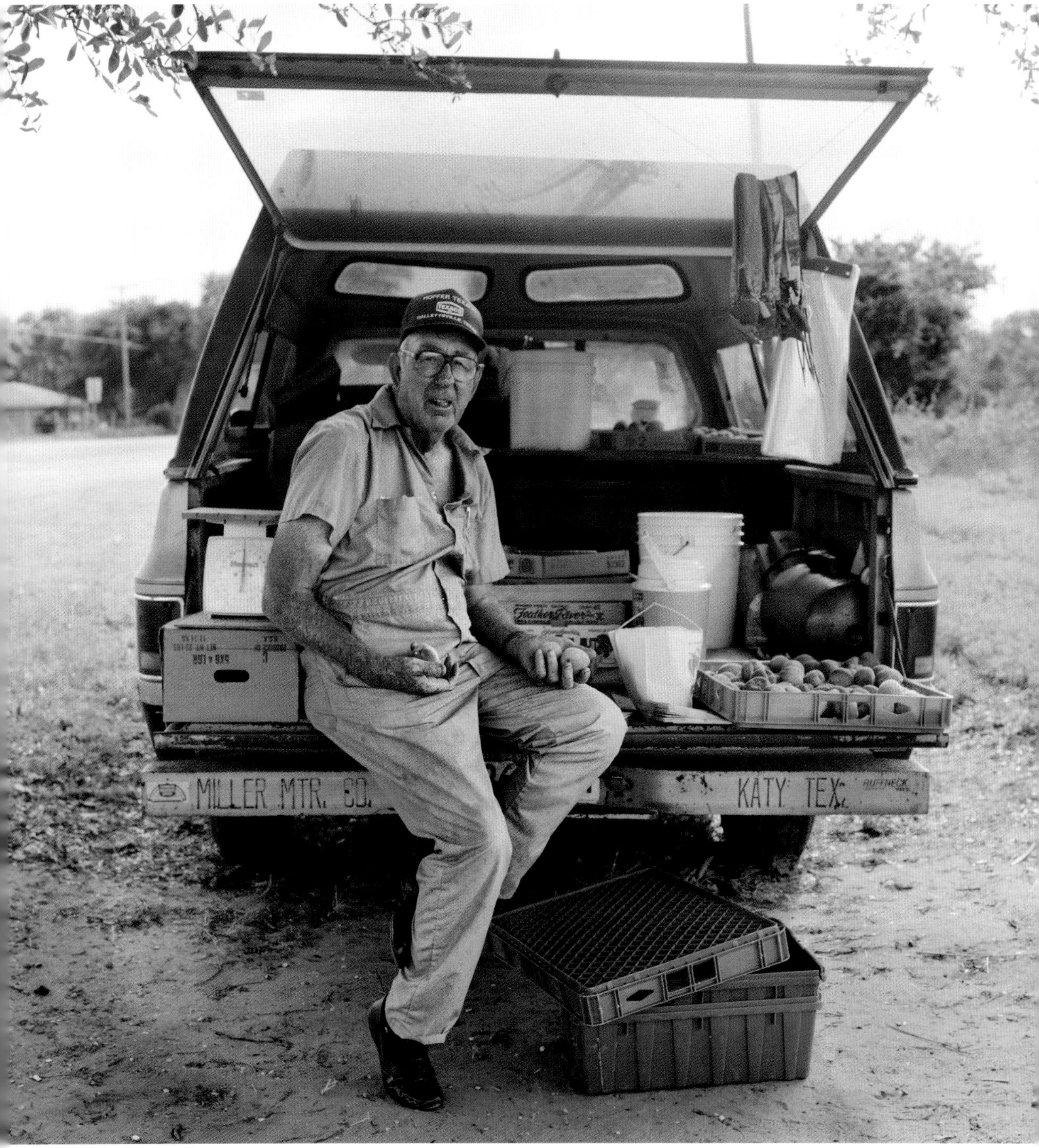

Ernest Brown, "the Man on the Hill"

And then I was raised up there on the farm, and we worked with mules. I used to plow behind mules from daylight to dark. We was so poor till my daddy couldn't buy me a pair of tennis shoes. I had to plow in the field barefooted, hot or what. And fin'ly he got me a pair of tennis shoes he got in Hallettsville up here, back when he had to go to town in a wagon and all. And I was so proud of them pair of tennis shoes that my daddy bought me, and I wouldn't wear 'em for a long time. And I thought he give a good price for them, and come to find out it cost him only twenty-five cents!

"I was raised up, you might as well say, on a poor farm is what I was raised up, 'cause we didn't have nothin'! We had chickens, but we didn't have no money to buy feed, so the chickens couldn't lay. They come out there to us just a *stumblin',* they was so weak. *Wasn't nothing*—wasn't even an earthworm could live in that ole poor sand.

"I moved down to Edna with one of my sisters. They were diggin' water wells for people down there. So I went to work for them down there, and they paid me whatever they could 'ford to pay me.

"And was a fellow down there name of Emmett Cole, and I would drive a cattle truck for him from Edna to Houston and back, and he would pay me six dollars a load. And if I went from Edna to San Antone and back, well, he would pay me eight dollars. And that was a lot more money than I was makin' helpin' these farmers and all around here."

Then he worked for a while for another sister and her husband: "Yeah, that was right back 'cross the river, back over here. Well, it really wasn't her husband—it was her boyfriend was what it was. He was married and, you know, she was 'on the side' for him—you know what I'm talking about? And he was paying me like fifty cents a day to work for him. Well, then I went to work in the oil field down in the Vanderbilt flat down there, roughneckin', and that was payin' ninety-nine cents an hour. And I thought that was real good money.

"When we get married, Mother?" he asked Naomi, adding, "Well, I been married twice. Do you want the first marriage? Well, I'd rather not, 'cause I lived like three months being with her—was like eight years—just wasn't no good." He had been running a beer joint and dance hall in Edna when he married the first time—"but it turned out she was married to *every man.*" He caught her in bed with someone else. Ernest was 268 pounds of solid muscle at that time, and said he kicked in the wall, trying to break into their bedroom. Then he said to the poor man, "Get out, and take her with you." When the man said, "I don't want her," Ernest told him, "You've got her now!" and stomped out.

How did he and Naomi meet? "Well, me and another friend of mine was going to a dance at Ganader [Ganado]. And I didn't have no date, and he had a date with my wife what I got now. So he walked off and left her with me, and he went to dancin'.

So she was ready to go home, so I ask her if she wanted me to take her, and she said yes. So after I got on the road with her, I asked her for a date the next week and she said yes, and that is where it got started."

"Was she pretty?"

"Damn right! She didn't weigh much. She only weighed one hundred twenty-eight pounds when me and her married. She gained a little weight since then," he said, chuckling affectionately. Naomi smiled along with him, looking unbothered by her husband's comments on her weight.

"And so I asked her to marry me and she said yes. And I still got her now since"—since 1949.

Said Ernest, "Her family had it real rough like *we* did comin' up—pickin' cotton and cuttin' cedar posts and everything else. They lived in the bar ditches and everywhere else, I think, back then—in cars, wherever they could sleep."

At Naomi's urging, Ernest told the story about when they got engaged: "We were going over to the rodeo ground. And we was walkin'. I wanted to take a shortcut, and I walked off out there in the grass and weeds, and when I did, I went down there in the septic tank. And I had on cowboy boots, and I got a bootful! So I come back over there, and I was really smellin' *loud*! So what I did, well, I asked her if she would marry me. I figured then, if she would take me when I was smellin' like that, maybe she would keep me!"

Ernest added, "Well, she stayed at home most of the time with the kids, and I was roughneckin', and I wasn't making enough money to support them at home, so I had to sleep in the car or in a bar ditch so I could have money enough."

Naomi interrupted: "You didn't sleep in the bar ditch. You slept in the car a few times but not in a bar ditch." And Ernest countered, "Well, I did! You may not want to believe it."

Ernest continued: "So I've still been with her a little over fifty-one years, and we have raised our seven kids plus what we have helped raise up of our grandkids, and I still got her! Thank the Lord for that."

He remembered the babies being born. "One time, I was working in the field way out there in the country out of Edinburg, and she drove out there in the car. I went out there to see what did she want, and she said, 'Well, you've got to take me to town. I'm fixin' to have a baby.' And we was *way out there* at the rig. And I went and told the tool pusher, or driller, and he couldn't get me off the location fast enough, for me to get her back to town 'fore she'd have the baby out there at the rig! So then we had *kids*! We got seven in all!"

Another time, her labor started in the middle of a winter storm. "We was living over there at Victoria," Ernest recalled, "and one morning she said, 'I gotta go to the doctor. I'm fixin' to have a baby.' I went out there, me and her got in the car, and when we did, I couldn't see out of the windshield for the ice. I got some water and throwed it on it, and it was freezin' just as fast as I was puttin' it on there. Finally, we went on down to the Decatur hospital. And when we did, I pulled up there in front, and we got out from the car down to get in, when she said, 'Oh, oh, wait a minute, wait a minute—here it is!' And so she had a baby, holdin' it in her lap! And I broked and run into the hospital. If that glass door would have been locked, I guess I would have went through it, fast as I was runnin'! And I was hollering, 'Hurry, hurry! Help me. My wife is in the yard havin' a baby!' And so here they come out there in the frost in the yard. So they got her on the stretcher, and they was takin' her in to the hospital there. And when they did, she said, 'Oh, oh, oh!' She went through the door, and there was another born!"

Naomi said, "They always told me I wasn't gonna have but one." And Ernest added, "So we was surprised of everything. So that girl, we didn't know what we gonna name her. Fin'ly we decided we'd name her Candace Colleen, and I nicknamed her Frosty. And now she goes by that name—everybody calls her Frosty."

He looked fondly at Naomi as he said, "We were a pretty good incubator—a pretty good incubator, we was."

Ernest went back to driving a truck. "We went to work for Martinez—a dump truck," he said. "He had a gravel pit up there in Altair, and I drove a truck for him and run front-end loaders and different things there for him. And he was one hell of a nice guy to work for. Whether if I got to work and get a check or not, he would still give me a check to help us out."

Naomi chipped in, "And then he started doin' in the garden, sellin' vegetables, raisin' chickens, deliverin' eggs. Up till he had his heart attack, we had chickens to eat, duck, layin' hens." Ernest recalled, "I guess about five hundred head. Duck, geese, guineas, turkeys—you name it, we had it all. Rabbit. You ever eat a tame rabbit? Shoot! You don't know what's good! Oh, man! She could cook a tame rabbit. Shoot, I could eat a whole one. It was a pretty good little pot of meat there."

Naomi added, "His mom lived with us here, in that trailer over there. She killed two squirrels out here 'fore she died. I couldn't eat them squirrels. She sat there and ate all them squirrels. These were fried. And she never had a tooth in her head!"

Ernest was told he had to give up his garden, his chickens, and his egg business after his heart attack. He hated losing these things he enjoyed so much, and that explains why he disappeared from his place on the highway. The two Browns agreed that this was the worst thing that ever happened to him, because he had been going down in physical health and spirits ever since.

"Had five hundred hen layin' right here in the back, and I was sellin' eggs. And then I had a garden back down there at the back to sell out of. We'd eat and use what we had in here. And then I'd load up, and I'd go usually up there where you seen me—that's the best place that I ever found to sell there. Well, I'll tell you one thing, I miss that road since it ain't out there—I miss it."

As they sat telling their stories, Naomi said of Ernest, "He throwed his ciggy-rets away, and his alcohol too, in 1985. He gave it up without Alcoholics Anonymous, and

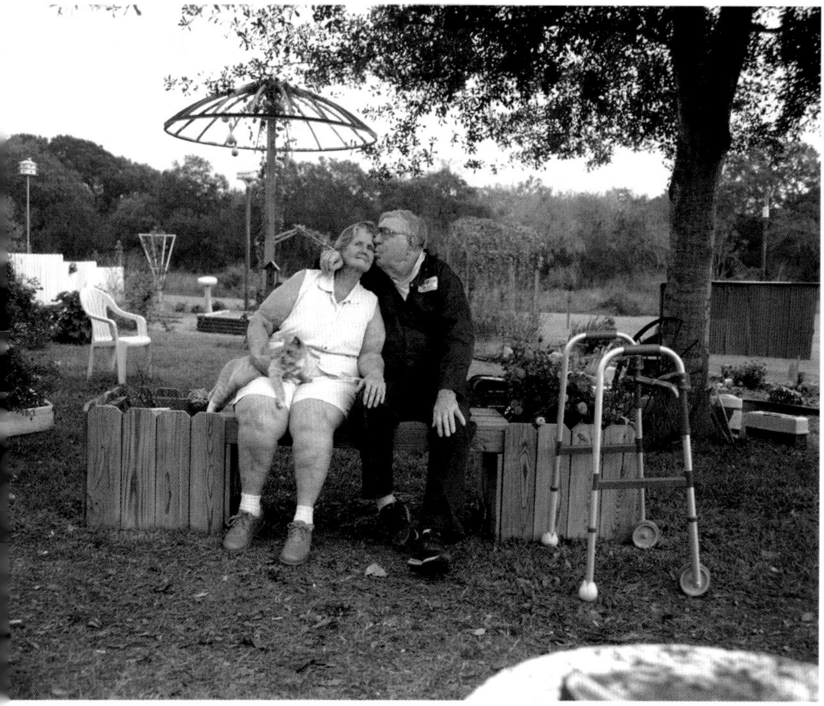
Naomi and Ernest Brown

he hadn't smoked or drunk anymore. He woke up in jail. When he heard that door clang, he knew that was it, and he had to give it up." Yet she said Ernest had always taken good care of his family and was always kind, even in his drinking days.

As I left, Ernest invited me to come back for dinner sometime. "And bring your own dinner," he said, laughing. "We'll sit together."

Emma Stancik

Emma Stancik said her name loud and clear when we introduced ourselves and then continued right on without any prompting. "May the eighteenth is my birthday," she announced. "Last Saturday was my birthday. Ninety-four. Yes, ma'am, ninety-four years old, born in 1897."

We were visiting in her bedroom at the Live Oak Nursing Center in Columbus, where Emma was a resident. She was totally relaxed and affable, clearly not wondering what a stranger was doing in her room with camera and tape recorder.

Calmly, she continued, "Born at Ellinger. I was so little, I couldn't tell you when we moved here. My family, all of 'em were farmers, and I was a farmer all of my life too. Um-hmm! I married Joe Stancik. I have seven chil'rens. I have five boys and two girls [pronounced 'gur-els']. I was sure that I was planned for it. I did always say I wanted lots of chil'rens. My mama had seven.

"I was not quite four when my mother died, and my daddy, August, raised us all up. He did a good job. He was a sweet daddy. I miss him today yet.

"I got a great big family. I got thirty-five gran'chil'ren and fifty-eight great-gran'chil'ren. I got a big family. My daughter said, 'Mama, when I get married, I ain't gonna be such a fool and have that many chil'rens like you!' She had more." Emma smiled and added, "She have eight. She say she never gone say somethin' like *that* again."

Emma's maiden name was Ahlgrim. "My daddy and my mother come from Germany," Emma said, "and my oldest sister come from Germany—she was born in Germany. I don't know why the old folks come here. All the family, all my kinfolks, all come out here—I guess they just wanted to leave Germany, come to United States. It was a big bunch what come together."

Did she speak German? "Yes, ma'am, I still do. I can talk Low German, High German. German, English, and Czech, I could talk. When I marry my husband, my mother-in-law couldn't talk no English, so I hadda do sump'tin. So I learned it. Yes, she was an awful sweet woman, awful sweet mother-in-law."

After Emma died, I talked to her daughter, Lillie Poenitzsch, who seemed as cheerful, warm, and upbeat as her mother. She described Emma as "a wonderful mother." Lillie Poenitzsch also was a farmer, living in the Shaw's Bend community, directly across from our family farm, where the Colorado River makes a deep bend on itself.

Emma Stancik continued, "We always was on a farm, just workin' in a field all the time. So many times we lost our crop with the flood take it all, and it was really bad.

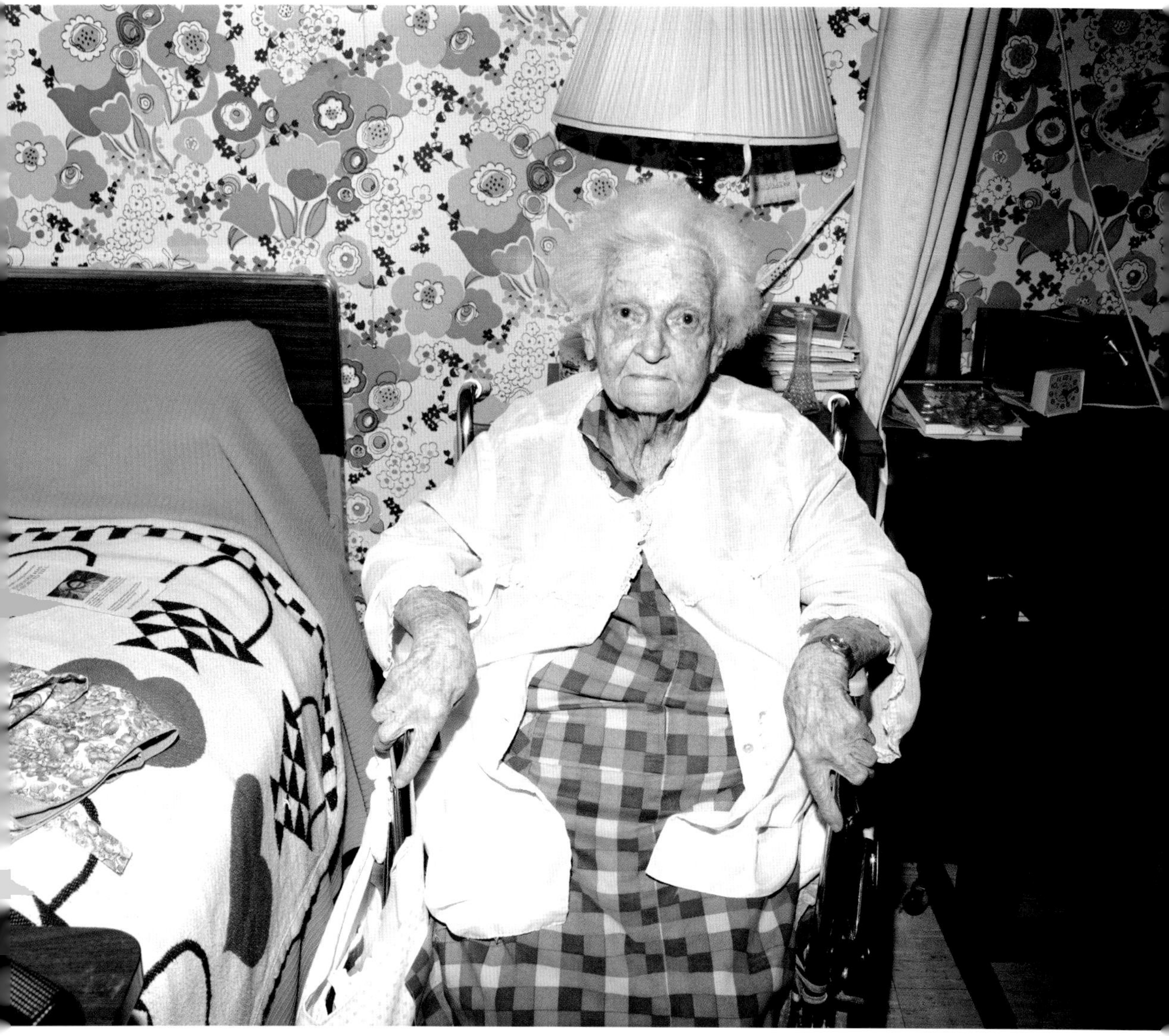

Emma Stancik in the nursing home

I say we really had a tough livin'. We picked our cotton yet on Sunday. My daddy said we better pick cotton today and get the bale out yet—tomorrow we ain't gon' get no more. And tomorrow was twenty foot of water on that same land. River took *everythin'*! We hadda make out, hadda eat less as we could, and hadda do what least we can.

"I worked on the farm every daytime, workin' all day. At night I washed clothes and ironed. I was happy married, that's all I could say. I was happy married. That was my best life. He was nice. He take me out. We went everywhere to visit [pronounced 'wisit']. We went to Port Lavaca and Galveston, all way round all the time.

"I lost three sons—all my sweet sons. Died—and my heart's bent." What a lovely phrase, so tender and evocative, to speak of a "bent heart."

"I just love it here [at the nursing home]. They all so nice. We got plenty to eat, and we got a nice bed to sleep. We should thank God we got a place to go like this. Always play dominoes, every day. Then we get some pah-ties, birthday pah-ties, and bingos and ice cream pah-ties. I feel *good*. And eats? I eat!" She smiled. "I feel good now, really good. Feel better than I did years ago."

Emma was a cheerful and inspiring model for old age.

Lillie Poenitzsch

Lillie Poenitzsch was a lot like her mom—open, friendly, and ready to share stories about her life. She began by talking about her marriage. "We'll be, on the twenty-second of this month, sixty-seven years! And I had birthday on the third. I was eighty-two. And he was ninety on the tenth. We have everything in one month. So they are plannin' on givin' us a little some kind of supper. We had supper. They surprised me. Everybody come with dishes Wednesday night, and we had supper here on mine. So they didn't want to leave him [her husband] out, so a bunch of them come round here. My kids, they come with a big pizza each one, so we had a pizza supper with him. So we celebrated it all." Lillie's husband, Lloyd, was suffering from physical and mental disabilities, conditions that kept him homebound and dependent on his family.

Lillie talked with pride about her grown children, "Well, my youngest one now—I had a younger one, but she passed away. I lost two of my daughters. Debbie—she was my youngest daughter—and Polly Ann, my second oldest daughter—lost with cancer. They both layin' there in the grave. We had our own cemetery here. She [Polly] paid the money to have it built and made—she wanted to come back home, the oldest one. She was such a lovely thing. And she taught school in Katy. She was Polly McRoberts. She married Mike McRoberts. And they built a big school in her name, in her honor. And we were all there and we were invited. We had a beautiful supper and everythin' that night. People was *so* friendly and good. They was so good to us all.

"I have never gone to a funeral that was more people there. Well, they turned Katy schools all out round there, just so they could all come. They loved her so much. It was a bunch of schools there that they turned out, just to have that half a day in the afternoon.

"Now, she was a teacher. I had five girls, and all teachers. And I have one in Columbus—the third one, Sandra O'Leary. She's teaching. Her husband is teaching. My oldest daughter and her husband both started teachin', but he is the principal now. And they got a daughter, and she is a principal already. So it's in the school, our whole family is."

Lillie added, "Well, *I* didn't have it—I was unlucky. And I loved school so much, but I didn't have the chance then 'cause we had a country school. I went through the sevens grade is all, to the eights grade. I had no way of gettin' to town—no kind of way."

Responding to a question about her school and how many children were there, she replied, "About twenty-five or twenty-four sometime, but the whole kids was in one

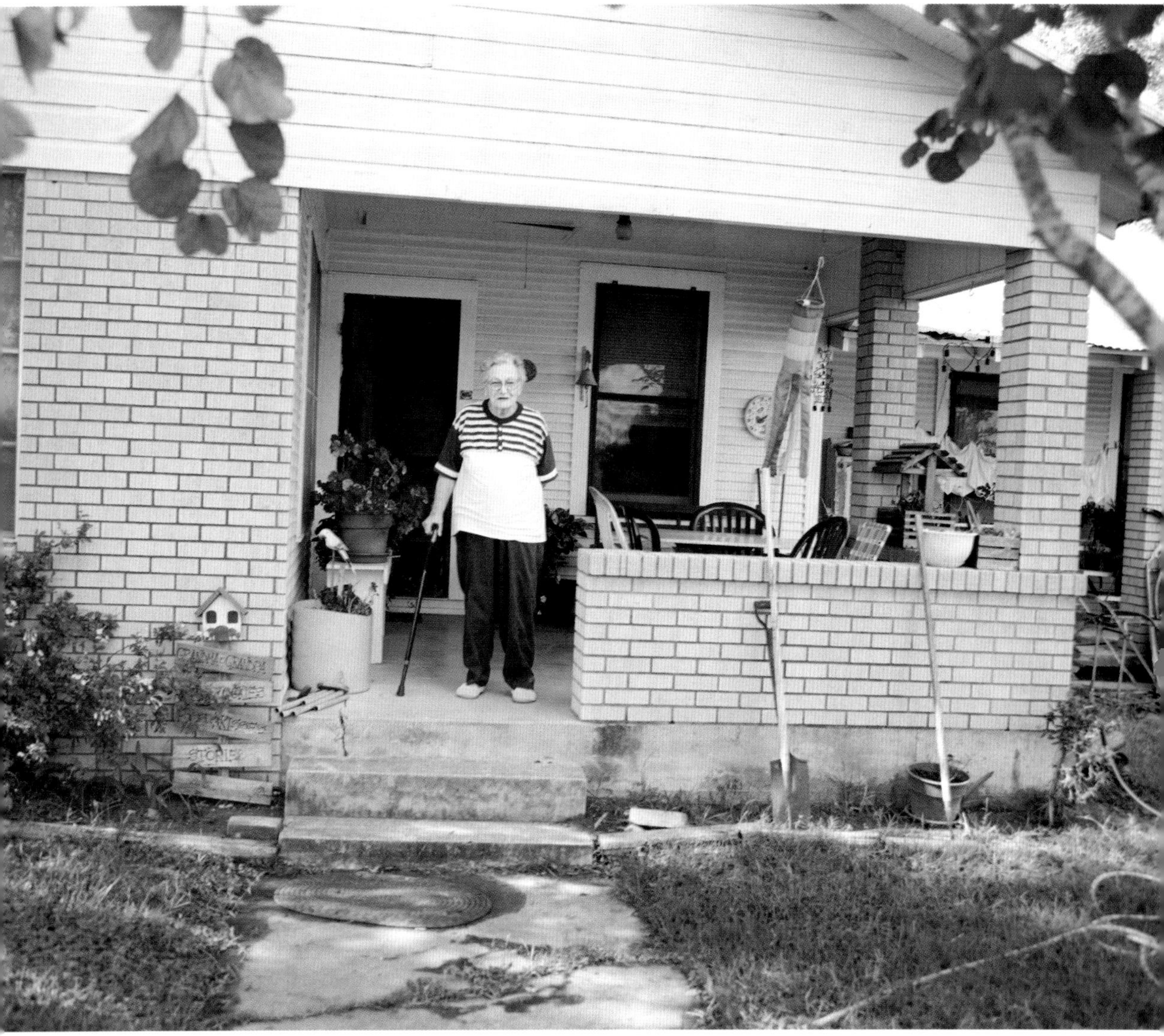

Lillie Poenitzsch

room. I walked to school. It was a long ways. Shoes, I usually kept mine on. I kept mine mostly on. But we had, at first, them long, black stockin's. None of 'em liked 'em, none of the kids. We'd get to the low-road gate, walk till there, and meet with the other ones, and we'd pull 'em off. When we come home, we put 'em on 'fore we got home, so Mama never knew that we didn't have 'em on.

"Miz Cora Rudicil was my teacher, and they all hated her, the other kids, 'cause she was strict and she was mean. But that's like all you need—you have to have teacher like that. She wouldn't whip or nothin', but she was strict. You had to study, and if you didn't do it, you got punished. Some of the boys would go run away, hide out in the bushes."

Lillie pointed down the lane that led to a small house a short distance away. "My parents, that was their home," she said, "that little brick one right there. That was their home. We built that just for them, to bring 'em here. You just should have saw Emma's, my mama's, face when we told her that it was theirs. They couldn't believe it. She was just like *in heaven* when she moved in that new house for herself. Everythin'—carpet on the floor and everythin' ready for her to just go and move in. They been farmers all their life, *all* their life. We're still farmin'."

Were all her sons farmers? "The oldest one," she answered. "None of the rest no more. My second oldest one helps 'im, but he's workin' at a machine shop here somewhere. He's got his own machine shop. And my younger son, he lives there now in that house here where Mama was, and they lives there today. They bought the house, and we deeded them two acres of land. He belongs to the Highway Department, and he works there. And she's a tax collector in Columbus Courthouse, his wife, Mary Jane. They have two sons. Here comes one now, come to visit us," she said, as a boy of ten or so ambled toward the house.

"Oh, Mama, she was a wonderful person. I always say she was my mama, but she was, to me, just a mama and a friend, a good woman to be with. A domino player! She played dominoes. We played a lot of dominoes. We'd have clubs. We'd have meetin's where we'd go together and play dominoes in the later years. But then she quit that. After she went to the rest home, she didn't come no more.

"She was always satisfied in the nursin' home. Always satisfied. Every time I'd come down, I'd ask her if I should bring her anythin' special. She said, 'No, they feed me good here.' Till the last, and the last she was really sick. Whatever it was, I don't know, but she got so sick, and then all at once, she come down. 'You go ahead and get yourself better and don't worry about me,' she said. 'Lillie, I am so ready to go see Papa,' she said. 'I am going to go see Papa now. I am ready to go.' We talked so much together at last, and she talked about goin'. She was ready to go.

"I feel the same way now already. I said if I had to go right now—I had such a good life already, I'm not afraid to go. I really am not. I wouldn't like to be tore up in the car or somethin' like that, but if it happens, it will happen like that too. But otherwise, I'm ready to go.

"I've had such a beautiful life. Hard. It was hard workin' and havin' eight children. And workin' in the field every day. For thirty years, I raked hay beside my husband—he baled it. I raked it, and he baled it. And for other people, we farmed."

What about her babies when they were little? "When they were nursin'?" she asked. "My two oldest girls—they'd drive 'em down to the field and I'd nurse them, and I'd go and rake, and rake again. Well, they stayed with the babies here at the house most of the time. And when they couldn't, I did. I had to then. But I felt so good in the field always. I never hated the job—I liked it. I'd get on that tractor and go from here. Do you know where Fayetteville is? I'd go to Fayetteville. And you'd go on that road—we'd turn off on this seventy-one [Highway 71] going to Fayetteville. And then you'd turn, and it's a big school there, and way up on the hill was a big patch. I'd go *way up there* and rake hay. That was so far. Yes, it was so easy to go. There was just no traffic like it's now.

"I was in the Home Demonstratin' Club. I'd take that half-day off, and we'd have dominoes. We'd have two tables together with five or six women at the table. We had good times—we were never bored. I wasn't, anyway. I had to quit. I just couldn't take care of that and my children and make a good home for them like that."

Speaking of her husband, Lloyd, who was disabled by Alzheimer's disease, she said, "Worked side by side, for every year that we lived here together. He was never mean to me, and I never was mean to him. And today he wouldn't say a bad word to me. Well, he talks very little now, but he's been a good husband. We were in love all the way through.

"Now I sit home here with him. I could get in the car and drive a little, I can drive here anywhere and visit. And it would feel good to talk with somebody. Well, Harvey, our son comes in, and he talks to his father.

"Now I'm tired, and ready to go to bed too, and I know I can't sleep. It's just too many things on your mind, I think. It's too many worries. And he gets up so often in the night—he can get up and walk around yet." When Lloyd came into the room, she introduced me as "from 'cross the river there, where the Rudicils used to live" and told him, "She used to go see Mama. She was a good friend with Mama together."

How did she and Lloyd meet? "Just meet like that," she said, "'cause he lived in that house, and we on the other side of the fence. And he was just walkin'. He never come courtin' me. He didn't have to have a car. He just walked across the pasture. And I was just sixteen when I got married. But I have never regretted it. Not *one time,* 'cause I had a good life from the first day we was married. We had a hard time, but we made a go of it. If you want to, you got to do it, and keep it goin'. And then we did have a lot of chil'ren, but I wouldn't trade *none* of 'em."

Lillie said good-bye and said she hoped for another visit soon. We agreed it would help if there were a bridge across the Colorado River. It would save the long drive back into Columbus and around, the twenty miles or more needed to go from our house to her house—frustrating when the two places were almost directly across the river from each other.

JoAnn Vornsand

JoAnn was a florist in Weimar in the 1990s. She owned her own flower shop, where she kept her fox terrier, Cookie, with her throughout the day. That is where this picture was taken.

JoAnn stated proudly that Borden was "my hometown." She provided a glimpse into the past of Borden, where today there is little to indicate that a living community ever existed. Other than a small road sign and the old Borden Store, nothing remains. "Borden" had always been simply the name on the sign for the turnoff to our farm until I learned more from JoAnn and the Simpsons, once the managers of the Borden Store.

JoAnn was born JoAnn Vasek in Borden, where her father, Joe, had built the Borden Store, a grocery, in the late 1930s, as well as a nearby dance hall to serve the local community. That was where JoAnn and her family lived from 1940 to 1946. It was a wonderful, two-story wooden building that housed both the Vasek family and their business. It still stood, spacious and welcoming, in the early twenty-first century, on the side of Old Highway 90, known as the San Antonio Highway until Interstate 10 was constructed. In 1949, Joe Vasek built the Lakeside Inn, a café on "the top of the hill," as JoAnn said, a few hundred yards away, and his family moved there. The café building was being rented by Isabel Garcia when I knew him, the old "Lakeside Inn" sign still standing, faded but readable, outside the house, speaking of its former use.

JoAnn summed up the rest of her life in a few short words: "I married and moved around some, went to West Texas, and I came back to Weimar." Period—leaving one to wonder what the intervening years had held.

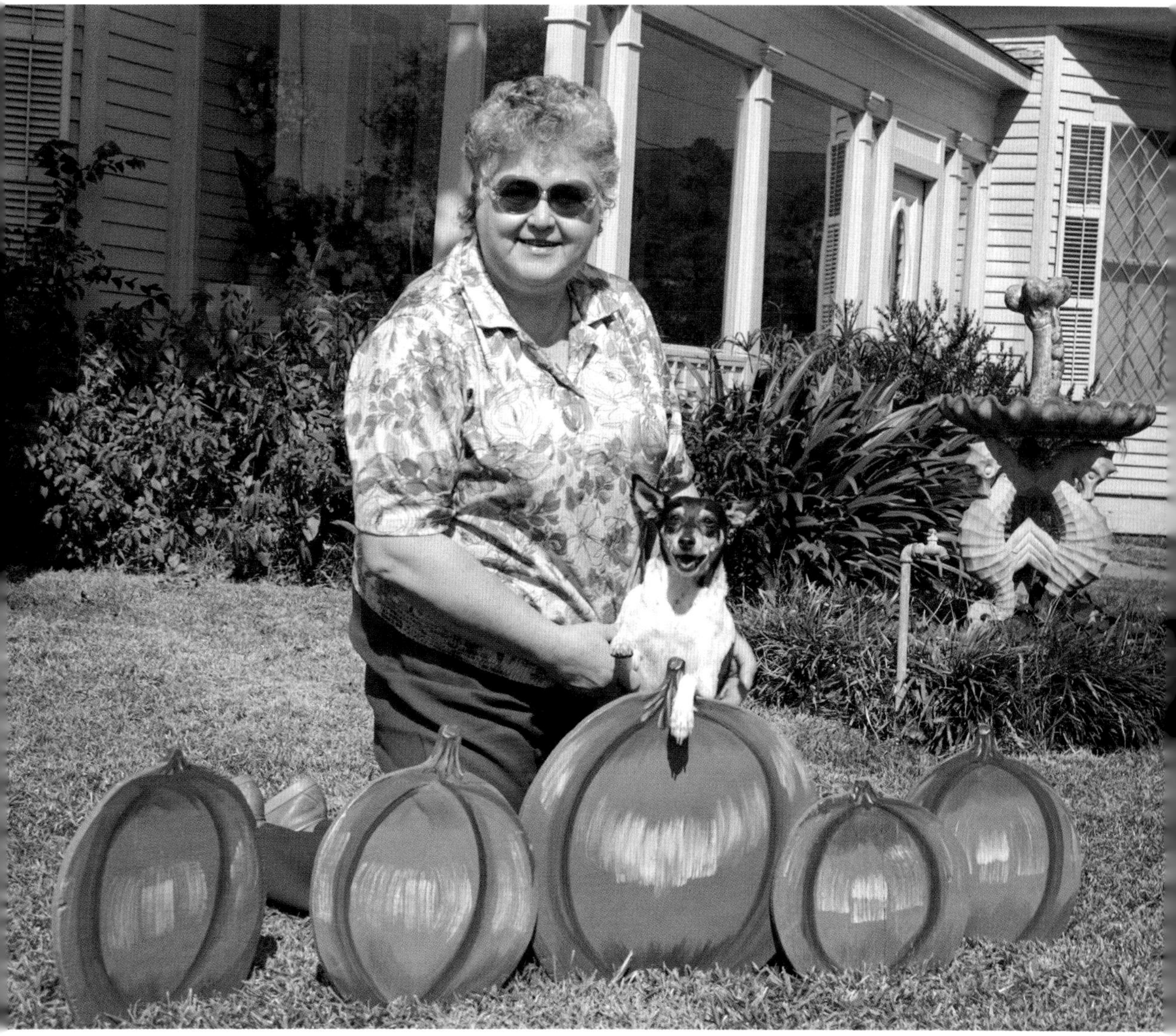

JoAnn Vornsand and her dog, Cookie

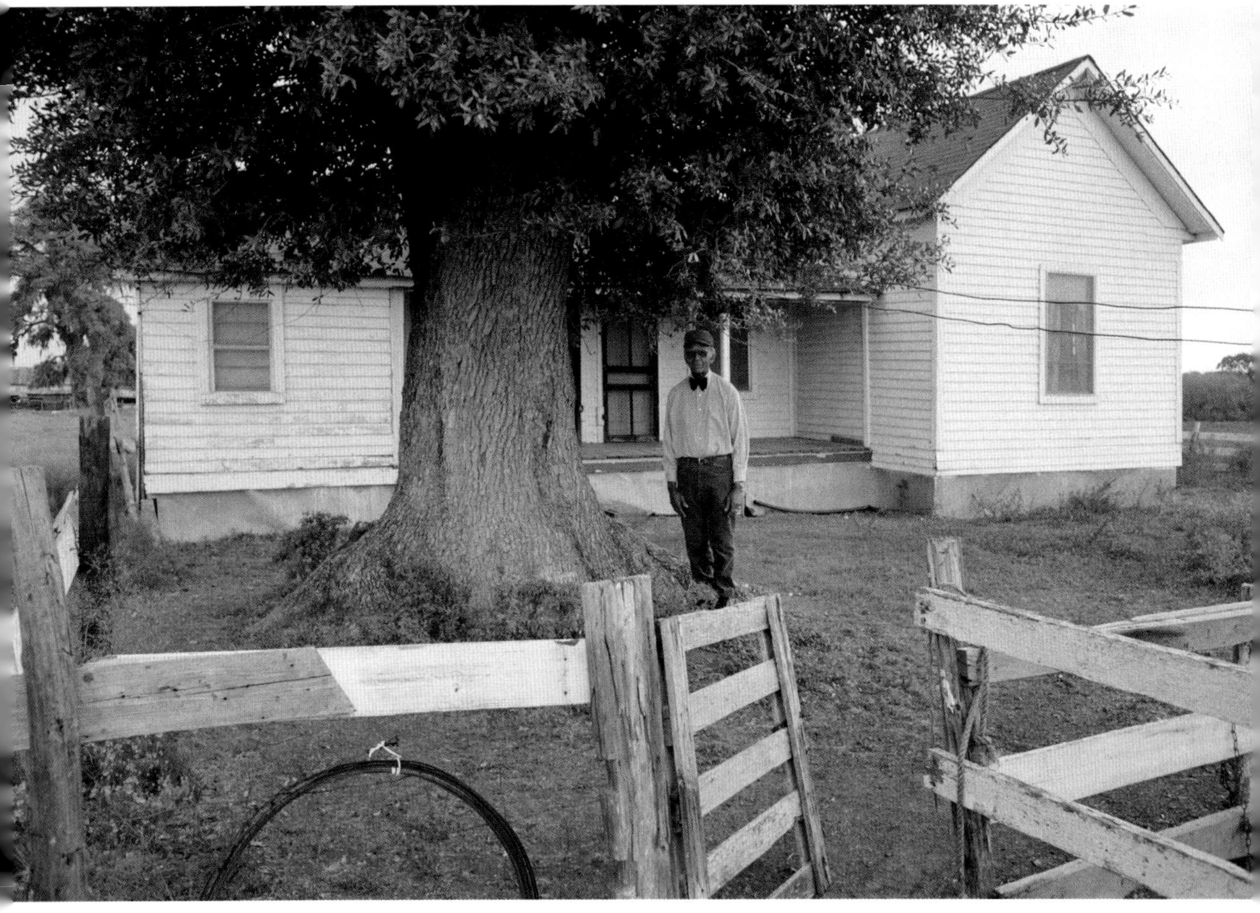

H.C. Taylor

H.C. Taylor

H.C. Taylor was born on July 9, 1905, in the same house where he was still living more than eighty years later. H.C. said proudly that the Old Spanish Trail had once passed close by his farm. He was born one of fourteen children, and he was the only survivor by the time we met. He knew that his daddy, Robert Taylor, had come from Tennessee to Texas on a wagon. Robert became a farmer and married Louise Nunn from New Bielau, a tiny community nearby.

H.C. too became a farmer, like his daddy. When H.C.'s wife, Callie Whitfield Taylor, died, H.C. was left to raise their three children and manage the farm alone. His son, Benjamin, continued to live on the place with his father, and he also farmed. The other two children, both daughters, moved to California when they were grown.

Visiting H.C. was a curious experience, because the steps to his front porch had broken off a while before, and he had never replaced them. You had to scramble up onto the porch any possible way in order to get into his house. That meant on hands and knees for me. It was a high porch and a tough reach. Maybe H.C. didn't have many short friends.

Asked what were his hardest times, he answered quickly, that *now* was the hardest time "'cause most of my friends dead and gone." He also was very deaf, a condition that would contribute to feelings of isolation and loneliness. But H.C. looked quite dashing in his bow tie, shiny boots, and tinted glasses and was said to be courting a lady in town. Maybe he would not be alone much longer.

H.C. proudly showed off large, formal black-and-white photographs of his parents, taken years before by an itinerant photographer. He and I were both struck by the elegance of his mother in her lacy white blouse. Sartorial pride seemed to run in the Taylor family.

It turned out that H.C. never remarried. He lived in a nursing home in his old age and died in 2001, at ninety-five, leaving behind his three grown children. He was a member of the St. James AME Church and had a graveside service at Paradise Gardens Cemetery.

Andrew Jackson Gillespie

Andrew Jackson Gillespie was born in Columbus in 1917, a member of a distinguished Columbus family, a fact meaningful in such a history-conscious town. His parents were Ruth Whitfield Youens and Robert Williamson Gillespie, and he had two siblings, Robert W. and George Duncan. His mother's maiden name, Youens, was an important name in Columbus.

"If you're not a native, you really don't quite fit in," Jack said with a mischievous smile. "You have to have been here a good while before you're fully accepted." This he said with no a trace of snobbery or criticism—it was just the way it was in Columbus. The former capital of Texas, Columbus was a lovely town of historic importance, spreading oaks, and gracious Victorian houses, where "Live Oaks, Live Folks" was once the town motto, and women dressed in antebellum hoop skirts during the annual Magnolia Homes Tour.

Gillespie, as Jack was known, left his hometown once he was an adult. He went to college at Texas A&M for a degree in landscape architecture, class of 1939, then attended and graduated from the Julliard School of Music in New York, with a rating of "exceptional." Julliard is where he received the nickname "Nimble Fingers Jack," for his skills on the piano keys. He returned to Columbus for a time and taught piano out of his grandmother's house, until enlisting in the Naval Air Corps after Pearl Harbor. But not for long. He was "washed out for reckless conduct with an airplane." He then trained as a weatherman (aerographer) and served in that capacity in the North Africa Campaign and the Pacific. "I've seen the Rock of Gibraltar from the air," he said, laughing lightly.

In 1945, at the end of World War II, Jack worked in weather forecasting in Japan and Washington, D.C. Then, because he retained an interest in plants, he studied botany at Texas A&M and worked for several years in a nursery in Houston. He returned home to Columbus in the 1950s to help his ailing mother, who had retired as the town librarian. Jack opened a nursery in his mother's house after her death in '57 and ran Gillespie Nursery in the family home for forty years, closing only when he became unwell and had to move into a care center.

The nursery is where we met when I stopped by on a whim to buy maidenhair fern and became enchanted by the way he spoke (musically) and gestured (like a dancer), and by his friendliness and charm. He gave no clue then about his musical training or his education. He appeared to be living on the edge of poverty, even had no electricity in his house. Yet it turned out he was keeping his musical talents alive, playing

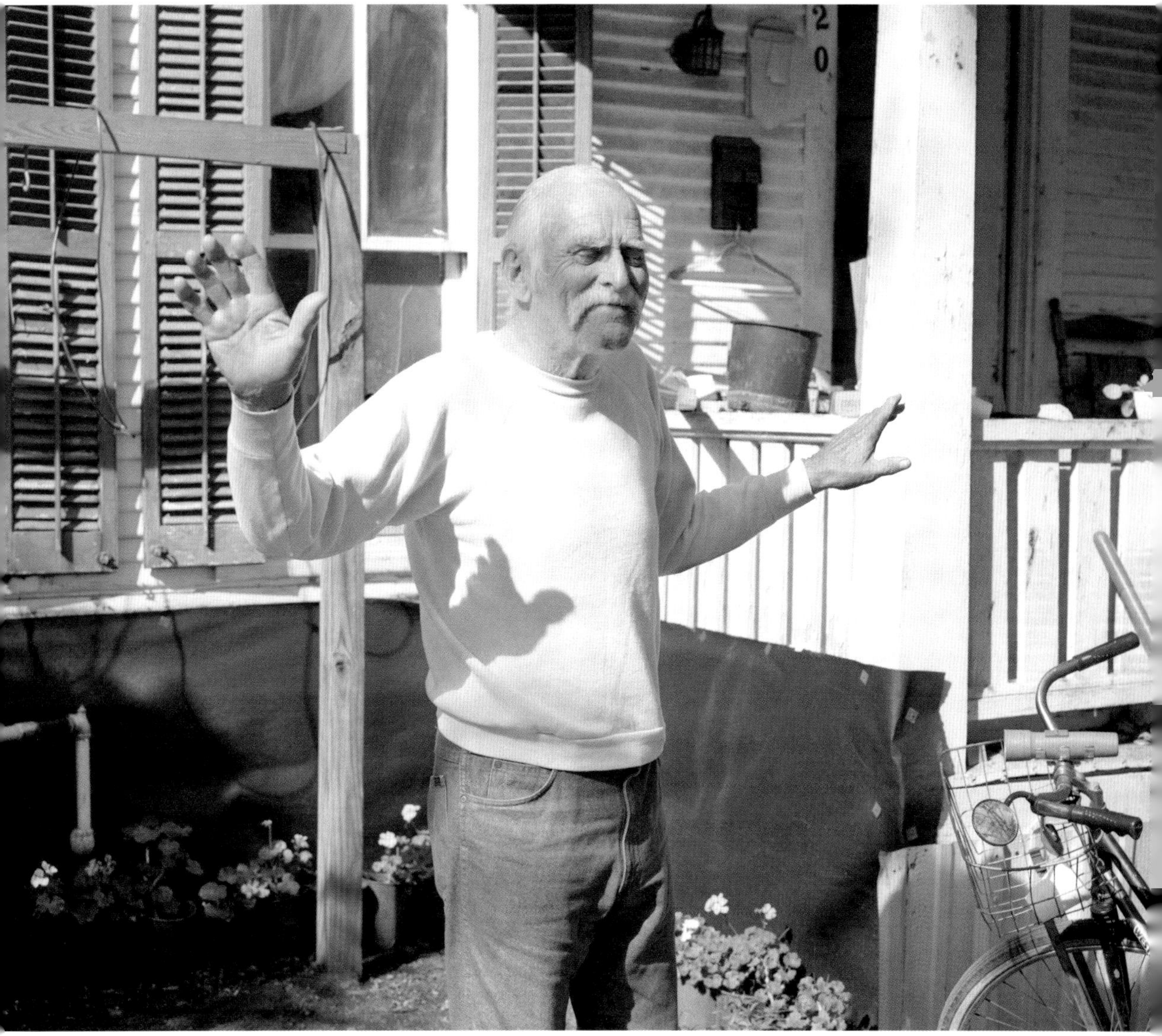

Jack Gillespie at his nursery

piano for his church, St. John's Episcopal, and for various social events around town. One thing was sure: Jack was well liked in town and had many caring friends.

The nursery gave him the pleasure of working with plants—Jack was reputed to talk to plants, which sounds reasonable. More importantly, the work provided him the enjoyment of meeting and talking to people, something he dearly loved. He said he hated the confinement of being indoors. It is impossible to imagine this free-spirited man in a nine-to-five job. He lived sometimes without heat or water in his little house at the nursery and was often given food and clothes by friends who looked out for him.

The best part of his life, he told me, was "right now actually." And he laughed and confided with a twinkle, "I don't say much, but I like to ad-lib and, like, say 'crazy things.' Kind of 'poco loco,' like the song, huh?"

Jack's nephew, who helped research this story, called his uncle "Nimble Fingers Jack" and wrote that Jack's "good times were dancing and a few beers," that he was "intelligent, well read and well spoken, a gentleman, an accomplished pianist, a raconteur, an individualist and friend to many. *Anyone* was welcome in his house"—a lovely remembrance of the man.

When I saw Jack occasionally in the streets on his three-wheel bike, I could understand the charges of reckless conduct—he drove even the bike like a wild man.

Jim Carter

Jim Carter was brought to my attention by a friend of mine who knew him from the Garwood Hunting Club, a duck-hunting club in the rice fields near Garwood, where Jim and his wife, Josephine, had worked for a long period of time. Jim and his friend Earl Dabney were guides and all-around assistants at the club; Josephine was the cook. My friend said he respected and liked all three of them because of their friendliness, their industry, and their general helpfulness. Besides, he confessed, he adored Josephine's cooking.

They were all retired by the time we met, and therefore had plenty of time to talk and tell their stories.

Jim told about meeting Josephine. "I am eighty-eight years old. And I was in a cotton field, close to where Josephine live, and her brother come out there and I wanted ta know who's the best cook. And he says, 'Josephine.' And I said, 'I want a *good* cook—that's why I ask the question.' So we met, and her auntie come after her, and we all rode together, went to a party, and that's how I got a chance to talk with her, right. I was twenty years of age." Was she a good cook after all? "Sho'," he replied, "she's a good cook. My mother said, 'Josephine gonna get married. You better get 'er if you want 'er.' And from that, went on and married 'er. Sixty-seven years to the same woman," he said in an awed voice.

The poor man listed the ailments of old age: blood clots, knee replacement, tumor on the spine. But nonetheless, he was "in pretty fair shape now," he said. "Walk around, doin' work—clean the yard, feed the cow, eat!"

Jim was born "in place you call Elm Grove." He continued, "That's where I went to school at, from my child days. And left that and move to Garwood. From Garwood, I move to Pin Oak and began workin' for a dollar and quarter a day—a *day*! For Mr. Henderson, workin' in the rice fields and cotton patch. From that, World War Two. They wanted to get me in the army. And he had to get me a hundred an' fifty acres of rice land to farm on halves with 'im. And I made a won'erful crop on that hundred an' fifty acres. And I was takin' care of five hundred for him at the same time. And I had a bunch of men workin'. And Mr. Henderson settin' on that tractor, and he got to mine—well, my rice come out better'n his. He said, 'This yours?' I told him, 'Yeah.' [Mr. Henderson replied,] 'You got a better crop than the boss. You did that good on that a hundred an' fifty, you take the whole five hundred on halves.' He furnished the water, the land, the seed rice. I furnished the labor and machinery.

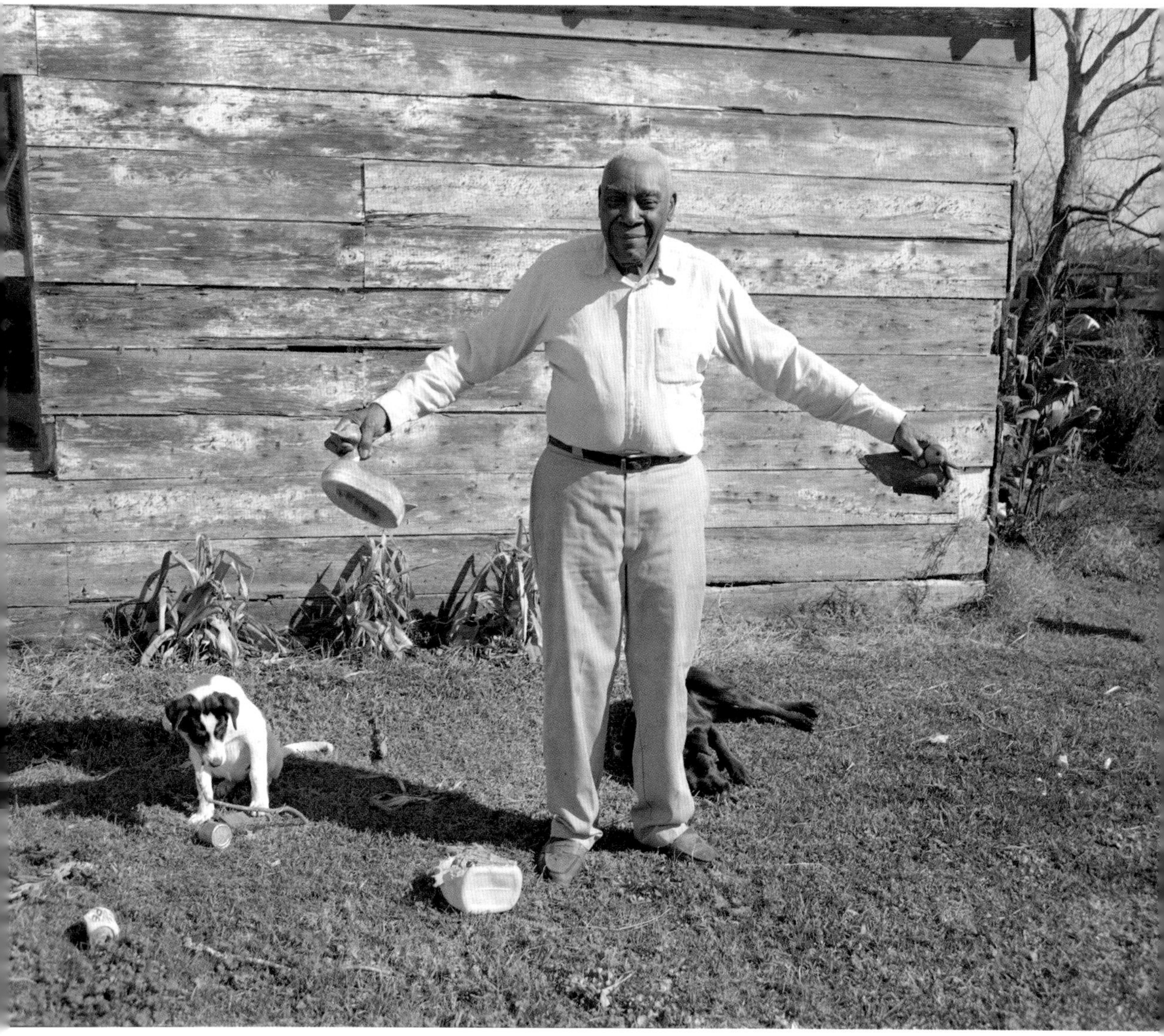

Jim Carter, holding duck decoys

"From that he moved to Jackson County. It was nine hundred fifty acres I had to farm on halves with 'im. I had hired hands too. Made 'em do a good job. But I had to go behind 'em at night with a lantern and check the place up. Had levees in there. They half put 'em up, didn't do a good job. So I go behind 'em at night, add more dirt in there, so's it won't break the field up. He furnish me money, Mr. Henderson, for to pay the hands off with. So we went to the bank in El Campo, and he deposit three or four thousand dollars in the bank. And the president said, 'You gonna trust this *boy* with that money?'" Jim said that Mr. Henderson replied coolly, "I trust 'im with *everythin'* but my wife." Jim continued, smiling, "That's what he said, yes, ma'am! So I made it like that. I'm a Christian person. By bein' honest, I made it like that, by bein' honest. Yes, ma'am, sho'. I never did crook, no kinda way. Never did crook.

"Whatever come up, see, I tell 'im 'bout it. I'd square with 'im. If he livin' today, he tell it too. He dead, Jesse Henderson.

"Today I don't have no money now. I live off social security. In my old age I can't work like I used to."

Did Jim go to school? "Just to the fourth grade, that's all," he said. "I had to get out and work and take care of Mama and the chil'ren. I had to send the school fifty cents a day. I had to work. I is the oldest. It was three girls and six boys of us. Nine of us in the fam'ly. I was thirteen years of age when I taken care of mother and the chil'ren, send them to school. Three dollars a week, yes, ma'am, three dollars a week, plowin'. They give me a hay meadow to work, twenty-five acres in johnsongrass. I made two won'erful crops on that. Then a white man wanted it; they give it to him. That's when I move. That was a hard time back then.

"It's better now. Yes, ma'am, it's better now. Didn't have that much then."

Josephine Carter

Josephine Carter was Jim's wife. The first time we three got together, Josephine stayed in the background, sitting silently across the room while Jim and I talked. Yet when Jim went out of the house and we were left alone, Josephine, in a soft voice and her typical abbreviated, low-key manner, talked boldly and clearly about her life.

"I was Josephine Farrow first," she began, "born in Colorado County. Nineteen oh-nine, I guess. Today—eighty. I feel pretty good. Then again, I feel pretty bad. I ain't stop goin' to church. But I don't go nowhere else. Go to church. The man—the pastor—and the sisters, they help me get up on the steps. Then I can sit down. Soon as they seen my face, preacher come to that door and come get me. We have church every week, second Sunday and fourth—New Hope Baptist.

"Now, when I come up, come up a chile, my daddy died. My mother married over—when I was just a young chile. And then she was havin' babies. She'd already had ten for my daddy. Then she had married my stepfather—she got three more. And her third one, she got *real* sick—taken with a stroke. So then after that—I was real young—I had to take care of my mother 'cause second husband wasn't *no earthly good*. He would make me stay there, and I needed to be goin' to school. She couldn't ever talk *no* more! She couldn't get up no more. She didn't *nothin'*! I had to lift her—I was just a little chile, 'bout eleven or twelve. I had to lift her up and down in the bed. He wasn't nothin' but a woman chaser. And my brothers and sisters—I was the third child—and they were all together, was twelve of us. My oldest brother, he left; second brother, he left; and my fourth brother, he stayed with me."

How about school? "I didn't get any—was just considerin', and my mother taken with that stroke. Lord, it was bad! *Really* hard for us.

"Then when she died, my oldest brother, he come to the funeral. I tried to get him to get a house and put all the chil'ren together. So he wouldn't do it. But Gus and Minnie, they already left home to stay with our aunt. So he tol' me, 'Sister, you go on there. Stay with Aunt Dolie.' It was hard for me to do, but I went ahead on, 'cause I didn't wanted to be the one would go rippin' and runnin' around. I wanted to be the good girl. And I *was,*" she said emphatically.

"She [Aunt Dolie] was so *mean* to those chil'ren!! My li'l sister, she would tie her hands behind her and tie her feets together and beat her with an eight-plait whip till ev'ry nail on her hand was purple. A eight-plait whip! She was *mean,* just *mean*. I should *say*!" Couldn't Josephine help her sister? "I didn't do nothin'" was her response.

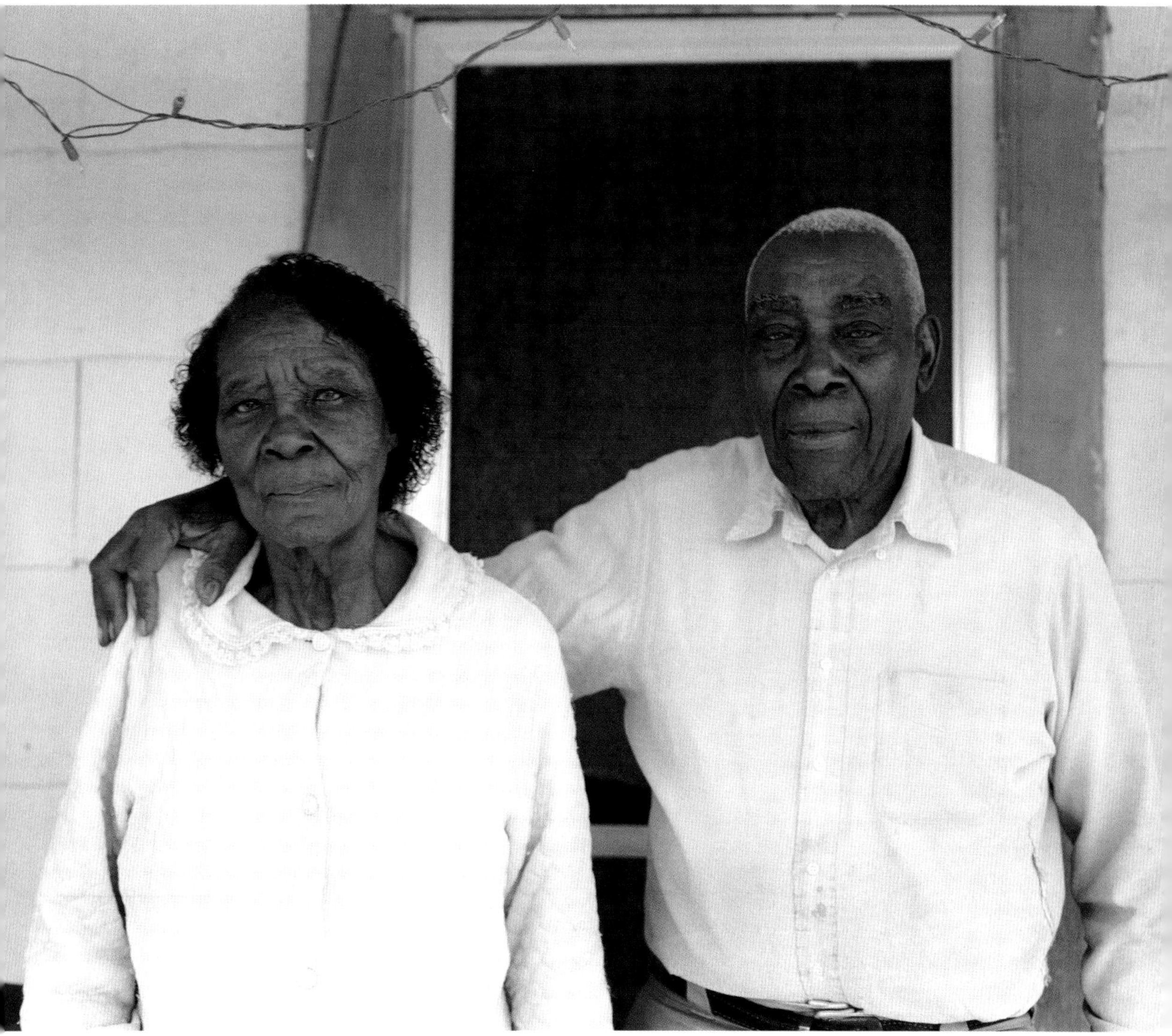

Josephine and Jim Carter

"When I got there, I knew cookin', housecleanin', washin', and all that. She just *sa' down*. I had to go to the cotton field, pick cotton, chop cotton, and all that. I'd go to the field, me and my two brothers—we'd chop cotton. She just settin' in the house. And we come back, I had to cook dinner. And my sister washed breakfast dishes whilst I cook. And when we eat, we had to go right back to the field. We come in, I'd cook supper, my sister'd wash, and my auntie didn't do *nothin'*. She was a mean woman.

"So I left her. Went to stay with my brother. My other brother and sister still there with her—gonna run away. The boy did run off.

"She died. She shoulda died *long* before she did. Oh my, she was mean! I'm tellin' you, she was so cruel to us!"

Josephine told a rambling story of a winter so cold that she had to cut up their old clothes to make some cover for the young ones. "I had set down and taken old britches and shirts and dresses and had pieced quilts and quilt them. The husband she had was so *triflin'*. She had a baby, and she didn't have *no* clothes on the bed. I took all the quilts and put 'em on 'er to try to keep 'er warm. Call my aunties—taken 'em a night and a day and a half to get there. Come in a wagon. It was *ice*! Was no cars then. Brought ole quilts—put 'em on the baby. That's the kind of life I had in my years.

"When my brother got married, I was twenty years old, and I got in touch with Jim, and I got married." I asked her if Jim was a good husband. She answered slowly, "He been *pretty* good—he just *wild* at first. But then he cooled down. Yeah, he *wild*! I tell it like it was. But fin'ly he cool down when he got older and realize what he had. He kinda cool now—but he done got old!" She chuckled lightly.

Did she have any fun in her life? "I never went to no picture show or nothin' like that. I never went no dancin'. I never had any kind of enjoyment. I just had a *hard* time till I married, hmm-hmm."

It was only in their older years that the couple worked at the Garwood Hunting Camp. "Out at the camp, where Dr. Crawford was, the help they got—the old lady died, and they wanted someone that was real *good,* could work and do all that," Josephine said. "Mr. John, he told 'em 'bout Jim and I. They hired us. That was '80 if I'm not mistaken. We worked till I took sick with this colon. Ahhh, they was *crazy* 'bout my cookin'! They *loved* my cookin'! Wanted send me to Houston, cook in a restaurant. Now I cain't hardly walk. I got this here arther-itis, poor circulation.

"Best time in my life—tell the truth—best time in my life? Since I married. That's the best time in my life. I tell you the truth, *I deserved it*.

"But I *always was* a churchgoer. Always will be." And Josephine remained a faithful church member until her death in 1998.

Harvey & Ruth Steward

When Lela and Lewis Steward, Harvey Steward's parents, lived on the land next to my parents' country home, we had to cross through their farm to get to ours, so we often saw them. I remember the old couple well, as friendly, cordial, and warm people.

In those days, back in the 1950s, the Steward place was cheerful, with flowerpots on the front porch, a profusion of narcissus waving in the grass around the house, cows all over the place, and one or both of the Stewards waving a hello as we drove by. I remember that Lewis plowed with mules and drove an old creaky wooden wagon with metal wheels. The Stewards died many years ago, both in their upper eighties, and were laid to rest in the Good Hope Cemetery. Their house was boarded up, the windows partially covered with sheets of tin, their belongings inside left to rot where they lay: mattresses, wall calendars, greeting cards, dishes, the wood-burning stove, Leila's dresses and hats—and no one has lived there since or tended the house. It looked sad and mournful after their deaths—the porch slowly, slowly, rotting away, the tin roof lifting off, flowered wallpaper peeling, the windows more cracked and opaque with dust each year.

Leila's scattering of narcissus bulbs kept on blooming bravely for years, making a cheery, perfumed presence, until the heedless trampling of cows' feet obliterated them. I used to pick the blossoms each winter. These days the house barely stands. It is going fast—the outbuildings have keeled over one by one, the plow is rusted, and cattle roam the yard. There is an air of sadness about it. And I still miss the Stewards' smiling faces and Leila's cheerful flowers.

Harvey's seven older brothers and sisters are also all gone. "All of 'em is dead now but me," Harvey said when we met to record his story. There had been three girls and five boys total. Several died before Harvey was born. "Some were thirty years older than me," he said. "Some of 'em caught the pneumonia and couldn't get to the doctor. It was *tough* back then. The roads was *so* bad. You walked to town or rode a horse or rode a wagon or buggy. Roads were mud. And if the weather was bad, even a car couldn't make it to town sometimes."

Harvey was now living in town but ran cattle on the old family place, so I sometimes got to see him as I drove through. He and his friends sometimes fished in his tank, which was also our dogs' favorite swimming hole and a choice spot for cows to cool off in the searing summer heat.

Leila was an accomplished quilter, and Harvey said he watched and helped her many times when he was a boy, being the baby and close to his mama. He learned

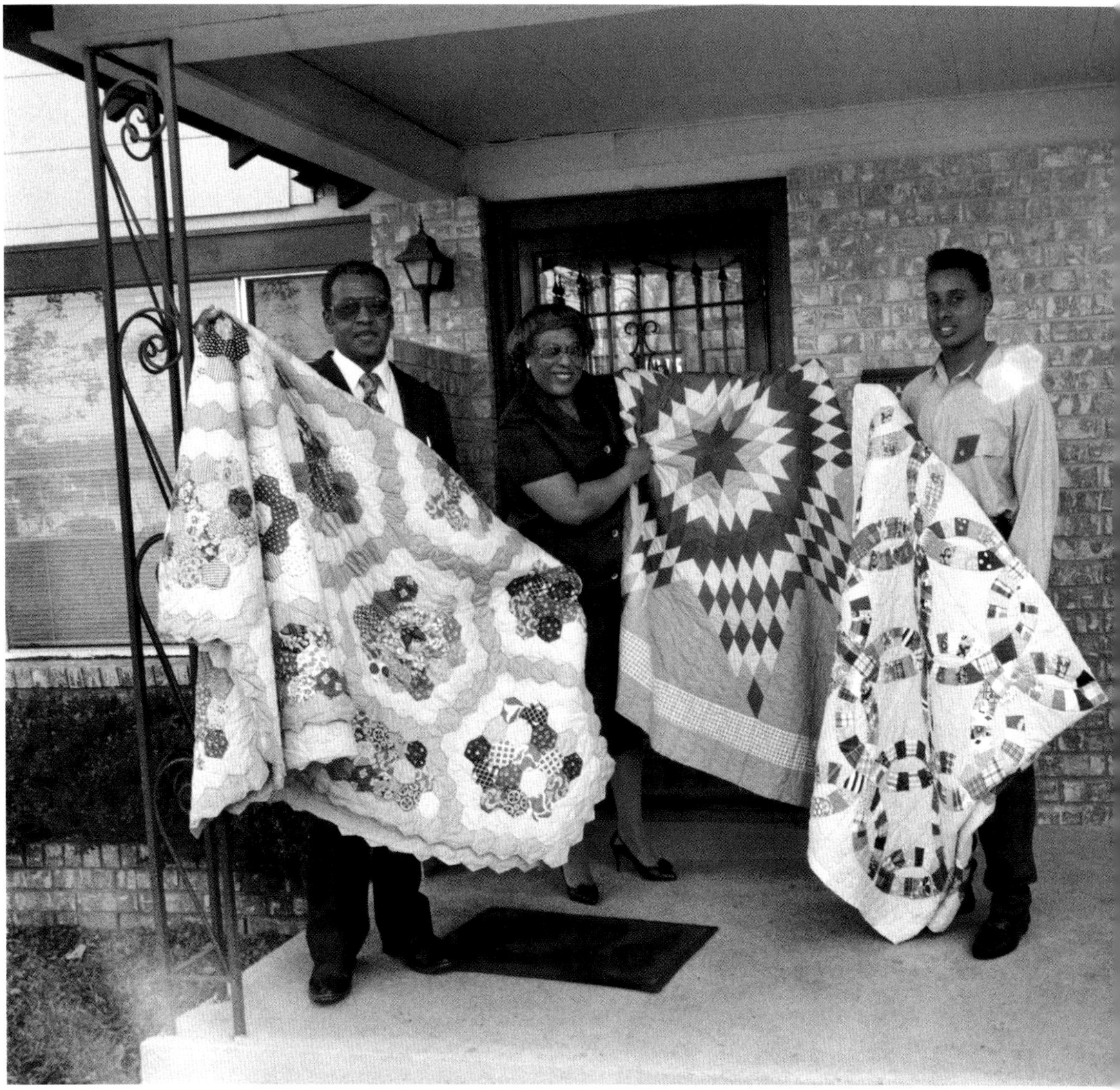

Harvey and Ruth Steward and their grandson, John Harvey Steward

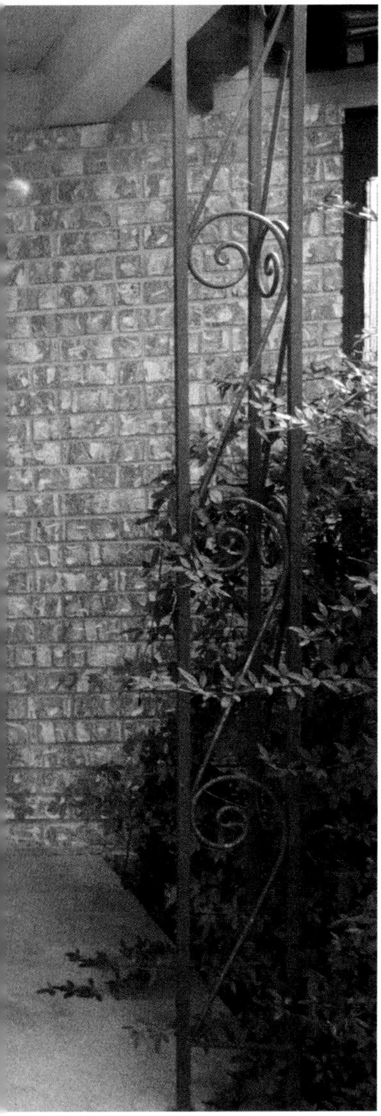

all the quilt patterns' names and still remembered them. It was one of his mother's quilts that he held for this photograph.

Harvey was drafted into the military service and sent to Corpus Christi for basic training, then on to Seattle, Oakland, and the Philippines. "It was bad in the Philippines," he recalled. "There was fightin' and mosquitoes and *hot!*" What was it like for an untraveled "country boy" to find himself suddenly halfway around the world? "I don't never regret it. I went out and come back. I didn't expect to get back. The Lord got us back," he declared firmly. What about crossing the Pacific Ocean? "Nothin' but water. Go to sleep on water, wake up on water," he replied.

Harvey realized other benefits from his time overseas. "Seen different countries I'd read about in school. And I learned to meet people, be around people." This experience no doubt helped him when he became a Weimar city councilman.

In 1951 he and Ruth married and moved from the country into Weimar proper. They had two children, a daughter who now lived in Houston and worked at Memorial City Hall, and a son, Ronald, who was a preacher at a Baptist church in Brooklyn, New York. "He's comin' back one day, hopefully comin' back soon," said his father wistfully of his only son, so far away.

Harvey reminisced on his childhood: "We had a lot of work. Somethin' to do all the time—hogs, cows, chickens to feed, cut wood, huntin', fishin'." He was another person who had missed a lot of school to work at home. But during his parents' time, it had been much worse. "It was a *rough* time," he said. "They hoped I wouldn't have it like that when I came up. Daddy was on his own—and my daddy made it. They made it. Sharecroppin'—never did make *anything,* just broke, year to year. *Never* cleared the books."

Harvey was a deacon at Mount Arie Missionary Baptist Church, where Ruthie was pianist and where he spent his time "pastorin' and workin' with charities." Harvey became the first black city councilman in Weimar in 1996. Sadly, Ruthie died in 1997, leaving Harvey alone and Mount Arie Church without a pianist.

Mary Mann & Rev. Melvin Jack Williams

Rev. Melvin Jack Williams was the twice-a-month pastor of Greater Macedonia Baptist Church for most of the years I was around the Weimar community. He was charming, eloquent, self-possessed, and very handsome when dressed for the Sunday service in his black silky robes trimmed in velvet. He appeared to have a sincere interest in and caring for his parishioners and to be a spiritual and devoted churchman. One could also appreciate his sense of humor and his playfulness. Once I went to Greater Macedonia Baptist to videotape the Sunday service. We had the church's permission to be there so, as we were leaving, I put a check in the plate to say "thank you" for allowing us to tape. Then Rev. Williams came over and, whispering, asking if he could announce the gift to the congregation. I answered reluctantly, "I guess so," at which he smiled disarmingly and said, "Good. I'm glad you said that, because I was going to tell them anyway. You know, you can never trust a preacher." What a charmer he was!

When I met Mr. Williams, he was married to Mary Mann, a lovely, independent-minded Weimar woman known in part by her outstanding church hats. Everyone adored her hats—they were all rhinestones and velvets, veils, frills, and feathers. She admitted she bought them at garage sales and offered to take me hat shopping. Only, no one could wear rhinestones and feathers the way Mary did! Mary's panache and sense of style were unique to her.

Once when she was sporting a cast, she said she had broken her wrist roping a calf. It was hard to imagine that glamorous woman roping a calf. Another time she hurt herself badly falling off a table she had climbed onto so that she could change a light bulb. Any woman who can rope a calf, climb on tables, dance well, wear sexy, distinctive hats—and look good doing them all—is special. Sad was the news of Mary's death at a young age.

Rev. Williams refused to be in the video *Coming Through Hard Times,* saying that he was too uneasy. He said he had a friend who had been beaten up for speaking out publicly in a newspaper. He did let me use a tape recorder for our only interview.

"Together we stand, and divided we fall. We got to be in unity with one another," he said, in his resonant voice. "And we got to love one another as the Bible taught us to love one another. Most of us *talk* love and don't *live* it. You got to *show* it, put love in action.

"We have a good group of young folks attend our service. They are active in the church program. And I tells 'em all the time, I say, all of us got to act like the church

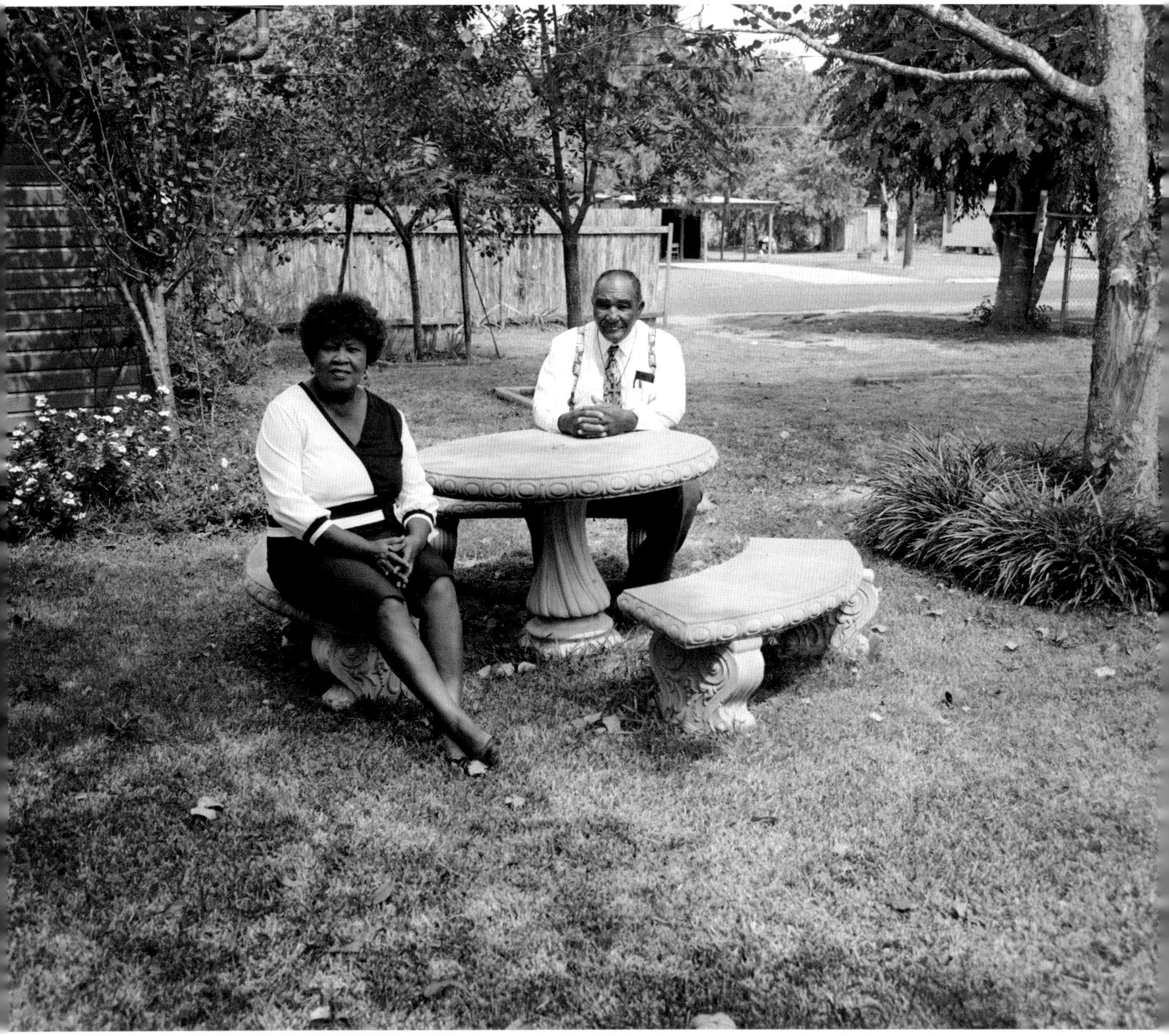

Mary Mann and Rev. Melvin Jack Williams

belongs to one individual. I say, we act like nobody got it but me. And you do that to the best of your understanding and ability, because if you don't, the church will never succeed. Whatever we are, just be the best, and that is what I try to teach our young folks, to be strong and have faith and confidence in yourself.

"Years ago, all of the black folk worked together. They were in harmony and unity with one another, and they loved one another. It wasn't no hypocrite love—it was pure love. If one was sick and wasn't able to work his crop out, the whole community would get together and go help and work his crop out, and wasn't no charges. But now, this younger generation, if they do a half-hour work for you, they wants pay for it. Back in years past, they were willing to do it on love.

"The Lord told us if we don't forgive, he will not forgive us. The forgiveness means you don't bring it up no more. When you ask me, 'Reverend, do you forgive me?' Well, truly you forgive, I'm through with it—that means there's *no more talkin' about it* no more. But if I bring it up again, I didn't forgive you."

Not long after Mary died, her husband moved away from Weimar. His presence was missed in the church, and many regretted the loss of these two fine people from their lives.

Selma & Walter "Jack" Johnson Jr.

"I'm a country man, country born, and I like the country best," declared Jack Johnson. "Was born in Colorado County, in old Borden, behind the cemetery"—in 1910, he said. He spent all but a short period of his life in Colorado County, where he said he was happiest.

"I was a kind of mischievous little boy," he recalled with a soft smile. "I'd mock the preacher in church, get up in the pulpit, and people would say, '*Git* that boy down!'" He chuckled at the memory. In his later days Jack was quiet and sedate, a senior member of the Pleasant Hill Missionary Baptist Church, and clearly respected by all. There was little trace of the mischievous boy he described. "They say I talk a lot, I talk too much now," he observed.

Like most of his contemporaries in rural Texas, black and white, he went no further than seventh grade. Farm families needed their children on the farm too much to allow them to stay in school for long. And some children missed so much school during busy times like planting and harvesting that they would be years older than their fellow classmates when they returned.

"Life was a struggle," he said, describing his childhood on the farm. The worst time in Jack's memory was the drought of 1925, when he had not yet married. The *best* time he said was after his marriage to Selma Burley, on his twenty-fourth birthday. He almost glowed with affection when he talked about Selma, who in turn smiled, saying nothing. He said of their marriage, "After that, it was *always* good. It brought me what we call good luck. I was proud to marry, and we lived happy and raised children." He and Selma had been together for fifty-four years and were still smiling and enjoying themselves when we talked.

Jack went from farming to spending a brief period on the Houston shipping wharves. He then served in the U.S. Army until he received a medical discharge for asthma. He later worked in the oil fields in El Campo and finally returned to Weimar to spend the next twenty-six years employed at Brasher Motors there, glad to be back home.

Selma wrote in 1999, "I, Selma Johnson, am the one whom was married to Walter Johnson Jr., on August 5, 1934. We were the proud parents of eight children. Four of them are now deceased. My maiden name is Burley. My date of birth is Oct. 11, 1914 and Walter was born August 5, 1910. My parents names were Seliana and Sylvester Burley."

Jack died in 1991, leaving Selma alone in their neat, white house just across the train tracks from Highway 90 and three doors down from the Pleasant Hill Missionary Baptist Church, their home church. Selma smiled less than before, kept on attending the Pleasant Hill church, and continued to say very little.

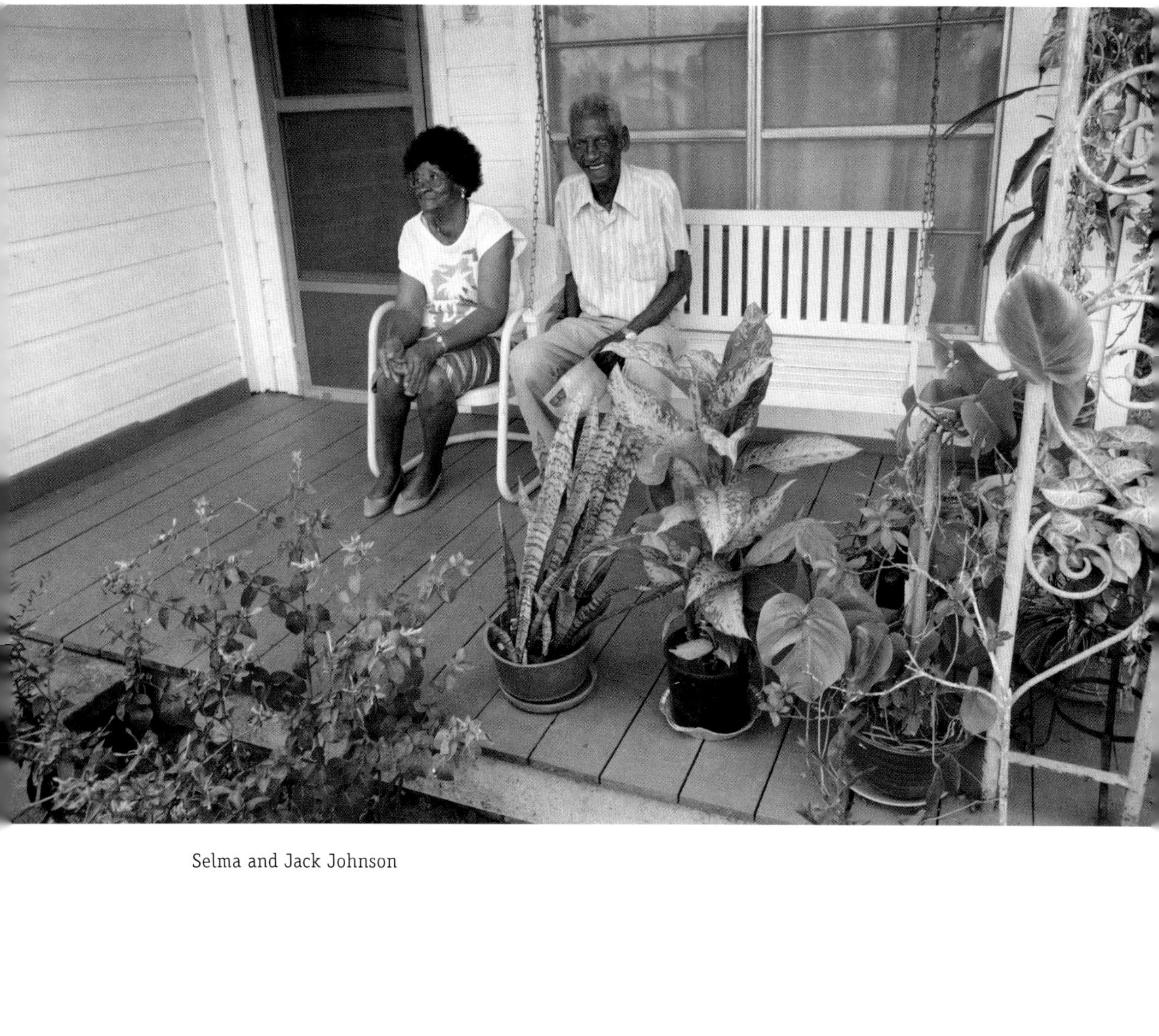

Selma and Jack Johnson

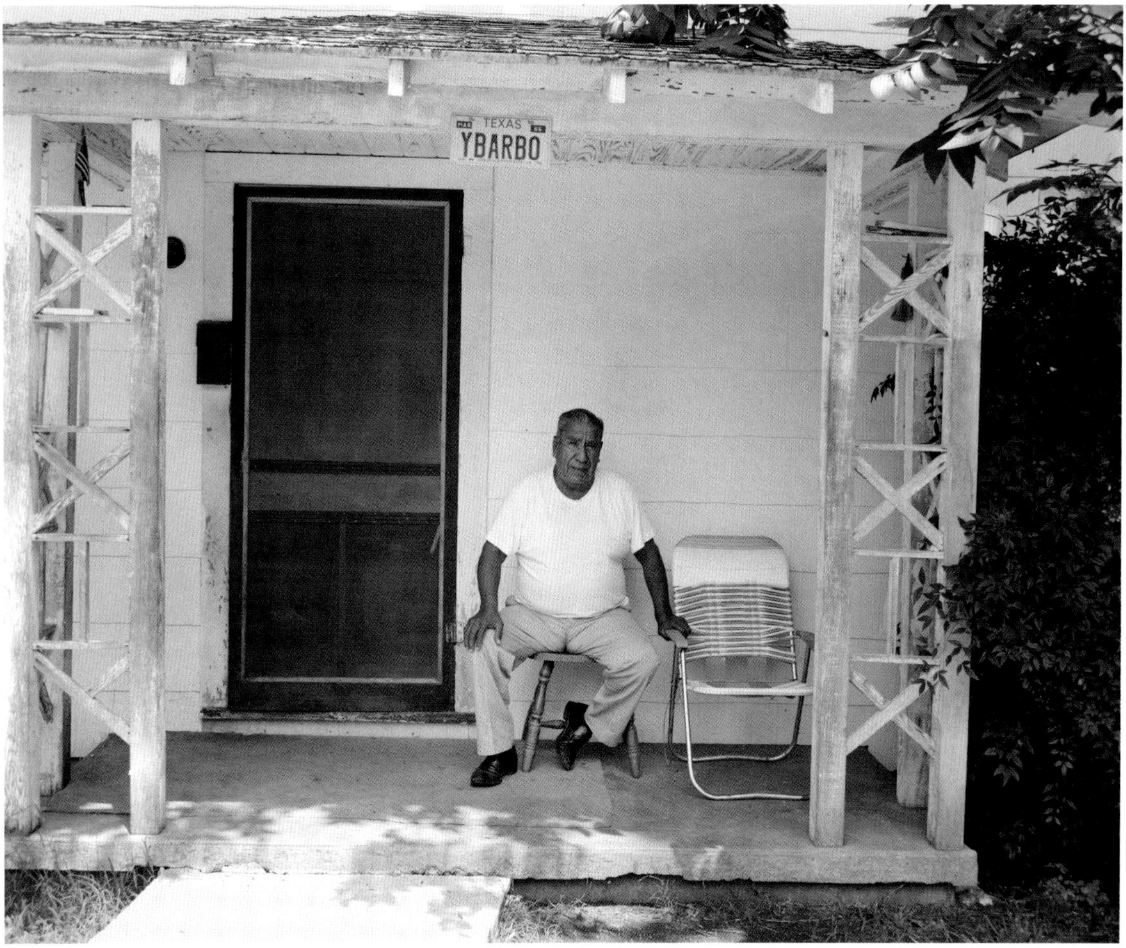

Juan Ybarbo, “the Old Elephant”

Juan Ybarbo

Juan Ybarbo called himself "the Old Elephant." So he said when I first walked up to him, unannounced and unknown, as he sat on his front porch, to ask for a visit and a photograph. I'd seen him several times before, sitting on the porch of his small house tucked in between two larger, grander houses, like an afterthought. I was struck by the name "Ybarbo" imprinted on the license plate that hung over the door and by the man's calm, still posture as he sat there looking serenely out at the street. It was as though he had all the time in the world.

He agreed to a photograph that first day, but the second visit was harder—he was always out. Finally, the day came when I simply left a copy of his picture and a telephone number at his door. And that did it. Juan called and told me how much he liked the picture. He said it was his first photograph for over forty-six years, since World War II, and that he wanted to thank me and was ready to talk.

This is how he began: "We can kick off with this here. This is my Civilian Conservation Corps discharge. That's back in 1940. And this is a nice piece of paper there, my honorable discharge. I went in the army on my twenty-first birthday. I volunteered. My oldest brother, him and another buddy, were the first volunteers in Goliad County. His name is Victor. He's got a lot of beautiful medals, citations, shakin' hands with the general, because he was a *big, brave* man.

"I was born in Victoria, and Daddy moved to Goliad in February 1923. I stayed in Goliad forty-seven years. I was born in 1922, and Daddy must have been in a hurry 'cause my sister's just one year older than I am. Daddy's Lupe and Mama's Alberta. We're all citizens, all-the-way American citizens. No wetbacks. Oh, sure, they call me all kinds of names, but I know better than that. You know 'wetback' and all—but on the jokin' side. I don't let them go too far. That's one thing about me—I have a bad temper, a *bad* temper.

"We had a hard life—*very*—durin' Depression time, back in the early thirties. But I was workin' for fifty cents a day, ma'am. Not for eight hours—a day! From *way* dark in the mornin' to *way* dark in the evenin', fifty cents! And I was workin' for the richest man in Victoria County. I bring home two dollars and fifty cents. I kept fifty cents and give Mama two dollars. Then I was the country jailer, makin' two dollars and board. I didn't want the two dollars, I wanted the board, 'cause I was *hongry*. So every Saturday at noon, Mr. Clyde Harveson would write me a check—a dollar ninety-eight. He would take out two cents social security. I used to buy a blue work shirt, forty-nine cents. When I had to buy shoes, it took all my check, a dollar ninety-eight. That week Mama didn't get none, and I didn't get none.

"I quit school when I was in the fifth grade, 1937. Daddy went blind on us. Daddy stayed blind five years, and then they wouldn't take me back in school. But I thought I was too smart, because I was makin' two fifty a week. I didn't go back." Asked if he missed his schooling, Juan replied, "Sure, a whole lot! I want to do it for my grandson, because I love him to have an education. I'm gonna give him all I can.

"We had a *hard* daddy, ma'am. He was pretty hard on us, but I'm glad he was, 'cause now I know how to live with people, work, bring home money. He whipped me still when I was fifteen years old—that was my fault.

"This Ybarbo is not a Mexican name," he said proudly. "It's Spaniard. This name, 'Ybarbo,' right there in fifth-grade history. Way back in the 1700s in that book, and the name is Gil Ybarbo."*

Juan volunteered for the army at twenty-one years old and served in the 266th Battalion as a gunner, or cannoneer. He served in Normandy, the Ardennes, and Northern France and fought in Paris and the Battle of the Bulge with General George Patton. He was awarded five Bronze Stars and a Victory Medal. "What counts is that Bronze Star," he said. "Five of 'em, little bitty stars on a ribbon.

"We went over there with twenty-five thousand personnel on that ship—the biggest, *Queen Elizabeth*. Come back, *Queen Mary*. After three days we were travelin', they said. 'At this point, we call your attention just to tell you that the ocean is twenty-five miles deep.' Three days from land and you couldn't see nothin' but water. All around you. And twenty-five miles deep! That's the distance from here to Sealy! *Really!*

"I was all the time by myself in the service with two Polanders from the North. We went through the war, and we didn't get hurt. Them, my most popular friends. Over there, you don't got but one *real* friend—that's God. That's the only buddy you have. The other, well, it's just a buddy, but the *real* friend is God. He's the one takes care of you. Them two boys were Polish boys, and we run together through the war. We used to dig a hole as big as a blanket. Dig the hole just where a bullet couldn't hit you. We used to sleep together in the same hole and eat what Mama and Daddy used to send. The cake wasn't nothin' but crumbs, but those crumbs were pretty good, 'cause sometimes we had nothin' to eat two or three days, 'cause the war was pretty hot.

*Gil Ybarbo was one of the original Texas settlers, described in *Spanish Texas, 1519–1821,* by Donald E. Chipman, as "the most prominent citizen in the East Texas settlements, Gil Antonio Ybarbo," "a trader and rancher who lived near the Ais Mission." Gil Ybarbo "became the chief spokesman for the repatriated Texans" in their dealings with the governor who represented Spain in Bexar, when the East Texans were ordered by the king to abandon their homes and lands. Chipman wrote that "Ybarbo and Gil Flores were their leaders . . . who traveled to Mexico City to seek relief from the imperial order" and finally received permission to build a new town, Nuestra Señora del Pilar de Bucareli, on the Trinity River in 1773.

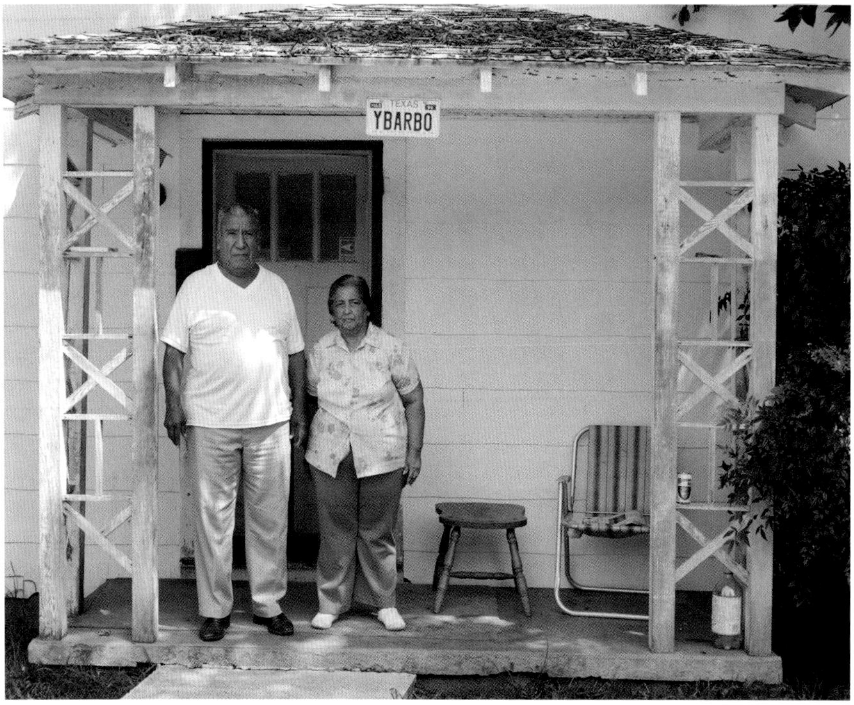

Juan Ybarbo and his wife, Esther

"I call 'em my Polanders—they're my brothers. I call them *my* Polanders. They're *mine* till I die!" he said emphatically.

Asked how he remembered dates so well, Juan smiled, and said, "Like a' old elephant. I'll be sixty-nine next birthday. I'm fixin' on makin' thirty-five more years, if I keep on like that."

The Ybarbos married on December 27, 1945, in South Texas and moved to Columbus in 1968 to be near their grown children and their only grandchild. Juan worked at Mikeska's Bar-B-Q as a butcher, on construction sites as a pipe layer, and in a marble business. He resented the retirement he was forced to take when he had a light heart attack, his first illness ever. He was proud to be a lifetime member of the Veterans of Foreign Wars, Post 2784, in Goliad.

Juan Ybarbo died on December 13, 1999, one day before I dropped by again, eager for another visit. His wife of fifty-four years, Esther, remained living in their house, looked after by their daughters.

Stella Taylor

"My name is Stella Taylor. I was born in New York City, and I came from the New York Foundlings' Hospital. My mother put me in there when I was three days old. She left me with a document from the doctor stating that she was emotionally and financially unable to care for me," Stella Taylor related, matter-of-factly. "When I was a year and a half old, I was placed in the Orphan Train, and I came to Texas, to Weimar."

I had never heard of the Orphan Trains until the day someone in Weimar mentioned to me that there were a couple of older women living there who had stories of coming to Weimar on the trains, known also as the Baby Trains. I went looking for them. The first woman burst into tears at the first mention of the train. She absolutely refused to let her picture be taken or have her story recorded, but she did tell some horrific tales of abuse, deprivation, loneliness, and the slavelike conditions she had endured as a child from the train. She told how she and her "brother," another Orphan Train child, were fed leftovers off the same plate, sitting on the floor, after their adoptive family had dined, and how they were treated like chattel. Clearly, these memories were hurting deeply even after more than seventy years. And that was the only time we spoke.

The second woman was Stella Taylor, and she was willing to talk. Stella was not exactly loquacious, but she was generous—and cautious—with her story, saying, "I don't want to hurt anyone." She also shared books, photographs, and newsletters she'd collected from the Orphan Train Heritage Society of America, which gave a fuller sense of the enormous scale of the project.

The Orphan Trains were a social experiment of the Children's Aid Society, which sought homes for orphaned, abandoned, and impoverished children. The program began in the middle of the nineteenth century, out of New York City, running from 1854 until 1929, "when the government stopped it," said Stella. It handled infants and children from Catholic foundling homes, "poor farms," sweatshops, the streets, asylums, penal institutions, and desperate parents, carrying them by train from town to town and seeking placement for them with adoptive families. One estimate of the number of homeless children on New York streets in the mid-nineteenth century is 10,000. And more than 150,000 youngsters were placed in homes during the seventy-five years that the program existed. The train traveled all over the United States, to the western states and the eastern states," said Stella.

"Well," she continued, "on Ellis Island, there were a lot of people—a lot of immigrants landed in Ellis Island—and it was very unfortunate for some 'cause they

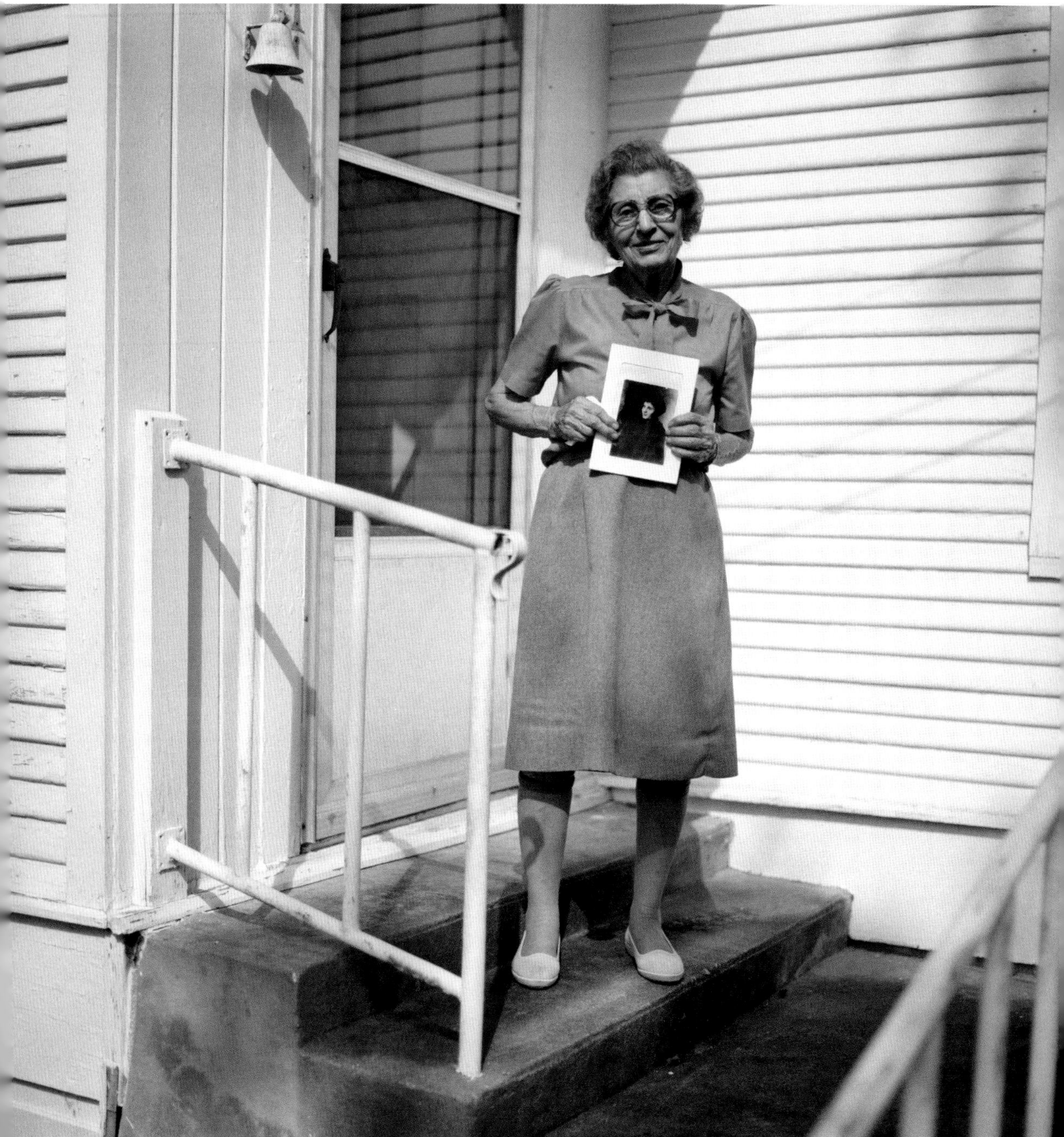

Stella Taylor, rider of the Orphan Train

had wives and children, and there were no jobs to go to. So I'm sure that is the reason why some people gave up their children." The results were sometimes tragic and sometimes successful. Stella's placement was happy.

When I met her, Stella had only recently learned anything concrete about her origins. She said she had been writing, fruitlessly, to the Catholic Diocese in New York for information on her birth for a long time, trying to get a passport. Time after time there was no reply. "So one day I thought, I'm gonna try again. So I put a twenty-dollar bill in there, and I told 'em"—she laughed—"that 'One day I would like to see Rome, the Holy City of God,' and I got it right back!" The answer was immediate. She laughed again, enjoying her own cleverness.

This was the reply she received: "According to the records of New York Foundling Hospital, you, Stella Joseph, were born on November 29, 1904 in New York City. You were brought here on December third by your mother because she was financially and physically unable to care for you." Stella sat silent, pondering the letter. "But," she said finally, "she put me in there, and she never asked about me again, so, well . . ." Her voice tapered off, leaving us in silence.

"Well, this is the story I was told, that, you know, the immigrants had no food, no nothin'. So the immigrants come to this country with their families, and the farmers, the ranchers, and whoever needed a laborer was standin' there waitin' for 'em [at the docks]. They would pick up the men and take 'em, leavin' the women over there, standin' there with little children. Didn't have anyplace to go. And those people never did give those men enough to get back. So what were those people supposed to do? What was Mama supposed to do? The kids were hungry, and they didn't have no jobs. God, they probably didn't even speak the language!"

So parents often had no recourse but to place their offspring in the care of whoever would take them. Then Charles Loring Brace, the innovative and caring director of the Children's Aid Society, came up with the idea of finding foster homes in the "healthy, wide open" western states. He would thereby populate the territories and at the same time provide the children with "salutary and redemptive" labor, an idea both romantic and practical. There were some clear abuses to the system and to some children. But, on the whole, it was a lot better than life in an asylum or on the streets.

The Orphan Trains carried their young charges to towns throughout the country. Stella continued, "When the train stopped, it was loaded with little children. Well, the children got off the train and went into the courthouse lawn or city hall lawn, and people that were waiting to adopt some children, then they could make up their mind. They'd take all those kids off, line 'em up, and the families that wanted 'em would come and pick out what they wanted. Some wanted little babies, some wanted bigger children, some still larger so they'd be large enough to do chores around the house or work in the fields. And sometimes some of 'em wasn't picked and wasn't picked, and then they felt terrible, and they had to take 'em back. They told me that in some places those farmers that needed laborers, they'd get out and feel the muscles of those poor little boys to see if they was strong, so they would be large enough to help with their chores around the house and to help in the fields.

"I said that over and over again, 'How *could* they *do* that!'" Stella declared with passion. "The church, once a year, the New York Foundling Hospital sent, I guess it was a supervisor or whoever he was, from the orphanage to check on those children, and see how well they were doing, and if they went to church, and if they had good homes. Some stories were not happy, but we had a very good home. And so did a lot of other people—and then some had homes that were not so good. But I imagine that works the same way with people's own children, you know."

So baby Stella arrived in Weimar and was chosen, along with a three-year-old boy, by a local German family. "I stayed in the orphanage until I was a year and a half old, and then I was placed on the Orphan Train, and I came to Weimar. I was placed in the home of David and Ada Teltschik, who were my parents." The Teltschiks' natural children were grown and gone, with the exception of one son. The two orphan kids were warmly welcomed into their new home as if they were their own.

"I had beautiful parents. They had eight children of their own, and when the youngest child was sixteen years old, they decided they wanted two more children, so they adopted a boy and a girl. There were just two children got off, because my father made up his mind after the train left New York. He went to the railroad station and told them, and the telegrapher wired to the train in New Orleans and wired to stop the train here. And only two little children got off here—was a little boy and myself.

"They were very good parents. My father was a prince in shining armor, and my mother had a beautiful soul that reached to the high heavens. We lived out on the farm. We had plenty of everything. Everybody worked. On Saturdays we did the washing. We tried our best to go to church every Sunday. And when I was big enough to go to school, I walked two and a half miles a day, and so did a lot of other children. And the days that it was too muddy to walk, we went horseback.

"Mr. and Mrs. Teltschik were both born in Germany. When they first adopted me, I couldn't talk German, and then when I started school, I couldn't talk English." She brought out a large book on the Teltschik family lineage, written in German, telling their history since 1301. Stella proudly showed a photograph of herself with her adoptive brother and their new parents.

"My father loved me so much that I was fourteen years and still sitting on his lap, and Mama could've killed us both! And then he had a stroke when I was about nineteen." Her voice dropped, "And one of his children—he was a kook—he looked at my father lyin' there, and he said, 'If that old man dies, you gonna work for me.' Just like that!" She snapped her fingers. "And my father said to me, 'If you wanna get married, get married, because when I leave here, it may not be so good for you.' So I married a peace officer.

"My husband died in '55. He was a disabled war vet'ran. He had got mustard gas. Anyway, I can't complain—I had a good life." Leslie Taylor worked as a deputy sheriff and also for the Liquor Control Board in Galveston during the wild years of gambling and illegal gaming under the influence of the Maceo brothers.

Stella's husband warned her to look out for herself after his death: "Don't let people tell you what to do. Make up your own mind." To one man who offered to help Stella with her money shortly after her husband's death, she replied, "No, thanks. I work and I make my own money. If I can work and handle someone else's money, I can take care of myself." And she added firmly, "You have to be independent when you're by yourself.

"I always got good jobs," she noted. She was still working at eighty-seven years of age. Why? "It's not for the money, but I have to keep my mind alert," she said, laughing. "I have stomped out of there, where I work, and I said, 'I don't need this damned job!' Nobody answers me, and I say, 'Hey, hey. Can I quit?' 'No,' my boss said, 'What would you do if you quit? Just go home!' He put that in my head—'You're just gonna sit there, like some of those other people who just sit there at home?' So I stay." And Stella laughed joyously at herself, filled my arms with bread and pie, and sent me off with an invitation to come talk again and to stay longer next time.

There was no next time. Stella entered a nursing home not long after this visit and died there on February 18, 1997.

Tracy Vlasta Koller

It was a rare day when I passed Tracy Koller's place and she was not in the fields working at something, usually picking pecans. Tracy loved to pick up pecans, and she also loved to talk. So she would always pause in her work when anyone driving by stopped, and she would come to the fence and have a visit. There was something very special about the way Tracy talked and the way she put herself together. She wore old, washed-out work clothes, worn shoes, gingham sunbonnets, and always, surprisingly, nail polish in a modest pink color on the fingers that peeked out from her half-fingered work gloves.

Asked on that first day for her name, she said, "Tracy Koller. And my middle name too? Vlasta, I guess. I don't know myself!" She laughed. "I done a lot of work, you know. Since I grew up, I am livin' on a farm. Never quit. And here I am! Guess how old I am?" She laughed delightedly as she said, "I'm eighty-five, going on eighty-six!

"I'm the oldest one, you know. It's five girls of us, whatcha call it, and I had three brothers, you know. Two of 'em passed away, you know, and the one what comes pick me up, he's living in town, whatcha call it. His wife died too. He picks me up, you know, picks me every seven, eight months, you know, to town, whatcha call it. You know."

Tracy was born a Vlasta. Her mother was a Marek, of Czech descent. "I come from Lavaca County," she said. She pronounced it "LAA-vaka," so that it took the longest time to figure out just what she was saying. "When I married, you know, I hid in Colorado, and I'm in that Colorado all that time, whatcha call it."

Tracy talked about her childhood. "Like them days—why, we had it hard! It was eight of us kids and Mama and Daddy. And Daddy had Grandpa. But his mother and his daddy had a brother and a sister—Daddy fed them all! And that time, we made two bales, cuttin' on ninety acres, you know. No pecans! And here I make money on pecans, whatcha call it! And them days, wasn't nothin'! I remember how I used to carry eggs, you know, to the store for nine, eight cents a dozen. You know. And two miles I walked with two big water buckets, hmmm, hmmm, hmmm!"

Tracy showed some marvelous old black-and-white photographs of herself and her sisters, formal studio shots as well as snapshots. Weddings, engagements, first communion—she was not sure what they all represented. They showed several healthy, solid-bodied, pretty young blond women in white dresses, often with ringlets of flowers in their braided hair, looking very sturdy, traditional, and northern European.

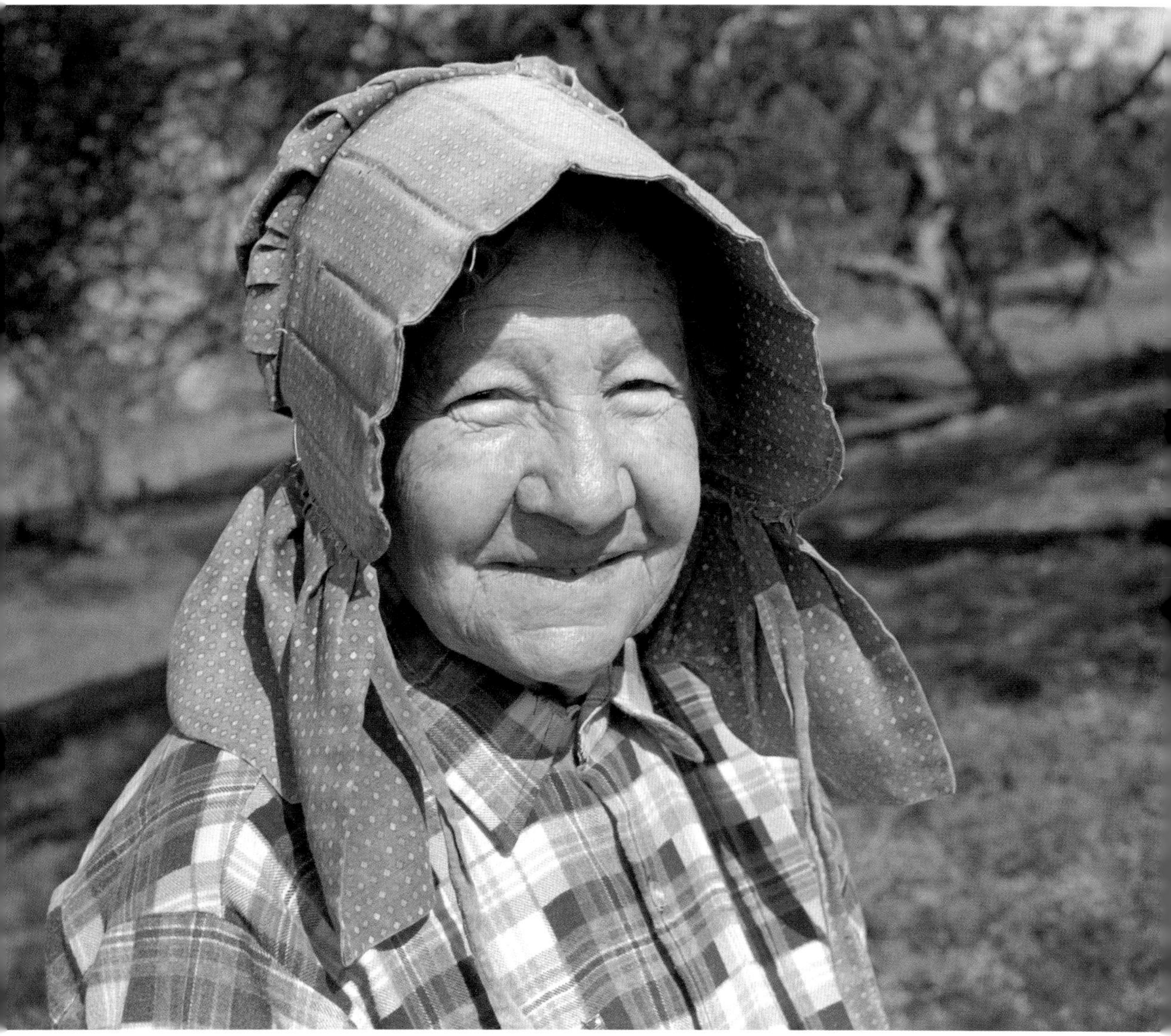

Tracy Koller in her sunbonnet

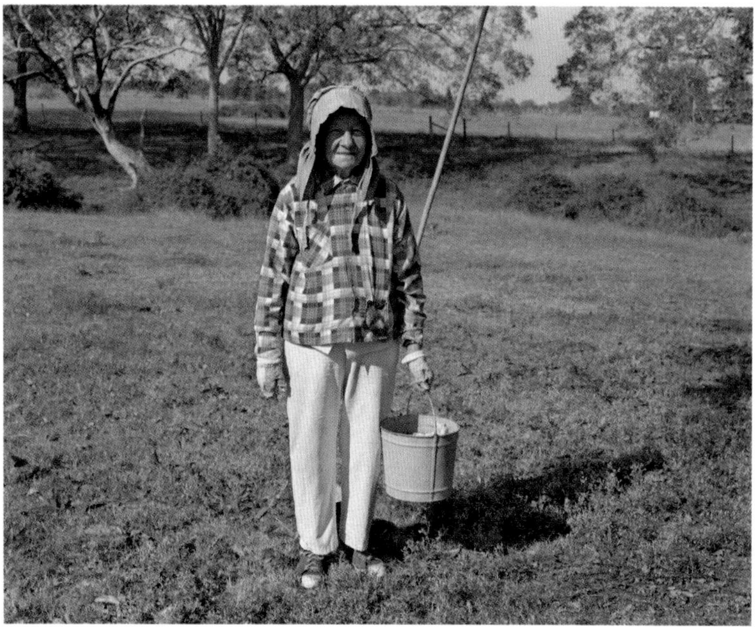

Tracy Koller, picking pecans

"I married in 1925—dry year, you know. We married, you know. My husband be six years passed away this December twelfth. I'm livin' here, you know. I'd rather get out of the house, you know—*lonesome* in the house! Miss him, kind of, you know?" Her voice dropped softly, and she looked away.

Her husband, Henry Koller, lost his mother when he was six and was raised by his sisters. "He was short-lookin', fat, and quiet. He listened while the rest of 'em talked. He was a fisher and a squirreler," Tracy said, smiling with pride and affection.

Tracy clearly loved her "squirreler." They were married more than sixty years, until his death. She says some things have changed since then. "You know, I don't bake. I don't cook. I eat sandwiches, you know. I used to bake kolaches, and good ones, you know. And you know, when my husband passed away, I got through with all of it. Just quit, you know. And pies, how I used to make 'em! I buy my stuff in town now—I don't care."

After she and Henry married, "We was, you know, everywhere! We lived in New Bielau three years, then we moved—you know where Needville is? That's where we lived. Three years, come back, you know. I started worryin'—too far away from Weimar!" She laughed. "So we come back, you know. We went to Schulenburg, to work for Frank Koller in a café. We lived with Frank, two families in one house. We worked there two years. And we farmed with a team—there was no tractors, you know. And how I worked! Doctor in Schulenburg tol' me, 'You gonna live, Miz Koller, for ninety years!'

"I'm gonna miss the farm, yeah. We bought this thing in 1946, right round before Christmas. It was in December. We moved here, whatcha call it, and we here since that."

When asked why she didn't have a dog for company, now that she was alone, Tracy said, "Somebody dropped a dog here—a big one. And I said, 'Ummm, if he barked, I would be scared.' This way I got it peaceful. I got just a cat, and that cat is old too, you know. She, in the morning, when I get up, round my feet, you know. She's, I guess, used to the place. Yes, she likes me, you know. In the mornin', when I get up, round my feet, she's rubbin' around, whatcha call it." Tracy wouldn't go out at night. "I'm scared, you know," she said. "Could be a man under the bed. If the phone rings at night, nine, eleven, one time, I said, 'Forget it'—could have been a man."

So Tracy kept on alone. She picked pecans, worked her farm, greeted passersby, fed her cat, and enjoyed her pecan trees. If only her dear "short-lookin', fat, and quiet" Henry had been there, life would have been perfect.

Tracy went into a nursing home not long after this photograph. She never returned to her farm and her beloved pecan trees, but died in the nursing home.

Father Victor Schmidtzinsky

The Reverend Monsignor Victor Schmidtzinsky was born and raised among pecan trees in Fredericksburg, Texas—"where the streets are one hundred and twenty feet wide and they *still* have accidents," as he put it. He grew up along the Pedernales River. Both his father and uncle were champion pecan growers who started teaching him tree culture as a young boy. When he was grown and became Father Victor, he was assigned to the parish of the Church of the Nativity of the Blessed Virgin Mary in Nada, near Columbus. There he planted forty-four pecan trees around his church and parish home, and there he continued in his twin callings of nurturing his parishioners' souls and tending his beloved pecan trees.

Father Victor's trees had always attracted attention because of their high yield and top-quality fruit. And the priest had been joyfully winning pecan prizes and teaching others the refinements of pecan growing for years.

Father Victor earned his first money, one silver dollar, picking pecans at the tender age of nine. He was receiving more reward for his work in his latter days. He was awarded the Lone Star Degree of the State of Texas from the Future Farmers of America and the Golden Spur from the 4-H Club. He was voted Texas Rural Minister of the Year in 1963 and was one of only two priests inducted into the South Central Texas Baseball Hall of Fame, among other honors.

Father Victor spoke with passion about his trees, and it appeared that his was a passion for all of the earth's creatures. Even when he was explaining a simple procedure such as placing a pipe at a tree's roots to catch rainwater, or soaking leaves in water to make a nutritious "tea" for the tree, it seemed he was speaking of spiritual matters.

The name "Nada" always seemed like a funny name for a town, since the word means "nothing" in Spanish. It turned out the town's name is not Spanish at all but instead originated from the name of the Czech village Nadja—a word that means "hope." Nada was founded in 1890 and was part of Stephen F. Austin's colony. It's a tiny place. St. Mary's, whose formal name is Nativity of the Blessed Virgin Mary, dominates the landscape, just as the churches do in many European towns and villages. The church was one hundred years old in 1990, and the people of Nada put on a big anniversary celebration with two bishops in attendance—and lots of pecan pie.

In 1996, Father Victor retired and moved to San Antonio to a Catholic retirement home.

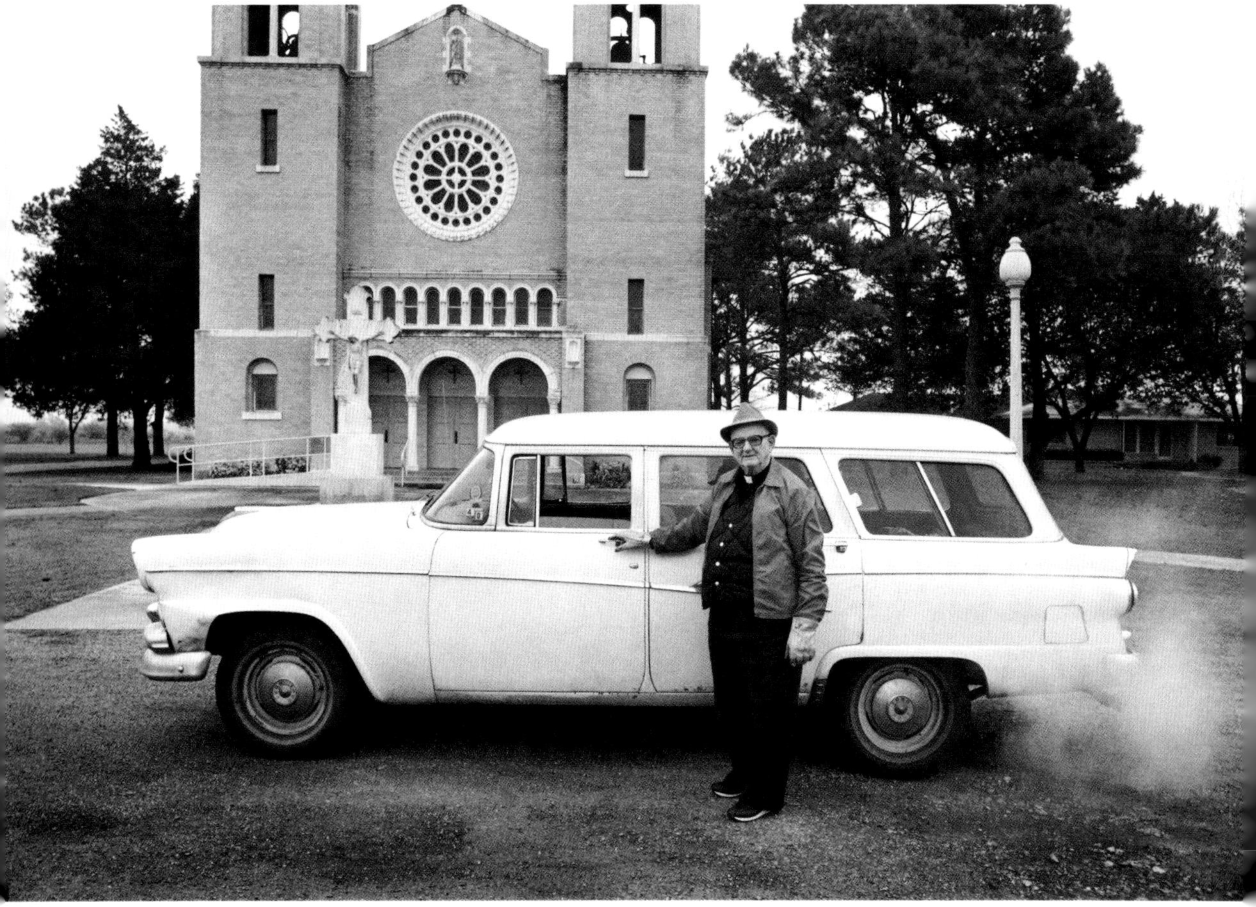

Father Victor Schmidtzinsky, the pecan-pickin' priest

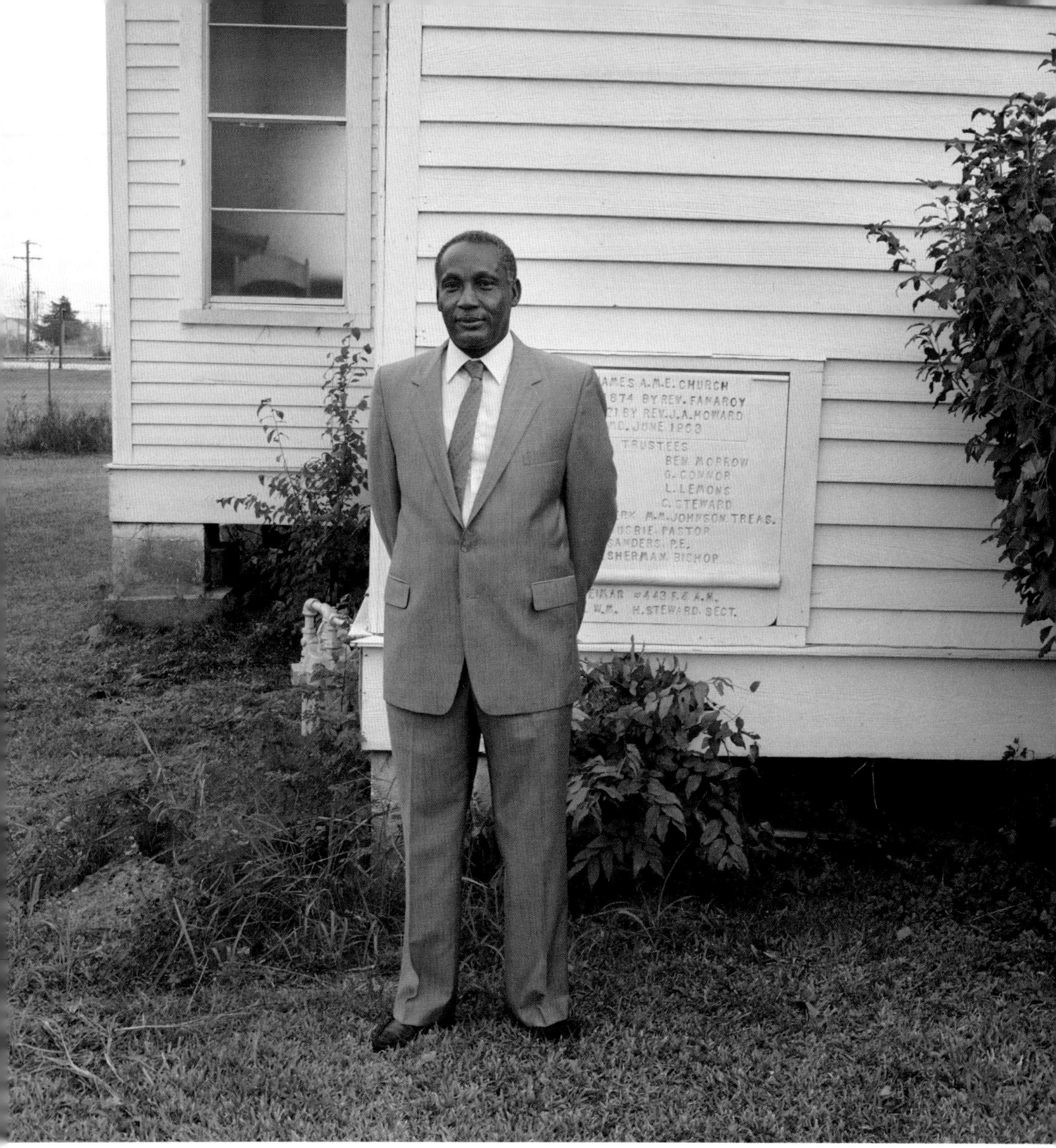

Melvin Houston at his church, St. James AME

Melvin Houston

Melvin Houston seemed reluctant to tell me his story. "I didn't live no hard life," he said dismissively, "didn't live no bad life." Melvin clearly believed that life had been good to him and without much drama. And so here is what he offered, the bare facts as he outlined them.

Melvin was born in the High Hill area of Fayette County in 1934. His mother died when he was five, and his siblings one and three. The youngsters were raised by their daddy, an "auntie," and a grandfather. Leo Houston was a sharecropper who also worked part-time in a dairy. Young Melvin attended J. A. Green High School in Schulenburg, until he left to find work.

When we met, Melvin had been living in Weimar for thirty years, moving there when he married his wife, Gloria, a Weimar resident. He worked at McCall Sanders Egg Company in the feed store and, later, as a truck driver for Schindler Brothers Steel Company, fifty-five miles from home, in Sealy. Like a lot of others during economic hard times, he was glad to have work, even if it meant traveling long distances every day. And, like lots of others, he was abruptly laid off from his job after thirteen years, when the steel mills closed in Sealy. Those were hard, hard times in small towns in the 1980s and 1990s.

Melvin and Gloria had two children. They belonged to St. James African Methodist Episcopal Church, housed in the oldest church building in town, a lovely, spacious, Victorian-style, white-plank structure. Melvin served his church faithfully as steward, trustee, and choir member. His daughter served as the church pianist.

Melvin commented, "Weimar is dying," noting that 60 percent of the young people had to leave town to find work. He considered himself lucky since his children were still living in Weimar. Yet there was no relief in sight.

Gloria told me that it was Melvin's dream to retire and live in the country, that he had a place just south of Weimar, in the Clear Creek area. "He goes every chance he gets, every day if he can." It was clear that Melvin, this meticulously dressed man, was a person with more than one side to him. And it was also clear that Gloria preferred town life to country life. Laughing over the phone, she said that when he's retired, "he can come home on the weekends to see me."

In the fall of 2000, Melvin stated that he was "still workin'—sort of retired *and* still workin'," at a barbecue restaurant in Schulenburg. And he said proudly that all three of his son's children were in college, quite an accomplishment against tough odds.

Heine & Earlyne Beken

The name of Heine Beken was given to me by a friend, who had been saying for several years that I needed to meet and talk to this "old cowboy" who was a great fellow with a lovely wife and many good stories. Heine and Earlyne turned out to be as described, truly nice folks, warm with others and affectionate with each other. They laughed comfortably together, reminiscing about their past and clearly enjoying the present moments as well.

"I lived a pretty hard life you know," said Heine. "When I was a young fellow, I went to help Mr. Cornelius down at Markham [a town near the Texas coast]. And the mosquitoes were so bad—and we slept on the ground down there in them swamps, you know. I tell you, it was *pretty tough* for me, and I was young. I don't believe I could stand it now."

Earlyne inserted more background for the story, remembering that it was Johnny Walker and Mr. Cornelius together whose cattle Heine was working. Heine's job was to travel from Weimar, past Nada, to Markham and on to the Gulf with hundreds of head of cattle, a much longer, tougher trip than Heine had indicated.

With Earlyne's urging, he filled in: "Markham is between El Campo and Bay City. I was helpin' him work cattle. He had about ten thousand cattle, and I was helpin' him. I worked for him for about a year, and then he said, 'I want you to go to work for me full-time,' and I says, 'What do you pay?' and he said, 'Thirty a month,' and he'd feed me. I tell him, I said, 'Well, I can go back to Weimar and pick cotton and make that much.' So, so he paid me a little more. He was givin' those other hands just a dollar a day, but I got *two* dollars—otherwise, I was goin' home.

"It was pretty tough. Oh, but he was a tough old guy, I guarantee you. And he had lots of cattle and lots of debts, but they didn't seem to bother him. He could get enough to pay me, so that was all right.

"We drove the cattle from Markham to Sargent, and we had to cross the Intercoastal Canal to get to that winter grazing. And that was somethin'! You might have ten or twelve men behind a thousand cattle, and when you got within a mile of that crossing where they had to swim, you couldn't hold the cattle. And lots of times, the smaller calves would—they'd drown. But you just couldn't hold them. I almost got bumped into the Intercoastal Canal. I was sittin' right here with a horse, you know, to hold them over there, and they *hit* that horse. It was somethin'!

"We'd drive twelve hundred head. And sometime I didn't see the front cowboy, and the one on the side and back—never got to see them all day from four o'clock in the

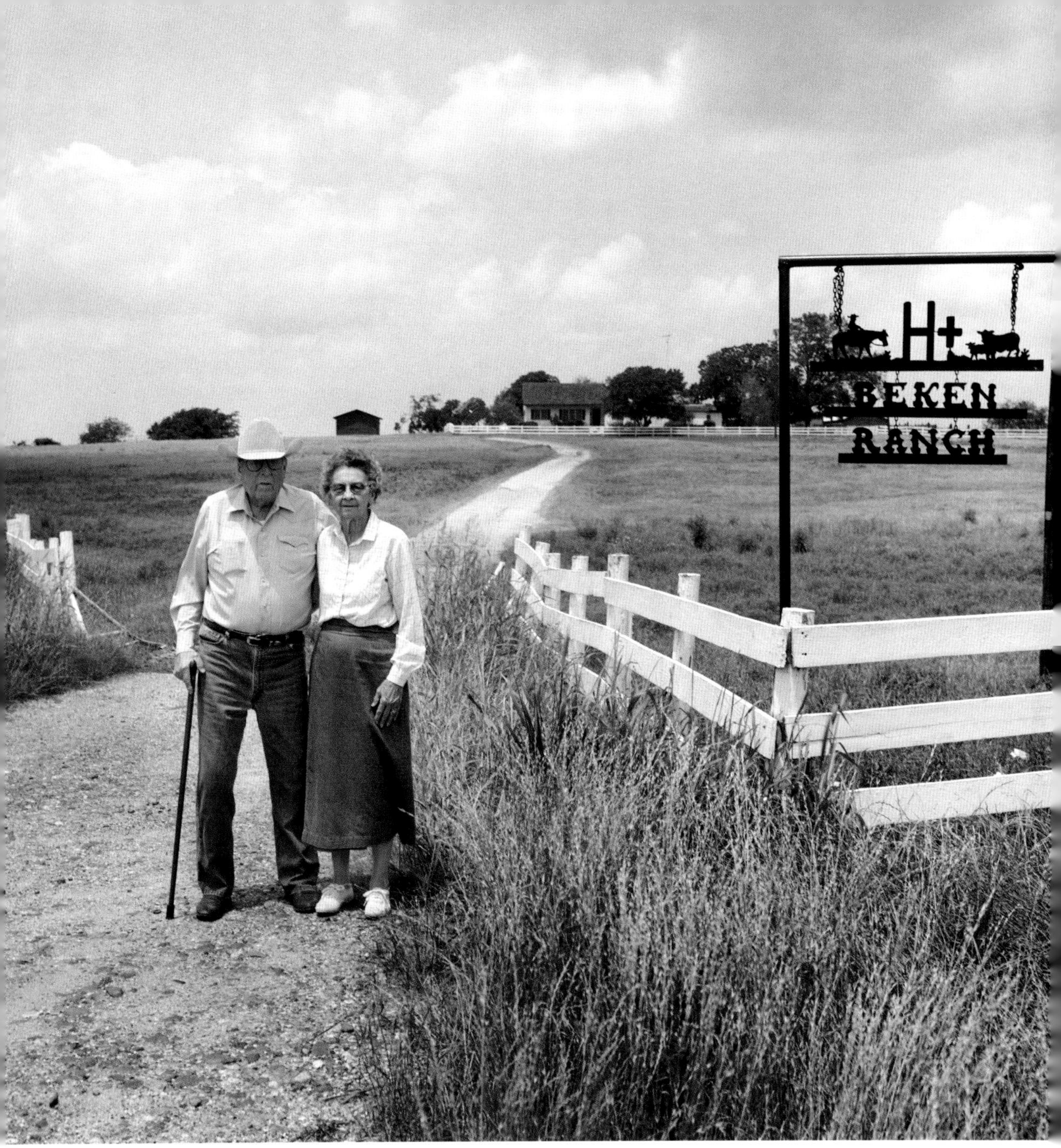

Heine and Earlyne Beken

mornin' till 'bout sundown. He wanted his cattle to stay in good shape, you know, while they were travelin', so he had a big trap, you know. He had places to stop, you know, and he'd let 'em graze, you know. If he had to go from here to Kansas, and he could start here with a poor cow, and he' get up there, and they'd be fat!

"If a cow was grazin', and he see you move that cow, that little man, he would raise some sand! 'Let her eat! Let her eat! Please let her eat!' He was on someone else's territory, you know—wasn't costin' *him* nothin'. And last time I worked for him, the other ranchers wouldn't let him cross their place anymore. It'd be all right if he would drive 'em on, but he grazed 'em. Heck, he didn't even make five miles a day when he could have made twenty. He was a tough old guy!

"Long days? From four till dark! It wasn't no problem—I was young. That's what you call 'from can to can't!' Heine laughed. "Man, I tell you! I got awful tired, and then have to sleep with the mosquitoes."

He said he had sat on a horse "most of my life—never did like *nothin'* else." Was he retired yet? "I don't know," he said. "I guess. I'm eighty-six years old, and it's 'bout time, isn't it? I got 'bout a hundred and twenty-five cows. But if it wasn't for Henry, my son, and them helping me take care of them, I'd have to get rid of 'em."

By 2000, Heine had had several pretty serious surgeries for various injuries he had sustained in rodeoing, on his hips and knees especially. He was walking with a walker or a cane and looked stiff, yet determined.

Heine talked about finding his passion for rodeoing as a child: "When I started, I had an arena down here right at the cattle guard. When we worked cattle and we'd drive them, I would get behind these younger calves—you know, they would lag behind—and I would rope 'em and get down and turn 'em loose. And you talk about somebody catches the blues—I did for that! They would give out, and I would rope 'em, and my daddy said, '*Please* let them alone. They ain't gonna make it the way it is.' But if he wasn't lookin', I'd catch another one. That's where I learned how to rope. Started competing in rodeos when I was about eighteen or nineteen. Yeah, then I went and roped in competition. I could beat 'em then, but the older I got, the tougher I got." He smiled benignly.

"I fell lots of times, but it was 'cause I was in such a hurry, tryin' to beat somebody. And gettin' off a horse—you know, you hit the ground pretty hard. And then you meet a calf bigger than you are, and he runs over you. I was good enough to make it all the time.

"Did the girls like rodeo men?" I asked. With a sideways glance at Earlyne, Heine answered, "I guess my wife did. Otherwise I wouldn't have had her.

"I went to Port Lavaca to a rodeo, and I told her I was goin', and she made her old boyfriend bring her on down there. That was the loosenin'-up part!" They laughed together. "I won the saddle down there in Port Lavaca, and she said some pretty nice things." He smiled affectionately at his wife.

Earlyne said she was first taken by Heine when she saw him win the saddle, the prize of all prizes. "Along the line," she added, "I found out he was this famous cowboy, you know. And I don't know why I liked cowboys, because I was raised so I couldn't even ride a horse—and can't even ride a horse to this day yet. Horses are afraid of me, and I'm afraid of them. And it just fascinated me because I thought he was famous, and finally we got together, you know, and made it, like he says."

Added Heine, "Poor Daddy and Mother wanted us to have a big wedding, you see. And Earlyne didn't want none, and I didn't either. So, so we go away to Schulenburg and get married right quick. Soon as we could get back to the car, we went to Port Lavaca and never stopped. Got out of the county."

Earlyne explained, "We were going into Mexico, but we couldn't get there. We got halfway down there. They stopped him and wanted to see his draft card—thought he was evading the draft." Heine added, "Thought I was running away from the draft. I ain't running away from nobody. And I ain't got enough money to stay over there very long, so we had to come back."

About being in the armed services, Heine said, "That was so sad. I don't believe I can tell all of that. When we *just* got married, I stayed at San Francisco, what, about six months, and then they shipped me overseas. I was a buck sergeant." Earlyne said, "We were married in April, and he went into the service on June the tenth."

"And then after that they shipped me overseas from there," Heine continued, "and you talk about the foghorns on the ship—why, that's the saddest thing I *ever* heard in my life. That's a wwwwhhhooooo. And I was on it, and the water was almost splashin' up on the deck. And I had to take the mop and clean up everything 'cause I was the only one left—rest of them was, boy, they was sick—they'd just look through a peephole, and they'd get sick. I was twenty-nine.

"But in the fall of 1942, I got on a ship and went to Australia. Then to New Guinea. There we were stationed pretty close to the airstrip. And that's a bad place to be 'cause they always bombed those airstrips. And, man, we had an alert—we had a siren, you know. You'd be, man, sleeping good and wasn't nothin' but brush out there. Man, when the siren went off, everybody got to runnin' and fallin' over everybody.

"We was just shipped from one place to another. And I had a pretty good voice, you know, to count the cadence, so I got to be a pretty good job. I was in command of the platoon—I was drill sergeant. Man, I was standing out on that parade ground, and I'd say, 'Hup, hup, hep, ho, ho, hoy, hoy.' Well, you had to holler that loud 'cause sometime I'd let them get that far, from here to the cattle guard, and I'd holler at them. Man, I had a good voice."

Heine came home in 1945. "Four years—I was *sure* glad to see you," said Earlyne tenderly.

Following his return, Heine went back to ranching. "And the rodeo," he said. "That's all I did. I was good enough to make it all the time. I didn't have no other money."

In fact, Heine was a charter member of the Cowboys' Turtle Association, the first professional cowboys' association, in 1937. Later, it became the Rodeo Cowboys Association. Said Heine's son Henry Junior, "What I've read is they called it the Turtles, 'cause they were so slow in getting organized. And there was a rodeo in Madison Square Garden and [somebody] rode off with all the entry fees and didn't pay any of the cowboys."

His father added, "You know, there were some son of a guns when I was coming up. Ooohh, they would crook you out of anything."

A sad note in the family's happiness was the loss of their only other son, John. Earlyne said, "Heine was waiting until the two boys got big enough. Then he'd quit ranching and let the boys run it." Heine said of John, "He was a pretty good roper. He was killed in a car wreck." And Henry Junior contributed these memories: "My brother won three or four saddles. We grew up roping right here at the arena, and we rode before school. And we all played sports, and so we'd come in from football and we'd come home and rope at night. We had lights at the arena. And at the end of the season, we were going to the rodeos." John's photo stayed on the living room wall, over our heads, smiling toward us.

Earlyne said, "We even have a daughter that rode barrels for a little bit. She didn't ride a whole lot, but she rode a little bit. Henry and John were very, very good ropers and that was kind of our lifestyle. We still go to all the ropings together around. It's kind of in the family."

Son Henry continued, "When Dad was in his carefree single days, he lived to rodeo. And his brothers, Arthur and Edgar, who were in the cattle-buying business, they would tell me that he would work for them until he got enough money for an entry fee. And then he would take off to the rodeo, and if he won, he would continue going to rodeos until he ran out of money. He'd come back and work for them until he got enough money for another entry fee."

The Bekens had been married for fifty-eight years. "A nice fifty-eight years," offered Heine lovingly, as Earlyne added, with feeling, "We've had lots of fun together. Lots of fun."

The Pesak Brothers

The three Pesak brothers—Kenneth, Robert, and Douglas—were carpenters and builders. They worked together in construction, and they remained close to each other into adulthood, "Well, we're not only brothers—we're best friends," said Kenneth emphatically. "We get along real good. We've been living together all of our lives. One room and three bunk beds." He smiled as he described their childhood.

Surely they fought when they were children? "We never started. We never got in any kind of argument where we were upset with each other for more than thirty minutes. You might be mad for a few minutes, but then you resolved the problem. It's something that you got to learn, to give and take." These were again the words of Kenneth, at age thirty-one the oldest and probably the most outgoing of the three. Robert was thirty, and Douglas twenty-nine.

He spoke proudly of his family's long history in Colorado County:, "I know from my dad's side, we've been here for over one hundred years. And from my mother's side, we've been here for longer than that. There were the Voscamps and Trojans and they were the two that were my grandmother's side. Our grandpa Tucko was from up around the Waco area. And we've all lived here, around Borden. The Voscamp is German; the other may be Polish.

"Well, my grandmother told us a lot of history for a hundred years back," Kenneth continued. "She took care of us while my mother and dad worked. And we're proud of our ancestry. At the time, you're not that interested, you know—you don't really go in depth and write it down or anything. Now that she's passed on, well, the people at the Voscamp reunions, they all say it would have been nice if they had written some of those stories down." Although Grandma Voscamp died in 1987 and was buried in the Miller Cemetery outside of Weimar, she clearly had not been forgotten.

"I think they all did whatever there was to do to make a living. If it was farming, or if they worked with the neighbor to fix this fence or fix that barn, the neighbors came and helped them. Every week they'd kill a calf and divide it with that neighbor. They called it a meat club. Then, there was more caring for people. It was a lot slower life, a lot more time to stop and smell the flowers, or whatever you might call it. Today it's just hustle and bustle, rush here, rush there, and hurry so you can pay this bill and hurry so you can pay that bill.

"And they used to go to great effort to go to church. It would take hours to ride in an old car or even with horse and buggies, and they had to leave two hours ahead of

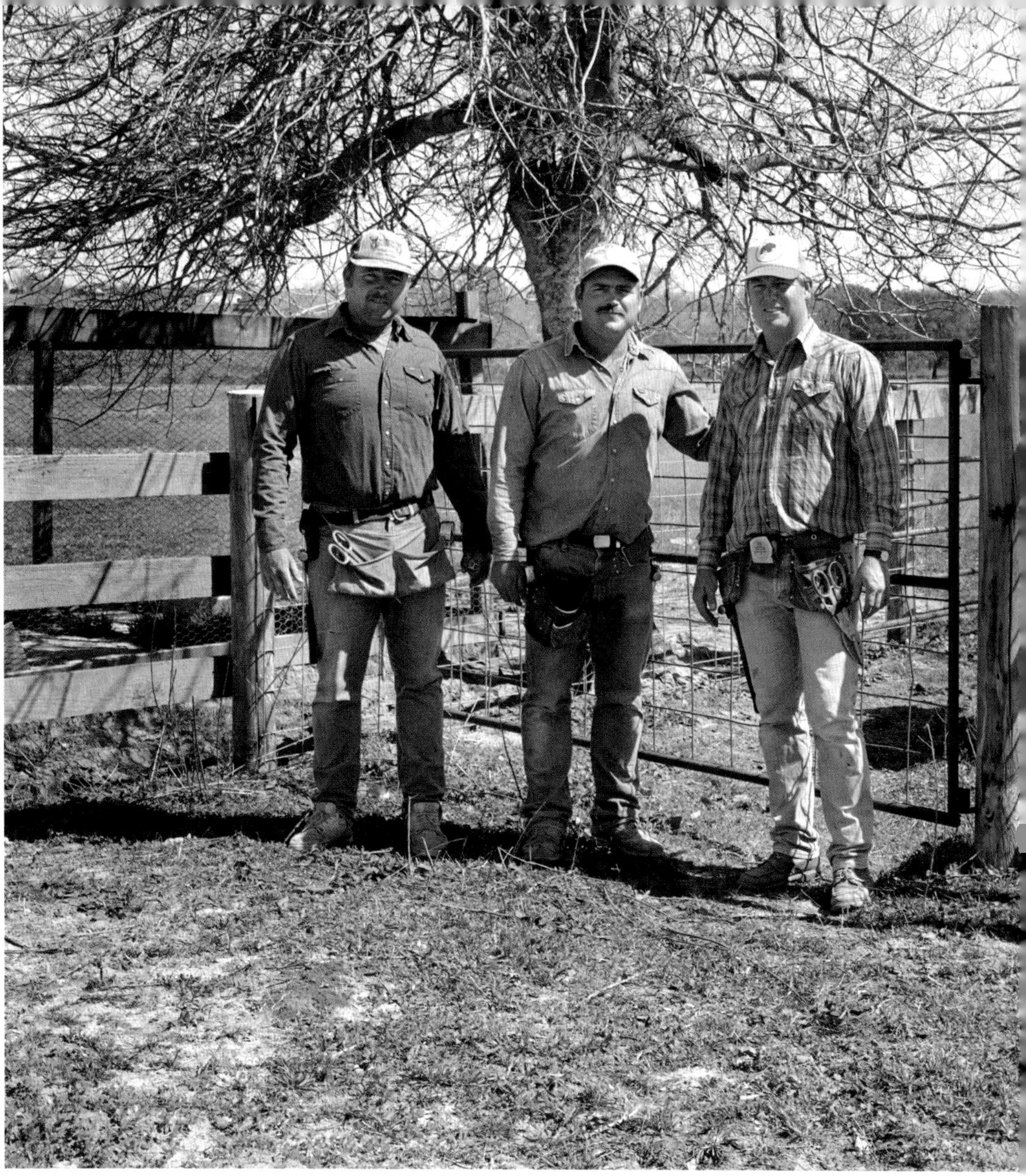

The Pesak Brothers—Kenneth, Douglas, and Robert

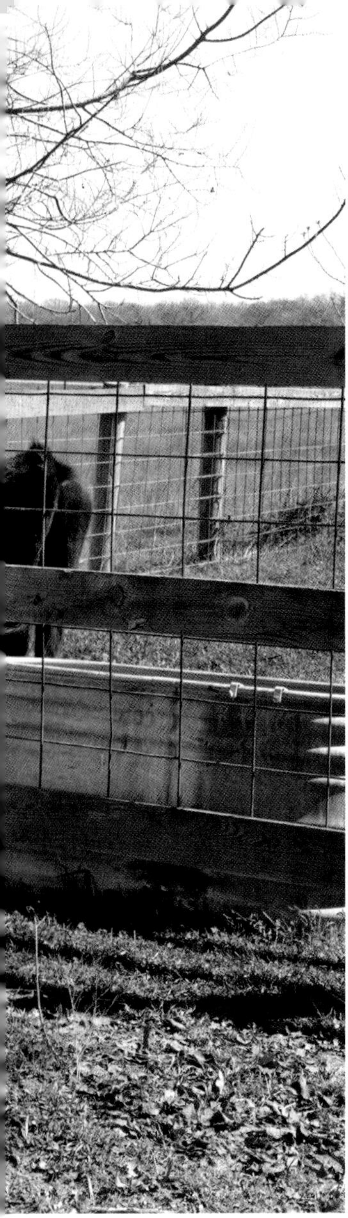

time. And my grandmother used to pick up a lot of the children on the way, where the parents didn't have time or couldn't get off the farm to do it."

Of himself and his brothers, Kenneth observed, "I would say we're not a lot different. We all have children and wives and are trying to raise our family. Keep our bills paid and try to get along with people as much as we can."

I heard a rumor—clearly said with affection, since the Pesak brothers were both liked and respected—that they were nicknamed "the Brains, the Brawn, and the Bullshit." I see the brains and the brawn in all three. As for the bullshit, that hasn't surfaced yet—or else I missed it.

Olga Mae Hefner

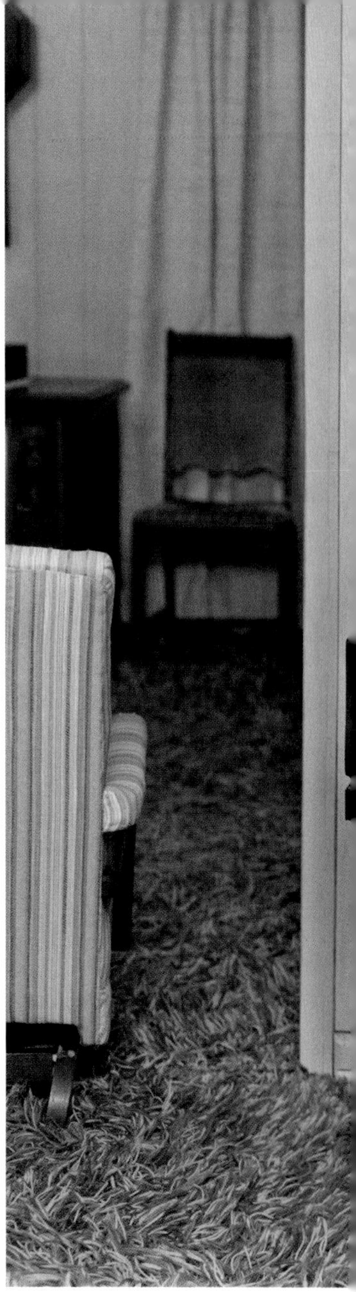

Olga Mae Stallman Hefner was happily married for forty-nine years to her loving husband and friend, W. A. Hefner. When W.A. died, Olga Mae found herself bereft and needing "something to keep my mind busy." So she became the justice of the peace of their small hometown, Garwood, a position W.A. had held for over twenty-five years, with Olga May's assistance. In fact, she had always been active. She had taught school for twenty-nine years, receiving more teaching awards than any other teacher in her school. She raised five children, three boys and two girls, one of whom was severely brain-damaged in infancy yet lived to adulthood at home.

Olga Mae was about to start down another road as she faced retirement from the JP post in 1991. She said she was planning to "just bum around."

Olga Mae described her father, August Stallman, as a man "respected and liked by all. He always had such a good relationship with the black people," she said proudly. "And if any of 'em had any trouble, it was always 'Mr. August,' and they'd come get 'im. And lot of times he would help 'em financially when he couldn't hardly help himself. Mother'd get so put out at him sometimes! She said that he'd give 'em the shirt off his back. Mother wasn't quite as easygoing, but Daddy just had a heart of gold."

Olga Mae reminisced about her parents' courtship. As a young single woman, her mother had attended a teaching workshop, a "summer normal," where "she met a lady from Garwood." Olga continued: "The lady said, 'Ida, you'll have to come home with me one weekend. There're six young men who live next door to us, across the fence. They're all grown, and none of 'em are married, and you can have your pick—except August. I'm gonna get August someday.' And Mother told her before she'd ever seen Daddy, 'That's the one I'm gonna get.' And Mother did." Olga Mae laughed.

"Mother taught school," Olga Mae said. "There were seven girls in their family, and six of them were schoolteachers. And then, in W.A.'s family, his dad had five sisters,

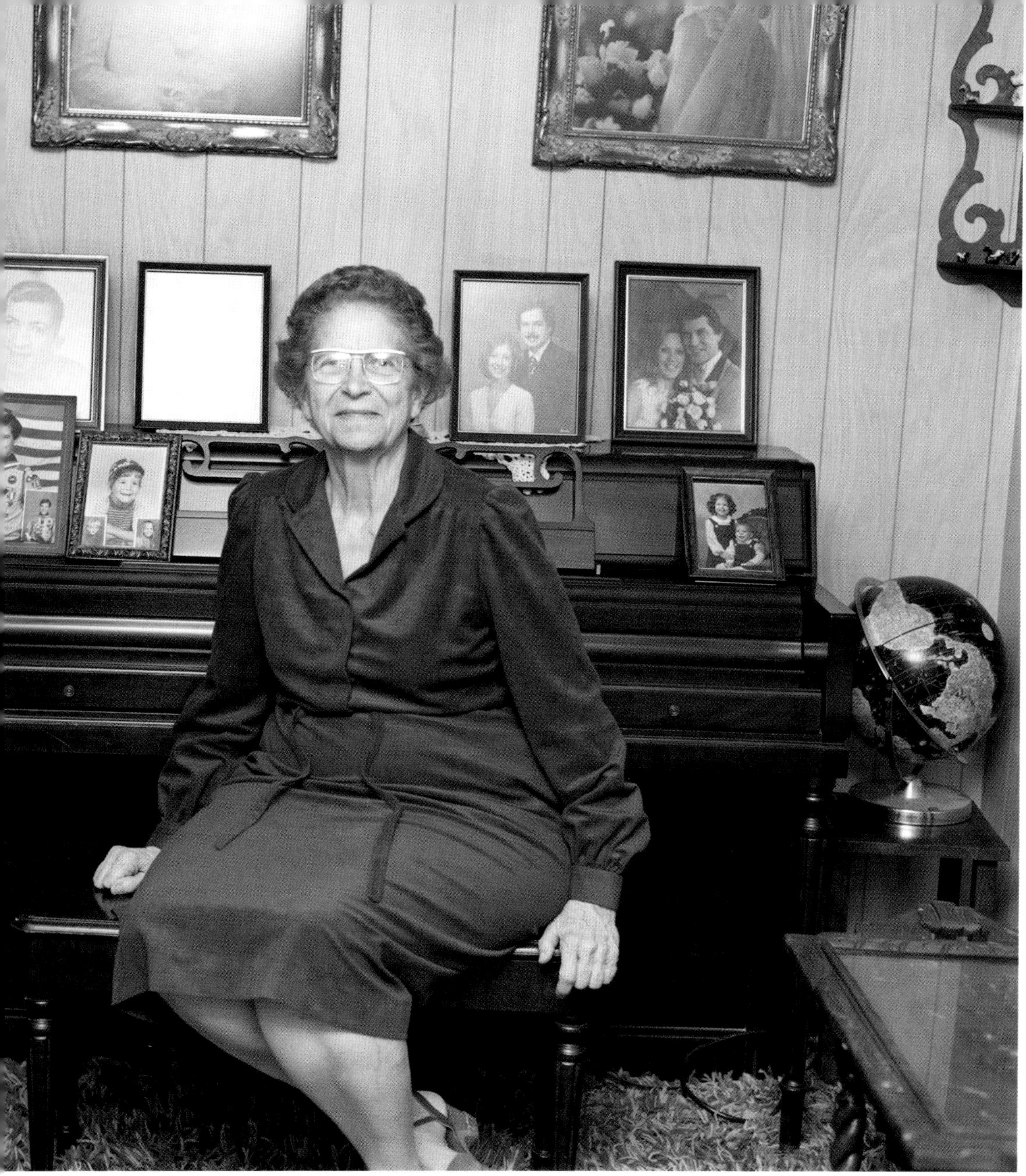

Olga Mae Hefner, lady JP

and four of *them* were schoolteachers. I mean there were teachers all around us—so it was just kinda natural that everybody was gonna be a teacher.

"And of course, we were poor people, and Mother and Dad did good to send me to college. And they were determined that we should have that opportunity. So I worked real hard in college to please 'em. And of course, I fell in love when I was in college and married W.A. And the first two years that we were married, we didn't even live together because he was behind me in college 'cause he had to stay out and work some. And I taught at China, near Beaumont, that little town. And then after he'd finished, we were real lucky. We got a little country school in Wharton County, and we taught there two years.

"And then the war business came up, and my brother was drafted. And he had a crop in the field that summer. And Daddy wanted us to come help get the crop out. And so we just did—that's how it worked. So, originally, it hadn't been our plan to farm, because we figured we'd keep on teaching school. But W.A. was reared on a ranch, and he liked, you know, country life too."

When W.A. died, Olga Mae cried so long that her daughter finally lost her cool. "I was sittin' there bawlin' one night," Olga Mae recalled, "and she said, 'Mother, you're cryin' again!' And I said, 'Yes, and I'm *gonna be cryin'!*' And she said, 'You know Daddy's gone, and he's not comin' back. And we all need you.' And it kind of made me think—W.A. would never have wanted me to sit and grieve." And so she got up and went back to work.

Olga Mae spoke with great tenderness about her children and said of Bubby, the child whose brain had been damaged by whooping cough and encephalitis, "He was like a three- or four-year-old—that's as far as his mind developed. He was affectionate and needed to be loved. He slept by his parents' bed and held his mama's hand each night as he fell asleep." Bubby died at twenty-eight.

"I think it's not just Bubby, but most retarded kids crave affection and love, nearly all of 'em do. And so many times they don't get it. I counseled with quite a few parents. And so many of 'em, it's so hard to accept. And a lot of times it's harder for a man to accept a retarded child than a mother. But W.A. never was ashamed of Bubby and was, you know, just very congenial with him. Bubby was never vicious or mean. He was easy to live with. But, oh, you do a lot of living in a lifetime!"

Olga Mae taught special-needs kids for twenty-two years in El Campo. "Bubby died in '78." she said. "I was out ten years when he was sick so much. Then Mother and W.A. sensed I needed something else, 'cause I always enjoyed being out with people. So I went back to college three summers to get my master's and taught college labs, and W.A. kept the kids. I'd drive up Tuesday morning and come home Saturday afternoon. I guess I might have had a nervous breakdown—things were closing in on me with Rodney [Bubby]. I needed to get out of the house by then, *real bad*." It was the same with the JP job: "I needed something that would really take my mind. Now I don't need it anymore."

She recalled some funny cases she had handled as the justice of the peace, like "the cows in the corn patch," when one farmer complained that his neighbor's cows were in his corn patch; the neighbor said no, it was deer in the corn, not cows. When neither would give in, Olga Mae sent her deputy to the scene, and he came back saying there's no way to confuse deer droppings and cow droppings. And the case was settled. She tried to resolve as many cases as possible over the phone, reminding people that they might make the newspaper if their case went to court. In a town as small as Garwood, that usually brought an agreement.

"I try to keep so busy I can't think," she said in 1990. But by early '91, Olga Mae admitted she had lost her incentive to work and just wanted to travel, visit her kids in Florida, Houston, and Australia, and enjoy her life.

Then a friend who was also widowed took Olga Mae aside and talked to her. "You know what you've got to do?" asked her friend. "You've got to convince yourself that you can live alone. Learn to live alone and accept it." Olga Mae responded, saying, "And I thought, well, I guess that was it, 'cause I was *fightin'* bein' alone, you know. And I still don't like it, 'cause I never was alone. Oh, but you do a lot of living in a lifetime!"

Em Hay

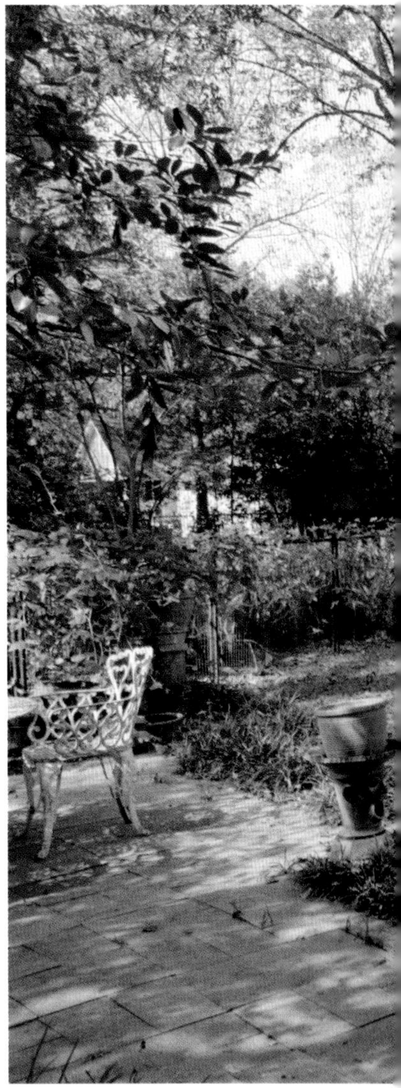

Em Hay said with no reserve that she had never been bored a day in her life.

She was born Emma Bowen in 1911 in Colorado County. "In that era of small-town thinking, I was a total adventuress. I was ready to go anywhere," she said. Em left home in 1931 when she married and didn't return to Colorado County for forty-eight years. In the meantime, she led a life of travel and adventure that should have made her retirement days in Columbus seem dull—but not for Em. She said she was too busy to be bored, although she did complain, laughingly, that "old age is *so* inconvenient!"

Em's first husband was a geologist and mining engineer who moved with her to Mexico City, where they spent the war years, later living in Monterrey, where he worked in mining. After Monterrey, they lived in mining camps near Saltillo for fourteen years. There in the camps, Em was often the only Anglo woman. She had arrived in Mexico speaking no Spanish but, over time, became comfortable in Spanish and able to have both American and Mexican friends. The mines where her husband worked were in very remote places, reachable only by narrow-gauge railroad on an electric cart (called *un garmon*), by freight caboose, or by horseback. She said she spent her days there reading, helping the Chinese cook, riding horseback, doing handiwork, and talking to the Mexican soldiers who guarded the compound. Although the guards would not let her leave the compound—"there was no exit," as she put it—"I loved it all. I've never been bored in my life."

Her husband died in Mexico in 1973 after they had been married for forty-two years. Eight years later, she married an old friend who also died, after only one and a half years. She was fortunate at this time to find work managing an art gallery in El Paso and as a business manager for a well-known artist, Frederic Taubes, whose paintings filled her house in Columbus. Her favorite activities in retirement were art-

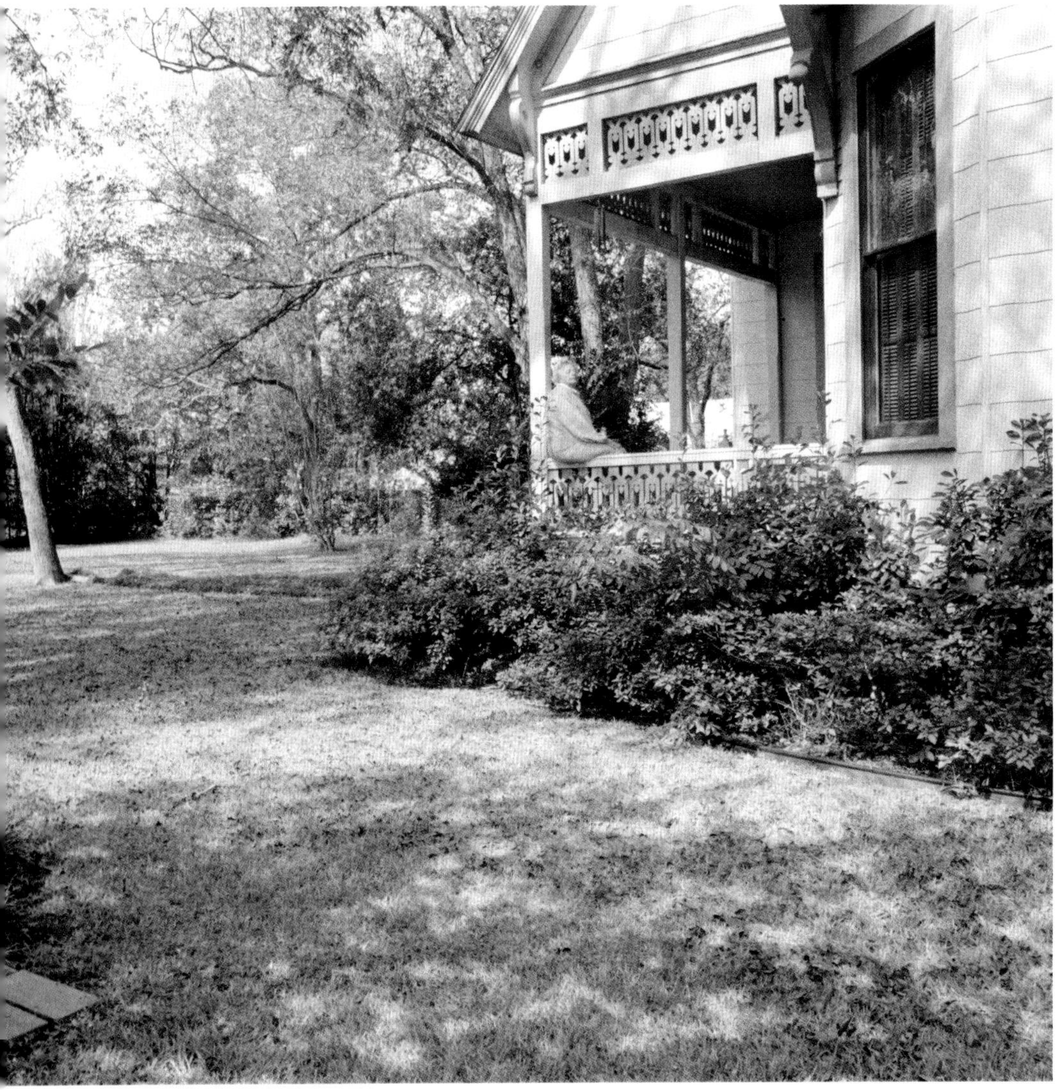

Em Hay at home

related, especially helping the town of Columbus develop a functioning art center. Em spearheaded the purchase of a Columbus building that had been a saloon and theater from 1891 on. And this was where the Live Oak Art Center found its home. She helped raise enough money in nine months to purchase the old building. The completed center has shows for local artists as well as traveling exhibits from New York, Mexico, Austin, and Houston. Plans for holding classes there for children and adults were in the works. "We're building this art center for future generations," said Em, with resolve and pride in her voice.

Of herself, she said, "I'm of an era of quiet, small-town people, but I was always a little adventurous. I was always ready to go anyplace, do *anything*."

For such an adventurous, bold woman, Em was surprisingly shy when it came to cameras, and she flatly refused to get within decent range of mine. You can *just* see her in the distance if you look hard, sitting on her porch railing.

Herbert Baines

Herbert Baines was born and raised in Oakland, where he was the owner and proprietor of the Oakland Mini-Mart when we met in the early nineties. He said he had spent twenty-one years away from Oakland in the Air Force, serving in France, Vietnam, Germany, and Guam. After returning to Texas with his family, he was determined to settle in one place and stop roaming. The other man pictured is Frank Strange, Herbert's beer-drinking friend from Crockett, in East Texas.

Once upon a time, Herbert said proudly, Oakland had been a thriving town. The local economy was based on cotton, and Oakland was where the cotton gins were. Then cotton "died" in the mid-1960s, and so did Oakland. Other locals disagreed with Herbert's explanation for Oakland's decline, citing the building of Highway 90 and the railroad, which was routed through Weimar, bypassing Oakland. It was likely that both events had killed the town.

When we talked, there was nothing to show Oakland's past glory—it was all simply gone. It was possible to drive into town and see not a soul, not even a dog in the street. Herbert's Mini-Mart seemed to be the hub of the action on that particular day.

Herbert Baines reminisced about when times were good. In the 1970s, he had a roping arena and remembered making two thousand dollars on opening night alone. People "come from all over, by the hundreds." Now, of course, times were hard for everyone, everywhere. And he named one other major difference between now and then: "Then, people helped each other out—you don't have that now," he lamented, a thought echoed by many.

Herbert was a well-spoken man and seemed educated even though he had had to quit school before finishing. He briefly attended both Marquette University in Milwaukee and Blinn College in Brenham, Texas. He worked as an aircraft mechanic in the service and believed he learned the most from traveling and from the schooling he received in the Air Force.

Herbert returned to Colorado County in 1975, when he worked as a carpenter and ran the Mini-Mart, Oakland's only market. Did he miss traveling? "No, had enough of it," he said. "I like the country life, the slow pace."

In the photograph, the wall behind the two men is the exterior wall of the store, giving a glimpse of the mural created by Frank one night. The two men were sitting around drinking beer, when Frank bragged about his skills as a painter, and Herbert had a brainstorm and challenged Frank to paint the store wall. Frank agreed, and

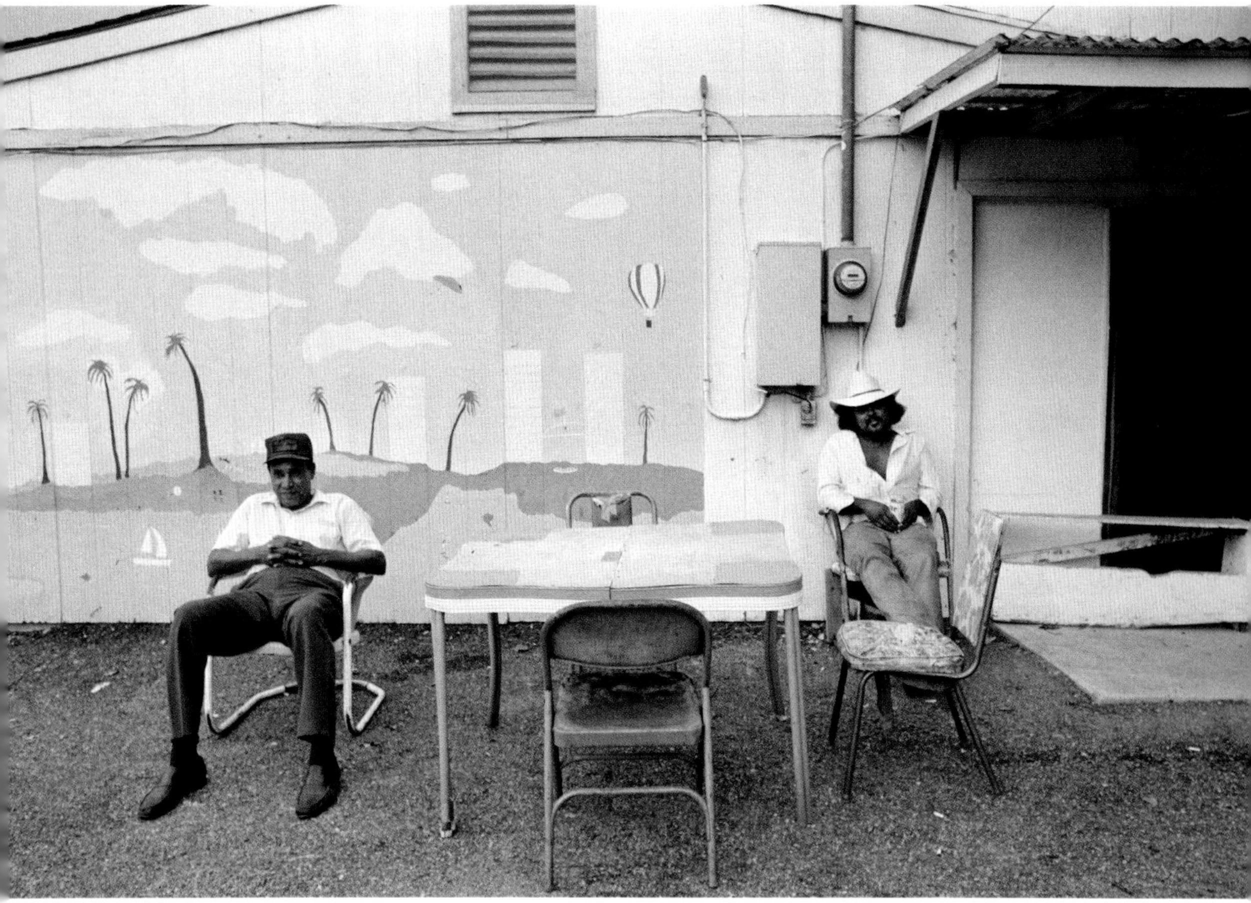

Herbert Baines and his friend, Frank Strange

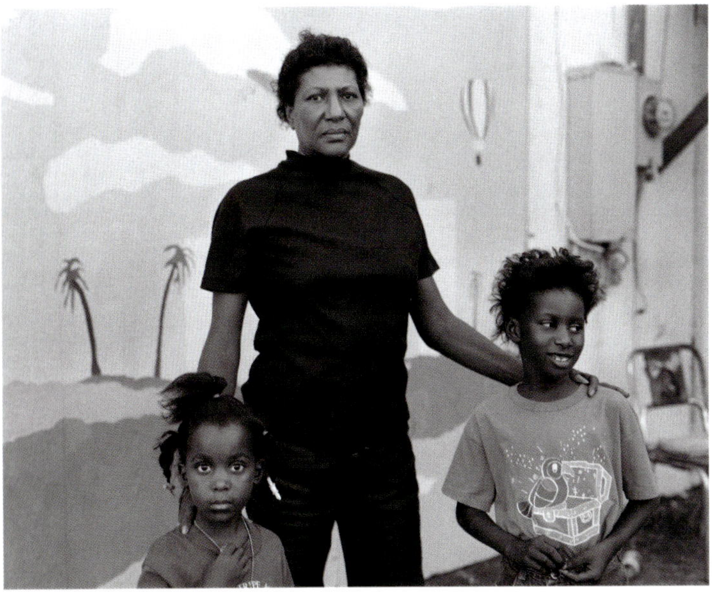

Joyce Baines, Herbert's wife, with her granddaughters

here it is, minus the tropical luscious colors—a scene of islands in a pale blue sea. It gives Oakland a slightly exotic air and is what caught my eye and brought me to the Baines family. Frank says he can paint anything. He just needs the chance.

When I returned in 2000, the Mini-Mart was closed. It appeared that Herbert might have been living in the shuttered store, but he never answered letters to tell what was going on. Oakland was as silent and vacant as ever.

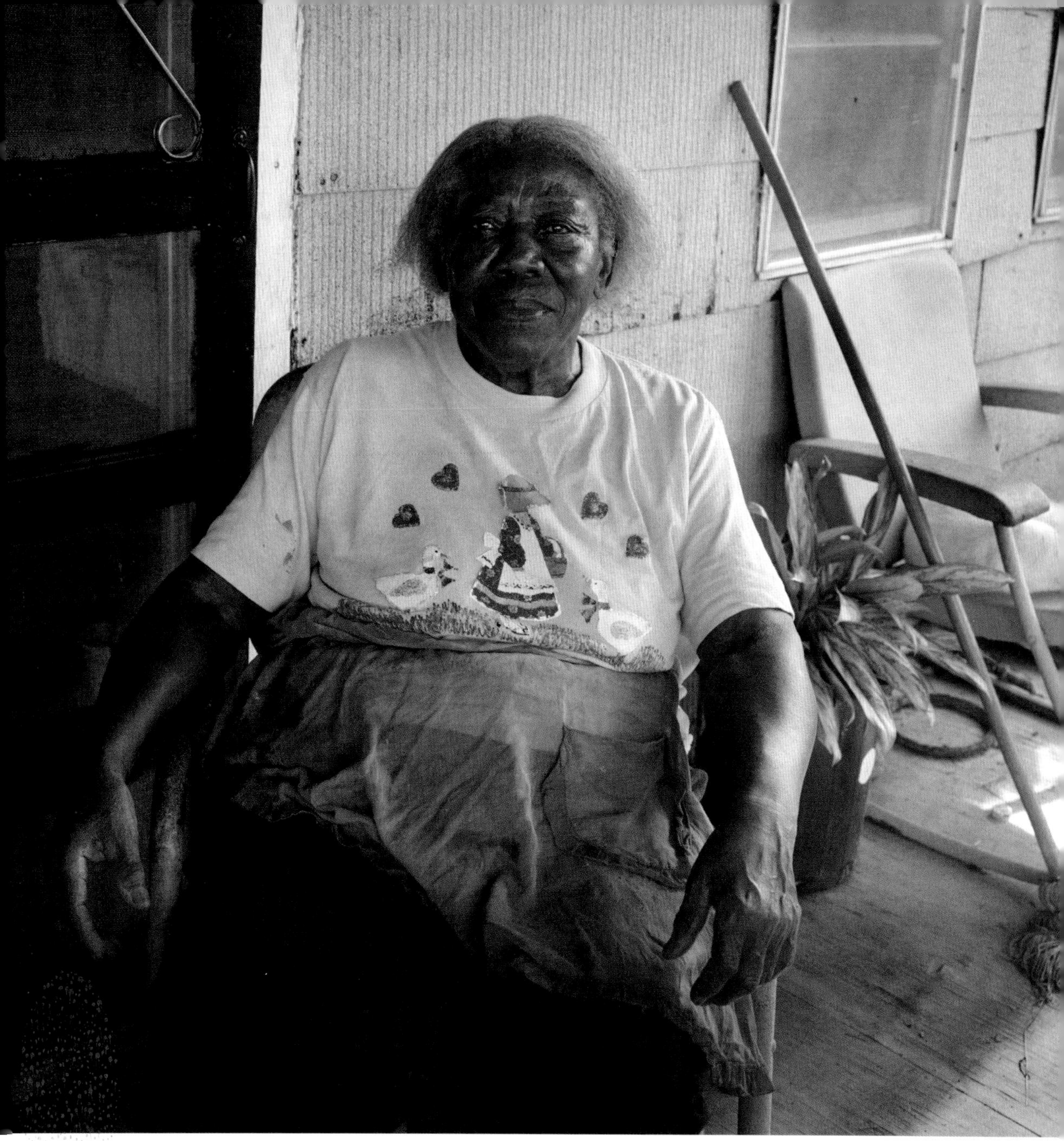

Leila Jackson

Leila Jackson

I met Leila Jackson through Eva Mae Glover, my friend and source for special African American women in rural Colorado County. It was Eva Mae who took me to Altair and Vox Populi to meet two of her closest friends, who were living in these two tiny communities, places so small they were virtually invisible from the nearby highway. They had no street names, no road signs, no indication at all that there were houses and people living a short distance away, off the farm-to-market road between Columbus and Garwood.

We went expressly to meet Leila Jackson and Dora Devlin. But Dora was never at her home in Vox Populi. Although she was over one hundred years old, Dora still drove a car, and she was always out in her car when we got to her house. Leila, thankfully, stayed home.

So we found Leila in Altair, in a house that stood off by itself, with only grassy fields around it and a single ornament in the front yard, a bottle tree she had made. An abandoned rice dryer stood nearby, the only other building in sight. The formerly healthy town of Altair had almost disappeared when the town's main business, the rice dryer, had closed. Yet Leila seemed content in her solitude. Friends came by to visit, and she had her church and her phone for company, her faith and her songs for pleasure. It seemed incredibly lonely, but Leila was in good spirits—and also very glad to see us.

"What'ew want me to tell ya?" she began, turning to Eva Mae with a smile after the introductions. "I can think of a whole lot of things, and some of them, I might not can get them so good. She be here the night if I be tellin' her everythin' I ever knowed or did! I be done forgot some of these things I'm gonna try to tell you.

"I was a Brooks when I'se born. My father was a Brooks. Well, I better tell where I'se born, right down there on Colorado River in nineteen and three. Right down there on that river. And I was raised right across on the arm over in there, like a bottom, like I was raised there.

"Well, I don't know—I live pretty good. You want to know some things I did? Well, I'll tell you what I did. For one thing, my daddy put me in the field when I was eight years old—that's when I went to the field. And I stayed in that field 'till I don't know.

"Well, I'm goin' tell you the truth. I have really picked cotton for forty cents a hundred, forty cents a hundred now, cotton pickin'. Choppin', seventy-five cents a day. I have *did* that!

"It was nice till mama whupped us 'bout doin' wrong now. Yes, I got whuppin's in my days. These chil'ren ain't getting' no whuppin's now—*they* raisin' their parents! Look, *my mama* raised me. And I raised my chil'ren. My mama raised me, and I raised my chil'ren," she emphasized.

"My father's mother, I didn't know her. But my mother's mother, I knowed her. And I knowed my mother's grandmother, and I knowed my mother's grandpa. I was nine years old when she died, and she was born in slavery.

She used to tell how they were treatin' them over there, in slavery. Well, Grandma Jenny—that was my mother's grandma now, and they was in slavery. Well, she said in slavery, had jobs for you to work. You'd go out in the field and work, do all that. But healthy-lookin' womens, they didn't put them out in the field. They breed them just like you breed somethin'. That's just how this color mixed up. That's how the color mixed up, 'cause when you breed 'em, see they breeded 'em to them bosses, you know, and *they* was white.

"They had to do what they said there, and she said, healthy, sportly-lookin' womens, they breeded them. And my mother and my mother's father—well, there's some [family name] in Columbus, and I'm tellin' it like it is. It's some T---s* up there in Columbus—I don't know where they are but they might be dead—but *his* father and *my* mother's father, they was first cousins. Now, my mother's father, he was a black man, and the T---s* was white."

Moving forward, she said, "All right, I married when I'se seventeen years old. And I been in this house right here seventy-six years. Seventy-six years I been here. I married in 1921. And this house was a new house, two years old, when I moved here, two years old."

"All right, later up in the '21, I had a baby. My son was born. Then, my daughter, she was born in 1922. My son, he died in 1969, my daughter in '89.

"Well, I'll tell ya, I don't know—I done good with my husban'. I don't know 'bout some of them and they husban's, but I did good with mine. Lee Jackson. He been dead—he died in 1971. I been here all my life 'round Altair. I lived pretty good.

"My daddy put me in the field when I was eight years old. My chil'ren, got big-sized chil'ren, so they could go do it. We'd work out, me and my chil'ren. We worked out, go workin' where we'd get paid for it. After I quit goin' out to the field and all that stuff, I washed and ironed for thirty-five years for three white women live right here—show you the big house now. But they dead. They gone. They were sisters. They died there in a Eagle Lake home. And I washed and ironed thirty-five years for them women, and I didn't have no 'lectric iron neither! I had what you called smoothin' irons—they was iron irons.

"Made you a fire, made you a log fire. In the wintertime, like now, we had wood heaters—we didn't had no 'lectric. We had wood heaters, and when I had to iron, I

*Leila named one of Columbus' most illustrious families.

could put my irons on this wood heater and heat that iron to iron them clothes. In the summertime, go on out there and make me a little log fire, a little log fire, set the irons up there to get hot."

What was Leila's hardest job? "Lord have mercy!" she exclaimed. "What was it? Really, the hardest workin' I ever done was pickin' that cotton 'cause it made your shoulders so sore, pickin' and draggin' them sacks. And some of them were so heavy! And if there was any men folks out in the field, they wouldn't pack your sacks for you. They did not.

"I was fifteen years old when I joined the church. And I was baptized in—well, it's a gravel pit down there back of my house. We used to catch fish down there when Miz Carrie Stafford was livin', but after she died, them young folks, the white people, wouldn't let us fish. We used to walk down there and fish many a day. I was baptized in that hole of water right down there when I was fifteen."

Leila and Eva Mae shared a love of laughter and good stories, and the two women could talk and joke together without end. But it wasn't until the second visit that Leila got comfortable enough to bring up the "good stuff," like the stories of which slave owner had sired which mixed-blood child. She seemed both outraged and amused by this. Like her friend Eva Mae, Leila had the courage to speak up, tell the "other" stories, and tell them with wit, flavor, and honesty.

Leila's granddaughter Shirley wrote about her adored grandmother. She told how she loved the summers when she would visit her grandparents and they would give her dimes rolled up in paper. As an adult, Shirley's favorite of her grandmother's colorful expressions was "Never let a man lay his hat." Commented Shirley, "And now I know what she meant by that."

She also said that one of Leila's favorite things in all her life was her church, Wright Glow Baptist, where she had served proudly as choir president for over sixty years. About church, Leila said, "Did I tell you about me? When I first joined the church at fifteen years, they didn't have too much work for children to do, but in 1926 our first choir was organized. And they made me president of that choir. And I was president of that choir sixty-somethin' years. It might be a little longer than that. I'll tell you what about it and the reason why we don't have a choir. We *could* have a choir, but some of our women has to work, you know, and we really don't have enough to hold up the choir like we used to. But anyway, that's how long I was there, and that ain't all I did.

"I taught the little number five–class children. Oh Lord, I must have been about sixty-some years with 'em. From the time that they elected me from dem children, I had two treasures: the mission and the Sunday school. I took care of the money, kept it from one end of the month to the other. Once the month, they would always report in church. And I'd keep it until the reportin' time every first Sunday. And I kept the mission's money, kept the Sunday school money over fifty years, I know. Mighta been longer than that.

"And I had a tribe. In those days, they had tribe leaders in the church. And you had so many members in your tribe. And it was a deacon—he was a tribe leader—but he died. But I musta kept that tribe, I reckon, 'bout thirty years, number five tribe. And always on a Sunday, I'd have the biggest report, when they'd report the money for the church. We paid dues, like dues.

"First and third, and Sunday school—we don't have it like we used to 'cause we don't have 'nough of 'em. Some of them goes to work, have to do their work. And me, I done got too old to walk down there to that church house 'cause I done made a many track at that church house, day and night. I used to walk down there at night to prayer meeting and all of that by myself.

"'Cause when I first married my husband, he used to belong to the church, but he had done got out. But before he died, he was an usher in the church. He went back to church a long time 'cause I told him, 'If you don't be in no church, when the Lord call you, *I ain't gonna carry you* to that church house—to the *graveyard* you goin'!' And he went and got back in the church, and when he died, he was an usher in the church—stood at the choir room door.

"In 1971 we had a house full of members. But oh, so many of them is gone. We have a lot of them is gone, oh Lord, yes! I done sure outlived 'em."

Medie Mae Scott

Lovely Medie Mae and I met by good luck when I went searching one day for Henry Grays, whom it had been suggested that I meet. In a small, somewhat creaky house backed up to the railroad track that runs through the middle of Columbus, I found him and his companion, Medie Mae, along with a large array of cats and dogs, some of which can be seen under Medie's chair in the picture.

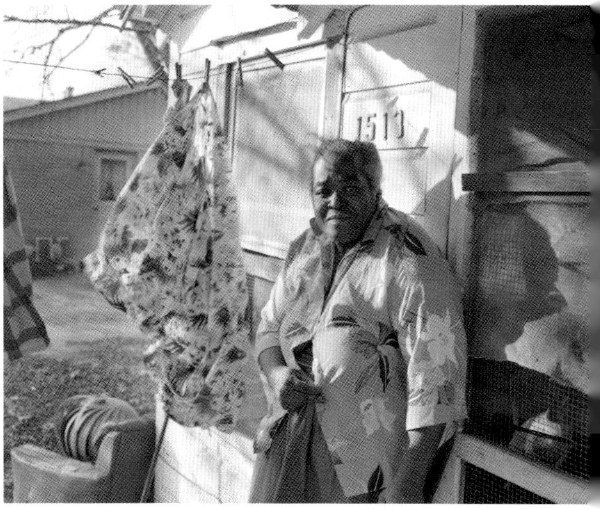

Medie Mae Scott

Medie seemed reserved, collected, and at ease. There was a calm expression in her eyes, an openness and a luminosity. She had a graceful smile. In spite of her overwashed, worn dress, callused feet, and disheveled hair, Medie showed self-assurance and a real beauty within herself.

We had only the shortest visit. Sadly, both Medie and Henry Grays died soon after that, before we could talk more. There was only time enough to take a copy of her photograph to her in the hospital where she was then a patient. So Medie Mae remains something of a mystery, and there is little to write about her—only what was learned from her niece, Linda Giles, the daughter of Medie's twin sister.

Linda said that Medie Mae and her twin sister, Modie Mae, were born in 1932 in Columbus, two of the Ned Whites' six children. Medie spent her entire life in her hometown, and there she raised two sons, William Scott Junior and Bennie Scott. That's all I know, other than that she was kindhearted and her niece loved her dearly. Linda described Medie as a person who was as kind and generous-spirited as she appeared to be.

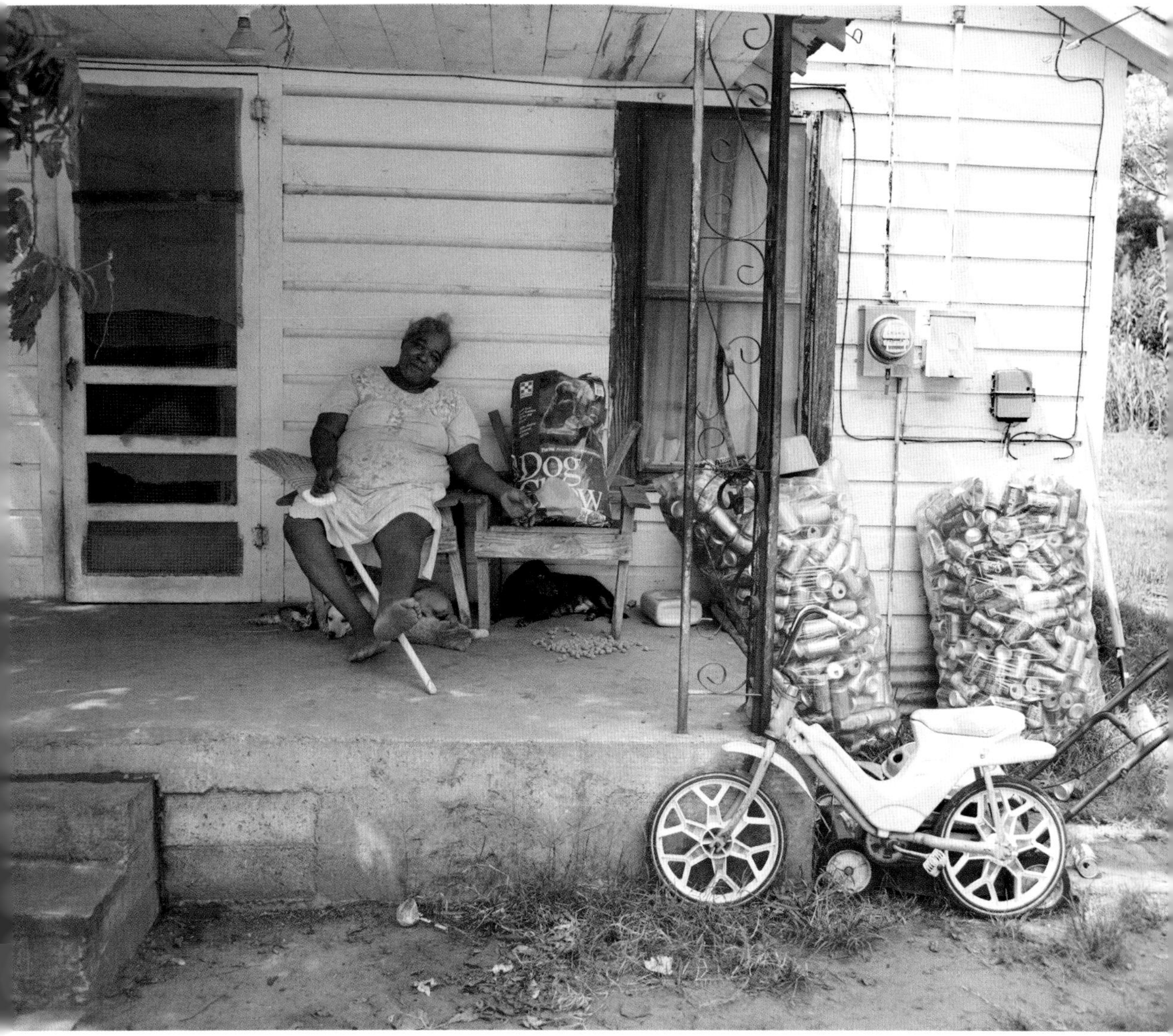

Medie Mae Scott and her pet dogs

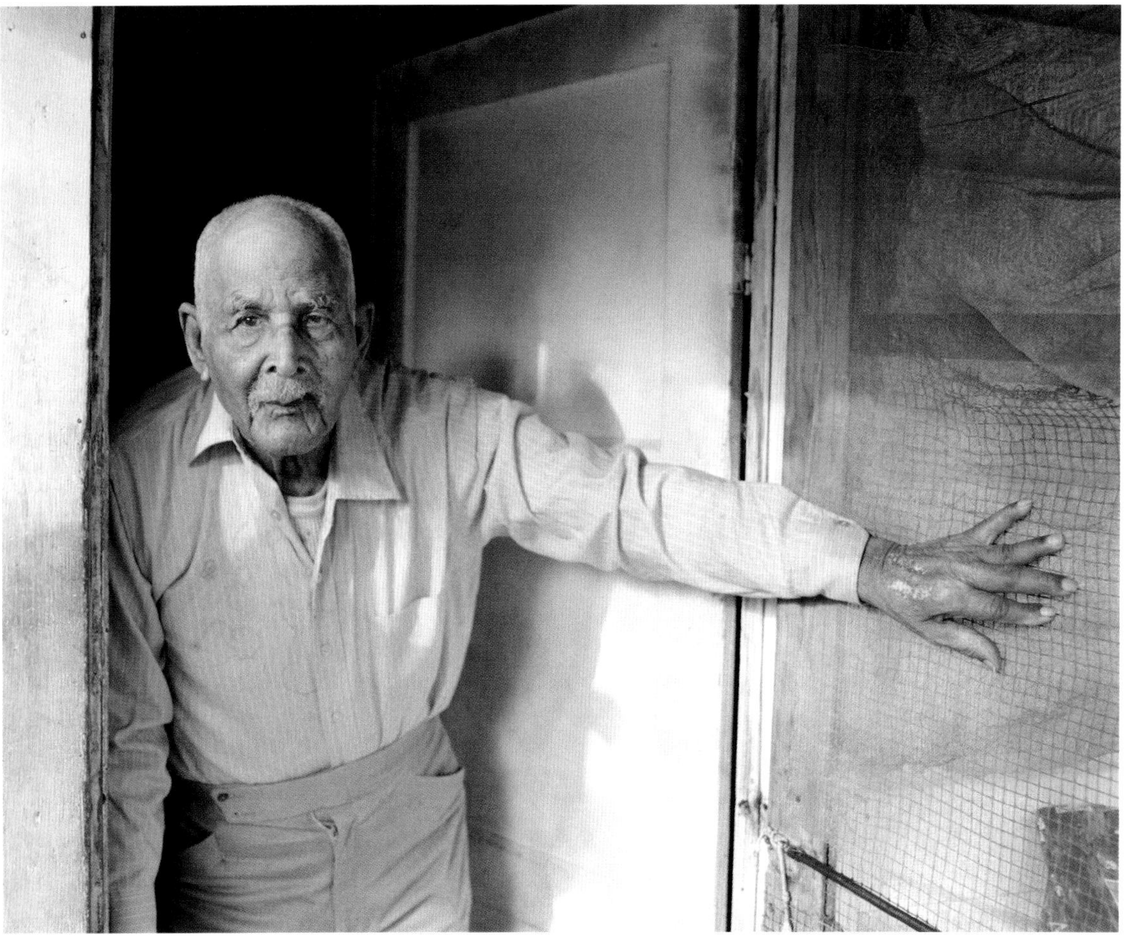

Henry Grays

Henry Grays

Henry Grays was ninety-seven years old when we met, a handsome older gentleman. He said he was born in "eighteen and ninety four." He lived to be ninety-nine, meaning that we talked not long before his death. The one time we met, we met at his house. A woman at the Nesbitt Memorial Library had steered me to him, naming Henry as a man worthy to meet and interview, a distinguished member of the black community.

Henry was living quietly with his companion, Medie Mae Scott, and their host of dogs. He looked frail and strong at the same time: wobbly on his feet, but with a tall, muscular frame and an elegant air. He walked with a cane, yet gave the impression that the cane he carried was more a matter of style than physical support. His face was alive and attractive, even at his advanced age.

Asked how he was feeling at ninety-seven, he simply said, "Oh, sometime I feel pretty good, and sometime I feel pretty bad."

He began to tell his story: "I was born in Colorado County, out in the country, 'bout four miles from here. Way b'tween here and Garwood. My mama was Della Grays and my father was named Henry Grays. I sure don't know where they come from, but my mother was a baby in slavery time. The onliest thing I heard her say [was that] when she was a baby, she was crippled—a horse stepped on her while she was crawlin'. And she remained crippled long till she lived." Henry was unsure where either parent had been born, except that it was somewhere in Texas. He said of his mother's family, "They was freed."

His father "worked on shares ever since I can remember—farmin', raisin' cotton and corn, potatoes, watermelon, chickens, and hogs," Henry said. "He worked for so many." Henry named his father's employers as Jeff Smith, Harry Tallman, Charlie Page, and Forest Miller—"and that where he was buried at," Henry said. "I been there lots of times, but there ain't no more cemetery. They done plowed it up." How did Henry feel about the loss of his father's grave? "I don't got no feelin's about it at all," he said.

Henry described his childhood: "We didn't have too many clothes and didn't have much food. They raised the biggest portion of our food. They raised corn and had it ground into meal. And they cured the hogs. And when that was gone, you had to do just as you could. Daddy would 'job around.'" Henry was one of six children. "One named Susan, one named Molly, one named Sally, one named Henrietta, and one named Ellen. And that got on to me, Henry. Only boy. I would like for it to have been a little brother. But I appreciated all of my sisters. They didn't want me to do nothin', but Daddy wouldn't stand for that, said he wanted Henry to do his part." Did his parents spank their kids? "They put a quirt on me—not no spankin'. *All over,* wherever they wanted, 'cept upside the head. It hurt so *bad*! I just think it made me a better man. I been here in Colorado County and never get in no trouble since I been here."

Asked if he was spoiled by his sisters, he answered, "Yes'm. *Still* spoiled." Did he like women to take care of him? "Yes'm. Married four times. Too old for that now," he added solemnly.

"Ought to have been goin' to school, I wasn't where no school was at," Henry said. "And when I got to where a school was at, I was big enough to plow. My daddy didn't have but one boy. I had to plow and go to school where church is. That's hard. I can read—I learned enough to work for Mr. Perry. Joe D. Perry, right down the road there, I'd haul all his cotton pickers and all his cotton and weights, and everythin'. And *nothin'* didn't ever turn up wrong.

"I spent my life on the rice fields. I worked for one man down on the rice fields for fifteen years. One I worked for is a dentist. He had a big ranch and I worked on that ranch three days a week and worked in the yard two days in that week. Till it got so I couldn't see how to do the yard in order to trim the trees and like that—then I had to give it up."

On sharecropping, Henry had this to say, "All I know, when I was a share farmer, one year I had to pick my own cotton for forty cents a hundred. The cotton I raised. Most folks, they getting' from ten, sometimes fifteen cents. There was a man come in here, by the name of Bill. He bought all the cotton he could buy for thirty cents. The pickin' wasn't hard as raisin' it."

The hardest time of his life, Henry said, was when he was in the service: "World War I, France. Didn't do nothin' but hard work. Cuttin' wood, diggin' holes, all such as that. I was in 332nd LB, Labor Battalion. We was all black. Just hard work. Always it was rainin' and snowin'. You had to work through all that. We left from Newport News, Virginia." Asked if he was scared crossing the ocean, he replied, "No, I wasn't scared, 'cause when we left, we went upstairs to bed till about twelve o'clock the next day. We went up top and couldn't see nothin' but water and sky—*then* I was scared!

"We landed in France and stayed two months. Then we went to no-man's-land"—the land between the armies ("a dangerous place," he allowed). Henry stayed in the service two years. "I tried to volunteer for World War II," he lamented. "Said I was too old."

Asked when was the best time of his life, Henry said, "Well, gamblin' and drinkin' I *thought* was my best time. But after that, I joined the church. I found out *that* was a *better* time. Now I go to church ev'ry Sunday and go to prayer meetin' every Tuesday." Friends came regularly to carry him to church.

He talked about joining the church as a young man: "I joined the church once and told them I had religion, but I didn't. I told them that. But I was still doin' everythin'

I was doin' 'fore I got in the church. And I said that wouldn't work. So now I haven't taken a strong drink since 1931. I don't drink, and I don't gamble, and I don't go to no cafés and nothin'. I don't go nowhere but to church, go to prayer meetin' every Tuesday. Dorothy Fitzgerald and Lucy O'Chase and Sister Conner [Luveen Conner], they go to prayer service and take me 'long."

When asked about his children, Harry replied: "All my children dead. I didn't have but three, and all of 'em dead. I got a bunch of grandchildren." He added, "I'm forgetful. I can't think long."

What little more I know about Henry Grays comes through his granddaughter: that he was a farmer all his life, that he had once worked for the Potasch family and for a Dr. Miller. One friend who drove Henry to church said the church was very important to him in his last years. He and she were in a Bible study group together, and she said he spoke often and always wisely. She also shared that Henry had a melodious singing voice.

Joe & Nicolasa Ramirez

Nicolasa and Joe Ramirez had been together for over eighteen years when we met. He had first seen her at his cousin's house, where she was babysitting. She was only fourteen, but "he must have liked what he saw, 'cause he just started hangin' 'round"—these were her smiling words. Eight children later, the two were still together and still enchanted with each other, holding hands, heads together, looking into each other's eyes, touching, touching all the time. "But no more babies," she added, with a seductive smile. "Eight's enough!"

I discovered the Ramirez family by chance one day, driving between Columbus and Weimar on Old Highway 90. There, where a roadside junkyard had once been a shambles, I saw that it had been cleaned up and was looking surprisingly neat and well tended. Someone had transformed that old junk heap into an attractive spot. Stopping to investigate, I discovered that Joe Ramirez had arrived. The grass was cut. A healthy-looking heifer grazed contentedly in the field among some abandoned cars, which were neatly placed in a line. Pieces of scrap were placed about for effect—metal hoops rested on end like arches, wagon wheels and hubcaps hung from trees and fences, flowers were sitting in odd pots and discarded tires. A painted ceramic burro peeked out from behind a lantana bush. It was clear that Joe had an artist's eye.

A surly-looking, serious-faced man, Joe would have none of this "artist" nonsense. He continued to treat me and my camera with a wary suspicion that never lessened. On the other hand, Nicolasa and the dogs were welcoming. She loved having their photographs taken and was proud that one of them was hung in the Columbus library during an exhibition.

There seemed to be children everywhere, quietly playing. They looked like happy kids—a little reserved, like their father. The family was living in a trailer home, parked to one side. Joe said he was worried about losing his lease and having to move his family. Their move would be a loss for all who drove that stretch of highway, which had been made cheerier by their presence.

Nicolasa, forty years old, had been born in Oakland, where her mother was living. Joe, fifty-something, was from Mexico. He had worked first in Houston in food markets, then had been a truck driver—"done almost everything," Nicolasa proudly explained.

The device on Joe's arm in this picture was holding together the bones of a broken wrist. He had broken the wrist and also an ankle in late 1990, and in April 1991 he

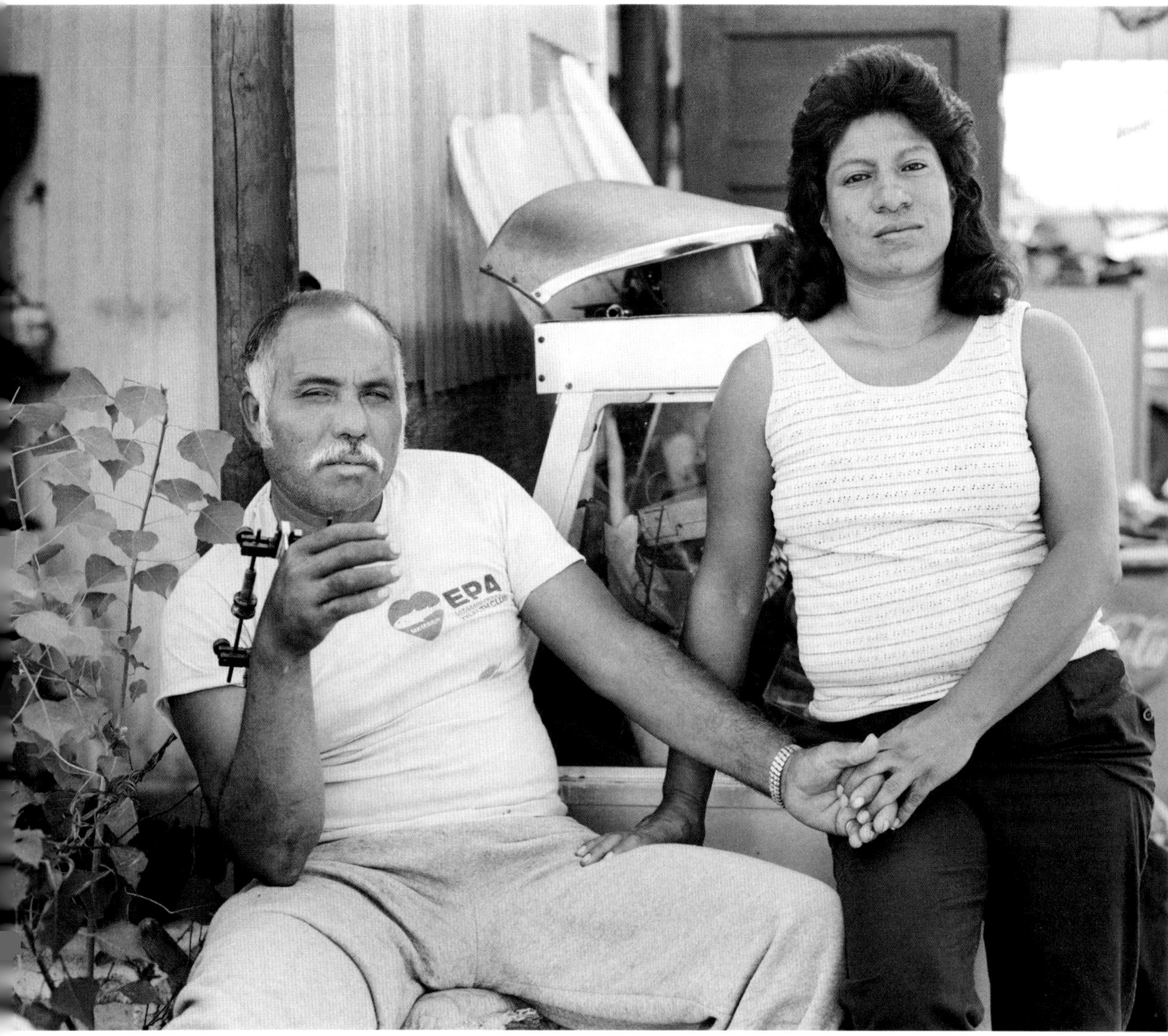

Joe and Nicolasa Ramirez

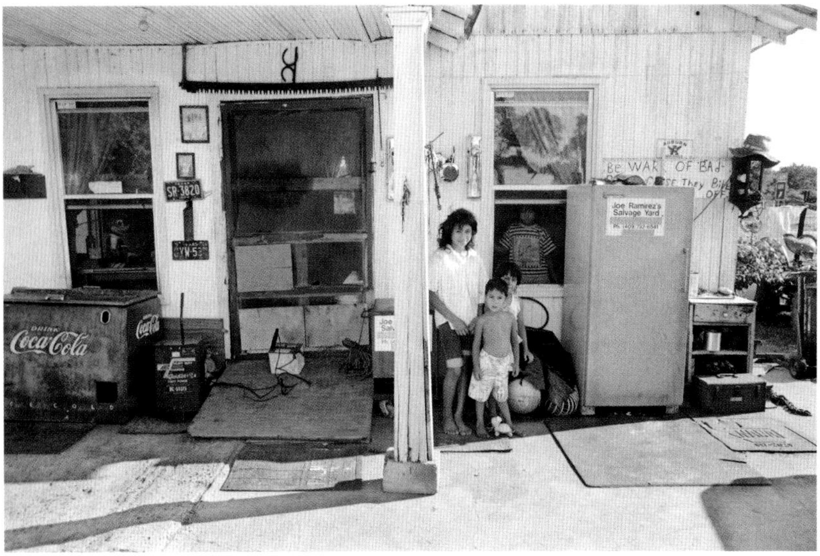

The Ramirez children

still couldn't make a fist with that hand. "Sometimes I touch his hand, and it's cold, cold, cold,' said Nicolasa sadly. "He don't feel *nothin'*!"

Soon afterwards, the trailer home was a charred ruin (no one could say why), and Joe, 50-something, and Nicolasa had moved. I learned later that Joe had died, and Nicolasa was working at a restaurant in Weimar. When we spoke once, she and the kids were doing all right.

RoseLee Ann & Frankie Neiser

RoseLee weighed only three pounds when she was born in 1941, so tiny that her daddy, Leo Wick, made her a crib from an apple box. "I fitted it with a light to warm her—like a chicken," he said with pride and tenderness. She fit in the palm of his hand, his one and only child.

"I was so small when I was born, my daddy, he put me in an apple box and fed me from an eyedropper," declared RoseLee Ann Neiser, describing her arrival on this earth.

As can be seen in the picture, RoseLee survived, and thrived, on her parents' loving care. She grew up, got a job at Elsie's coffee shop, and eventually met Frankie Neiser at the market where he was working, the Weimar Food Market, where they would work together for over twenty years. They married when she was twenty-two and he was twenty-six. They moved next door to her daddy, into a small, yellow brick house on the road between Weimar and Holman, where they remained. In time. David and Lisa were born. What did RoseLee think of Frankie when they first met? "Oh, he was okay, I guess," she said, with a wiggle and a giggle, not being one for wasting words.

Frankie's parents were Frank and Martha Mazock Neiser. RoseLee's parents were Leo and Annie Wick. Frank Senior was born in Austria, and Martha in the United States. You could catch a trace of a Czech accent in their son's voice. Frankie's father died one day in a car parked at Kmart, with no warning, in RoseLee's arms, his rosary in his hand.

Frankie served in the infantry from 1958 to 1961, in the Second Armored Division, known as Hell on Wheels. He trained at Fort Hood and served in Germany for two years, his only time ever to be away from his hometown.

The Neisers were living with their son, David, when this picture was taken. Lisa and Len, unlike her parents, had lived in many places, including England, Pennsylvania, and Hawaii—wherever Len, a career Air Force officer, was stationed. Lisa said she was *"sure glad"* to get out of Weimar. "A lot of people *never* got out of Weimar," she said, clearly relieved that she wasn't one of them. She said she liked moving around the world.

Amazingly, RoseLee and Frankie, these two small-towners, flew to England on their twenty-fourth wedding anniversary to visit Lisa and Len. "I always wanted to see the sun come up, or the sun go down, or somethin'!" RoseLee complained afterward. "But we were sittin' in the middle of the plane, and I never did get to see it come up. Coming home, what made me mad was they keep these windows closed,

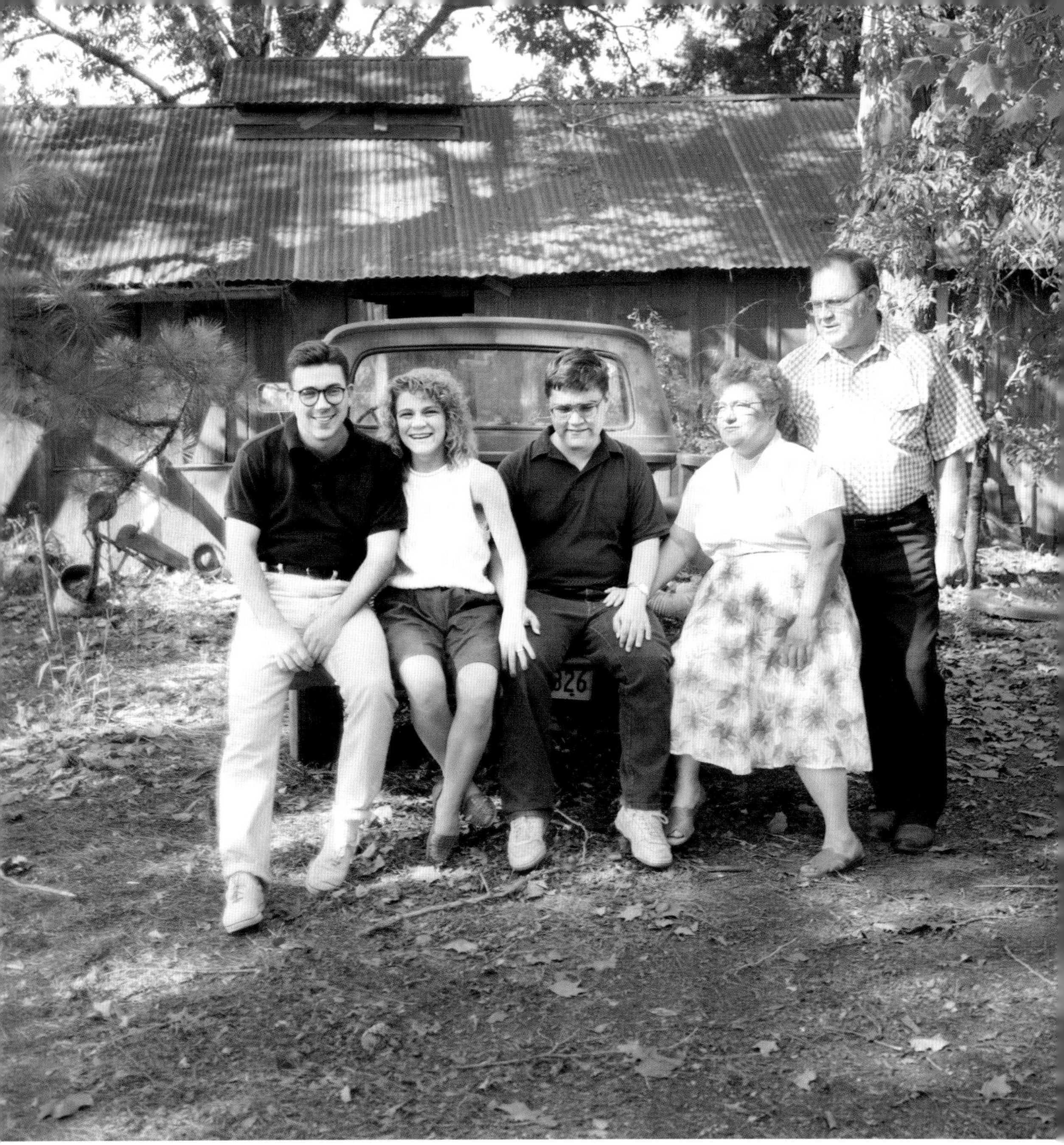

The Neiser family: son-in-law Len Gertner, daughter Lisa, son David, and RoseLee and Frankie Neiser

you know—they're showin' these movies, you know. But once in a while I'd open it up a little—I told Frankie, 'Gosh darn, I'm *payin'* for this trip, I wanna see where I'm going!' And it was dark!"

RoseLee and Frankie owned and ran the Weimar Food Market for years. The store was for sale when this photograph was taken in 1990. Business had been terrible all over Weimar. The chain stores that opened in nearby Columbus had proved to be unbeatable competition for many small businesses in nearby towns. Frankie said he was ready to retire anyway, "I *need* to rest," he said. He looked like he meant it.

When next I saw the Neisers, they were having trouble finding *any* kind of work, one of the risks of living in such a small town. There seemed to be very few jobs, and most were low-paying.

In late 2000, RoseLee called and gave an update. She was working in a local bakery, and Frankie was employed at Gallip's Super Market, in nearby Schulenburg. Len and Lisa were finishing a term of duty in Hawaii and soon coming back to the States. Len was in his eighteenth year in the Air Force. David was going with his mom to her job, rather than sit home alone. All was well.

Henry Lee Williams

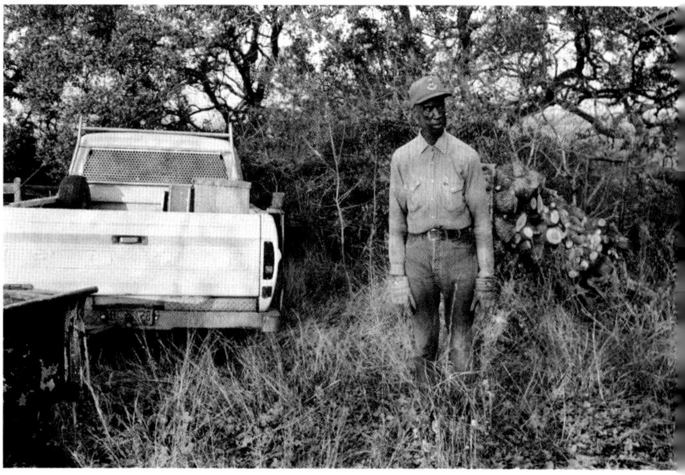

Henry Lee Williams

"This is my home. No place like home," said Henry Lee, with firmness and conviction when I first visited him at the house on the Williamses' family farm near our place, where he had lived his entire life.

Henry Lee was our 'across-the-road' neighbor in Osage. His mother, Nancy, who was born near the old Borden Store, had lived there with him until her death a few years earlier. After her death, Henry Lee lived on in the same house alone. He'd once had a job in Houston, for two years, at Magnolia Paper, and he did farm and yard work after his return to Weimar.

"I'm the only colored left here. All the coloreds left. Moved to town," he said. Asked if he was lonely out there by himself, Henry stood quite still and quiet, looking down and to the side. "Well," he mused thoughtfully after some time, "some of the neighbors treat me almost like family."

Some folks called Henry "strange." I always thought of him as simply different. He was certainly guarded, shy, and solitary in his habits. But he thought clearly enough and could be quite firm in his beliefs. Lacey Henry said, "He's just slow. They say his mama looked at a horse when she was carryin' 'im, and then she watched a horse havin' a colt, and somethin' fell on the baby," she explained caringly.

As a loner, Henry coped well with his solitude. He had friends in town and held a position in his church, Pleasant Hill Missionary Baptist. He seemed to enjoy his work, which was mowing yards. He loved going to church and visiting his friends in town, especially "Cousin Lacey," his favorite of all.

When I first knew him, Henry drove a car that had no reverse gear, so he had to do some fancy maneuvering at times to get out of tight situations. This caused hilarity among some of the white citizens of the town.

A while back, when I gave Henry a photograph of himself, he took the picture in his hands and looked at it long and hard, turning it round and round, upside down,

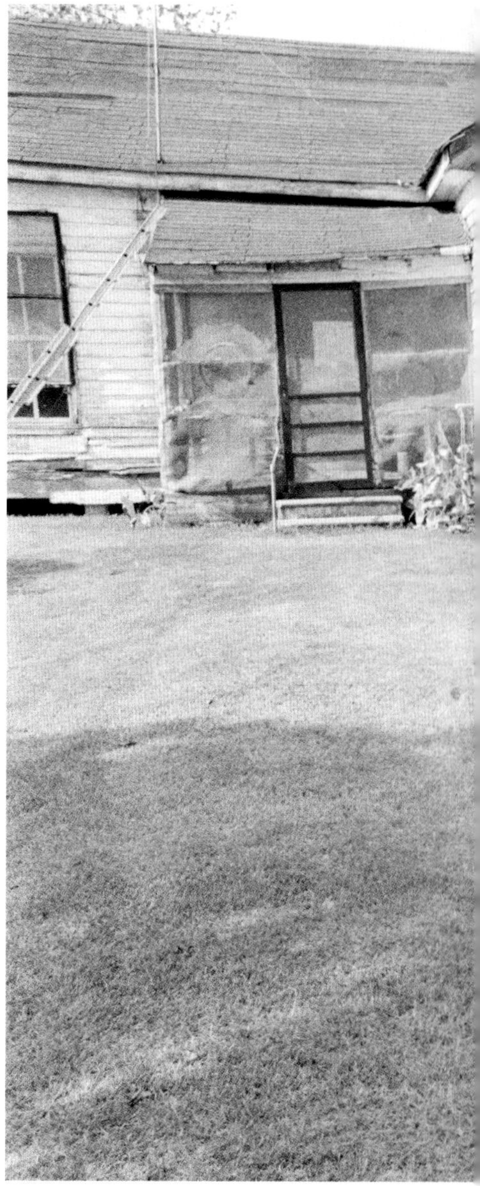

Henry Lee Williams at home

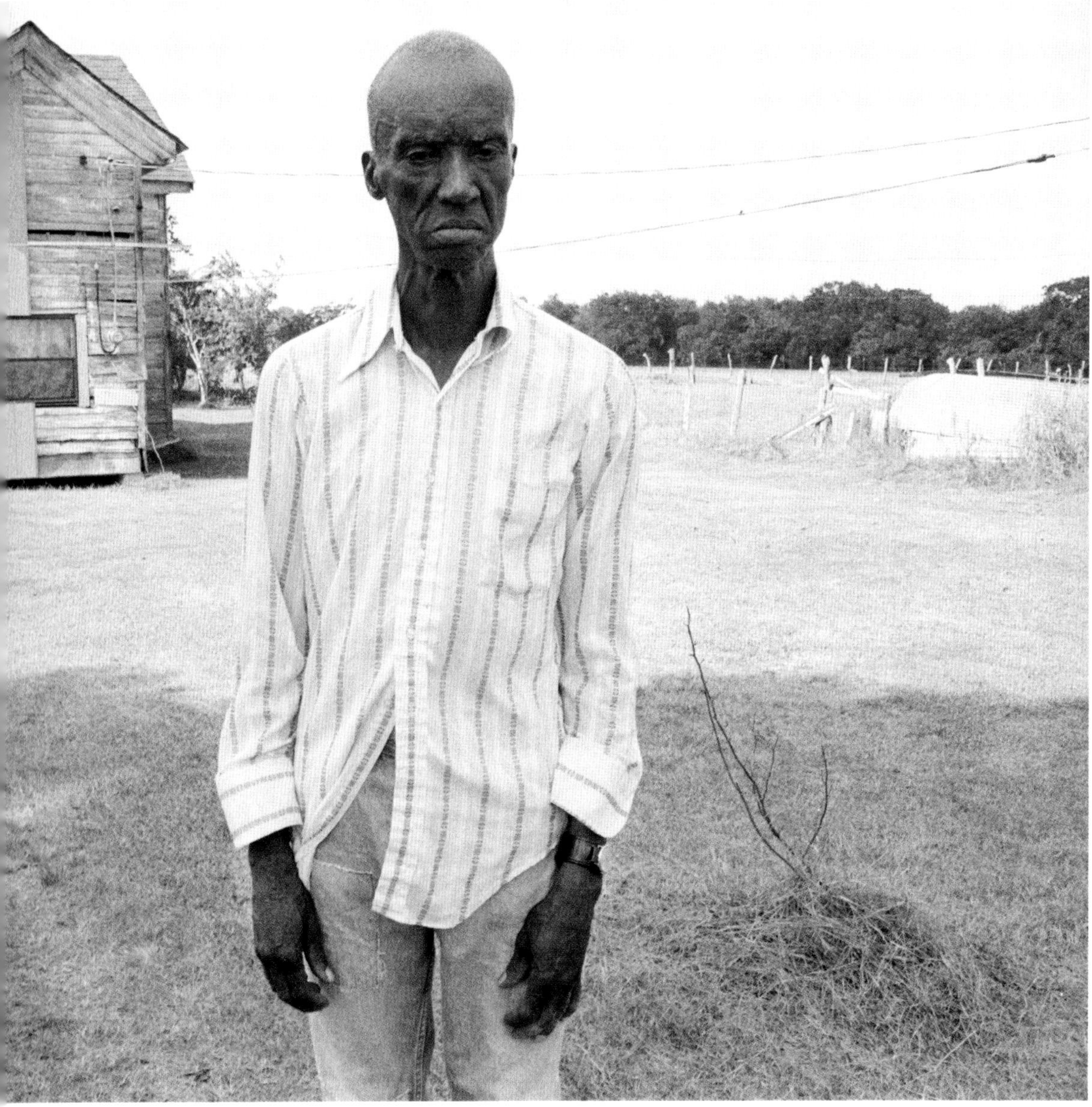

and sideways. Then he looked at it again and said solemnly, "That's Henry." It may have been his first ever photograph of himself.

Henry Lee was always a serious man. The only time I remember seeing him *really* smile was when he was told that his photograph would be in an exhibit at the Weimar Heritage Society Museum. Then, to my surprise, Henry began to grin, and still looking at the floor as he always did, but smiling, he walked to the door, saying over and over, "That's good, thank you—that's good, thank you, that's good." It was very moving and one of the nicest thank-yous a person could receive.

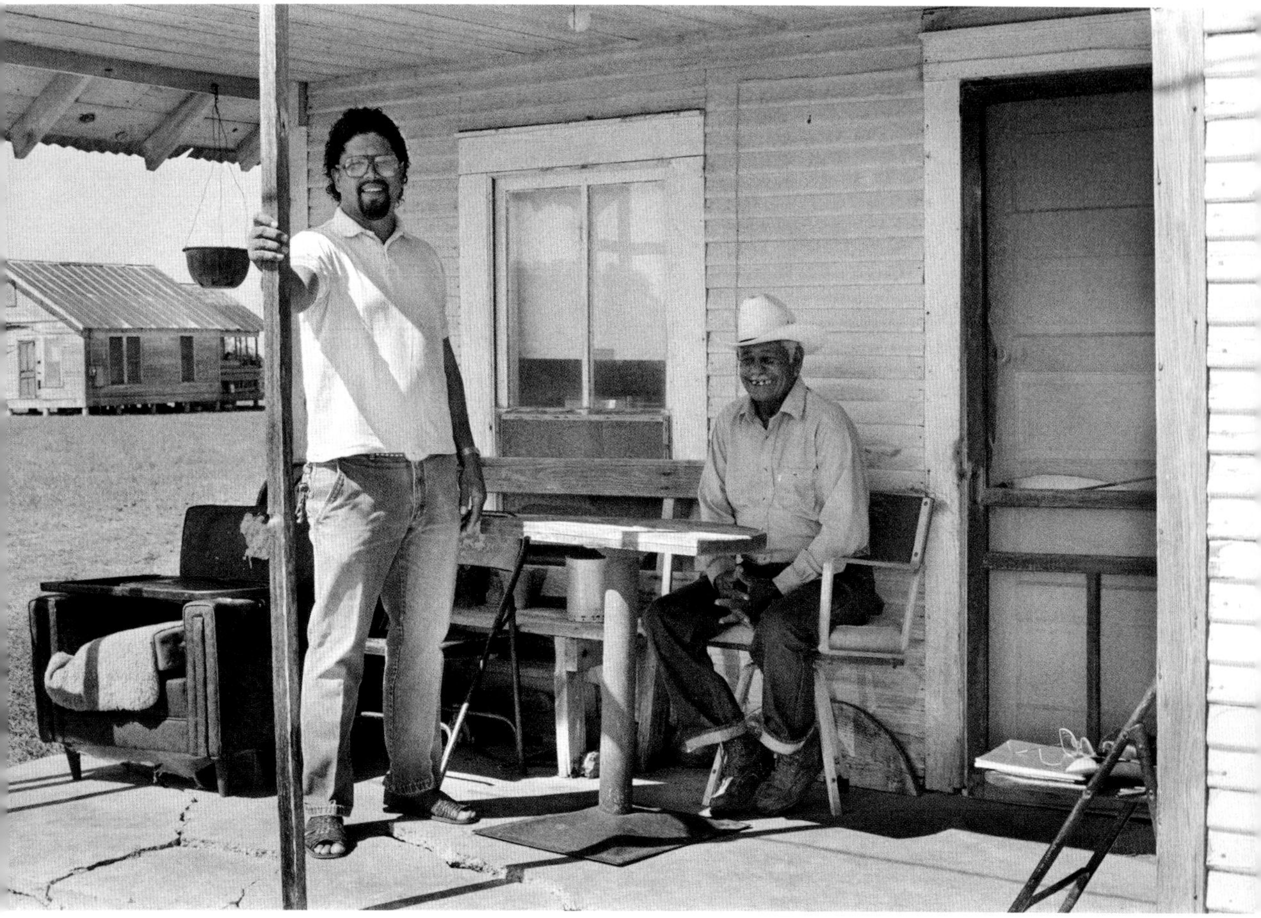

Gabriel Almeida, visiting John Webb

Gabriel Almeida

Gabriel Almeida was a rarity among my acquaintances in Weimar. Clearly a city man, he seemed confident, polished, and traveled. From the time we met at the house of his older friend John Webb, I was eager to learn what Gabriel, a sophisticated person of African American extraction, was doing in small-town Texas in the 1990s, where he didn't seem to fit the mold. Who was he, and why was he there?

Gabriel's friendship with John was a blessing for the elderly widower who had been so lonely and despondent after the death of his wife, Isabel. Thankfully the two men had become close, even with their more than forty-year age difference. Gabriel often drove several miles to John's place to visit, acting as a sort of guardian angel for his older, grieving friend.

It turned out that Gabriel had been born not in Weimar but in Houston, to a father of Mexican origin and an African American, Weimar-born mother. Gabriel moved to Weimar as an adult because of his mother's connections there and because he wanted his family raised in a safer environment than that of the city. As a youngster, he had lived in both Galveston and Houston, and he knew firsthand the fighting, drugs, and other kinds of trouble a boy could get into there.

Gabriel, who was born in 1954, attended school in Houston, playing football and running track. He spent two years after school in the army in Germany, France, and Spain, where he said, laughingly, that people asked him, "Where'd you get that great suntan?" He married at eighteen and moved to Weimar with his wife, Emma. There he worked for the Southern Pacific Railroad on the "tie gang," traveling between New Orleans and El Paso in two-month shifts. When he was home, he looked out for the older men and women in his neighborhood, including Marie and Lillie Williams who lived across the street.

How was it being a city-raised man with black blood in this white-run town? Gabriel replied that whites act friendlier in Weimar than in Houston, but their friendliness was only superficial. "Basically, Houston is more open to blacks. Here it's 'their way or no way' in these small towns of Germans and Bohemians," he said matter-of-factly. He stayed on anyway, content to work and make a good life for his family and himself.

John Webb

John Webb spoke with deep caring and passion about his wife, Isabel, who had died five years earlier. He said they were inseparable during their forty-seven years of marriage. "We were *never* apart. No separation of any kind—when you saw me, you saw her," John stated clearly, in words echoed by their friends. "You seen one, you seen the other," agreed Mamie Johnson, ninety-eight, speaking tenderly of John and Isabel. "You wouldn't know one from the other."

They were so close that they even worked together throughout their marriage. "She was all-round lady," John said. "Cowboy, field work, city work, cook." The only thing he would not allow Isabel to do was "brush ride, down in the bottoms—it was too rough."

Life was desperately bleak and lonely for John after Isabel died in 1987. He visited her grave every day and said she visited him two or three times a night in his dreams. "She talks to me. I wake up," John said, wonderingly.

John was in his teens and Isabel only nine or ten when they first saw each other on the streets of Weimar. He would ride his horse into town, wearing shiny boots, a big hat, and spurs, looking handsome and rakish. He would canter his horse fast through the dirt streets, kicking up dust and showing off. And Isabel followed him around on foot, he remembered happily. Dazzled by this dashing older boy, she told her sister she "had found her boyfriend and he's a cowboy."

"And ever since then, we been courtin'," John smiled fondly. The only thorn in the rosebush was that Isabel had set her goals on college, and she refused to marry him until she'd finished her education. This meant they courted for fourteen years. "She worked herself through school" in Hempstead and Austin, John said proudly. Isabel and John were twenty and twenty-six when they finally married in 1941 and began their happy life together.

Isabel was described by others as strong, determined, and intelligent. She looked all of this and also quite beautiful in the photograph that John held when I took this picture. John himself was a man of many talents: horseman, hunter, cook, bartender, maker of gunstocks and chairs, hide tanner, plaiter of whips, cowboy, carpenter, and more. He reminisced on his childhood, recalling how, when he was about six, he loved to watch the mail plane as it flew low and slowly over his house on its daily route from Houston to Austin and back. The young boy studied the plane carefully, lying on his back in the grassy fields, memorizing every detail. Then he went to a blacksmith shop down the road and asked to learn some blacksmithing skills.

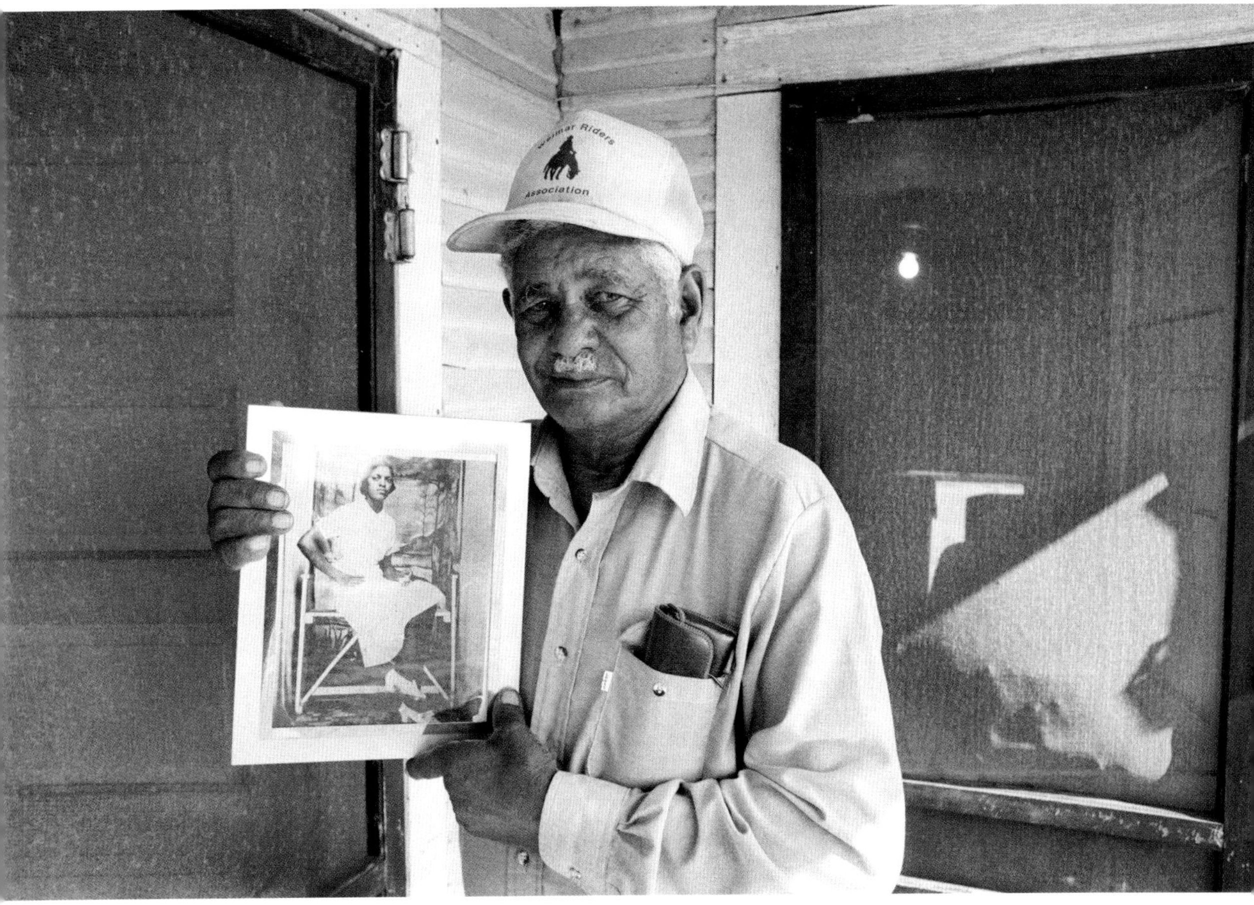

John Webb, widower, holding a picture of his wife, Isabel

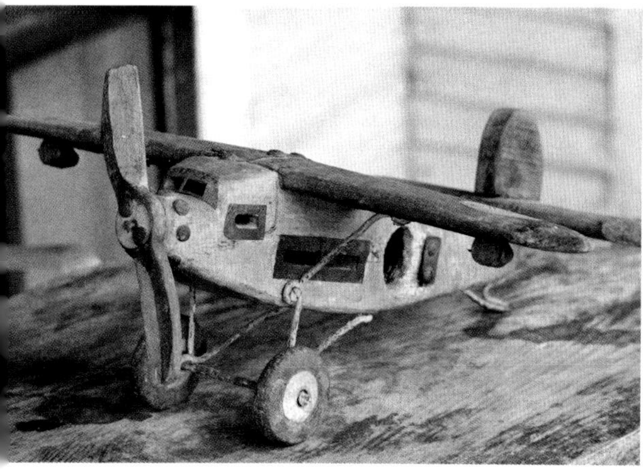

John's handcrafted airplane

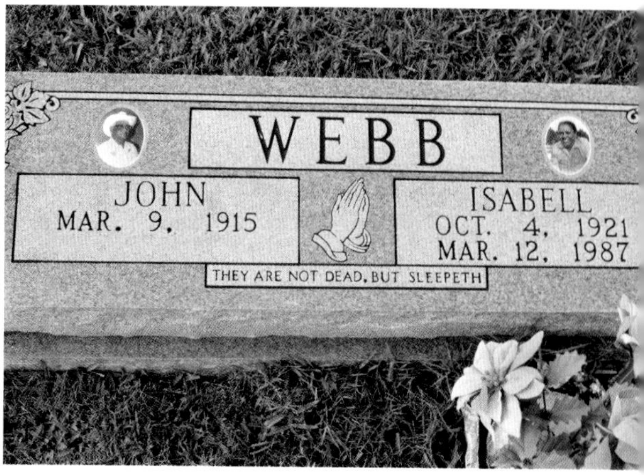

John and Isabel's gravestone

It took John three years of carving and metalwork to fashion a replica of the plane, accurate in every way he could manage. He treasured his model plane and said he wouldn't give it up for anything or anybody.

John asked me please to take a photograph of Isabel's grave for him to keep. We went together to the cemetery, and he showed me where the two lovers would rest, side by side, smiling in their matching, oval, never-fade color photographs.

One day he asked if I could come for a longer visit, and I, in turn, asked him to wait awhile for me to consider it. "There ain't nothin' for me but to wait," he countered, in a forlorn voice, as though life held little for him. He showed me his guest room and told me what a good cook he was and what good company. In time, a young woman entered his life and treated him very badly, it was said, taking advantage of this lonely older man. She took his money, some of his possessions, and, worse, his fragile tranquillity.

On August 2, 1990, John called a close friend to say he could not go on anymore—he was finished. And John shot and killed himself.

He was buried at Isabel's side, as he wanted to be. Mamie Johnson said, with heaviness, in grief and solemnity, "A cloud of gloom settled over the town that day." No one knew what became of John's model plane, that treasure and a rare piece of folk art. It simply disappeared.

Afterword

Bob Patten

Black and White The earliest photographs were in black and white. Not really: they were in silvery shadowy grays. None of the initial mediums—bitumen, silver chloride, or gallic acid on iodized paper—could develop the full range of intensity and tone from black to white. But photographers thought these images were the closest things yet to reality. The French called them "sun pictures," heliographs. People believed that nothing—no human agency or imaginative manipulation—got in between the sun, the object, and the photographic plate. Nature photographed herself. She drew her own picture, fixed in time and space on paper, for all to see, in black and white. Reality seemed color-blind.

Black and White The nineteenth century saw in black and white. Literally, not only in photographs but also in etchings and engravings and in an explosion of printed materials, black inked alphabets and shapes on bleached paper. Figuratively, too: there were whites, and there were other races. Blacks counted as three-fifths of a person. Morality was black and white, and the devil less often was imaged as a bringer of false light than as a bringer of darkness. Over the course of a century, Western cultures discovered more in-between values. Abolitionists portrayed slaves as brothers, not others. Laws began to recognize shades of gray.

Black and White But even in twentieth-century America, black and white, for many decades, defined our films and our way of representing the human condition. Blacks may have been freed, but they were still "colored," not white. Their worlds may on occasion have been glamorized—Harlem, Memphis, New Orleans—but all the brightness shone against a night sky. During the day, as Ralph Ellison reminded the world, blacks were invisible.

Black and White Patsy Cravens's black-and-white photographs, with their accompanying printed texts, show the black and white citizens of Colorado County, Texas, in all their shades of difference and similarity. Nuancing the binaries of race, these pictures tell us about colorful lives—lives of hardship and humor, field work and singing, flirting and families, religion and lynching.

Of all her meticulously framed and developed portraits, none is more moving to me than that of John Webb. It is at once a composition in gray, a narrative history, and a reflection on memorial imagery and photography itself.

No man was more beloved in the community than John. When he died, Mamie Johnson said, "A cloud of gloom settled over the town that day." His face radiates sensitivity as well as bone-deep sorrow. The brightness of his life was a girl he saw passing by in a small-town parade. She became his wife and partner through hard times, and she predeceased him.

He holds a picture of her—the black-and-white image of all that brought color to him. Even reduced to a photograph in a photograph, this woman attracts. Beautiful and proud, wearing a white dress and white shoes and seated on a white metal chair, she looks almost defiantly at the camera, challenging it to contain, frame, know, or fix all that she is in a single image.

When she died, John's life turned gray. And he is a gray image, from cap to shirt, holding on to his memories and showing them to another camera. John's expression seems to ask a question: "Do you see what I had and lost?" Vulnerable and trusting, he lets the photographer in beyond the blacks and whites of cultural difference, lets Patsy in to the infinite shades of gray that depict the world and our shared experiences.

Around John are doors. They are shut. Sunlight slants across the surface of a screen. Inside a bare bulb shines. Those closed black doors angling in on both sides speak to me of the bleakness John felt. There were to be no more parades, no more color. No doors open onto those worlds any more. Within months, John would close his life.

Patsy's print foretells the future. It deploys traditional imagery: portraits of widowers holding images of their beloved ones have been a visual trope for memory, possession, and loss since the Renaissance. Patsy uses that trope to make a new picture, about someone whose life would once have been invisible. Her images illustrate the power of photography to remind us simultaneously of life and of loss. And it captures a past, in black and white, far richer and more moving than our blind simplifications could ever discover or the sun alone illuminate.

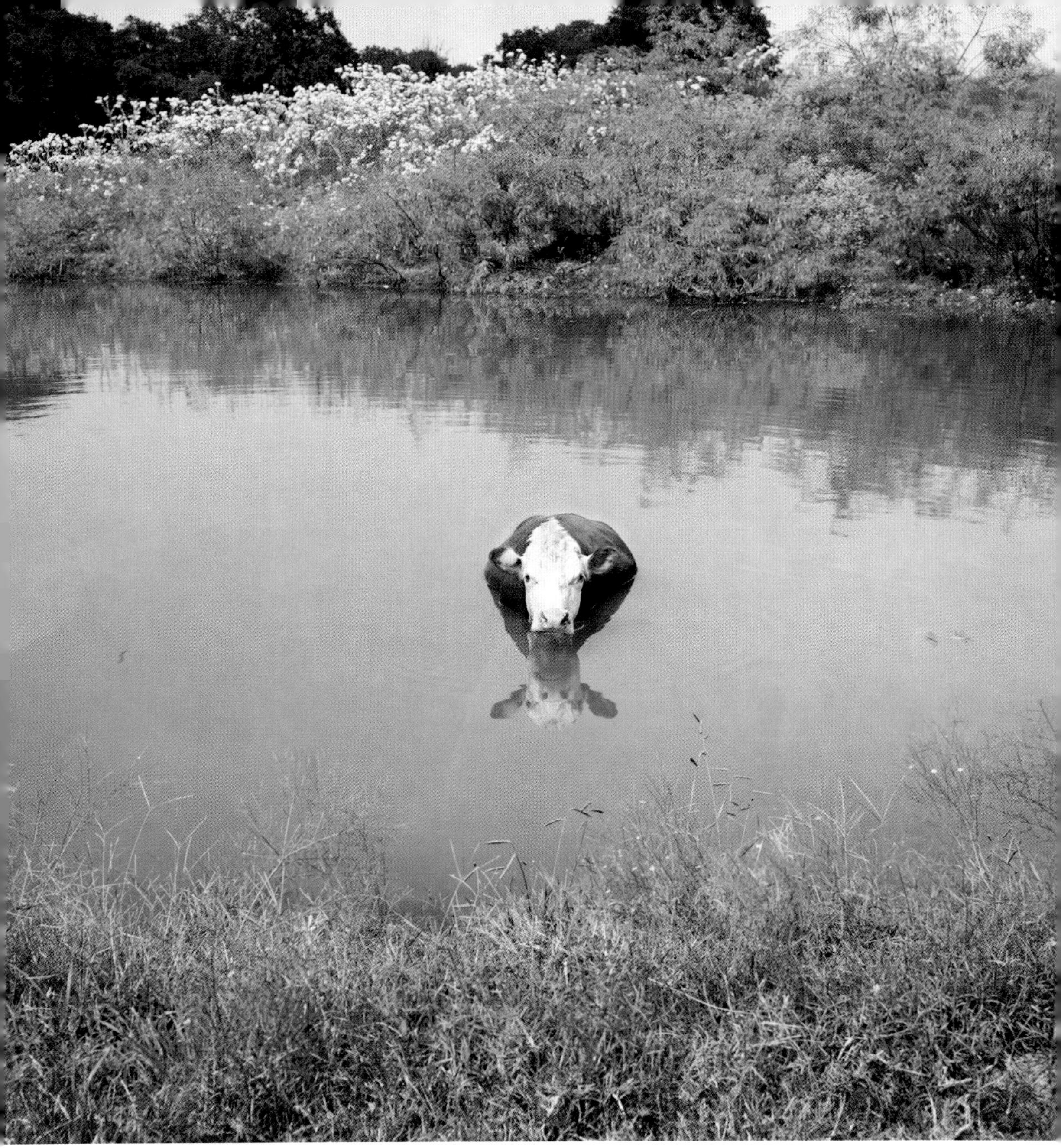

Odalisque